T0260088

From Traditional Fault Tolerance to Blockchain

Scrivener Publishing
100 Cummings Center, Suite 541J
Beverly, MA 01915-6106

Publishers at Scrivener
Martin Scrivener (martin@scrivenerpublishing.com)
Phillip Carmical (pcarmical@scrivenerpublishing.com)

From Traditional Fault Tolerance to Blockchain

Wenbing Zhao
Cleveland State University

Scrivener
Publishing

WILEY

This edition first published 2021 by John Wiley & Sons, Inc., 111 River Street, Hoboken, NJ 07030, USA and Scrivener Publishing LLC, 100 Cummings Center, Suite 541J, Beverly, MA 01915, USA
© 2021 Scrivener Publishing LLC
For more information about Scrivener publications please visit www.scrivenerpublishing.com.

Wiley Global Headquarters
111 River Street, Hoboken, NJ 07030, USA

For details of our global editorial offices, customer services, and more information about Wiley products visit us at www.wiley.com.

Limit of Liability/Disclaimer of Warranty

Library of Congress Cataloging-in-Publication Data

ISBN 978-1-119-68195-3

Cover image: Pixabay.Com
Cover design by Russell Richardson

MIX
Paper from
responsible sources
FSC
www.fsc.org   FSC® C013604

To My Parents

Contents

List of Figures

List of Tables

Acknowledgments

This book is dedicated to my parents. They tried their best to help me pursue my dreams through so many years' financial hardship. They took their life savings to pay the government so that I could be free to emigrate to the greatest country on earth. When I stumbled and had nowhere else to go, they took me under their wings and took care of me. I am forever in their debt.

I also would like to thank my beautiful wife, Hao, and my lovely children Dorothy, Emily, and Arthur. It is them that make my life so enjoyable and meaningful.

W. Z.

Preface

Cloud services are playing an ever increasingly important role in all aspects of our society, governments, businesses, and individuals alike. We depend on these services on a daily basis, such as financial (*e.g.*, online banking and stock trading), e-commerce (*e.g.*, online shopping), civil infrastructure (*e.g.*, electric power grid and traffic control), entertainment (*e.g.*, online gaming and multimedia streaming), and personal data storage (*e.g.*, various cloud services such as Dropbox, Google Drive, and OneDrive). Behind these cloud services is distributed computing, which addresses many critical issues in making the services dependable and trustworthy. The most important of all is to build consensus in its internal operations that span many different computing nodes.

Distributed consensus has been studied for several decades, at least starting in 1970s. The reason why distributed consensus is important is that a distributed system would span over many computing nodes, and these nodes must maintain a common view on the system state so that each can operate as planned towards the objectives of the system. Prolonged inconsistency among different components of the system would damage the integrity of the system and ultimately would result in system-level failures that are visible to end users.

The cost of system failures is enormous. If a data center is brought down by a system failure, the average cost for downtime may range from $42,000 to about $300,000 per hour [2, 6]. The cost can be estimated by summing up the wasted expenses and the loss of revenue. While the labor cost of downtime may be estimated relatively easily (*i.e.*, roughly, wasted expenses per hour = number of employees × average salary per hour) [13], it is much harder to estimate the loss of revenue, especially due to the damages on the reputation of the business and the loyalty of its potential customers [2].

Ensuring high availability of distributed systems is not cheap. In [7], the cost of data center is estimated to range from $450 per square foot for 99.671% availability (*i.e.*, 28.8 hours of downtime per year), to $1,100 per square foot for 99.995% availability (*i.e.*, 0.4 hours of downtime per year).

That is perhaps one reason why about 59% of Fortune 500 companies suffer from 1.6 hours or more of downtime per week [2].

All classical consensus algorithms rely on a concept referred to as membership, that is, every node would know how many nodes are in the current membership, the logical role of each node, and how to reach other nodes. Another important construct is voting via the sending of messages to each other. Typically, one of the members would assume a special role, which is referred to as the primary or the coordinator. The coordinator might fail or become compromised, in which case, a new coordinator would be elected through voting. As such, classical distributed consensus algorithms are expensive, highly complex, and not scalable due to the heavy use of multiple rounds of message exchanges among the members.

In January 2009, the launch of the first practical cryptocurrency, Bitcoin [12], has completely changed the picture. The most essential prerequisite for a cryptocurrency is the assurance that it is virtually impossible for anyone to double-spend the money (i.e., cryptocurrency) one has. Bitcoin addressed this requirement by introducing an immutable distributed ledger in the form of a chain of blocks where each block aggregates hundreds or even thousands of transactions. This distributed ledger is often referred to as the blockchain. The immutability of the blockchain is achieved by several means: (1) cryptographic protection of the blockchain, such as digital signature, one-way hash function, and chaining of the blocks; (2) massive degree of replication of the blockchain across many nodes in the Bitcoin network; and (3) a novel probabilistic consensus algorithm that is completely different from classical consensus algorithms.

The consensus algorithm used in Bitcoin does not involve any explicit form of voting, therefore, there is no extra message exchange among the nodes in the Bitcoin network for the purpose of reaching consensus. In Bitcoin, the consensus building process is converted into a lottery-like stochastic process where the winner of the lottery gets the right to create a new block of transactions and collects an award [22]. To ensure fairness and to ensure the process to be a stochastic process, every participating node would work on a Proof-of-Work (PoW) based puzzle, and the first one that finds a solution becomes the winner. The PoW puzzle has a predefined target difficulty, and a participating node would experiment with different ways of making the hash of the block header meet the target difficulty. This is a CPU-intensive process. Hence, the only way a node could gain advantage over other nodes is to invest in better hardware that can perform the hash operation faster. The Bitcoin consensus algorithm is referred to as PoW and sometimes as the Nakamoto algorithm, named after Bitcoin's creator, which is apparently a pseudonym. This novel form of consensus algorithm has aroused huge interest in the research and application of the blockchain technology [20]. Some even expressed the hope that the blockchain technology would lead to a new-form of economy, just like what the Internet has transformed our society [16].

This book contains two parts. The first part consists of the first 7 chapters and it covers the most essential techniques for building dependable distributed systems. The last 3 chapters form the second part, which covers the blockchain technology.

Chapter 1 introduces the basic concepts and terminologies of dependable distributed computing, as well as the primary means to achieve dependability.

Chapter 2 describes the checkpointing and logging mechanisms, which are widely used in practice to achieve some form of fault tolerance. Checkpointing and logging enable the recoverability of the system but do not prevent service disruption. These mechanisms are relatively simple to implement and understand, and they incur minimum runtime overhead while demanding very moderate extra resources (only stable storage). Furthermore, checkpointing and logging also serve as the foundation for more sophisticated dependability techniques.

Chapter 3 covers research works on recovery-oriented computing, including fault detection and diagnosis, microreboot, and system-level undo and redo. Recovery-oriented computing aims to facilitate faster recovery after a system failure and thereby improving the availability of the system. Similar to checkpointing and logging, the mechanisms for recovery-oriented computing do not prevent service disruption, hence, it is a promising approach for many e-commerce application, but not suitable for applications that require high reliability.

Chapter 4 outlines the replication technique for data and service fault tolerance. This is the fundamental technique to ensure high reliability. Through active replication (*i.e.,* the use of multiple redundant copies of the application processes), the system would be able to mask the failure of a replica and continue to process clients' requests (this is actually not entirely true, as we will show in later chapters, some failures may cause extended period of unavailability of the system). With replication comes the complexity of consistency issue. Ideally, the replicas should always maintain consistency with each other. However, doing so might not incur too much runtime overhead to be acceptable for some applications, or may cause extended period of system unavailability. Hence, strict consistency may have to be compromised either for better performance [15] or for better availability [19].

Chapter 5 explains the group communication systems, which can be used to implement active replication. A group communication system typically offers a totally ordered reliable multicast service for messages, a membership server, and a view synchrony service. These set of services help the replicas to maintain consistency even in the presence of failures, which would reduce the development cost of building dependable systems with active replication.

Chapter 6 discusses the consensus problem and describes several Paxos algorithms, including the Classic Paxos, Dynamic Paxos, Cheap Paxos, and Fast Paxos. While it is easy for a group of processes to agree on the same value if all processes can communicate with each other promptly and if none of them fails, distributed consensus is an incredibly hard problem when processes might fail and there might be extended delay to send or receive a message. The classical Paxos algorithm solves the consensus problem (under the non-malicious fault model) in a very elegant and efficient manner by separating the safety concern and the liveness concern [9]. Additional Paxos algorithm are developed to minimize the resources required, and to reduce the latency for achieving consensus by using a higher redundancy level [10, 18].

Chapter 7 introduces the problem of Byzantine fault tolerance. A Byzantine fault is synonymous with a malicious fault. Because a malicious faulty component may choose to behave like any of the non-malicious faults, the Byzantine fault model encompasses any arbitrary fault. The distributed consensus problem under the Byzantine fault model was first studied several decades ago by Lamport, Shostak, and Pease [11]. A much more efficient algorithm for achieving fault tolerance under the Byzantine fault model (referred to as Practical Byzantine fault tolerance) was proposed by Castro and Liskov in 1999 [5]. Since then, the research on Byzantine fault tolerance exploded. With the pervasiveness of cyberattacks and espionages, dealing with malicious faults becomes an urgent concern now compared with several decades ago.

Chapter 8 provides an overview of cryptocurrency and the blockchain technology, including the early conception of cryptocur rency, the first implementation of cryptocurrency in Bitcoin [12], the concept of smart contract and its implementation in Ethereum [4], as well as the vision of decentralized organizations [16] powered by smart contract and the blockchain technology.

Chapter 9 explains the consensus algorithms used in the blockchain technology in depth. Since the original PoW algorithm was introduced in Bitcoin, there has been great effort on improving PoW in various aspects, and on finding alternative algorithms that do not consume as much energy. A common set of requirements for such algorithms is laid out [22] and different proposals are examined with respect to the requirements [17].

In this chapter, we also discuss the Proof-of-Stake (PoS) consensus algorithm, which is the second most well-known algorithm behind PoW for blockchain. We will explain the PoS implementation in PeerCoin [8]. It is the first implementation of PoS in a practical cryptocurrency (*i.e.,* PeerCoin) in 2013 and it has gone through several revisions to address its initial vulnerabilities.

Chapter 10 presents the applications of the blockchain technology and issues that will directly impact on how widely the blockchain technology can be adopted, including the value of the blockchain technology and the efforts to increase the throughput of blockchain systems [1, 3, 14, 21]. We primarily focus on blockchain applications in the area of cyber-physical systems (CPS) [20]. CPS is evolving rapidly and the integration of blockchain and CPS could potentially transform CPS design for much stronger security and robustness.

Wenbing Zhao
Cleveland, USA
March 2021

References

1. E. Akbari, W. Zhao, S. Yang, and X. Lou. The impact of block parameters on the throughput and security of blockchains. In *Proceedings of the 2020 International Conference on Blockchain Technology*, pages 13–18. ACM, 2020.
2. A. Arnold. Assessing the financial impact of downtime, April 2010. http://www.businesscomputingworld.co.uk/assessing-the-financial-impact-of-downtime/.
3. A. Back, M. Corallo, L. Dashjr, M. Friedenbach, G. Maxwell, A. Miller, A. Poelstra, J. Timón, and P. Wuille. Enabling blockchain innovations with pegged sidechains. *URL: http://www. opensciencereview. com/papers/123/enablingblockchain-innovations-with-pegged-sidechains*, 72, 2014.
4. V. Buterin *et al.* Ethereum white paper. https://ethereum.org/en/whitepaper/, 2013.
5. M. Castro and B. Liskov. Practical byzantine fault tolerance. In *Proceedings of the third symposium on Operating systems design and implementation*, OSDI '99, pages 173–186, Berkeley, CA, USA, 1999. USENIX Association.
6. Channel Insider. Unplanned it outages cost more than $5,000 per minute: Report. http://www.channelinsider.com/c/a/Spotlight/Unplanned-IT-Outages-Cost-More-than-5000-per-Minute-Report-105393/, May 2011.
7. J. Clark. The price of data center availability, October 2011. http://www.datacenterjournal.com/design/the-price-of-data-center-availability/.
8. S. King and S. Nadal. Ppcoin: Peer-to-peer crypto-currency with proof-of-stake. https://www.peercoin.net/assets/paper/peercoin-paper.pdf, 2008.
9. L. Lamport. Paxos made simple. *ACM SIGACT News (Distributed Computing Column)*, 32(4):18–25, December 2001.
10. L. Lamport. Fast paxos. *Distributed Computing*, 19(2):79–193, 2006.
11. L. Lamport, R. Shostak, and M. Pease. The byzantine generals problem. *ACM Transactions on Programming Languages and Systems*, 4:382–401, 1982.
12. S. Nakamoto. Bitcoin: A peer-to-peer electronic cash system. https://bitcoin.org/bitcoin.pdf, 2008.
13. T. Pisello and B. Quirk. How to quantify downtime, January 2004. http://www.networkworld.com/careers/2004/0105man.html.
14. J. Poon and T. Dryja. The bitcoin lightning network: Scalable off-chain instant payments, 2016.

15. Y. Saito and M. Shapiro. Optimistic replication. *ACM Comput. Surv.*, 37(1):42– 81, Mar. 2005.
16. M. Swan. *Blockchain: Blueprint for a new economy.* "O'Reilly Media, Inc.", 2015.
17. W. Wang, D. T. Hoang, P. Hu, Z. Xiong, D. Niyato, P. Wang, Y. Wen, and D. I. Kim. A survey on consensus mechanisms and mining strategy management in blockchain networks. *IEEE Access*, 7:22328–22370, 2019.
18. W. Zhao. Fast paxos made easy: Theory and implementation. *International Journal of Distributed Systems and Technologies (IJDST)*, 6(1):15–33, 2015.
19. W. Zhao. Optimistic byzantine fault tolerance. *International Journal of Parallel, Emergent and Distributed Systems*, 31(3):254–267, 2016.
20. W. Zhao, C. Jiang, H. Gao, S. Yang, and X. Luo. Blockchain-enabled cyber-physical systems: A review. *IEEE Internet of Things Journal*, 2020.
21. W. Zhao, S. Yang, and X. Lou. Secure hierarchical processing and logging of sensing data and iot events with blockchain. In *Proceedings of the 2020 International Conference on Blockchain Technology*, pages 52–56. ACM, 2020.
22. W. Zhao, S. Yang, and X. Luo. On consensus in public blockchains. In *Proceedings of the 2019 International Conference on Blockchain Technology*, pages 1–5, 2019.

1

Introduction

Distributed systems bring many benefits to us, for example, we can share resources such as data storage and processing cycles much more easily; we can collaborative on projects efficiently even if the team members span across the planet; we can solve challenging problems by utilizing the vast aggregated computing power of large scale distributed systems. However, if not designed properly, distributed systems may appear to be less dependable than standalone systems. As Leslie Lamport pointed out: "You know you have one (a distributed system) when the crash of a computer you've never heard of stops you from getting any work done" [10]. In this book, we introduce various dependability techniques that can be used to address the issue brought up by Lamport. In fact, with sufficient redundancy in the system, a distributed system can be made significantly more dependable than a standalone system because such a distributed system can continue providing services to its users even when a subset of its nodes have failed.

In this chapter, we introduce the basic concepts and terminologies of dependable distributed computing and system security, and outline the primary approaches to achieving dependability.

1.1   Basic Concepts and Terminologies for Dependable Computing

The term "dependable systems" has been used widely in many different contexts and often means different things. In the context of distributed computing, **dependability** refers to the ability of a distributed system to provide correct services to its users despite various threats to the system such as undetected software defects, hardware failures, and malicious attacks.

To reason about the dependability of a distributed system, we need to model the system itself as well as the threats to the system clearly [2]. We also define common attributes of dependable distributed systems and metrics on evaluating the dependability of a distributed system.

1.1.1   System Models

A system is designed to provide a set of **services** to its users (often referred to as clients). Each service has an **interface** that a client could use to request the service. What the system should do for each service is defined as a set of **functions** according to a *functional specification* for the system. The status of a system is determined by its **state**. The state of a practical system is usually very complicated. A system may consist of one or more processes spanning over one or more nodes, and each process might consist of one or more threads. The state of the system is determined collectively by the state of the processes and threads in the system. The state of a process typically consists of the values of its registers, stack, heap, file descriptors, and the kernel state. Part of the state might become visible to the users of the system via information contained in the responses to the users' requests. Such state is referred to as **external state** and is normally an abstract state defined in the functional specification of the system. The remaining part of the state that is not visible to users is referred to as **internal state**. A system can be recovered to where it was before a failure if its state was captured and not lost due to the failure (for example, if the state is serialized and written to stable storage).

From the structure perspective, a system consists of a one or more **components** (such as nodes or processes), and a system always has a **boundary** that separates the system from its **environment**. Here environment refers to all other systems that the current system interact with. Note that what we refer to as a system is always relative with respect to the current context. A component in a (larger) system by itself is a system when we want to study its behavior and it may in turn have its own internal structures.

1.1.2   Threat Models

Whether or not a system is providing correct services is judged by whether or not the system is performing the functions defined in the functional specification for the system. When a system is not functioning according to its functional specification, we say a service failure (or simply failure) has occurred. The failure of a system is caused by part of its state in wrong values, *i.e.*, **errors** in its state. We hypothesize that the errors are caused by some **faults** [6]. Therefore, the threats to the dependability of a system are modeled as various faults.

A fault might not always exhibit itself and cause error. In particular, a software defect (often referred to as software bug) might not be revealed until the code that contains the defect is exercised when certain condition is met. For example, if a shared variable is not protected by a lock in a multithreaded application, the fault (often referred to as race condition) does not exhibit itself unless there are two or more threads trying to update the shared variable concurrently. As another example, if there is no boundary check on accessing to an array, the fault does not show up until a process tries to access the array with an out-of-bound index. When a fault does not exhibit itself, we say the fault is **dormant**. When certain condition is met, the fault will be **activated**.

When a fault is activated, initially the fault would cause an error in the component that encompasses the defected area (in programming code). When the component interacts with other components of the system, the error would propagates to other components. When the errors propagate to the interface of the system and render the service provided to a client deviate from the specification, a service failure would occur. Due to the recursive nature of common system composition, the failure of one system may cause a fault in a larger system when the former constitutes a component of the latter, as shown in Figure 1.1. Such relationship between fault, error, and failure is referred to as "chain of threats" in [2]. Hence, in literature the terms "faults" and "failures" are often used interchangeably.

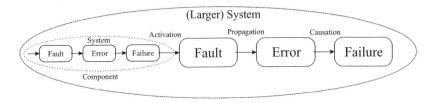

Figure 1.1   An example of a chain of threats with two levels of recursion.

Of course, not all failures can be analyzed with the above chain of threats. For example, a power outage of the entire system would immediately cause the failure of the system.

Faults can be classified based on different criteria, the most common classifications include:

- Based on the source of the faults, faults can be classified as:

    - Hardware faults, if the faults are caused by the failure of hardware components such as power outages, hard drive failures, bad memory chips, etc.

    - Software faults, if the faults are caused by software bugs such as race conditions and no-boundary-checks for arrays.

    - Operator faults, if the faults are caused by the operator of the system, for example, misconfiguration, wrong upgrade procedures, etc.

- Based on the intent of the faults, faults can be classified as:

    - Non-malicious faults, if the faults are not caused by a person with malicious intent. For example, the naturally occurred hardware faults and some remnant software bugs such as race conditions are non-malicious faults.

    - Malicious faults, if the faults are caused by a person with intent to harm the system, for example, to deny services to legitimate clients or to compromise the integrity of the service. Malicious faults are often referred to as commission faults, or Byzantine faults [5].

- Based on the duration of the faults, faults can be classified as:

    - Transient faults, if such a fault is activated momentarily and becomes dormant again. For example, the race condition might often show up as transient fault because if the threads stop accessing the shared variable concurrently, the fault appears to have disappeared.

- Permanent faults, if once a fault is activated, the fault stays activated unless the faulty component is repaired or the source of the fault is addressed. For example, a power outage is considered a permanent fault because unless the power is restored, a computer system will remain powered off. A specific permanent fault is the (process) crash fault. A segmentation fault could result in the crash of a process.

- Based on how a fault in a component reveals to other components in the system, faults can be classified as:
  - Content faults, if the values passed on to other components are wrong due to the faults. A faulty component may always pass on the same wrong values to other components, or it may return different values to different components that it interacts with. The latter is specifically modeled as Byzantine faults [5].

  - Timing faults, if the faulty component either returns a reply too early, or too late alter receiving a request from another component. An extreme case is when the faulty component stops responding at all (*i.e.*, it takes infinite amount of time to return a reply), *e.g.*, when the component crashes, or hangs due to an infinite loop or a deadlock.

- Based on whether or not a fault is reproducible or deterministic, faults (primarily software faults) can be classified as:
  - Reproducible/deterministic faults. The fault happens deterministically and can be easily reproduced. Accessing a null pointer is an example of deterministic fault, which often would lead to the crash of the system. This type of faults can be easily identified and repaired.

  - Nondeterministic faults. The fault appears to happen nondeterministically and hard to reproduce. For example, if a fault is caused by a specific interleaving of several threads when they access some shared variable, it is going to be hard to reproduce such a fault. This type of software faults is also referred to as Heisenbugs to highlight their uncertainty.

- Given a number of faults within a system, we can classify them based on their relationship:
  - Independent faults, if there is no causal relationship between the faults, *e.g.*, given fault A and fault B, B is not caused by A, and A is not caused by B.
  - Correlated faults, if the faults are causally related, *e.g.*, given fault A and fault B, either B is caused by A, or A is caused by B. If multiple components fail due to a common reason, the failures are referred to as common mode failures.

When the system fails, it is desirable to avoid catastrophic consequences, such as the loss of life. The consequence of the failure of a system can be alleviated by incorporating dependability mechanisms into the system such that when it fails, it stops responding to requests (such systems are referred to as **fail-stop** systems), if this is impossible, it returns consistent wrong values instead of inconsistent values to all components that it may interact with. If the failure of a system does not cause great harm either to human life or to the environment, we call such as system a **fail-safe** system. Usually, a fail-safe system defines a set of safe states. When a fail-safe system can no longer operate according to its specification due to faults, it can transit to one of the predefined safe states when it fails. For example, the computer system that is used to control a nuclear power plant must be a fail-safe system.

Perhaps counter intuitively, it is often desirable for a system to halt its operation immediately when it is in an error state or encounters an unexpected condition. The software engineering practice to ensure such a behavior is called fail fast [9]. The benefits of the fail-fast practice are that it enables early detection of software faults and the diagnosis of faults. When a fault has been propagated to many other components, it is a lot harder to pinpoint the source of the problem.

1.1.3   Dependability Attributes and Evaluation Metrics

A dependable system has a number of desirable attributes and some of the attributes can be used as evaluation metrics for the system. We classify these attributes into two categories: (1) those that are fundamental to, and are immediate concern of, all distributed systems, including availability, reliability, and integrity; and (2) those that are secondary and may not be of immediate concern of, or be applicable to all systems, such as maintainability and safety.

The availability and reliability of a system can be used as evaluation metrics. Other attributes are normally not used as evaluation metrics because it is difficult to quantify the integrity, maintainability, and safety of a distributed system.

1.1.3.1 Availability

Availability is a measure of the readiness of a dependable system at a point in time, *i.e.*, when a client needs to use a service provided by the system, the probability that the system is there to provide the service to the client. The availability of a system is determined by two factors:

- Mean time to failure (MTTF). It characterizes how long the system can run without a failure.
- Mean time to repair (MTTR). It characterizes how long the system can be repaired and recovered to be fully functional again.

Availability is defined to be $MTTF/(MTTF + MTTR)$. Hence, the larger the MTTF, and higher the availability of a system. Similarly, the smaller the MTTR, the higher the availability of the system.

The availability of a system is typically represented in terms of how many 9s. For example, if a system is claimed to offer five 9s availability, it means that the system will be available with a probability of 99.999%, *i.e.*, the system has 10^{-5} probability to be not available when a client wants to access the service offered by the system at any time, which means that the system may have at most 5.256 minutes of down time a year.

1.1.3.2 Reliability

Reliability is a measure of the system's capability of providing correct services continuously for a period of time. It is often represented as the probability for the system to do so for a given period of time t, *i.e.*, $Reliability = R(t)$. The larger the t, the lower the reliability value. The reliability of a system is proportional to MTTF. The relationship between reliability and availability can be represented as $Availability = \int_0^\infty R(t)$. Reliability is very different from availability. If a system fails frequently but can recover very quickly, the system may have high availability. However, such a system would have very low reliability.

1.1.3.3   Integrity

Integrity refers to the capability of a system to protect its state from being compromised under various threats. In dependable computing research, integrity is typically translated into the consistency of server replicas, if redundancy is employed. As long as the number of faulty replicas does not exceed a pre-defined threshold, the consistency of the remaining replicas would naturally imply the integrity of the system.

1.1.3.4   Maintainability

Maintainability refers to the capability of a system to evolve after it is deployed. Once a software fault is detected, it is desirable to be able to apply a patch that repairs the system without having to uninstall the existing system and then reinstall an updated system. The same patching/software update mechanism may be used to add new features or improve the performance of the existing system. Ideally, we want to be able to perform the software update without having to shutdown the running system (often referred to as live upgrade or live update), which is already a standard feature for many operating systems for patching non-kernal level components. Live upgrade has also be achieved via replication in some distributed systems [12].

1.1.3.5   Safety

Safety means that when a system fails, it does not cause catastrophic consequences, i.e., the system must be fail-safe. Systems that are used to control operations that may cause catastrophic consequences, such as nuclear power plants, or endanger human lives, such as hospital operation rooms, must bear the safety attribute. The safety attribute is not important for systems that are not operating in such environments, such as for e-commerce.

1.2   Means to Achieve Dependability

There are two primary approaches to improving the dependability of distributed systems: (1) *fault avoidance*: build and use high quality software components and hardware that are less prone to failures; (2) fault detection and diagnosis: while crash faults are trivial to detect, components in a practical system might fail in various ways other than crash, and if not detected, the integrity of the system cannot be guaranteed; and (3) *fault tolerance*: a system is able to recover from various faults without service interruption if the system employs sufficient redundancy so that the system can mask the failures of a portion of its components, or with minimum service interruption if the system uses less costly dependability means such as logging and checkpointing.

1.2.1   Fault Avoidance

For software components, fault avoidance aims to ensure correct design specification and correct implementation before a distributed system is released. This objective can be achieved by employing standard software engineering practices, for example:

- More rigorous software design using techniques such as formal methods. Formal methods mandate the use of formal language to facilitate the validation of a specification.
- More rigorous software testing to identify and remove software bugs due to remnant design deficiency and introduced during implementation.
- For some applications, it may be impractical to employ formal methods, in which case, it is wise to design for testability [2], for example, by extensively use unit testing that is available in many modern programming languages such as Java and C#.

1.2.2   Fault Detection and Diagnosis

Fault detection is a crucial step in ensuring the dependability of a system. Crash faults are relatively trivial to detect, for example, we can periodically probe each component to check on its health. If no response is received after several consecutive probes, the component may be declared as having crashed. However, components in a system might fail in various ways and they might respond promptly to each probe after they have failed. It is nontrivial to detect such faults, especially in a large distributed system. Diagnosis is required to determine that a fault indeed has occurred and to localize the source of the fault (*i.e.*, pinpoint the faulty component). To accomplish this, the distributed system is modeled, and sophisticated statistical tools are often used [3]. Some of the approaches in fault detection and diagnosis are introduced in Chapter 3.

A lot of progress has been made in modern programming language design to include some forms of software fault detection and handling, such as unexpected input or state. The most notable example is exception handling. A block of code can be enclosed with a try-catch construct. If an error condition occurs during the execution of the code, the catch block will be executed automatically. Exceptions may also be propagated upward through the calling chain. If an exception occurs and it is not handled by any developer-supplied code, the language runtime usually terminates the process.

The recovery block method, which is designed for software fault tolerance [8], may be considered as an extension of the programming language exception handling mechanism. An important step in recovery blocks is the acceptance testing, which is a form of fault detection. A developer is supposed to supply an acceptance test for each module of the system. When the acceptance test fails, a software fault is detected. Subsequently, an alternate block of code is executed, after which the acceptance test is evaluated again. Multiple alternate blocks of code may be provided to increase the robustness of the system.

1.2.3   Fault Removal

Once a fault is detected and localized, it should be isolated and removed from the system. Subsequently, the faulty component is either repaired or replaced. A repaired or replaced component can be readmitted to the system. To accommodate these steps, the system often needs to be reconfigured. In a distributed system, it is often necessary to have a notion of membership, *i.e.*, each component is aware of a list of components that are considered part of the system and their roles. When a faulty component is removed from the system, a reconfiguration is carried out and a new membership is formed with the faulty component excluded. When the component is repaired or replaced, and readmitted to the system, it becomes part of the membership again.

A special case of fault removal is software patching and updates. Software faults and vulnerabilities may be removed via a software update when the original system is patched. Virtually all modern operating systems and software packages include the software update capability.

1.2.4   Fault Tolerance

Robust software itself is normally insufficient to delivery high dependability because of the possibility of hardware failures. Unless a distributed system is strictly stateless, simply restarting the system after a failure would not automatically restore its state to what it had before the failure. Hence, fault tolerance techniques are essential to improve the dependability of distributed systems to the next level.

There are different fault tolerance techniques that can be used to cater to different levels of dependability requirements. For applications that need high availability, but not necessarily high reliability, logging and checkpointing (which is the topic of Chapter 2), which incurs minimum runtime overhead and uses minimum extra resources, might be sufficient. More demanding applications could adopt the recovery oriented computing techniques (which is the topic of Chapter 3). Both types of fault tolerance techniques rely on *rollback recovery*. After restarting a failed system, the most recent correct state (referred to as a checkpoint) of the system is located in the log and the system is restored to this correct state.

An example scenario of rollback recovery is illustrated in Figure 1.2. When a system fails, it takes some time to detect the failure. Subsequently, the system is restarted and the most recent checkpoint in the log is used to recover the system back to that checkpoint. If there are logged requests, these requests are re-executed by the system, after which the recovery is completed. The system then resumes handling new requests.

For a distributed system that requires high reliability, *i.e.*, continuous correct services, redundant instances of the system must be used so that the system can continue operating correctly even if a portion of redundant copies (referred to as replicas) fail.

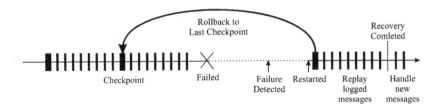

Figure 1.2   The rollback recovery is enabled by periodically taking checkpoints and usually logging of the requests received.

Using redundant instances (referred to as replicas) also makes it possible to tolerate malicious faults provided that the replicas fail independently. When the failed replica is repaired, it can be incorporated back into the system by rolling its state forward to the current state of other replicas. This recovery strategy is called *rollforward recovery*.

An example scenario of rollforward recovery is shown in Figure 1.3. When the failure of the replica is detected and the replica is restarted (possibly after being repaired). To readmit the restarted replica into the system, a nonfaulty replica takes a checkpoint of its state and transfer the checkpoint to the recovering replica. The restarted replica can rollforward its state using the received checkpoint, which represents the latest state of the system.

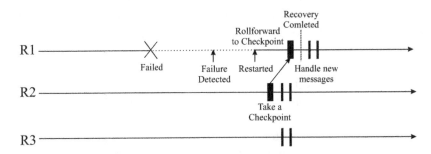

Figure 1.3   With redundant instances in the system, the failure of a replica in some cases can be masked and the system continue providing services to its clients without any disruption.

To avoid common mode failures (*i.e.*, correlated faults), it helps if each replica could execute a different version of the system code. This strategy is referred to as n-version programming [1]. Program transformation may also be used to achieve diversified replicas with lower software development cost [4]. A special form of n-version programming appears in the recovery block method for software fault tolerance [8]. Instead of using different versions of the software in different replicas, each module of the system is equipped with a main version and one or more alternate versions. At the end of the execution of the main version, an acceptance test is evaluated. If the testing fails, the first alternate version is executed and the acceptance test is evaluated again. This goes on until all alternate versions have been exhausted, in which case, the module returns an error.

1.3   System Security

For a system to be trustworthy, it must be both dependable and secure. Traditionally, dependable computing and secure computing have been studied by two disjoint communities [2]. Only relatively recently, the two communities started to collaborate and exchange ideas, as evidenced by the creation of a new IEEE Transactions on Dependable and Secure Computing in 2004. Traditionally, security means the protection of assets [7]. When the system is the asset to be protected, it includes several major components as shown in Figure 1.4:

- *Operation*. A system is dynamic in that it is continuously processing messages and changing its state. The code as well as the execution environment must be protected from malicious attacks, such as the buffer-overflow attacks.
- *System state*. The system state refers to that in the memory, and it should not be corrupted due to failures or attacks.
- *Persistent state*. System state could be lost if the process crashes and if the process is terminated. Many applications would use files or database systems to store critical system state into stable storage.
- *Message*. In a distributed system, different processes communicate with each other via messages. During transit, especial when over the public Internet, the message might be corrupted. An adversary might also inject fake messages to the system. A corrupted message or an injected message must be rejected.

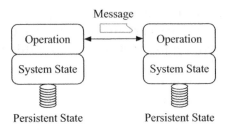

Figure 1.4   Main types of assets in a distributed system.

When we say a system is secure, we are expecting that the system exhibits three attributes regarding how its assets are protected [2]: (1) confidentiality, (2) integrity, and (3) availability. Confidentiality refers to the assurance that the system never reveals sensitive information (system state or persistent state) to unauthorized users. The integrity means that the assets are intact, and any unauthorized modification to the assets, be it the code, virtual memory, state, or message, can be detected. Furthermore, messages must be authenticated prior to being accepted, which would prevent fake messages from being injected by adversaries. The interpretation of availability in the security context is quite different from that in the dependable computing context. Availability here means that the asset is accessible to authorized users. For example, if someone encrypted some data, but lost the security key for decryption, the system is not secure because the data would no longer be available for anyone to access. When combining with dependable computing and in the system context, availability is morphing into that defined by the dependable computing community, that is, the system might be up and running, and running correctly so that an authorized user could access any asset at any time.

An important tool to implement system security is cryptography [11]. Put simply, cryptography is the art of designing ciphers, which scrambles a plaintext in such a way that its meaning is no longer obvious (*i.e.*, the encryption process) and retrieves the plaintext back when needed (*i.e.*, the decryption process). The encrypted text is often called cipher text. Encryption is the most powerful way of ensuring confidentiality and it is also the foundation for protecting the integrity of the system. There are two types of encryption algorithms, one is called symmetric encryption, where the same security key is used for encryption and decryption (similar to household locks where the same key is used to lock and unlock), and the other one is called asymmetric encryption, where one key is used to encrypt and a different key is used to decrypt. For symmetric encryption, key distribution is a challenge in a networked system because the same key is needed to do both encryption and decryption. The asymmetric encryption offers the possibility of making the encryption key available to anyone who wishes to send an encrypted message to the owner, as long as the corresponding decryption key is properly protected. Indeed, asymmetric encryption provides the foundation for key distribution. The encryption key is also called the public key because it can be made publicly available without endangering the system security, and the decryption key is called the private key because it must remain private, *i.e.*, the loss of the private key will cripple the security of the entire system if built on top of asymmetric encryption. To further enhance the security of key distribution, a public-key infrastructure is established so that the ownership of the public key can be assured by the infrastructure.

Symmetric encryption is based on two basic operations: substitution and transposition. Substitution replaces each symbol in the plaintext by some other symbol aiming at disguising the original message, while transposition alters the positions of the symbols in the plaintext. The former still preserves the order of the symbols in the plaintext, while the latter produces a permutation of the original plaintext and hence would break any established patterns of the symbols. The two basic operations are complementary to each and would make the encryption stronger if used together. This also dictates that the symmetric encryption is going to work on a block of plaintext at a time, which is often referred to as block ciphers. When encrypting a large amount of plaintext using block ciphers, they must be divided into multiple blocks. A naive way of doing encryption would be to encrypt each block separately. Although the encryption can be done in parallel and hence can be quickly done, doing so like this would create a problem: an adversary can reorder some of the cipher texts so that the meaning is completely altered, and the receiver would have no means to detect this! To mitigate this problem, various cipher modes were introduced, such as the cipher block chaining mode and the cipher feedback mode. The essence of the cipher modes is to chain consecutive blocks together when encrypting them. As a result, any alteration of the relative ordering of the cipher texts would break the decryption.

However, encryption alone is not sufficient to build a secure system. We still need mechanisms for authentication, authorization, and for ensuring non-repudiation, among many other requirements. Highly important cryptographic constructs include cryptographic hash functions (also referred to as one-way or secure hash functions) such as secure hash standard (SHA-family algorithms), message authentication code, and digital signatures.

A cryptographic hash function would hash any given message P and produce a fixed-length bit-string, and it must satisfy a number of requirements:

- The hash function must be efficient, that is, given a message P, the hash value of P, $Hash(P)$, must be quickly computed.
- Given $Hash(P)$, it is virtually impossible to find P. In this context, P is often referred to the preimage of the hash. In other words, this requirement says it is virtually impossible to find a preimage of a hash. It is easy to understand that if P is much longer than $Hash(P)$ in size, this requirement can be easily satisfied because information must have been lost during the hash processing. However, even if P is shorter than $Hash(P)$, the requirement must still hold.
- Given a message P, and the corresponding hash of P, $Hash(P)$, it is virtually impossible to find a different message P' that would produce exactly the same hash, that is, $Hash(P) = Hash(P')$. If the unfortunate event happens where $Hash(P) = Hash(P')$, we would say there is *collision*. This requirement states that it should be computationally prohibitive to find a collision.

The cryptographic hash function must consider every single bit in the message when producing the hash string so that even if a single bit is changed, the output would be totally different. There has been several generations of cryptographic hash functions. Currently the most common ones used are called secure hash algorithms (SHA), which are published as a federal information processing standard by the US National Institute of Standards and Technology. The SHA family of algorithms have four categories: SHA-0, SHA-1, SHA-2, and SHA-3. SHA-0 and SHA-1 both produce a 160-bit string, which are now considered obsolete. SHA-2, which produces a 256-bit string or a 512-bit string, is used commonly nowadays.

Digital signature is another very important cryptographic construct in building secure systems. A digital signature mimics a physical signature in legal documents, and it must possess the following properties:

- The receiver of a digitally signed document can verify the signer's identity. This is to facilitate authentication of the signer. Unlike in real world, where an official could verify the signer identity by checking for government-issued identification document such as driver's license or passport, the digital signature must be designed in a way that a remote receiver of the digital signature can authenticate the signer based on the digital signature alone.
- The signer of the digital signature cannot repudiate the signed document once it has been signed.
- No one other than the original signer of the signed document could possibly have fabricated the signature.

The first property is for authenticating the signer of a signed document. The second and the third properties are essentially the same because if another person could have fabricated the digital signature, then the original signer could in fact repudiate the signed document. In other words, if the original signer cannot repudiate the signed document, then it must be true that no one else could fabricate the digital signature. Digital signatures are typically produced by using public-key cryptography on the hash of a document. This hash of a document is typically called message digest. The message digest is used because public-key cryptography must use long-keys and it is computationally very expensive compared with symmetric cryptography. In this case, the no-collision requirement for secure hash functions is essential to protect the integrity of digital signatures.

Message authentication code (MAC) is based on secure hash function and symmetric key encryption. More specifically, the sender would concatenate the message to be sent and a security key together, then hash it to produce a MAC. It is used pervasively in message exchanges to both authenticate the sender and to protect the integrity of the message. The basis for authentication is that only the sender and the receiver would know the security key used to generate the MAC. Because of the characteristic of the secure hash function, if any bit in the message is altered during transmission, the transmitted MAC would differ from the one recomputed at the receiver. Hence, the MAC is also used as a form of checksum with much stronger protection than traditional checksum method such as CRC16.

In conventional systems, communication between a client and server is done over a session. Hence, security mechanisms were designed around this need. At the beginning of the session, the client and the server would mutually authenticate each other. Once the authentication step is done, a session key would be created and used to encrypt all messages exchanged within the session. For a prolonged session, the session key might be refreshed. For sessions conducted over the Web, the secure socket layer (SSL) (or transport layer security) protocol is typically used. The server authentication is done via a digital signature and public-key certificate protected by a public-key infrastructure. Client authentication is typically done via user-name and password. Some enterprise systems, such as directory services, adopt much more sophisticated authentication algorithms based on the challenge-response approach.

REFERENCES

1. A. Avizienis and L. Chen. On the implementation of n-version programming for software fault tolerance during execution. In *Proceedings of the IEEE International Computer Software and Applications Conference*, pages 149–155, 1977.

2. A. Avizienis, J. C. Laprie, B. Randell, and C. Landwehr. Basic concepts and taxonomy of dependable and secure computing. *IEEE Transactions on Dependable and Secure Computing*, 1(1):11–33, 2004.

3. M. Y. Chen, E. Kiciman, E. Fratkin, A. Fox, and E. Brewer. Pinpoint: Problem determination in large, dynamic internet services. In *Proceedings of the 2002 International Conference on Dependable Systems and Networks*, DSN '02, pages 595–604, Washington, DC, USA, 2002. IEEE Computer Society.

4. M. Franz. Understanding and countering insider threats in software development. In *Proceedings of the International MCETECH Conference on e-Technologies*, pages 81–90, January 2008.

5. L. Lamport, R. Shostak, and M. Pease. The byzantine generals problem. *ACM Transactions on Programming Languages and Systems*, 4:382–401, 1982.

6. P. M. Melliar-Smith and B. Randell.   Software reliability: The role of programmed exception handling. In *Proceedings of an ACM conference on*

Language design for reliable software, pages 95–100, New York, NY, USA, 1977. ACM.

7. C. P. Pfleeger, S. L. Pfleeger, and J. Margulies. *Security in Computing (5th Ed.)*. Pearson, 2015.

8. B. Randell and J. Xu. The evolution of the recovery block concept. In *Software Fault Tolerance*, pages 1–22. John Wiley & Sons Ltd, 1994.

9. J. Shore. Fail fast. *IEEE Software*, pages 21–25, September/October 2004.

10. A. S. Tanenbaum and M. V. Steen. *Distributed Systems: Principles and Paradigms*. Prentice Hall, 2nd edition, 2006.

11. A. S. Tanenbaum and D. J. Wetherall. *Computer Networks (5th Ed.)*. Pearson, 2010.

12. L. Tewksbury, L. Moser, and P. Melliar-Smith. Live upgrade techniques for corba applications. In *New Developments in Distributed Applications and Interoperable Systems*, volume 70 of *IFIP International Federation for Information Processing*, pages 257–271. Springer US, 2002.

2

Logging and Checkpointing

Checkpointing and logging are the most essential techniques to achieve dependability in distributed systems [7]. By themselves, they provide a form of fault tolerance that is relatively easy to implement and incurs low runtime overhead. Although some information could be lost (if only checkpointing is used) when a fault occurs and the recovery time after a fault is typically larger than that of more sophisticated fault tolerance approaches, it may be sufficient for many applications. Furthermore, they are used in all levels of dependability mechanisms.

A checkpoint of a distributed system refers to a copy of the system state [7]. If the checkpoint is available after the system fails, it can be used to recover the system to the state when the checkpoint was taken. Checkpointing refers to the action of taking a copy of the system state (periodically) and saving the checkpoint to a stable storage that can survive the faults tolerated.

To recover the system to the point right before it fails, other recovery information must be logged in addition to periodical checkpointing. Typically all incoming messages to the system are logged. Other nondeterministic events may have to be logged as well to ensure proper recovery.

Checkpointing and logging provide a form of rollback recovery [7] because they can recover the system to a state prior to the failure. In contrast, there exist other approaches that accomplish roll-forward recovery, that is, a failed process can be recovered to the current state by incorporating process redundancy into the system. However, roll-forward recovery protocols typically incur significantly higher runtime overhead and demand more physical resources.

2.1   System Model

In this section, we define the system model used in the checkpointing and logging algorithms introduced in this chapter. The algorithms are executed in a distributed system that consists of N number of processes. Processes within the system interact with each other by sending and receiving messages. These processes may also interact with the outside world by message exchanges. The input message to the distributed system from the outside world is often a request message sent by the user of the system. The output message from the system is the corresponding response message. An example distributed system consisting of 4 processes is shown in Figure 2.1.

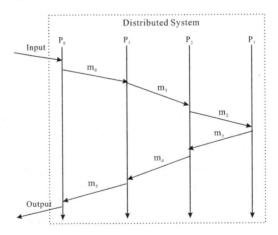

Figure 2.1   An example distributed system.

2.1.1   Fault Model

In such a distributed system, a failure could occur at a process. However, it is assumed that when a process fails, it simply stops execution and loses all its volatile state (*i.e.*, the fail-stop model [18] is used). In addition, it is assumed that any two processes can establish a reliable connection (such as a TCP connection) for communication. Even though the network may lose messages, the reliable channel can effectively mask such losses. Naturally, the reliable connection ensures the first-in first-out (FIFO) property between the two endpoints of the reliable connection. This assumption also implies that the network does not partition, *i.e.*, it does not prevent two or more processes in the system from interacting with each other for extended period of time.

2.1.2   Process State and Global State

The state of an individual process is defined by its entire address space in an operating system. A generic checkpointing library (such as Condor [23]) normally saves the entire address space as a checkpoint of the process. Of course, not everything in the address space is interesting based on the application semantics. As such, the checkpoint of a process can be potentially made much smaller by exploiting application semantics.

The state of a distributed system is usually referred to as the global state of the system [5]. It is not a simple aggregation of the states of the processes in the distributed system because the processes exchange messages with each other, which means that a process may causally depend on some other processes. Such dependency must be preserved in a global state. Assume that each process in the distributed system takes checkpoints periodically, this implies that we may not be able to use the latest set of checkpoints for proper recovery should the processes fails, unless the checkpointing at different processes are coordinated [5]. To see why, considering the three scenarios illustrated in Figure 2.2 where the global state is constructed by using the three checkpoints, C_0, C_1, C_2, taken at processes P_0, P_1, and P_2, respectively.

Figure 2.2(a) shows a scenario in which the checkpoints taken by different processes are incompatible, and hence cannot be used to recover the system upon a failure. Let's see why. In this scenario, P_0 sends a message m_0 to P_1, and P_1 subsequently sends a message m_1

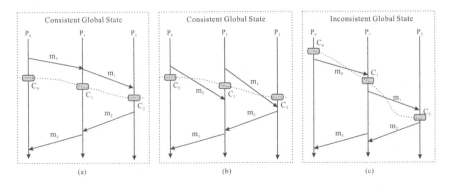

Figure 2.2   Consistent and inconsistent global state examples.

to P_2. Therefore, the state of P_2 potentially depends on the state of P_1 after it has received m_1, and the state of P_1 may depend on that of P_0 once it receives m_0. The checkpoint C_0 is taken *before* P_0 sends the message m_0 to P_1, whereas the checkpoint C_1 is taken *after* P_1 has received m_0. The checkpoints are not compatible because C_1 reflects the receiving of m_0 while C_0 does not reflect the sending of m_0, that is, the dependency is broken. Similarly, C_2 reflects the receiving of m_1 while C_1 does not reflect the sending of m_1.

▪ EXAMPLE 2.1

To understand the problem better, consider the following example. Assume that P_0 and P_1 represent two bank accounts, A and B respectively. The purpose of m_0 is to deposit \$100 to account B after P_0 has debited account A. P_0 takes a checkpoint C_0 *before* the debit operation, and P_1 takes a checkpoint C_1 *after* it has received and processed the deposit request (*i.e.*, m_0), as illustrated in Figure 2.2(a). If P_0 crashes after sending the deposit request (m_0), and P_1 crashes after taking the checkpoint C_1, upon recovery, P_1's state would reflect a deposit of \$100 (from account A) while P_0's state would not reflect the corresponding debit operation. Consequently, \$100 would appear to have come from nowhere, which obviously is not what had happened. In essence, the global state constructed using the wrong set of checkpoints does not correspond to a state that could have happened since the initial state of the distributed system. Such a global state is referred to as an inconsistent global state.

Next, let's look at a scenarios (shown in Figure 2.2(b)) in which the set of checkpoints can be used to properly recover the system to an earlier state prior to the failure. The checkpoint (C_0) taken by P_0 reflects the sending event of m_0. The checkpoint C_1 is taken by P_1 after it has received m_0, therefore, the dependency on P_0 is captured by C_1. Similarly, the dependency of P_2 on P_1 is also preserved by the checkpoint C_2 taken by P_2. Such a global state is an example of consistent global state. Of course, the execution after the checkpoints, such as the sending and receiving of m_2 and m_3, will be lost upon recovery.

The scenario described in Figure 2.2(c) is the most subtle one. In this scenario, P_0 takes a checkpoint *after* it has sent message m_0 while P_1 takes a checkpoint *before* it receives m_0 but *after* it has sent m_1, and P_2 takes a checkpoint *before* it receives m_1. This means that the checkpoint C_0 reflects the state change resulting from sending m_0 whereas C_1 does not incorporate the state change caused by the receiving of m_0. Consequently, this set of checkpoints cannot be used to recover the system after a failure because m_0 and m_1 would have been lost. However, the global state reconstructed by using such a set of checkpoints would still be qualified as a consistent global state because it is one such that it could have happened, *i.e.*, messages m_0 and m_1 are still in transit to their destinations. To accommodate this scenario, an additional type of states, referred to as channel state, is introduced as part of the distributed system state [5].

To define the channel state properly, it is necessary to provide a more rigorous (and abstract) definition of a distributed system. A distributed system consists of two types of components [5]:

- A set of N processes. Each process, in turn, consists of a set of states and a set of events. One of the states is the initial state when the process is started. Only an event could trigger the change of the state of a process.

- A set of channels. Each channel is a uni-directional reliable communication channel between two processes. The state of a channel is the set of messages that are still in transit along the channel (*i.e.*, they have not yet been received by the target process). A TCP connection between two processes can be considered as two channels, one in each direction.

A pair of neighboring processes are always connected by a pair of channels, one in each direction. An event (such as the sending or receiving of a message) at a process may change the state of the process and the state of the channel it is associated with, if any. For example, the injection of a message into a channel may change the state of the channel from empty to one that contains the message itself.

Using this revised definition, the channel states in the third scenario would consist of the two in-transit messages m_0 and m_1. If the channel states can be properly recorded in addition to the checkpoints in this scenario, the recovery can be made possible (*i.e.*, m_0 will be delivered to P_1 and m_1 will be delivered to P_2 during recovery).

2.1.3 Piecewise Deterministic Assumption

Checkpoint-based protocols only ensure to recover the system up to the most recent consistent global state that has been recorded and all executions happened afterwards, if any, are lost. Logging can be used to recover the system to the state right before the failure, provided that all events (that could potentially change the state of the processes) are logged and the log is available upon recovery. This is what is referred to as the piecewise deterministic assumption [21]. According to this assumption, all nondeterministic events can be identified and sufficient information (referred to as a determinant [1]) must be logged for each event. The most obvious example of nondeterministic events is the receiving of a message. Other examples include system calls, timeouts, and the receipt of interrupts. In this chapter, we typically assume that the only nondeterministic events are the receiving of a message. Note that the sending of a message is not a deterministic event, *i.e.*, it is determined by a nondeterministic event or the initial state of the process [7].

2.1.4 Output Commit

A distributed system usually receives message from, and sends message to, the outside world, such as the clients of the services provided by the distributed system. Once a message is sent to the outside world, the state of the distributed system may be exposed to the outside world. If a failure occurs, the outside world cannot be relied upon for recovery. Therefore, to ensure that the recovered state is consistent with the external view, sufficient recovery information must be logged prior to the sending of a message to the outside world. This is what so called the output commit problem [21].

2.1.5 Stable Storage

An essential requirement for logging and checkpointing protocols is the availability of stable storage. Stable storage can survive process failures in that upon recovery, the information stored in the stable storage is readily available to the recovering process. As such, all checkpoints and messages logged must be stored in stable storage.

There are various forms of stable storage. To tolerate only process failures, it is sufficient to use local disks as stable storage. To tolerate disk failures, redundant disks (such as RAID-1 or RAID-5 [14]) could be used as stable storage. Replicated file systems, such as the Google File Systems [9], can be used as more robust stable storage.

2.2 Checkpoint-Based Protocols

Checkpoint-based protocols do not rely on the piecewise deterministic assumption, hence, they are simpler to implement and less restrictive (because the developers do not have to identify all forms of nondeterministic events and log them properly). However, a tradeoff is that the distributed systems that choose to use checkpoint-based protocols must be willing to tolerate loss of execution unless a checkpoint is taken prior to every event, which is normally not realistic.

2.2.1 Uncoordinated Checkpointing

Uncoordinated checkpointing, where each process in the distributed system enjoys full autonomy and can decide when to checkpoints, even though appears to be attractive, is not recommended for two primary reasons.

First, the checkpoints taken by the processes might not be useful to reconstruct a consistent global state. In the worst case, the system might have to do a cascading rollback to the initial system state (often referred to as the domino effect [16]), which completely defeats the purpose of doing checkpointing. Consider the following example.

EXAMPLE 2.2

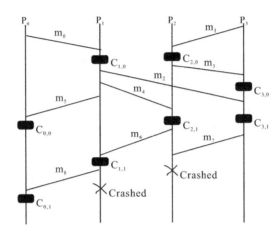

Figure 2.3   An example of the domino effect in recovery with uncoordinated checkpointing.

In the example illustrated in Figure 2.3, process P_1 crashed after it has sent message m_8 to P_0, but before it has a chance to take a checkpoint. The last checkpoint taken by P_1 is $C_{1,1}$. Furthermore, P_2 also crashed concurrently. Now, let's examine the impact of the failure of P_1 and P_2:

- The most recent checkpoint at P_0, $C_{0,1}$, cannot be used because it is inconsistent with $C_{1,1}$. Therefore, P_0 would have to rollback to $C_{0,0}$.
- The most recent checkpoint at P_1, $C_{1,1}$, cannot be used because it is inconsistent with $C_{2,1}$, *i.e.*, $C_{1,1}$ reflected the receiving of m_6 but $C_{2,1}$ does not reflect the sending of m_6. This means that P_1 would have to rollback to $C_{1,0}$.
- Unfortunately, $C_{2,1}$ is not consistent with $C_{1,0}$ because it recorded the receiving of m_4 while $C_{1,0}$ does not reflect the sending of m_4. This means P_2 would have to rollback to $C_{2,0}$.
- This in turn would make it impossible to use any of the two checkpoints, $C_{3,1}$ or $C_{3,0}$, at P_3. This would result in P_3 rolling back to its initial state.

- The rollback of P_3 to its initial state would cause the invalidation of $C_{2,0}$ at P_2 because it reflects the state change resulted from the receiving of m_1, which is not reflected in the initial state of P_3. Therefore, P_2 would have to be rolled back to its initial state too.
- The rollback of P_1 to $C_{1,0}$ would invalidate the use of $C_{0,0}$ at P_0 because of m_5. This means that P_0 would have to rollback to its initial state too.
- Finally, the rollback of P_0 to its initial state would invalidate the use of $C_{1,0}$ at P_1, thereby forcing P_1 to rollback to its initial state. Consequently, the distributed system can only recover to its initial state.

Second, to enable the selection of a set of consistent checkpoints during recovery, the dependency of the checkpoints has to be determined and recorded together with each checkpoint. This would incur additional overhead and increase the complexity of the implementation [2]. As a result, the uncoordinated checkpointing is not as simple as and not as efficient as one would have expected [3].

2.2.2   Tamir and Sequin Global Checkpointing Protocol

In this coordinated checkpointing protocol due to Tamir and Sequin [22], one of the processes is designated as the coordinator and the remaining processes are participants. The coordinator must know all other processes in the system. The coordinator uses a two-phase commit protocol to ensure that not only the checkpoints taken at individual processes are consistent with each other, the global checkpointing operation is carried out atomically, that is, either all processes successfully create a new set of checkpoints or they abandon the current round and revert back to their previous set of checkpoints. The objective of the first phase is to create a quiescent point of the distributed system, thereby ensuring the consistency of the individual checkpoints. The second phase is to ensure the atomic switchover from the old checkpoint to the new one. When a participant fails to respond to the coordinator in a timely fashion, the coordinator aborts the checkpointing round.

2.2.2.1   Protocol Description.

The finite state machine specifications for the coordinator and the participant are provided in Figure 2.4 and Figure 2.5, respectively.

Final State Machine for Coordinator

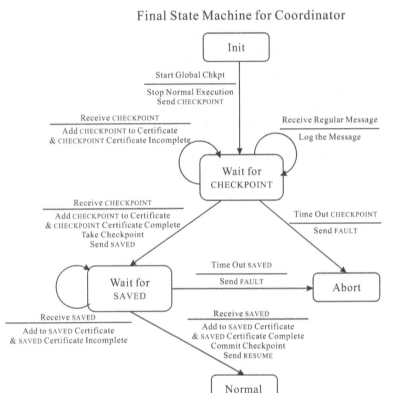

Figure 2.4   Finite state machine specification for the coordinator in the Tamir and Sequin checkpointing protocol.

Note that in the finite state machine specification for the coordinator as shown in Figure 2.4, the normal state is shown twice, once at the beginning (as 'init') and the other at the end, for clarity.

More detailed explanation of the protocol rule for the coordinator and the participant is given below. In the description of the protocol, the messages exchanged between the processes in between two rounds of global checkpointing are referred to regular messages (and the corresponding execution is termed as normal execution), to differentiate them from the set of control messages introduced by the protocol for the purpose of coordination:

– CHECKPOINT message. It is used to initiate a global checkpoint. It is also used to establish a quiescent point of

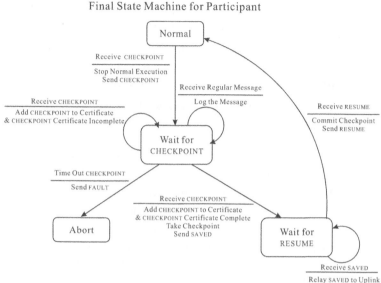

Figure 2.5   Finite state machine specification for the participant in the Tamir and Sequin checkpointing protocol.

the distributed system where all processes have stopped normal execution.
- SAVED message. It is used for a participant to inform the coordinator that it has done a local checkpoint.
- FAULT message. It is used to indicate that a timeout has occurred and the current round of global checkpointing should be aborted.
- RESUME message. It is used by the coordinator to inform the participants that they now can resume normal execution.

Rule for the coordinator:

- At the beginning of the first phase, the coordinator stops its normal execution (including the sending of regular messages) and sends a CHECKPOINT message along each of its outgoing channel.
- The coordinator then waits for the corresponding CHECK-POINT message from all its incoming channels.
  - While waiting, the coordinator might receive regular messages. Such messages are logged and will be appended to the checkpoint of its state. This can only

happen from an incoming channel from which the coordinator has not received the CHECKPOINT message.

- The coordinate aborts the checkpointing round if it fails to receive the CHECKPOINT message from one or more incoming channels within a predefined time period.

- When the coordinator receives the CHECKPOINT message from all its incoming channels, it proceeds to take a checkpoint of its state.
- Then, the coordinator waits for a SAVED notification from *every process* (other than itself) in the distributed system. It aborts the checkpointing round if it fails to receive the SAVED message from one or more incoming channels within a predefined time period. It does so by sending a FAULT message along each of its outgoing channel. Note that it is impossible for the coordinator to receive any regular message at this stage.
- When the coordinator receives the SAVED notification from all other processes, it switches to the new checkpoint, and sends a RESUME message along each of its outgoing channel.
- The coordinator then resumes normal execution.

Rule for the participant:

- Upon receiving a CHECKPOINT notification, the participant stops its normal execution and in turn sends a CHECKPOINT message along each of its outgoing channel.
- The participant then waits for the corresponding CHECKPOINT message from all its incoming channels.

    - While waiting, the participant might receives regular messages. Such messages are logged and will be appended to the checkpoint of its state. Again, this can only happen from an incoming channel from which the participant has not received the CHECKPOINT message.

    - The participant aborts the checkpointing round by sending a FAULT message along each of its outgoing channel if it fails to receive the CHECKPOINT message from one or more incoming channels within a predefined time period.

- Once the participant has collected the set of CHECKPOINT messages, it takes a checkpoint of its state.

- The participant then sends a SAVED message to its upstream neighbor (from which the participant receives the first CHECKPOINT message), and waits for a RESUME message.

- Upon receiving a SAVED message (from one of its downstream neighbors), it relays the message to its upstream neighbor.

- When it receives a RESUME message, it propagates the message along all its outgoing channels except the one that connects to the process that sends it the message. The participant then resumes normal execution.

EXAMPLE 2.3

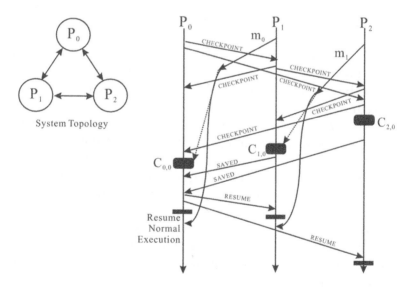

Figure 2.6 Normal operation of the Tamir and Sequin checkpointing protocol in an example three-process distributed system.

To see how the checkpointing protocol works, consider the example shown in Figure 2.6. In this example, we assume that the distributed system consists of three processes, where the three processes are fully connected, *i.e.*, P_0 has a connection with P_1, P_1 has a connection with P_2, and P_2 has a connection with P_0. Therefore, each process has two incoming channels and two outgoing channels connected to its two neighbors.

Assume process P_0 is the checkpointing coordinator. It initiates the global checkpointing by sending a CHECKPOINT message to P_1 and P_2, respectively, along the two outgoing channels. In the mean time, P_1 sends a regular message m_0 to P_0, and P_2 sends a regular message m_1 to P_1.

Upon receiving the CHECKPOINT message from P_0, P_1 stops normal execution and sends a CHECKPOINT message along each of its outgoing channel to P_0 and P_2, respectively. Similarly, P_2 sends the CHECKPOINT message to P_0 and P_1, respectively, once it receives the first CHECKPOINT message.

Due to the FIFO property of the connections, P_0 receives m_0 before it collects all the CHECKPOINT messages from all its incoming channels, and P_1 receives m_1 before it receives the CHECKPOINT messages from P_2. According to the protocol rule, such regular messages are logged instead of delivered because normal execution must be stopped once the global checkpointing is initiated. These logged messages will be appended to the local checkpoint once it is taken. In fact, such messages reflect the channel states of the distributed system. These messages won't be delivered for execution until a process resumes normal execution.

When P_0 receives the CHECKPOINT messages from P_1 and P_2, it takes a local checkpoint, $C_{0,0}$ and append the message log to the checkpoint. Similarly, P_1 takes a local checkpoint when it receives the CHECKPOINT messages from P_0 and P_2, and P_2 takes a local checkpoint when it receives the CHECKPOINT messages from P_0 and P_1.

Subsequently, P_1 and P_2 send their SAVED messages to P_0, i.e., the global checkpointing coordinator. P_0 then informs P_1 and P_2 to resume normal execution with a RESUME message to each of them.

A more complicated distributed system in which some processes do not have direct connection with the coordinator will require some of the coordinator's neighbors to relay the SAVED notification to the coordinator.

2.2.2.2   Correctness of the Protocol.

It is easy to see why the protocol always produce a set of checkpoints that can be used to reconstruct a consistent global state in the absence of failures. As shown in Figure 2.2(a) and (b), a consistent global state consists of only two scenarios with respect to each pair of local states:

1. All messages sent by one process prior to its taking a local checkpoint have been received and executed before the other process takes its local checkpoint.
2. Some messages sent by one process prior to its taking a local checkpoint might arrive after the other process has checkpointed its state, however, these messages are logged at stable storage for replay.

In the Tamir and Sequin protocol, if neither the coordinator nor any of the participants receives any regular message once the global checkpointing is initiated, then the scenario 1 holds. On the other hand, if a process receives one or more regular messages, it logs them and append them to the local checkpoint, ensuring their replayability. Hence, the scenario 2 holds. Because the protocol prohibits any process from continuing normal execution (including the sending of a message) as soon as it initiates (if it is the coordinator) or receives the very first CHECKPOINT message (for a participant), no process would receive a message prior to its checkpointing that has been sent by another process after that process has taken its local checkpoint in the same round. That is, the inconsistent global state scenario shown in Figure 2.2(a) does not occur.

2.2.3   Chandy and Lamport Distributed Snapshot Protocol

The Tamir and Sequin global checkpointing protocol is very elegant. However, it is a blocking protocol in that normal execution is suspended during each round of global checkpointing. For applications that do not wish to suspend the normal execution for potentially extensive period of time, the Chandy and Lamport distributed snapshot protocol [5] might be more desirable.

The Chandy and Lamport distributed snapshot protocol [5] is a nonblocking protocol in that normal execution is not interrupted by the global checkpointing. However, unlike the Tamir and Sequin protocol, the Chandy and Lamport distributed snapshot protocol only concerns on how to produce a consistent global checkpoint, and it prescribes no mechanisms on how to determine the end of the checkpointing round, and how to atomically switch over to the new global checkpoint.

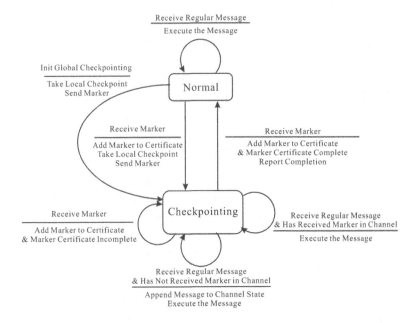

Figure 2.7   Finite state machine specification for the Chandy and Lamport distributed snapshot protocol.

2.2.3.1   *Protocol Description.*

The finite state machine diagram for the Chandy and Lamport distributed snapshot protocol is given in Figure 2.7. A process will be in the Normal state between two rounds of global checkpointing, and in the Checkpointing state during a global checkpointing round. A process may encounter a number of events:

- The global checkpointing can be initiated by any of the processes in the distributed system. Once a process decides to initiate a global checkpointing round, it takes a local checkpoint and sends a Marker message to each of its outgoing channels. The state of the process changes from Normal to Checkpointing as a result.
- A process undergoes the same state transition (from Normal to Checkpointing) and take the same actions upon receiving the Marker message for the first time, except

that it logs the Maker in a data structure referred to as the Marker Certificate in the finite state machine diagram. The Marker Certificate data structure keeps track of which incoming channel has received a Marker and whether or not all incoming channels have received the Marker. The Marker Certificate is called complete when every incoming channel has received a Marker.

- When a process receives the Marker message from a channel when it is in the Checkpointing state, it adds the Marker message to the Marker Certificate and checks whether or not the Marker Certificate is complete. If the Marker Certificate is now complete, the process transits to the Normal state (and possibly reports the completion of the global checkpointing to some predefined server). Otherwise, the process will remain in the Checkpointing state.

- In either the Normal or Checkpointing state, the process may receive a regular message. The regular message is always executed immediately. This is drastically different from the Tamir and Sequin global checkpointing protocol. The regular message will be appended to the channel state from which it is received only when the process is in the Checkpointing state and it has not received the Marker message in this channel.

EXAMPLE 2.4

An example run of the distributed snapshot protocol in a three-process distributed system is shown in Figure 2.8. P_0 is the initiator of the round of the global checkpointing. P_0 takes a local checkpoint and sends a Marker message along each of its outing channels. Upon receiving the Marker message, P_1 immediately takes a local checkpoint and in turn sends a Marker message to each of its outgoing channels. Similarly, P_2 takes a local checkpoint when it receives the first Marker message (from P_1) and sends a Marker message to each of its outgoing channels connecting to P_0 and P_1, respectively.

Upon taking a local checkpoint, a process starts logging messages, if any, arrived at each incoming channel. The process stops logging messages for a channel as soon as it has received a Marker message from that channel. The messages logged will

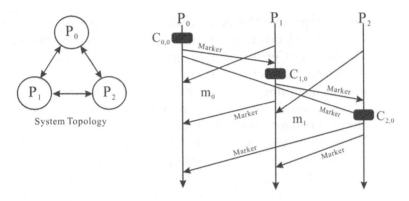

Figure 2.8   Normal operation of the Chandy and Lamport global snapshot protocol in an example three-process distributed system.

become the state for each channel. For P_0, the channel state consists of a message m_0. For P_1, the channel state consists of a message m_1. The channel state for P_2 is empty because it did not receive any message prior to the receipt of the Marker message from each of its incoming channels. Note that the regular message received (such as m_0 or m_1) is executed immediately, which is drastically different from the Tamir and Sequin global checkpointing protocol.

2.2.4   Discussion

The two global checkpointing protocols introduced in this section share a number of similarities.

- Both rely on virtually the same system model, and use a special control message to propagate and coordinate the global checkpointing.
- They both recognize the need to capture the channel state to ensure the recoverability of the system.
- The mechanism to capture the channel state is virtually the same for both protocols, as shown in Figure 2.9.
    - In both protocols, a process starts logging messages (for the channel state) for each channel upon the initiation of the global checkpoint (at the initiator) or upon the receipt of the first control message (*i.e.*, the Marker message in the Chandy and Lamport protocol and the CHECKPOINT message in the Tamir and Sequin protocol).

    – In both protocols, the process stops logging messages and conclude the channel state for each channel when it receives the control message in that channel.

- The communication overhead of the two protocols is identical (*i.e.*, the same number of control messages is used to produce a global checkpoint).

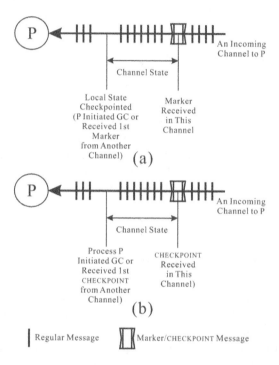

        An Incoming
        Channel to P

Channel State

Local State
Checkpointed
(P Initiated GC or
Received 1st
Marker
from Another
Channel)

Marker
Received
in This
Channel

(a)

An Incoming
Channel to P

Channel State

Process P
Initiated GC or
Received 1st
CHECKPOINT
from Another
Channel)

CHECKPOINT
Received
in This
Channel)

(b)

| Regular Message   Marker/CHECKPOINT Message

Figure 2.9 A comparison of the channel state definition between (a) the Chandy and Lamport distributed snapshot protocol and (b) the Tamir and Sequin global checkpointing protocol.

The two protocols also differ in their strategies in producing a global checkpoint.

- The Tamir and Sequin protocol is more conservative in that a process suspends its normal execution as soon as it learns that a global checkpointing round has started. In light of the Chandy and Lamport protocol, the suspension of normal execution could have been avoided during a global checkpointing round.

- The reason for the blocking design in the Tamir and Sequin protocol is that a process captures the channel states prior to taking a local checkpoint. While capturing the channel state, a process cannot execute the regular messages received because doing so would alter the process state, thereby potentially rendering the global checkpoint inconsistent. On the other hand, in the Chandy and Lamport protocol, a process captures the channel state *after* it has taken a local checkpoint, thereby enabling the execution of regular messages without the risk of making the global checkpoint inconsistent.

- The Tamir and Sequin protocol is more complete and robust because it ensures the atomicity of the global checkpointing round. Should a failure occurs, the current round would be aborted. The Chandy and Lamport protocol does not define any mechanism to ensure such atomicity. Presumably, the mechanisms defined in the Tamir and Sequin protocol can be incorporated to improve the Chandy and Lamport protocol.

2.3   Log Based Protocols

Checkpoint-based protocols only ensure to recover the system up to the most recent consistent global state that has been recorded and all executions happened afterwards, if any, are lost. Logging can be used to recover the system to the state right before the failure, provided that the piecewise deterministic assumption is valid. In log based protocols, the execution of a process is modeled as consecutive state intervals [21]. Each state interval is initiated by a nondeterministic event (such as the receiving of a message) or the initialization of the process, and followed by a sequence of deterministic state changes. As long as the nondeterministic event is logged, the entire state interval can be replayed.

As an example, three state intervals are shown in Figure 2.10. The first state interval starts at the initialization of the process P_i and ends right before it executes the first message, m_1 received. Note that the sending of message m_0 is not considered a nondeterministic event. The second state interval is initiated by the receiving event of message m_1 and ends prior to the receipt of m_3. Similarly, the third state interval starts with the receiving event of m_3 and ends prior to the receipt of m_5.

In the remaining of this section, we assume that the only type of nondeterministic events is the receiving of application messages. Therefore, logging is synonymous with message logging.

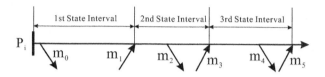

Figure 2.10   Example state intervals.

For all practical purposes, logging is always used in conjunction with checkpointing to enjoy two benefits:

1. It limits the recovery time because to recover from a failure the process can be restarted from its last checkpoint (instead from its initial state) and its state can be recovered prior to the failure by replaying the logged nondeterministic events.
2. It limits the size of the log. By taking a checkpoint periodically, the logged events prior to the checkpoint can be garbage collected.

Logging protocols can be classified into three types [7]:

- Pessimistic logging. A message received is synchronously logged prior to its execution.
- Optimistic logging. To reduce the latency overhead, the nondeterministic events are first stored in volatile memory and logged asynchronously to stable storage. Consequently, the failure of a process might result in permanent loss of some messages, which would force a rollback to a state earlier than the state when the process fails.
- Causal logging. The nondeterministic events (and their determinant, such as delivery order of messages received at a process) that have not yet logged to stable storage are piggybacked with each message sent. With the piggybacked information, a process can have access all the nondeterministic events that may have causal effects on its state, thereby enabling a consistent recovery of the system upon a failure.

In both optimistic logging [21, 19, 20] and causal logging protocols [1], the dependency of the processes has to be tracked and sufficient dependency information has to be piggybacked with each message sent. This not only increases the complexity of the logging mechanisms, but most importantly, makes the failure recovery more sophisticated and expensive because the recovering process has to find a way to examine its logs and determines if it is missing any messages and often causes cascading recovery operations at other processes.

On the other hand, pessimistic logging protocols are much simpler in their design and implementation and failure recovery can be made much faster [11] (specific advantages will be elaborated in section 2.3.1 below). Therefore, our discussion will focus on the pessimistic logging techniques and there will be no further elaboration on optimistic and causal logging.

2.3.1   Pessimistic Logging

The most straightforward implementation of pessimistic logging is to synchronously log every incoming message to stable storage before it is executed at a process. Each process can checkpoint its state periodically at its own pace without the need to coordinate with other processes in the distributed system. Upon recovery from a failure, a process restores its state using the last checkpoint and replays all logged incoming messages to recover itself to the state right before it fails.

EXAMPLE 2.5

Consider the example shown in Figure 2.11. Process P_1 crashes after sending message m_8. Process P_2 crashes after sending message m_9. Upon recovery, P_1 restores its state using the checkpoint $C_{1,0}$. Because it will be in the state interval initiated with the receiving of message m_0, messages m_2, m_4, and m_5 will be deterministically regenerated. This should not be a problem because the receiving processes should have mechanism to detect duplicates. Subsequently, the logged message m_6 is replayed, which triggers a new state interval in which m_8 would be deterministically regenerated (and discarded by P_0. Similar, upon recovery, P_2 restores its state using the checkpoint $C_{2,0}$. The restored state is in the state interval initiated by

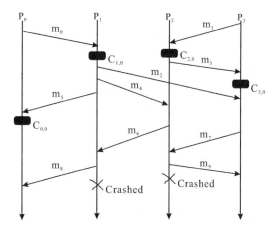

Figure 2.11 An example for pessimistic logging.

the receiving of m_1, and message m_3 will be deterministically regenerated and sent to P_3. Again, P_3 would detect that it is a duplicate and discard it. Furthermore, the logged messages m_4 and m_7 is replayed, causing the sending of messages m_6 and m_9, which will be ignored by P_1 and P_3.

Pessimistic logging can cope with concurrent failing and recovery of two or more processes, as illustrated in the example shown in Figure 2.11. Messages received while a process is recovering (*i.e.*, while it is restoring its state using the latest checkpoint and by replaying all the logged messages), can be buffered and examined when the process completes its recovery. It is possible that while a process is engaging in a recovery, another process fails and recovers itself concurrently, as the above example shows. In this case, P_1 would receive a duplicate message (m_6) regenerated by another recovering process P_2 and temporarily buffers it. P_1 then would discard it as soon as it is done recovery. Similarly, P_2 would receive the duplicate message m_4 regenerated by P_1, which will be discarded after the recovery is completed.

2.3.1.1 *Benefits of Pessimistic Logging.*

It is apparent that pessimistic logging has a number of very desirable characteristics:

- Processes do not need to track their dependencies. The relative ordering of the incoming messages to each process is naturally reflected in the log (*i.e.*, during recovery, the messages in the log will be replayed in the order in which they are logged). Hence, the pessimistic logging mechanism is straightforward to implement and less error prone.

- Output commit is free with pessimistic logging. This is a great fit for distributed applications that interact with their users frequently.

- There is no need to carry out coordinated global checkpointing because by replaying the logged messages, a process can always bring itself to be consistent with other processes in the system. This further reduces the complexity of adding rollback recovery support to applications. Furthermore, a process can decide when it is the best time to take a local checkpoint, for example, when its message log is too big.

- Recovery can be done completely locally to the failed processes. The only impact to other processes is the possibility of receiving duplicate messages and discard them. Hence, the recovery is simpler and in general faster than optimistic and causal logging. The localization of failure recovery also means that pessimistic logging supports concurrent failure recovery of multiple processes.

2.3.1.2   Discussion.

There are three issues that warrant additional elaboration: reconnection, message duplicate detection, and atomic message receiving and logging.

Reconnection. A process must be able to cope with temporary connection failures and be ready to accept reconnections from other processes. This is an essential requirement for recoverable distributed system. This calls for a design in which the application logic is independent from the transport level events. This can be achieved by using a event-based [8] or document-based distributed computing architecture such as Web services [15], in conjunction with appropriate exception handling.

Message duplicate detection. As mentioned above, a process must be capable of detecting duplicate messages because it may receive such messages replayed by another process during recovery. Even though transport-level protocols such as TCP have build-in mechanism to detect and discard duplicate messages, such mechanism is irrelevant because it works only within the established connection. During failure recovery, the recovering process will inevitably re-establish the connections to other processes, hence, such mechanism cannot be depend on. Furthermore, not all application-level protocols have duplicate detection support (they often depend on the underlying transport-level protocol to do so). In this case, the application-level protocol must be modified to add the capability of message duplicate detection. For XML-based protocols, such as SOAP [15], it is straightforward to do so by introducing an additional header element that carries a <sender-id, sequence-number> tuple, where the sender-id is a unique identifier for the sending process and sequence-number is the sequence number of the message issued by the sending process. The sequence number establishes the order in which the message is sent by a process P_i to another process P_j. It must start from an initial sequence number (assigned to the first message sent) known to both processes and continuously incremented for each additional message sent without any gap. The Web Services Reliable Messaging standard [6] specifies a protocol that satisfies the above requirement.

Atomic message receiving and logging. In the protocol description, we implicitly assumed that the receiving of a message and the logging of the same message are carried out in a single atomic operation. Obviously the use of a reliable communication channel alone does not warrant such atomicity because the process may fail right after it receives a message but before it could successfully log the message, in which case, the message could be permanently lost. This issue is in fact a good demonstration of the end-to-end system design argument [17]. To ensure the atomicity of the message receiving and logging, additional application-level mechanism must be used. (Although the atomic receiving and logging can be achieved via special hardware [4], such solution is not practical for most modern systems.)

As shown in Figure 2.12(a), a reliable channel only ensures that the message sent is temporarily buffered at the sending side until an acknowledgement is received in the transport layer. The receiving side sends an acknowledgement as soon as it receives the message in the transport layer. The receiving side buffers the message received until the application process picks up the message. If the application process at the receiving side fails either before it picks up the message, or before it completes logging

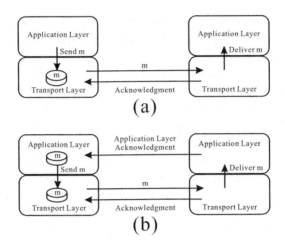

Figure 2.12   Transport level (a) and application level (b) reliable messaging.

the message in stable storage, the sending side would receive no notification and the message sent is no longer available.

To ensure application level reliable messaging, the sending process must store a copy of the message sent (in the application level) for possible retransmission until it receives an explicit acknowledgment message from the receiving process in the application level, as shown in Figure 2.12(b). Such an application level reliable messaging protocol does exist in some distributed computing paradigm, such as Web services [6]. Incidentally, the sender-based message logging protocol [13], to be introduced in a later subsection, incorporates a similar mechanism, albeit for a slightly different purpose.

We should note that the use of such an application level reliable messaging protocol is essential not only to ensure the atomicity of message receiving and logging, but also to facilitate the distributed system to recover from process failures (for example, the failure of the process at one end point of a transport level connection, which would cause the breakage of the connection, would have no negative impact on the process at the other end of the connection, and a process is always ready to reconnect if the current connection breaks).

Furthermore, the use of an application level reliable messaging protocol also enables the following optimization: a message received can be executed immediately and the logging of the message in stable storage can be deferred until another message is to be sent [13]. This optimization has a number of benefits, as shown in Figure 2.13:

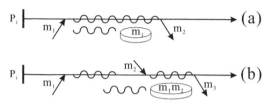

Figure 2.13   Optimization of pessimistic logging: (a) concurrent message logging and execution (b) logging batched messages.

- Message logging and message execution can be done concurrently (illustrated in Figure 2.13(a)), hence, minimizing the latency impact due to logging.
- If a process sends out a message after receiving several incoming messages, the logging of such messages can be batched in a single I/O operation (illustrated in Figure 2.13(b)), further reducing the logging latency.

2.3.1.3   Pessimistic Logging Cost.

While much research efforts have been carried out to design optimistic and causal logging to avoid or minimize the number of logging operations (on disks) assuming that synchronous logging would incur significant latency overhead [1, 19, 20, 21] . In this section, we present some experimental results to show that such assumption is often unwarranted. The key reason is that it is easy to ensure sequential disk I/Os by using dedicated disks. It is common nowadays for magnetic disks to offer a maximum sustained data rate of 100MB or more per second. Such transfer rate is approaching or exceeding the effective bandwidth of Gigabit Ethernet networks. Furthermore, with the increasing availability (and reduced cost) of semiconductor solid state disks, the sequential disk I/Os can be made even faster and the latency for random disk I/Os can be dramatically reduced. By using multiple logging disks together with disk striping, Gigabytes per second I/Os have been reported [10].

In the experiment, a simple client-server Java program is used where the server process logs every incoming request message sent

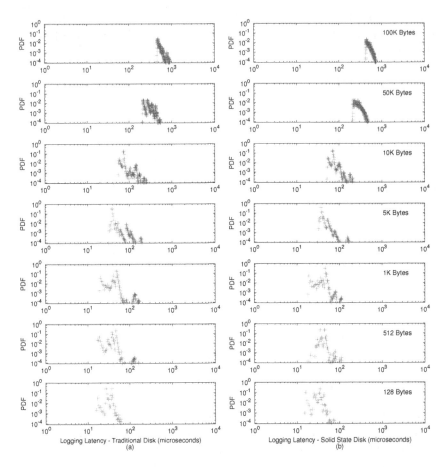

Figure 2.14 Probability density function of the logging latency.

by the client and issues a response to the client. The response message is formed by transforming the client's request and it carries the same length as the request. The server node is equipped with a 2nd generation core i5 processor running the Windows 7 Operating system. The client runs on an iMac computer in the same local area network connected by a Gigabit Ethernet switch. The server node has two hard drives, one traditional magnetic hard drive with a spindle speed of 7,200 RPM, and the other a semiconductor solid state drive. In each run, 100,000 iterations were performed. The logging latency (at the server) and the end-to-end latency (at the client) are measured.

Figure 2.14 shows the logging latency for various message sizes using the traditional disk (on the left), and the solid state disk (on the right), respectively. The experimental results are presented here in the form of a sequence of probability density functions (PDF) [12] of the logging latency for various message lengths. The PDFs give much more details on the cost of logging operation than a simple average value. As can be seen, on both the solid state disk and the traditional disk, the far majority of the logging operation (for each incoming message) can be completed within 1000 μs for messages as large as 100KB, which means the logging can be done with a rate of over 100MB per second, approaching the advertised upper limit of the data transfer rate of traditional disks. For small messages, the logging can be done within 100 μs.

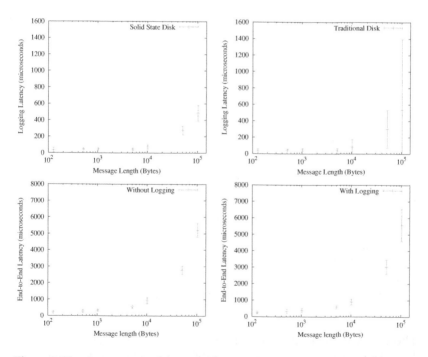

Figure 2.15   A summary of the mean logging latency and mean end-to-end latency under various conditions.

It is somewhat surprising to see that the performance on the solid state disk is not significantly better than that on the traditional disk, especially for small messages. For large messages, the solid state disk does make the logging operations more predictable in its latency, that is, the standard deviation [12] is much smaller than that on the traditional disk, as can be seen in Figure 2.15.

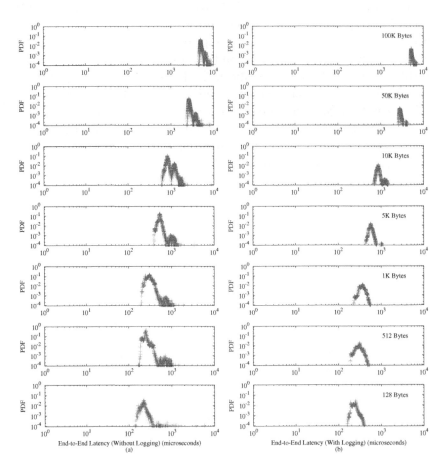

Figure 2.16   Probability density function of the end-to-end latency.

The end-to-end latency results shown in Figure 2.16 prove that indeed the pessimistic logging contributes very moderate (often less than 10%) overhead to the performance of the system as observed by the client. For messages of up to 100KB, the end-to-end latency with and without pessimistic logging falls within 10ms. For small messages, the end-to-end latency can go down as low as about 100μs. In all circumstances, the end-to-end latency is significantly larger than the logging latency. For the message size of 100KB, the oneway transfer latency over the network is esti-mated to be around $2600\mu s$ (half of the end-to-end latency without logging). This implies that the network manages to offer slightly under 40MB per second transfer rate.

2.3.2   Sender-Based Message Logging

For distributed applications that do not wish to log messages synchronously in stable storage, the sender-based message logging protocol [13] can be used to achieve limited degree of robust-ness against process failures. The basic idea of the sender-based message logging protocol is to log the message at the sending side in volatile memory. Should the receiving process fail, it could obtain the messages logged at the sending processes for recovery. To avoid restarting from the initial state after a failure, a process can period-ically checkpoint its local state and write the message log in stable storage (as part of the checkpoint) asynchronously.

Unlike the receiver-based message logging protocol introduced in section 2.3.1, where the relative ordering of the messages received can be implicitly logged, such ordering information (*i.e.*, the determinant for the messages) must be explicitly supplied by the receiver of a message to the sender. Furthermore, after sending the ordering information, the receiver needs to wait for an explicit acknowledgment for the ordering message. Prior to receiving of the acknowledgment, the receiver must not send any message to other processes (however, it can execute the message received immediately without delay, similar to the optimization for pessimistic logging discussed in section 2.3.1.2. This restriction is put in place to prevent the formation of orphan messages and orphan processes [7], which would force the orphan processes to roll back their state during the recovery of another process.

An orphan message is one that was sent by a process prior to a failure, but cannot be guaranteed to be regenerated upon the recov-ery of the process [7]. An orphan process is a process that receives an orphan message. If a process sends out a message and subse-quently fails before the determinants of the messages it has received are properly logged, the message sent becomes an orphan message.

2.3.2.1   *Data Structures*

In the sender-based message logging protocol, each process must maintain the following data structures:

- A counter, *seq_counter*, used to assign a sequence number (using the current value of the counter) to each outgoing (application) message. The counter is initialized to 0 and incremented by one for each message sent. The sequence number is needed for duplicate detection (at the receiving process).
- A table used to carry out duplicate detection on incoming messages. The table consists of a collection of entries, one for each process with which the current one communicates. Each entry has the form $<process\_id, max\_seq>$, where max_seq is the maximum sequence number that the current process has received from a process with an identifier of $process\_id$. A message is deemed as a duplicate if it carries a sequence number lower or equal to max_seq for the corresponding process.
- Another counter, *rsn_counter*, used to record the receiving/execution order of an incoming message. The counter is initialized to 0 and incremented by one for each message received. The receiving order of a message is represented by the current value of the counter and it is sent back to the sending process of the message for logging.
- A message log (in volatile memory) for messages sent by the process. In addition to the message sent, the following meta data is also recorded for each message:
  - Destination process id, *receiver_id*;
  - Sending sequence number, *seq*;
  - Receiving sequence number, *rsn*.

  The destination process id, the sending sequence number, and the message will be logged prior to the sending of the message. However, the receiving order number will be logged after the process receives such information later.
- A history list for the messages received since the last checkpoint. Each entry in the list has the following information regarding each message received:
  - Sending process id, *sender_id*;
  - Sending sequence number, *seq*;
  - Receiving sequence number, *rsn* (assigned by the current process).

The history list is used to find the receiving order number for a duplicate message received. Upon receiving a duplicate message, the process should supply the corresponding (original) receiving order number so that the sender of the message can log such ordering information properly.

All the data structures described above except the history list must be checkpointed together with the process state. The two counters, one for assigning the message sequence number and the other for assigning the message receiving order, are needed so that the process can continue doing so upon recovery using the checkpoint. The table for duplicate detection is needed for a similar reason. However, the saving of the message log as part of the checkpoint might appear to be counter-intuitive because a major benefit of doing checkpointing is to truncate the message log (*i.e.*, garbage collect logged messages) for (receiver-based) pessimistic logging as described in section 2.3.1. For sender-based message logging, unfortunately this side benefit is no longer applicable. The message log is needed for the receiving processes to recover from a failure, and hence, cannot be garbage collected upon a checkpointing operation. Additional mechanism, which will be introduced towards the end of this section, is necessary to ensure that the message log does not grow indefinitely.

The reason why the history list can be garbage collected upon a checkpointing operation is because the receiving sequence number information in the list (*i.e.*, the receiving/execution order of the messages leading to the checkpoint) will no longer be needed for failure recovery. When a process receives a duplicate message and it cannot find the corresponding receiving sequence number in the history list because it has recently checkpointed its state, it may inform the sender that the message can now be purged from its message log – it is no longer needed for failure recovery due to the recent checkpoint.

In addition to the above data structures, the protocol uses the following types of messages:

- REGULAR message type. It is used for sending regular messages generated by the application process, and it has the form <REGULAR,*seq,rsn,m*>, where m refers to the message content. Obviously, at the time of sending of a message, its receiving sequence number, rsn, would not be known to the sending process, in which case, it assumes a special constant value (such as -1) indicating the unknown status. When a logged message is replayed to a recovering process, the sending process might have already learned the rsn value, in which case, a concrete rsn value is supplied.

- ORDER message type. It is used for the receiving process is notify the sending process the receiving/execution order of the message. An ORDER message carries the form <ORDER, $[m]$, rsn>, where $[m]$ is the message identifier consisting of a tuple <$sender\_id$, $receiver\_id$, seq>.
- ACK message type. It is used for the sending process (of a regular message) to acknowledge the receipt of the ORDER message. It assumes the form <ACK, $[m]$>.

2.3.2.2   Normal Operation of the Message Logging Protocol

The normal operation of the protocol is shown in Figure 2.17.

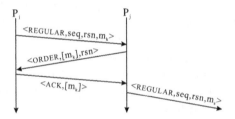

Figure 2.17   Normal operation of the sender-based logging protocol.

The protocol operates in three steps for each message:

1. A REGULAR message, <REGULAR,seq,rsn,m>, is sent from one process, $e.g.$, P_i, to another process, $e.g.$, P_j.
2. Process P_j determines the receiving/execution order, rsn, of the regular message and informs the determinant information to P_i in an ORDER message <ORDER, $[m]$, rsn>.
3. Process P_j waits until it has received the corresponding acknowledgment message, <ACK, $[m]$>, before it sends out any REGULAR message.

The original sender-based message logging protocol [13] was designed for use with unreliable channels. Since we have assumed the use of reliable channels, one might wonder if the third step in the protocol is still necessary. The answer is yes because transport-level reliability does not necessarily lead to application-level reliability, as we have argued in section 2.3.1.2. If a process sends the ordering message to a process and another regular message to a different process, and node on which the process runs subsequently crashes, the ordering message might not be delivered to its intended target successfully while the regular message might.

Furthermore, in the original sender-based message logging protocol [13] , the regular message and the ordering message must be retransmitted after a timeout before the expected acknowledgment message is received. With the use of reliable channels, such proactive retransmission becomes unnecessary because the only scenario in which a retransmission is necessary is when a process fails, in which case, the retransmission will be triggered by the recovery mechanism (more in section 2.3.2.3).

The use of a mature reliable communication protocol such as TCP in distributed applications is more desirable because the application developers can focus on the application logic and application-level messaging reliability without worrying about issues such as achieving high throughput and doing congestion control.

◧ EXAMPLE 2.6

In the example shown in Figure 2.18, the distributed system consists of three processes. Both the seq counter and rsn counter are initialized to be 0, and the message log is empty at each process. Process P_0 first sends a regular message, $<$REGULAR,0,?,$m_0>$, to P_1. Upon sending the message, P_0 increments its seq counter to 1 and log the message in its volatile buffer. At this point, the rsn value for the message is unknown, hence it is denoted as a question mark.

On receiving the regular message $<$REGULAR,0,?,$m_0>$, P_1 assigns the current rsn counter value, which is 0, to this message indicating its receiving order, increments its rsn counter to 1, and sends P_0 an ORDER message $<$ORDER,$[m_0]$,0$>$. When P_0 receives this ORDER message, it updates the entry in its message log to reflect the ordering number for message m_0, and sends an sc ack message, $<$ACK,$[m_0]>$, to P_1.

Once receiving the ACK message, P_1 is permitted to send a regular message, $<$REGULAR,0,?,$m_1>$, to P_2. The handling of the message and the corresponding ORDER and ACK messages are similar to the previous ones.

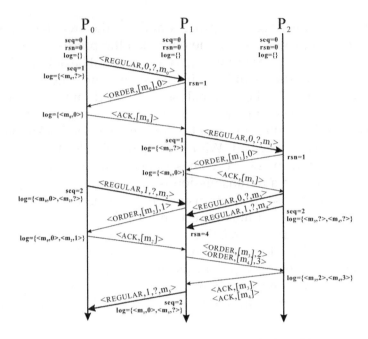

Figure 2.18   An example normal operation of the sender-based logging protocol.

Subsequently, P_0 and P_2 send three regular messages m_2, m_3, m_4, nearly concurrently to P_0. P_1 assigns 1 as the rsn value for the first of the three messages (for m_2) and sends an ordering message to P_0, and assigns 2 and 3 for the two back-to-back regular messages (for m_3 and m_4) from P_2. For the two messages from P_2, P_1 can batch the ORDER messages and sends them together to P_2, and P_2 can batch the corresponding the ACK messages to P_1 too. Upon receiving the ACK messages for all three ORDER messages, P_1 sends another regular message containing m_5 with sequence number 1, updates the seq counter to 2, and log the message.

2.3.2.3   Recovery Mechanism.

On recovering from a failure, a process first restores its state using the latest local checkpoint, and then it must broadcast a request to all other processes in the system to retransmit all their logged messages that were sent to the process.

Because the checkpoint includes its message log, and the regular messages logged and the corresponding ACK messages might not reach their the destination processes due to the process failure, the recovering process retransmit the regular messages or the ack messages based on the following rule:

- If the entry in the log for a message contains no rsn value, then a REGULAR message is retransmitted because the intended receiving process might not have received this message.
- If the entry in the log for a message contains a valid rsn value, then an ACK message is sent so that the receiving process can send regular messages.

When a process receives a regular message, it always sends a corresponding ORDER message in response. There are three scenarios:

- The message is not a duplicate, in which case, the current rsn counter value is assigned to the message as its receiving order, and the corresponding ORDER message is sent. The process must then wait for the ACK message before it sends any regular message.
- The message is a duplicate, and the corresponding rsn value is found in its history list, in which case, an ORDER is message is sent and the duplicate message itself is discarded. The process must then wait for the ACK message before it sends any regular message. Note that it is impossible for the process to have received the corresponding ACK message before because otherwise the recovering process must have logged the rsn value for the regular message.
- The message is a duplicate, and there is no corresponding entry in the history list. In this case, the process must have checkpointed its state after receiving the message and it is no longer needed for recovery. As a result, the process sends an ORDER message with a special constant indicating that the message is no longer needed and the sending processing can safely purge the entry from its message log.

The recovering process may receive two types of retransmitted regular messages: (1) those with a valid rsn value, and (2) those without. Because the rsn counter is part of the state checkpointed, the recovering process knows which message is to be executed next. During the recovery, the process executes the retransmitted regular messages with valid rsn values according to the ascending rsn

order. This ensures that these messages are replayed in exactly the same order as they were received prior to the failure. During the replay, the process may send regular messages to other processes. Such messages are logged at the recovering process as usual and they are likely to be duplicate. This is not a concern because of the duplicate detection mechanism in place and the duplicate message handling mechanism described above.

After replaying these messages, the process is recovered to a state that is visible to, and consistent with, other processes prior to the failure. For regular messages without rsn values, the recovering process can replay them in an arbitrary order because the process must not have sent any regular message since the receipt of such messages prior to its failure.

2.3.2.4   Limitations and Correctness.

The sender-based message logging protocol described above ensures proper recovery of a distributed system as long as a single failure occurs at a time. That is, after a process fails, no other processes fail until the failed process is fully recovered. Note that the protocol cannot cope with two or more concurrent failures. If two or more failures occur concurrently, the determinant for some regular messages (*i.e.*, the rsn values) might be lost, which would lead to orphan processes and the cascading rollback (*i.e.*, the domino effect).

■ EXAMPLE 2.7

Consider a distributed system consisting of three processes P_0, P_1, and P_2, shown in Figure 2.19. P_0 sends P_1 a regular message $<$REGULAR,k,?,$m_i>$. After the message is fully logged at P_0, P_1 sends P_2 a message $<$REGULAR,s,?,$m_t>$. Then, both P_0 and P_1 crashed. Upon recovery, although P_0 can resend the regular message $<$REGULAR,k,?,$m_i>$ to P_1, however, the receiving order information rsn is lost due to the failures. Hence, it is not guaranteed that P_1 could initiate the correct state interval that resulted in the sending of regular message $<$REGULAR,s,?,$m_t>$. P_2 would become an orphan process and be forced to rollback its state.

We prove below that the recovery mechanism introduced in section 2.3.2.3 guarantees a consistent global state of the distributed system after the recovery of a failed process. The only way the

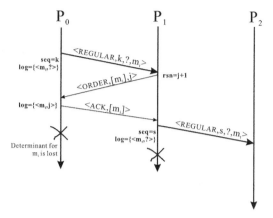

Figure 2.19   Two concurrent failures could result in the loss of determinant information for regular messages.

global state of a distributed system becomes inconsistent is when one process records the receipt of a (regular) message that was not sent by any other process (*i.e.*, the message is an orphan message). We prove that any regular message that is received at a process must have been logged at the sending process. For a pair of nonfailing processes, the correctness of this statement is straightforward because the sending process always logs any message it sends. The interesting case is when a nonfailing process received a regular message that was sent by a process that fails subsequently.

Let's assume a process P_i fails and another process P_j receives a regular message sent by P_i prior to the failure, we need to prove that the message must have been logged at P_i either prior to its failure or will have been logged before the end of the recovery.

If P_i checkpointed its state after sending the regular message prior to the failure, the message must have been logged in stable storage and is guaranteed to be recoverable. Otherwise, the message itself would have been lost due the failure because it was logged in volatile memory. However, we prove that the message will be regenerated during the recovery.

According to the protocol, a process cannot send any new regular message before it has received the ACK message for every regular message received. The fact that the message was sent means P_i must have received the ACK message for the regular message that triggered the state interval in which the message was sent. This in turn means that the sending process of the regular message, say P_k

must have received the corresponding ORDER message sent by P_i. Hence, upon recovery, P_k will be contacted by P_i and the regular message with a valid rsn value will be retransmitted to P_i. This would ensure the recovering process P_i to reinitiate the state interval in the correct order. The regular message received by P_j will be correctly regenerated and logged at P_i during recovery. This completes our proof.

2.3.2.5   Discussion.

As we have mentioned before, unlike the receiver-based pessimistic logging, performing a local checkpointing at a process does not truncate its message log because the log contains messages sent to *other* processes and they might be needed for the recovery of these other processes. This is rather undesirable. Not only it means unbounded message log size, but it leads to unbounded recovery time as well.

The sender-based message logging protocol can be modified to at least partially fix the problem. However, it will be at the expense of the locality of local checkpointing. Once a process completes a local checkpoint, it broadcasts a message containing the highest rsn value for the messages that it has executed prior to the checkpoint. All messages sent by other processes to this process that were assigned a value that is smaller or equal to this rsn value can now to purged from its message log (including those in stable storage as part of a checkpoint). Alternatively, this highest rsn value can be piggybacked with each message (regular or control messages) sent to another process to enable asynchronous purging of the logged messages that are no longer needed.

REFERENCES

1. L. Alvisi and K. Marzullo. Message logging: Pessimistic, optimistic, causal, and optimal. *IEEE Trans. Softw. Eng.*, 24(2):149–159, Feb. 1998.

2. B. K. Bhargava and S.-R. Lian. Independent checkpointing and concurrent rollback for recovery in distributed systems - an optimistic approach. In *Symposium on Reliable Distributed Systems*, pages 3–12, 1988.

3. B. K. Bhargava, S.-R. Lian, and P.-J. Leu. Experimental evaluation of concurrency checkpointing and rollback-recovery algorithms. In *ICDE*, pages 182–189. IEEE Computer Society, 1990.

4. A. Borg, W. Blau, W. Graetsch, F. Herrmann, and W. Oberle. Fault tolerance under unix. *ACM Trans. Comput. Syst.*, 7(1):1–24, Jan. 1989.

5. K. M. Chandy and L. Lamport. Distributed snapshots: determining global states of distributed systems. *ACM Trans. Comput. Syst.*, 3(1):63–75, Feb. 1985.

6. D. Davis, A. Karmarkar, G. Pilz, S. Winkler, and U. Yalcinalp. Web Services Reliable Messaging (WSReliableMessaging) Version 1.2, OASIS Standard. http://docs.oasis-open.org/ws-rx/wsrm/200702/wsrm-1.2-spec-os.pdf, February 2009.

7. E. N. M. Elnozahy, L. Alvisi, Y.-M. Wang, and D. B. Johnson. A survey of rollback-recovery protocols in message-passing systems. *ACM Comput. Surv.*, 34(3):375–408, Sept. 2002.

8. O. Etzion and P. Niblett. *Event Processing in Action*. Manning Publications, 2010.

9. S. Ghemawat, H. Gobioff, and S.-T. Leung. The google file system. *SIGOPS Oper. Syst. Rev.*, 37(5):29–43, Oct. 2003.

10. J. Gray and P. Kukol. Sequential disk io tests for gbps land speed record. Technical report, Microsoft Research, 2004.

11. Y. Huang and Y.-M. Wang. Why optimistic message logging has not been used in telecommunications systems. In *Proceedings of the Twenty-Fifth International Symposium on Fault-Tolerant Computing*, FTCS '95, pages 459–, Washington, DC, USA, 1995. IEEE Computer Society.

12. R. K. Jain. *The Art of Computer Systems Performance Analysis: Techniques for Experimental Design, Measurement, Simulation, and Modeling*. Wiley, 1991.

13. D. B. Johnson and W. Zwaenepoel. Sender-based message logging. In *The 7th annual international symposium on fault-tolerant computing*. IEEE Computer Society, 1987.

14. F. Miller, A. Vandome, and J. McBrewster. *Standard Raid Levels*. Alphascript Publishing, 2009.

15. E. Newcomer and G. Lomow. *Understanding SOA with Web Services*. Addison-Wesley Professional, 2004.

16. B. Randell. System structure for software fault tolerance. In *Proceedings of the international conference on Reliable software*, pages 437–449, New York, NY, USA, 1975. ACM.

17. J. H. Saltzer, D. P. Reed, and D. D. Clark. End-to-end arguments in system design. *ACM Transactions on Computer Systems*, 2(4):277–288, 1984.

18. R. D. Schlichting and F. B. Schneider. Fail-stop processors: an approach to designing fault-tolerant computing systems. *ACM Trans. Comput. Syst.*, 1(3):222–238, Aug. 1983.

19. A. P. Sistla and J. L. Welch. Efficient distributed recovery using message logging. In *Proceedings of the eighth annual ACM Symposium on Principles of distributed computing*, PODC '89, pages 223–238, New York, NY, USA, 1989. ACM.

20. S. W. Smith and D. B. Johnson. Minimizing timestamp size for completely asynchronous optimistic recovery with minimal rollback. In *Proceedings of the 15th Symposium on Reliable Distributed Systems*, SRDS '96, pages 66–, Washington, DC, USA, 1996. IEEE Computer Society.

21. R. Strom and S. Yemini. Optimistic recovery in distributed systems. *ACM Trans. Comput. Syst.*, 3(3):204–226, Aug. 1985.

22. Y. Tamir and C. H. Suin. Error recovery in multicomputers using global checkpoints. In *In 1984 International Conference on Parallel Processing*, pages 32–41, 1984.

23. T. Tannenbaum and M. Litzkow. Checkpointing and migration of unix processes in the Condor distributed processing system. *Dr Dobbs Journal*, February 1995.

3

Recovery-Oriented Computing

Recovery-oriented computing was pioneered by a joint research project of Stanford University and the University of California, Berkerly [7] in early and mid 2000. The main focus of the research is to develop guidelines, methodologies, and tools to enable fast recovery for Internet-based servers. This research complements other research efforts that aim to extend the mean time to failure (MTTF) of the software systems, for example, by using replication to mask low-level failures. The rational is that, by reducing the mean time to recover (MTTR), the system availability can be improved as well due to the inverse relationship between the availability and the mean time to recover (*i.e.*, Availability = MTTF / (MTTF+MTTR)).

The first step in achieving fast recovery is quick fault detection and localization. Fault detection means to determine if some component of a system has failed, and it may not pinpoint exactly which component has failed. Fault localization, on the other hand, is to find the exact component that has failed. While low level fail-stop faults can be quickly detected using mechanisms such as timeouts, most application level faults are more subtle (at least revealed by their symptoms during early stages) and much harder to detect and in general, even harder to localize. As reported in [13, 14, 22], for some Internet service providers, up to 75% of the recovery time is spent on application-level fault detection.

Although fault detection and localization have long been an active area of research [2, 12, 19, 29], the approaches employed in recovery-oriented computing are unique in that they target the application-level fault detection and localization based on application-agnostic machine-learning techniques. These approaches have several advantages: (1) they may be applied to many distributed systems with minimum development cost because they are not tied to any specific application and they do not depend on any specific application semantics, and (2) they can cope with unforeseen faults, which is very useful for large complex systems because it is impossible to develop fault models *a priori* for traditional fault diagnosis methods.

Once a failed component is located, the cheapest method to recover the component is to restart it, which is referred to as microreboot [11]. Microreboot is different from regular reboot in that only the suspected component is restarted instead of the entire server application. As such, microreboot is much faster than typically reboot. According to [7, 11], restarting an Enterprise Javabean (EJB) typically takes less than 0.6 seconds, while restarting the entire application server would take about 20 seconds. Microreboot is best at handling transient software bugs (often referred to as Heisenbugs) and resource (such as memory and file descriptors) leaks.

When microreboot is not capable of fixing the problem, such as in the presence of persistent software bugs and the corruption of persistent data, and in case of operator errors, more heavy-weight method must be used to recover the system. A system-level undo/redo methodology was developed to handle these difficult cases. Different from checkpointing and logging introduced in the previous chapter, the system-level undo/redo provides a more comprehensive recovery solution for several reasons: When resetting the state of a process (*i.e.*, undo), the operating system state is also reset. This is especially useful to handle operator error because any persistent effect on the operating system (*e.g.*, files modified, deleted, or created) due to the error must be reversed in order to correct the error. It aims to preserve the application's intent while performing replay. When replaying an operation, the system behavior might not be consistent with the view of an external user. Such paradoxes will have to be detected and properly addressed by using application-specific consistency rules and compensation methods.

3.1   System Model

An important step in failure recovery is to reconstruct the state of the recovering component or process so that it is consistent with other parts of the system and ready to provide services to its clients. For faster recovery, the best practice is to separate data management from application logic. The three-tier architecture [30], which is pervasively used in Internet-based applications, is a good example of this strategy.

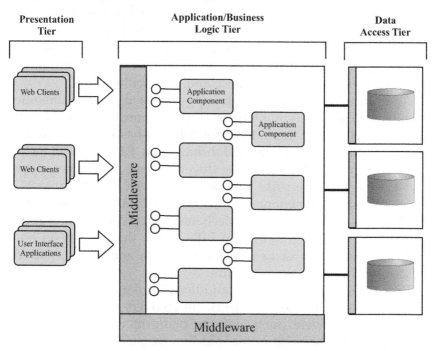

Figure 3.1   The three-tier architecture.

As shown in Figure 3.1, in this architecture, persistent state of an application is stored separately at the backend tier (typically a database server) while the middle-tier server (typically an application server) is responsible to handle clients' requests according to the application logic. As such, the application server at the middle-tier maintains only session state, which typically consists of temporary state that lasts only for the session (*e.g.*, between when a user logs in and when the user logs out). Examples of the session state include the user's shopping cart and the list of products that the user has viewed. The presentation tier consists of the client software that enables the users of the application to interact with the application via a graphic user interface. Sometimes, the Web server, which interacts with the client software directly and is stateless, is regarded as part of the presentation tier.

When an application server fails, only the session state is lost, which would impact the users of the active sessions this particular server was engaged in. To minimize the negative impact of a failed application server even further, the session state can be separated to a dedicated session state store, as did in [11]. The recovery-oriented computing techniques would work the best for applications using the three-tier architecture. This is especially the case for employing the microrebooting technique because the architecture enables the rebooting of components of an application server with minimum impact to the system performance and availability.

As indicated in Figure 3.1, an application using the three-tier architecture is usually implemented using some middleware platform. The dominating platform for Internet-based applications is the Java Platform, Enterprise Edition (Java EE). Java EE facilitates component-based software development. A key component construct is the Enterprise Java Bean (EJB). An EJB implements a specific business function. Java EE also enables the separation of mechanisms and policies [32]. Mechanisms in accomplishing application logic are programmed in EJBs, while the policies on how they are used are specified in terms of Java annotations and/or descriptor files at deployment time.

Java EE is still an evolving middleware platform. At the time when several of the seminal works in recovery-oriented computing [13, 22, 11] were published, the platform was referred to as J2EE and it was selected as the middleware platform of choice for recovery-oriented computing. Since then, the platform has evolved to be less complicated and more efficient.

As shown in Figure 3.2, in Java EE, the components are managed by containers. On the server side, there are two types of containers:

Java EE Application Server

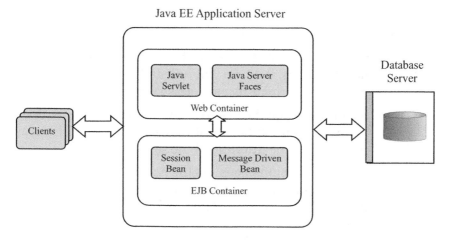

Figure 3.2   The Java EE architecture.

- Web container. This container manages Web components that are responsible to interact directly with clients and to generate Web pages for the clients. Example Web components include Java servlets and user interface objects produced by the Java Server Faces framework.
- EJB container. This container manages EJBs.

At deployment time, the components are installed in their respective containers. A container provides a set of system-level services to the components it manages. Some services are configurable, such as security, transaction management, and remote connectivity. Other services are not configurable, such as the life cycle management, data persistence, and database connection resource pooling. The container mechanism makes EJBs more portable and reusable. It also alleviates the burden of the component developers from writing code for the services provided to the component.

There are several types of EJBs:

- Session beans. A session bean represents an interactive session initiated by a single client (*e.g.,* by logging into an account) inside the application server. All client's interactions with the application server are done through remote invocation with the session bean. The session bean executes business tasks on behalf of the client. The state of the session bean is not saved automatically to the backend database server. There are three types of session beans:

- Stateless session beans. A stateless session bean does not maintain state for the client beyond the current invocation, similar to a stateless Web server.

- Stateful session beans. A stateful session bean does maintain state on behalf of the client across all invocations within the duration of the session.

- Singleton session beans. As the name suggests, a singleton session bean is instantiated only once during the life cycle of an application (that is, there is only a single instance for each singleton session bean). This is different from stateful and stateless sessions beans, which allow multiple instances being created. A singleton session bean typically represents a piece of state that is shared across the application.

• Message-driven beans. A message-driven bean is used in conjunction with the Java Message Service to enable J2EE applications to process messages asynchronously.

• Entity beans. Entity beans were introduced in J2EE and have been deprecated and replaced by the Java persistence application programming interface (API). An entity bean represents a business object (such as a customer or a product) whose state should be made persistent at the database server. The state persistency can be managed by the bean itself (which means the developer must explicitly write code for the database access), or by the container. Different entity beans might have relationships as they are defined in the database schema.

It is worth noting that an EJB is always executed within a single thread of control under the container.

3.2   Fault Detection and Localization

Much of the theory of fault detection in distributed systems has been focused on the detection of fail-stop faults. To detect a fail-stop fault, a fault detector relies on the use of timeouts, even though it may not be reliable in asynchronous systems. Nevertheless, detecting fail-stop faults is straightforward compared with the challenge of detecting application-level faults. This is because many application-level faults exhibit symptoms initially only at the application-level, which is not detectable by lower-level fault detectors.

Ideally, application-level faults can be detected by acceptance tests introduced in the recovery block approach for software fault tolerance [16]. Unfortunately, this approach would put undue burden on application developers to develop effective and efficient acceptance test routines. In general, it is regarded as impractical to monitor directly application-level functionality of Internet-based applications to see if it has deviated from its specification [22] because of their scale, complexity, and rapid rate of upgrades. Consequently, [14, 13, 22] propose to measure and monitor structural behaviors of an application as a way to detect application-level failures without *a priori* knowledge of the inner workings of the application.

This approach is based on the following insight. In component-based applications, each component typically implements a specific application function, *e.g.*, a stateful session bean may be used to manage a user's shopping cart and a set of singleton session beans are used to keep track of the inventory for each product that is on sale. Hence, the interaction patterns between different components would reflect the application-level functionality. This internal structural behavior then can be monitored to infer whether or not the application is functioning normally. To monitor structural behavior, it is necessary to log the runtime path of each end-user request, which entails to keeping track all internal events triggered by the request, *i.e.*, all incoming messages to, and outgoing messages from, each component, and all direct interactions between different components (in terms of method invocations), and their causal relationships.

EXAMPLE 3.1

Figure 3.3 shows an example runtime path of an end-user request.

In the example, the Web server component A, such as a Java servlet, issues a nested request (request-i1, event 1) to a component B in the application server, such as a session bean, in response to receiving an end-user request (request-i).

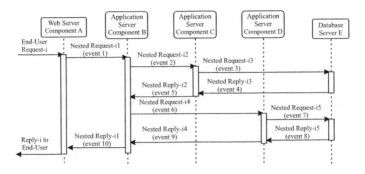

Figure 3.3   An example runtime path of an end-user request.

On processing the nested request (request-i1), the application server component B invokes a method of component C (nested request-i2, event 2), which is a singleton bean. In turn, component B persists the updated data to the database server E (nested request-i3, event3, and the corresponding reply-i3, event4) in response to the method invocation. Furthermore, A also invokes a method of component D, which in turn invokes on the database server E, before it sends back the nested reply to the Web component A (events 6 through 10). Hence, the runtime path for this end-user request spans across 5 components and consists of 10 events.

According to [13, 14, 22], the best way to keep track of the runtime path of each end-user request is to instrument the underlying middleware framework. Indeed, the availability of an open-source Java EE application server, JBoss, enables the tracking of runtime path in [13, 14, 22]. The advantage of this approach is that it is transparent to applications, which makes it easier to deploy and maintain than any application-specific solutions.

Once the runtime path logging is enabled, the next step for structural behavior monitoring is to perform the machine learning step. The objective of this step is to construct reference models for the application's normal behavior in terms of its structural interaction patterns. In [13, 14, 22], each reference model is further divided into two sub-models:

- Historical reference model. This model is built by using all the logged runtime path data. The objective of this model is to enable anomaly detection on components with respect to their past behavior.

- Peer reference model. This model is build by using the runtime path data obtained in the most recent period of time (*e.g.*, the last 5 minutes). The objective of this model is to enable anomaly detection with respect to the peer components.

While historical reference model can be built using synthetic workload that resembles real workload offline (it can also be constructed during runtime in the presence of real workload, of course), the peer reference model can only be built during runtime, which requires the assumption that the end-user requests arrive in high volume and they are mostly independent of each other for the statistical techniques to work.

After the machine learning step is completed, the structural behavior monitoring framework will be ready to monitor the health of the application by detecting anomalies, *i.e.*, by comparing the observed interaction patterns with those in the reference models using statistical techniques.

Two types of reference models are introduced in [13, 14, 22]. The first type models the component interactions while the second type models the runtime path shapes. The former focuses on detecting faulty components, and the latter focuses on detecting the end-user requests that are mishandled. These two types of models are complementary to each other because they each may detect anomalies undetectable using the other model, as explained in the following example given in [22].

EXAMPLE 3.2

A temporary fault in a component might affect only a few requests. This fault can be detected by the path shape reference model because the runtime paths of the affected requests would be significantly deviated from their normal paths. However, the fault might not be detectable by the component reference model because the number of requests affected is too statistically insignificant.

As another example, a faulty component might reject a large portion of authentication requests with valid credentials. This fault can be detected by component interaction reference model because the component interaction pattern would significantly deviate from its normal pattern (*e.g.*, only a very small fraction of authentication requests are rejected normally). However, because the rejection of an authentication request is one of several valid paths, the fault cannot be detected by the path shape reference model.

Recently, an inference-based fault diagnosis method was proposed in [20]. It is designed for small enterprise networks that consist of both Web-based applications and networking components (such as firewalls). Similar to [13, 14, 22], the method is designed to be application-agnostic and it uses a dynamically constructed dependency graph of the entities in the enterprise networks. The basic idea is to determine if the current state of an entity is abnormal by comparing against the history of that entity, and to infer the root cause of the abnormality using the dependency graph, again, by analyzing the history information of the entities in the network. The fault diagnosis method as presented in [20] is on coarser granular entities such as hosts and processes than that of [13, 14, 22], which can be as small as an EJB. However, there does not appear to have intrinsic difficulty to extend the method to perform fault diagnosis on finer-granular components in the EJB-level. Hence, in the detailed description of the inference-based fault diagnosis method in Section 3.2.3, we still use the term "component" to refer to the fault diagnosis granularity.

3.2.1 Component Interactions Modeling and Anomaly Detection

To model the component interactions, it is necessary to differentiate a component class and an instance of a component. For example, each type of EJB as defined by the corresponding Java class can be considered as a component class. Except for singleton beans, multiple instances of an EJB class may be created to handle different users, which constitutes as the component instances.

In the model introduced into [22], only the interactions between a component instance and all the other component classes are considered. One reason is that the level of interactions between different component instances is not the same for individual instances of a component class [22]. Perhaps it is also due to the use of the Chi-square test for anomaly detection (explained shortly). This decision also makes the modeling process more scalable because the number of instances for each component class could potentially be large for

Internet-based applications (to handle large number of concurrent users).

Given a system with n component classes, the interaction model for a component instance consists of a set of $n-1$ weighted links between the component instance and all the other $n-1$ component classes (one for each component class). Here we assume that the component instances of the same component class do not interact with each other. We also assume that the interaction between two components are symmetric in that the interaction is either a local method invocation, or a remote method invocation with a request being sent and the corresponding reply received).

The weight assigned to each link is the probability of the component instance interacting with the linked component class. The sum of the weight on all the links should be equal to 1 (*i.e.*, the component instance has probability of 1 to interact with one or more other component classes).

◼ **EXAMPLE 3.3**

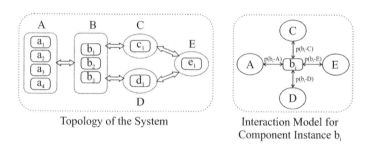

Topology of the System   Interaction Model for
                                Component Instance b_i

Figure 3.4   Component class and component instances.

Consider the example system shown in Figure 3.4. The system consists of 5 component classes:

- A Web component class A. Its instances (a_1 through a_4) handle requests from the end-user.
- An application logic component class B. It consists of several stateful session bean instances (b_1, b_2, b_3), which are used to handle the conversations with the end-users.
- Application logic component classes C and D. Each class has only a single instance (*i.e.*, singleton session bean instance), representing the state to be shared, such as the inventory of a product, in the system.

- Database server component class E. It represents the specific table (*i.e.*, persistent state) involved when handling the end-user requests.

As shown in the system topology, A only directly interacts with B, B interacts with C and D, C and D interact with E. The interaction model for a component instance of B is shown on the right-side of Figure 3.4. The weight on each link is denoted as $p(b_i - C_j)$, where C_j is the class with which component instance b_i interact. According to the system topology, it is apparent that $p(b_i - E) = 0$ because there is no direct interaction between B and E.

The weight for other links depends on the observed interactions. Assume that the following interactions occurred at component instance b_1 during the learning period:

- A issued 400 remote invocations on b_1.
- b_1 in turn issued 300 local method invocations on C and 300 local method invocations on D.
- For the interaction model for b_1, it is not important what happened between C and E, and D and E.

The total number of interactions occurred at the component instance b_1 is 1,000. Therefore, the weight $p(b_1 - A) = 400/1000 = 0.4$, $p(b_1 - C) = 300/1000 = 0.3$, and $p(b_1 - D) = 300/1000 = 0.3$. The total weight on all links sums up to be 1.

To detect anomalies, the deviation between a component instance's behavior and the reference model is measured. In [22], the chi-square (χ^2) test [18] is used. The chi-square test is one of the most commonly used tests to determine whether or not a set of observed data satisfies a particular distribution. Furthermore, the chi-square test can be used for any distribution.

To perform the chi-square test, it is necessary to prepare the observed data set as a histogram [18]. The deviation between the observed data and the expected distribution is then calculated according to the following equation:

$$D = \sum_{i=1}^{k} \frac{(o_i - e_i)^2}{e_i} \tag{3.1}$$

where k is the number of cells in the histogram, e_i is the expected frequency in cell i, and o_i is the observed frequency in cell i.

Obviously, if e_i is 0 for a cell, the cell should be pruned off from the calculation.

In the context of the component interaction reference model, each link is regarded as a cell. Suppose the observation period is defined by a fixed total number of method invocations m for all the links of the component instance, the observed number of the interactions on link i is o_i. Then, the expected frequency for the same link i is:

$$e_i = mp_i \tag{3.2}$$

where p_i is the weight assigned to link i in the reference model.

When there is no anomaly, ideally o_i should match e_i, and the deviation D should be 0. However, in real system, D would not be 0 even if there is no anomaly because of randomness. In fact, D follows a chi-square distribution with $k - 1$ degrees of freedom (when using a histogram with k number of cells) [18]. Hence, we can declare an anomaly only if the computed D is *greater* than the $1 - \alpha$ quantile of the chi-square distribution with the freedom of degree of $k - 1$ at a level of significance α. The higher level of significance, the more sensitive of the test to deviations (as a tradeoff, the more prone to false positives).

▪ EXAMPLE 3.4

With respect to the example system and reference model introduced in Example 3.3, suppose the following has been observed for the most recent 100 method invocations with which component instance b_1 is involved:

- A issued 45 remote invocations on b_1.
- b_1 in turn issued 35 local method invocations on C and 20 local method invocations on D.

For the link between A and b_1, the observed value is 45, and the expected value is $100 \times 0.4 = 40$. For the link between C and b_1, the observed value is 35, and the expected value is $100 \times 0.3 = 30$. For the link between D and b_1, the observed value is 20, and the expected value is $100 \times 0.3 = 30$. Hence, the deviation from the reference model according to the chi-square test is: $D = (45 - 40)^2/40 + (35 - 30)^2/30 + (20 - 30)^2/30 = 4.79$.

This chi-square test has a degree of freedom of 2 (because there are only 3 cells in the histogram). For the level of significance $\alpha = 0.1$, the 90% quantile of the chi-square distribution

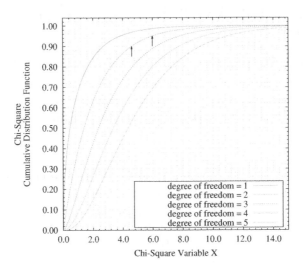

Figure 3.5   The chi-square cumulative distribution function for degree of freedom of 1, 2, 3, 4, 5.

with a degree of freedom 2 can be estimated from Figure 3.5 to be about 4.6 (as indicated by the arrow pointing to the 90% quantile value), which is slightly smaller than the observed deviation (4.79). Therefore, the component instance is behaving abnormally for the level of significance of 0.1. However, we could reduce the significance level to make the anomaly detection less sensitive, for example $\alpha = 0.05$. In this case, the threshold deviation for abnormality would be changed to about 6.0 (as indicated by the arrow pointing to the 95% quantile value), which would not trigger an anomaly report.

The arrows point to the 90% and 95% quantile values of the chi-square distribution, respectively.

3.2.2   Path Shapes Modeling and Root Cause Analysis

A complementary fault detection method to component interactions monitoring is to monitor the shapes of the runtime paths of the end-user requests. While serving an end-user request, in general multiple component instances are involved, as shown in Figure 3.3. The shape of a runtime path is defined to be the ordered set of component classes instead of component instances for modeling purpose. A path shape is represented as a tree in which a node represents a component class, and the directional edge represents the causal relationship between two adjacent nodes.

■ **EXAMPLE 3.5**

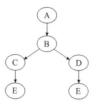

Figure 3.6   The path shape of the example runtime path shown in Figure 3.3.

As an example, the path shape of the runtime path shown in Figure 3.3 is illustrated in Figure 3.6. The root of the tree of the Web component class A. The directional edge from the root node to its child node (an application server component class B) implies that it is A that invoked a method of B. Other edges can be interpreted similarly.

The probabilistic context-free grammar (PCFG) is used in [14, 13, 22] as a tool to model the path shapes of end-user requests in the system during normal (*i.e.*, fault-free) operation. The grammar is inferred during the learning phase from the observed path shapes.

PCFG was originally used in natural language processing [25] and has recently been used to infer the structures of many networked systems [15, 24].

A PCFG consists of the following items:

- A list of terminal symbols, T^k, $k = 1, 2, ..., n$. In our concurrent context, the component classes that may be present in any path shape form the terminal symbols.
- A list of nonterminal symbols, N^i, $i = 1, 2, ..., m$. These symbols are used to denote the stages of the production rules. N^1 is the designated start symbol, often denoted as S. For path shapes modeling, a special nonterminal symbol, $, is used to indicate the end of a rule. All other nonterminal symbols are to be replaced by specific production rules.
- A list of production rules, $N^i \rightarrow \zeta^j$, where ζ^j represents a list of terminals and nonterminals.
- A list of probabilities $R_{ij} = P(N^i \rightarrow \zeta^j)$. Each production rule is assigned a probability, indicating the likelihood of

the transition defined in the rule. Furthermore, the sum of the probabilities of the rules at each stage must be 1, *i.e.*, for any N^i, $\sum P(N^i \to \zeta^j) = 1$.

For path shape modeling, the PCFG in the Chomsky Normal Form (CNF) [25] is derived to model the rules of the path shapes during the learning phase. A production rule involving two or more component classes is inferred if it is observed that one or more invocations are made from one component class to other component classes when handling the same end-user request. Subsequently, the probability of the detected pattern (*i.e.*, the corresponding rule) is then calculated when sufficiently large number of requests have been handled.

To understand how the production rules with the corresponding probabilities can be inferred from observing the path shapes, consider the following example.

EXAMPLE 3.6

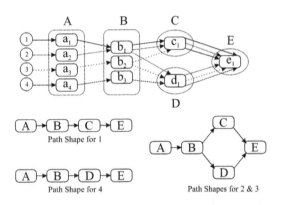

Figure 3.7   Component class and component instances.

Suppose we are going to infer the PCFG with only the traces of 4 end-user requests, as shown in Figure 3.7. The runtime paths of the 4 requests can be reduced to 3 different path shapes, also shown in Figure 3.7. The path shape of request 1 and the path shape of request 4 are unique, while the runtime paths of requests 2 and 3 share the same path shape.

From these path shapes, we can deduce that there is 100% probability for the call to transit from component class A to B, hence we can derive the following rules:

- R_{1j}: $S \to A$, p = 1.0
- R_{2j}: $A \to B$, p = 1.0

From B, there are 3 possible transitions: to C with 25% probability (due to end-user request 1), to D with 25% probability (due to end-user request 4), and to both C and D with 50% probability (due to end-user requests 2 and 3). Hence, we can deduce the following additional rules:

- R_{3j}: $B \to C$, p = 0.25 | $B \to D$, p = 0.25 | $B \to CD$, p = 0.5

Once a call reaches C, it is guaranteed to transit to E (due to requests 1, 2, and 3). Similarly, once a call reaches D, it will transit to E as well (due to requests 2, 3, and 4). Hence, the following rules are established:

- R_{4j}: $C \to E$, p = 1.0
- R_{5j}: $D \to E$, p = 1.0

Finally, component class E is the last stop for all requests, hence the following rule:

- R_{6j}: $E \to \$$, p = 1.0

Once the PCFG is learned from the traces, the path shapes of new requests can be judged to see if they confirm to the grammar. An anomaly is detected if a path shape is found not to conform to the grammar. One potential issue with using PCFG of anomaly detection is that the inferred PCFG from the runtime paths would form a superset of the observed paths because the grammar is context-free, as pointed out in [13]. This means it would regard many more paths as valid than those actually observed, which would lead to false negatives. On the plus side, the grammar is robust against false positives. However, it does not mean false positives would not happen. For example, if a legitimate path shape is not seen during the learning phase, an anomaly alert might be triggered.

Unlike the component interactions approach, which could pinpoint exactly which component is at fault when an anomaly is detected, the anomaly detected by the PCFG-based path shape analysis only tells that there is a fault in the system that impacted the flow of end-user request handling. Additional method is needed to pinpoint the likely faulty component, a process referred as the location of the fault. In [22], a decision tree based approach was used to locate the faulty component.

3.2.3 Inference-Based Fault Diagnosis

In this method, a richer set of information, such as CPU utilization, memory usage, in addition to the messages exchanged, regarding the operation of each component in the system is captured. Each type of information is captured as a state variable for the component. The number of state variables varies for each component and it depends on the instrumentation framework used. For the Windows Performance Counter framework (http://msdn.microsoft.com/en-us/library/ms254503.aspx),   it traces on average 35 variables for each component and the number of variables can go beyond 100 for components [20]. What is interesting is that the instrumentation framework can trace both generic state variables and application-specific variables (as long as the application exports them), and the fault diagnosis method would treat them equally without the need for their semantics.

The inference-based fault diagnosis method consists of three steps: (1) log component states, (2) construct the dependency graph, and (3) rank likely root causes for the abnormality observed. The details of each step is provided below.

3.2.3.1 Component States Logging.

The state variables are exported by the operating systems and the applications, and they are logged via an instrumentation framework. The states of the following types of components are logged:

- Node. For this type of components, the state variables consist of CPU utilization, memory usage, disk I/O, and network I/O.
- Process. For this type of components, both generic states such as CPU utilization, memory usage, the amount of messages exchanged, and application-specific states, such as the number of requests handled for each type are logged.
- Network path. For this type of components, the states are defined by the characteristics of the network path, such as loss rate and latency.
- Configuration. This refers to the configuration of the node or the process, and it is represented by a single state variable.
- Neighbor set. This is a virtual component that highlights the collective behavior of the communication peers of a

process, such as the total number of messages exchanged and the performance characteristics.

The states for each component are logged periodically into a multivariable vector data structure. In [20], the logging frequency is set to be once per minute. To monitor short-lived faults, a higher frequency may have to be used.

3.2.3.2   Dependency Graph Construction.

Once sufficient history data is logged, a dependency graph is constructed based on a set of pre-defined templates with one template for each component type. The templates used in [20] are shown in Figure 3.8 with the firewall components for the network path component in [20] omitted.

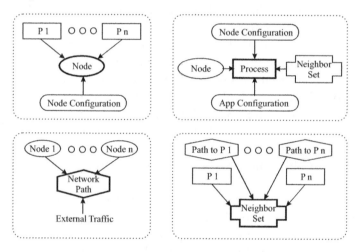

Figure 3.8   Dependency templates for nodes, processes, network paths, and the neighbor sets.

As defined in the template for the node component, the state of the node depends on the node configuration (such as the Windows registry if the node runs the Windows operating system), and the set of application processes (P1 through Pn). Hence, the edges from the configuration and the processes point to the node.

For the process component, its state depends on both the node configuration and the application configuration, the node at which it runs, and its neighbor set.

For the network path component, its state depends on the messages sent to the path by the nodes (Node 1 through Node n) along the path, as well as the network traffic injected to the path by external entities.

For the neighbor set component, its state depends on the set of the neighbor processes and the network paths that connect these processes.

▛ EXAMPLE 3.7

To see how to use the templates shown in Figure 3.8 to generate the dependency graph, consider the example illustrated in Figure 3.9 (to avoid cluttering, the configuration components are omitted in the graph). The example system consists of two nodes, Node 1 and Node 2. Node 1 has 2 application processes, P1 and P2. All three processes are neighbors of each other.

According to the template for the node component, P1 and P2 each has an edge that points to Node 1 (N1), and P3 has an edge that points to Node 2 (N2). According to the template for the process component, N1 and the neighbor set for P1 (NS1) each has an edge that points to P1. Similarly, N1 and the neighbor set for P2 (NS2) each has an edge that points to P2, and N2 and the neighbor set for P3 (NS3) each has an edge that points to P3. According to the template for the neighbor set, P2 and P3 each has an edge that points to NS1, P1 and P3 each has an edge that points to NS2, and P1 and P2 each has an edge that points to NS3.

Note that the example dependency graph contains many cycles. For example, P1 has an edge that points to NS2, which has an edge that points to P2, which in turn has an edge that points to P1's neighbor set NS1, which has an edge that points to P1 (*i.e.*, P1 → NS2 → P2 → NS1 → P1).

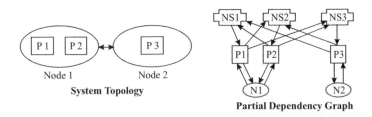

Figure 3.9   A partial dependency graph for an example system.

3.2.3.3   Fault Diagnosis.

Fault diagnosis involves three steps: (1) identifying components that are in abnormal states, (2) computing edge weights to facilitate finding the root cause of the fault, and (3) ranking likely faulty components as the root cause for the abnormal states observed.

The current state of a component is assessed by comparing the current values of the state variables against the corresponding historical values. The abnormality of the component is determined to be the highest abnormality value of any of its state variables. The history does not have to be error-free. As long as it is sufficiently long (in [20], the minimum history duration for good results is 30 minutes) and not dominated by the fault being diagnosed, the history will help produce reasonable good results.

For a state variable with a current value v, its abnormality $A(v)$ is defined to be:

$$A(v) = |erf(\frac{v - \mu}{\sigma\sqrt{2}})| \qquad (3.3)$$

where μ and σ are the mean value and the standard deviation of the state variable in the history, and $erf()$ is the error function, as shown in Figure 3.10. The abnormality calculated using this formula ranges from 0 to 1. The higher the value, the more abnormal the current state variable is. In [20], a heuristic threshold value of 0.8 is used to determine if a component is abnormal. The rational for choosing a higher threshold value is that it reduces the likelihood of producing false negatives. It is less desirable to declare an abnormal component normal than mistaken a normal component as an abnormal one. As shown in Section 3.3, the cost of false positives can be minimized using microreboot.

◼ **EXAMPLE 3.8**

Consider a state variable with a current value of 65. Assume the following 20 values are logged in the history of the variable: 35, 41, 52, 37, 48, 51, 60, 71, 52, 39, 43, 44, 53, 62, 55, 64, 71, 82, 36, 65 (the last being the current value).

The mean of the variable is 53.05 and the standard deviation is 13.20. Hence, $A(65) = erf(0.64) = 0.63$. Using 0.8 as the abnormality threshold as shown in Figure 3.10 (pointed by the arrow), this state variable is considered normal.

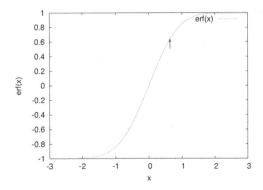

Figure 3.10   The error function.

The next step is to calculate the weight of each edge in the dependency graph. The objective of computing the edge weights is to facilitate the root cause analysis. Consider an edge with the source component S and the destination component D. If either S or D is normal, a minimum weight of 0.1 is assigned to the edge because it is unlikely that S has negative impact on D. Here the use of 0.1 instead of 0 as the weight is because the path weight calculation (needed for root cause predication) involves the multiplication of the edge weights along the path.

If both S and D are abnormal, the edge weight is calculated based on the joint historical behavior of S and D. The history where both S and D are present is divided equally into N chunks, with each chunk containing at least one set of logged values for S and one for D. If a chunk k contains multiple set of values (which is usually the case), the set that represents a state, S_k, that is most similar to the current state, S_{now}, for the source component S, is selected. Empirically, a small N, such as 10, is sufficient for accurate fault diagnosis [20].

The similarity of two states of a component C (except the configuration component) is calculated by computing their differences in the values of the component's state variables:

$$|C_k - C_{now}| = \sum_{n}^{i=1} \frac{|d^i|}{n} \tag{3.4}$$

where d^i is the difference of the i-th state variable, v^i, normalized by the observed range in the history, *i.e.*,

$$d^i = \frac{v^i_k - v^i_{now}}{v^i_{max} - v^i_{min}}$$ (3.5)

where v_{min} and v_{max} are the minimum and maximum values for v^i in the history. The normalization (which leads to a difference between 0 and 1) is important because it prevents a variable with a significant change of values from dominating the overall difference.

For the configuration component, the difference is either 0, if the configuration remains identical, or 1, if the configuration is different in anyway because even a slight change in configuration may result in a significant functional change in the node or application process.

The weight for the $S \rightarrow D$ edge is computed as follows:

$$E(S \rightarrow D) = \frac{\sum_{k=1}^{N}(1 - |D_k - D_{now}|) \times w_k}{\sum_{k=1}^{N} w_k}$$ (3.6)

where w_k is the weight assigned to chunk k and it is determined by the state differences for S:

$$w_k = \begin{cases} 1 - |S_k - S_{now}|, & \text{if } |S_k - S_{now}| \leq \delta \\ 0, & \text{otherwise} \end{cases}$$ (3.7)

where δ is heuristically set to be $1/3$ in [20]. The weighing scheme assigns a higher weight on historical states that are more similar. Furthermore, it excludes the chunks where the most similar state differs from S_{now} by more than δ. This is a rational decision because it is baseless to compute the state differences for D when the state for S is significantly different from S_{now}.

It may occur that no useable historical data can be found (*i.e.*, $w_k = 0$ for $k = 1, ...N$), the edge weight is set to be 0.8 (obviously Equation 3.6 cannot be used for the calculation in this case). The decision for assigning a high weight to the edge is based on the assumption that the abnormality is more likely caused by a component that has not been seen in a similar state before. This is consistent with the principle that we would rather see false positive than failing to diagnose a faulty component.

The final step is to predict the root causes of the abnormality. The causality of the abnormality of a component is inferred from the high weight of an edge. For example, if the weight for the edge $S \rightarrow D$ is high, and both S and D are abnormal, it is likely that S has caused the abnormality of D. However, a naive application of this idea may produce too many false positives, as shown in the following example.

EXAMPLE 3.9

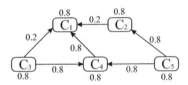

Figure 3.11   A hypothetical dependency graph with abnormality for each component and the weight for each edge labeled.

Consider the hypothetical dependency graph shown in Figure 3.11. Assume we want to find the root cause of component A, which is behaving abnormally. Because the edge weights for $D \rightarrow A$, $E \rightarrow D$, and $C \rightarrow D$ are all 0.8 (high), all three components C, D, and E would be labeled as the likely causes for A's abnormal behavior when in fact, E is the actual culprit.

In [20], a sophisticated ranking formula is introduced to help predict the real root causes. The rank of a component C_i with respect to its impact to an abnormal component C_j is based on the product of two factors:

- The direct impact of C_i on C_j, $I(C_i \rightarrow C_j)$, along one or more paths;
- The global impact of C_i, $S(C_i)$, on the entire system.

The rank assigned to a component C_i is inversely proportional to the product of the two factors. The component with the smallest rank value is regarded as the most likely culprit for the abnormal behavior of the affected component. Let $\{C_1, ..., C_K\}$ be the set of components in the system, and the affected component be C_j. The rank for a component C_i in the system with respect to its impact on C_j is determined by the ranking formula below:

$$Rank(C_i \rightarrow C_j) \propto \frac{1}{I(C_i \rightarrow C_j) \times S(C_i)} \tag{3.8}$$

$$I(C_i \to C_j) = \begin{cases} max(W(p)), \forall \text{acyclic paths p from } C_i \text{ to } C_j, & \text{if } C_i \neq C_j \\ 1 & \text{otherwise} \end{cases}$$

$$(3.9)$$

$$W(p) = (\prod_{k=1}^{n} E(e_j))^{\frac{1}{n}}, \quad \text{where } e_1, ..., e_n \text{ are edges of the path } p$$

$$(3.10)$$

$$S(C_i) = \sum_{k=1}^{K} I(C_i \to C_k) \times A(C_k), \quad \text{where } A(C_k) \text{is the abnormality of } C_k$$

$$(3.11)$$

It is possible that there does not exist an acyclic path between C_i and C_j, in which case, $I(C_i \to C_j)$ is set to 0. To see how the ranking formula works, consider the Example 3.9 again.

EXAMPLE 3.10

Here the component of interest is A. We want to determine which component in the system is the most likely cause for the abnormal behavior of A. Because of the low edge weight between B and A, we can easily rule out the possibility of B being the culprit. We only consider the three likely culprits, C, D, and E, and the component A itself.

We start with A itself. $I(A \to A) = 1$, and $S(A) = I(A \to A) \times A(A) = 1 \times 0.8 = 0.8$. Hence, $Rank(A \to A) = \frac{1}{1 \times 0.8} = 1.25$.

We next consider D. Because there is only one acyclic path between D and A,

$$I(D \to A) = E(D \to A) = 0.8$$

Because there exists only a single path from D to any other component in the system, which is A, the global impact of D is:

$$S(D) = I(D \to D) \times A(D) + I(D \to A) \times A(A)$$
$$= 1 \times 0.8 + 0.8 \times 0.8 = 1.44$$

Hence, $Rank(D \to A) \propto \frac{1}{0.8 \times 1.44} = 0.87$.

Next, consider C. To compute $I(C \to A)$, we need to consider two alternative paths: $C \to D \to A$, and $C \to A$.

$$W(C \to D \to A) = \sqrt{0.8 \times 0.8} = 0.8$$

$$W(C \to A) = 0.2$$

Obviously, $I(C \to A) = 0.8$. Because from C, we can only reach A and D, the global impact of C is:

$$S(C) = I(C \to C) \times A(D) + I(C \to A) \times A(A) + I(C \to D) \times A(D)$$
$$= 1 \times 0.8 + 0.8 \times 0.8 + 0.8 \times 0.8 = 2.08$$

Hence, $Rank(C \to A) \propto \frac{1}{0.8 \times 2.08} = 0.60$.

Finally, let's consider E. There are two acyclic paths from E to A: $E \to D \to A$ with a path weight of $\sqrt{0.8 \times 0.8} = 0.8$, and $E \to B \to A$ with a path weight of $\sqrt{0.8 \times 0.2} = 0.4$. Therefore, $I(E \to A) = 0.8$.

For the global impact of E, we need to consider the impact to D, B, A, and E itself:

$$S(E) = I(E \to E) \times A(E) + I(E \to A) \times A(A) +$$
$$I(E \to D) \times A(D) + I(E \to B) \times A(B)$$
$$= 1 \times 0.8 + 0.8 \times 0.8 + 0.8 \times 0.8 + 0.8 \times 0.8 = 2.72$$

Hence, $Rank(E \to A) \propto \frac{1}{0.8 \times 2.72} = 0.46$. Because $Rank(E \to A) < Rank(C \to A) < Rank(D \to A) < Rank(A \to A)$, component E is the most likely cause for the abnormality of A.

As can be seen from the example, the accuracy of the edge weight plays an important role in the root cause analysis. So far, in the edge weight calculation shown in Equation 3.6, we have assumed equal contribution from each state variable when in fact some of them play a more significant role than others for different types of faults (which may result in the dilution of component-level state differences), and some of the state variables might be redundant (which may result in over-emphasis on these variables). Therefore, the edge weight computation can be further improved by differentiating the state variables in the following ways:

- Filtering out redundant state variables. Some instrumentation framework capture some state variables in a redundant form. For example, in [20], the instrumentation framework exports used memory in units of bytes, kilobytes, and megabytes for the node, which would result in two redundant variables regarding the memory usage. The redundancy of the state variables can be identified using statistical methods [17], if hand-pick is impossible.

- Focusing on the relevant state variables. While the fault diagnosis is done in an application-agnostic manner, in some cases, if a fault is related to some generic symptom, such as the abnormality of CPU usage, it is possible to identify what state variables are the most relevant and give them more weight in the calculation (such as using the abnormality of these variables as the weight), or ignore the variables that are apparently irrelevant from the calculation all together, for example, when considering the impact of a node on one of its processes, we can ignore the exceptions returned from the remote processes.

- Identify aggregate relationships between state variables. Some of the state variables exported by the instrumentation framework are in fact aggregate of individual variables. For example, the CPU usage reported at the node-level is the sum of the CPU usage of all processes. Such aggregate relationships can be detected easily using the name of the variables (such as the CPU usage of node and processes) if the individual variables are time-synchronized. Even if they are not strictly synchronized, the relationship may be detected by allowing some margin of error.

  Once the aggregate relationships are established, the redundancy is removed from the edge weight calculation. For example, when calculating the edge weight from a node to one of its processes, the contribution from the process is omitted. More details for utilizing the aggregate relationships can be found in [20].

3.3 Microreboot

Restarting a fine-grained component can be a very efficient way to repair a system quickly. However, in order for the approach to work, the system has to be designed according to the guideline laid out in [11].

3.3.1   Microrebootable System Design Guideline

The main requirement for a microrebootable system include:

- Component based. The system should be constructed using a set of well-defined components instead of using a monolithic structure. Each component should be designed to accomplish a specific task. The Java EE is a well-known platform supporting this design guideline and it is used in [11] as the platform of choice. In Java EE, the EJB is used to encapsulate application logic and a Web component is used to take care of the presentation task to the clients.
- Separating of application logic execution and state management. Any important state that might be accessed by a component must be stored externally to the component in a database system or a dedicated state store [23]. This is necessary because otherwise the state kept in the component would be lost after a reboot.
- Loose coupling. The components in the system must be loosely coupled to enable localized microreboot of some components. The goal of loose coupling is to reduce the dependency among the components. Ideally, a component should be self-contained and be able to complete its designated task without referencing any other components. When this is not possible, the referencing to another component should be mediated, for example, via a Java EE container or a directory service, instead of direct invocation on a particular instance of another component. The key is that *any instance* of the referenced component (class) should be able to get the job done so that when one instance of a component undergoes a microreboot, another instance of the same component class can provide the necessary service potentially needed by other components. The Java EE platform allows such mediation.

  The middleware platform that provides even greater degree of loose coupling is Web services [21]. In Web services, a document-style messaging is used as the basic means of interaction between different components. As such, a component simply sends the document to a particular endpoint for processing, without the need to know which component instance would handle the request (*i.e.*, the document), and wait asynchronously for a response. Of course, the interface for the services provided by each component must be defined, and the request/response messages have to follow certain well-defined structure.

- Resilient inter-component interactions. Strictly speaking, this should be part of the loose coupling requirement. When a component (instance) undergoes a microreboot, all ongoing invocations on this component would be interrupted as a result. The invoking components must be prepared to retry the same invocation again (possibly on a different component instance via a mediator service) before declaring a failure. This is crucial to localize the impact of microrebooting.

  On the other hand, some of the invocations issued by the rebooting component (on other components) might be reissued again after rebooting. Unless such invocations are idempotent, the invocations must carry sufficient information for the invokees to perform duplicate detection. Otherwise, rebooting a component might lead to the rollback of all ongoing transactions in which the rebooting component is involved. In the worse case, compensating operations may have to be applied for transactions that have been committed before the rebooting. Obviously, this scenario should be avoided because it would significantly increase the cost of doing microrebooting.

- Lease-based resource management. Resources should be leased to a component instance so that if the component hangs, the resources can be released for other components and the component is rebooted. Such resources include file descriptors, memory, or even CPU.

3.3.2   Automatic Recovery with Microreboot

Automatic recovery can be made possible for a distributed system by equipping it with a fault monitor and a recovery manager [8]. The fault monitor implements some of the fault detection and localization algorithms described in the previous section. The recovery manager is responsible to recover the system from the fault recursively by microrebooting first the identified faulty component, if the symptom does not disappear, a group of components according to a fault-dependency graph. If microrebooting does not work, the entire system is rebooted. The final resort is to notify a human operator.

The fault-dependency graph (referred to as f-map in [10]) consists of components as nodes and the fault-propagation paths as edges. The f-map can be obtained by a technique called automatic failure-path inference (AFPI) [10]. In AFPI, an initial f-map of the system is constructed by observing the system's behaviors when faults are injected into the system. The f-map is then refined during normal operation. Because it is possible for multiple components to have mutual dependencies, there may be cycles in the f-map, in which case, the f-map is reduced to an r-map by grouping the components forming a cycle as a single node, as shown in Figure 3.12. During the recovery, the entire group of components will be microrebooted as a single unit.

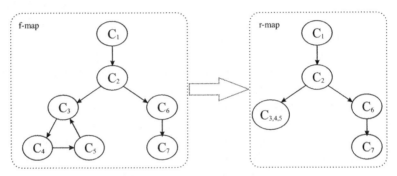

Figure 3.12   The components that form a cycle in the f-map are reduced to a single unit in the r-map for recursive recovery.

Upon detecting a faulty component, it is microrebooted by the recovery manager. A conservative approach is to microreboot both the reported faulty component and all the components that are immediately downstream from the component, as done in [9]. If the faulty symptom persists, it is reasonable to assume that the root cause of the fault observed must have come from the upstream component. Therefore, the upstream component in the r-map is also microrebooted. The recovery is carried out recursively in this fashion until the entire system is rebooted.

3.3.3   Implications of the Microrebooting Technique

Microrebooting has the following positive implications to dependable system design and fault management.

- Microreboot faulty components before node-level failover. Suspected faulty components should be rebooted first because it is a much faster way of repairing the system, as shown in [11]. Node-level failover should be attempted only if microrebooting suspected faulty components does not fix the problem.
- Tolerating more false positives. Because the cost of rebooting a suspected faulty component is so insignificant, the impact of false positives (*i.e.*, a normal component is labeled as faulty) in fault detection is minimized. Hence, the fault detection algorithm can be tuned to be more aggressive in suspecting faulty components. As a result, the false negative (*i.e.*, a faulty component is not detected) rate can be reduced and the overall dependability of the system is improved.
- Proactive microreboot for software rejuvenation. Proactive application-level reboot has been used as a way to reclaim leaked resources and to eliminate undetected transient errors in the system. This process is referred to as software rejuvenation. For microreboot-friendly applications, individual components can be periodically rebooted to achieve similar effect while causing minimum disruptions to the clients.
- Enhanced fault transparency for end-users. Process-level and node-level reboot would inevitably be visible to end-users because the reboot typically takes 10 or more seconds to complete. However, the reboot of an individual component usually takes less than a second in Java EE applications [11]. The fast recovery makes it possible to hide the microreboot from end-users with the facility provided by HTTP 1.1. A request that is disrupted by the microreboot would result in an HTTP response message with a status code 503, indicating that the server is temporarily unavailable, and a Retry-After header line, instructing the Web browser to retry after certain period of time.

3.4 Overcoming Operator Errors

Most sophisticated software systems require human operators to configure, upgrade, and sometimes manually recover from failures.

Unfortunately, human errors are inevitable and in many cases, the system dependability is significantly reduced because of human errors [4]. To overcome operator errors, the checkpointing and logging techniques introduced in Chapter 2 will be essential tools. However, these techniques alone are not sufficient because the side-effect of the operator errors might not be limited to the application itself. Furthermore, traditional checkpointing and logging techniques do not address the need for the state repair and selective replay issues. In this section, we describe the operator-undo approach [5, 6] in overcoming operator errors.

It is worth noting that there are numerous works that aim to prevent operator errors by automating tasks [31, 33], to reduce the likelihood of operator errors by providing operator guidance [1, 3], to contain operator errors (so that an error does not propagate to other parts of the system) by validation testing [26, 27] and by early detection based on machine learning [28]. These approaches are complementary to the operator-undo approach.

3.4.1   The Operator Undo Model

The objective of the operator undo model is to allow an operator to correct any mistake that was made by rolling back the system-wide state to a known correct point, reapplying the intended modification to the application (and/or the operating system), and then rolling forward again by replaying the logged operations. The model consists of three main steps:

- Rewind. Upon detecting a mistake, an operator can restore the system to a known correct state by applying a system-wide checkpoint that includes both the state of the application and the operating system. This is different from the rollback facility provided by modern operating system, which allows one to rollback only the operating system state to a previous restoration point.
- Repair. Once the system-wide state is rolled back, the operator can then attempt to reapply the intended changes to the application or the operating system, for example, installing the correct patches or reconfiguring the application in a correct way. The repair step also potentially involves the modification of the logged interactions so that the end-user's intention is preserved and externalized results are

consistent with what the user has seen prior to the undo during replay.

- Replay. Subsequently, all the logged end-user interactions, often in the form of request messages, are replayed to roll forward the state.

The main challenge of this model is how to ensure consistent replay of end-user interactions. For example, in an email application, the change of the spam filter could lead to previously reviewed messages to be removed from the inbox (and moved to the spam folder instead). Obviously, how to address the inconsistencies is highly application-dependent.

3.4.2   The Operator Undo Framework

The implementation of the operator undo model requires several key steps:

- Mediating end-user interactions. The operator undo framework must be able to intercept all end-user requests to the application, and be able to control the responses sent to the users.
- Application and operating system checkpointing.
- Logging of end-user interactions.

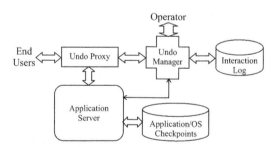

Figure 3.13   The architecture of an Operator Undo framework [5, 6].

Figure 3.13 shows the architecture of an operator undo framework implemented in [5, 6]. The main components of the framework include the Undo Proxy, which is used to mediate the end-user interactions and for replay, the Undo Manager, which is responsible to log the user interactions, and facilitate undo and replay as requested by the operator, and two storage facilities for state checkpoints and end-user interactions. The Undo Manager is also responsible to facilitate periodic system-wide checkpointing.

To help separate the application-dependent and the generic implementation of the framework, a key construct, called "verb" is introduced in [5, 6]. A verb assumes a generic data structure and its content encapsulates the logical intent of an end-user interaction with the application server. Hence, verbs are application-specific. However, the generic data structure of the verbs makes it possible to implement the Undo Manager and the log storage components in an application-independent fashion.

■ EXAMPLE 3.11

In [6], 13 verbs are defined an email system. These verbs captures the common operations for email transfer (SMTP protocol) and for end-user access of emails (IMAP protocol). Among these verbs, only 4 of them would cause externally visible changes:

- Fetch. It is used for an end-user to retrieve headers, flags, or the entire emails from a designated folder.
- Store. It is used for an end-user to set flags on emails, such as read or deleted.
- List. It is used to retrieve the list of IMAP folders.
- Expunge. It is used to purge all emails that have been flagged as deleted.

Other verbs defined include:

- Deliver. The only verb for SMTP to deliver an email to the mail store.
- Append. It is used to append an email to a designated IMAP folder.
- Copy. It is used to copy emails to another folder.
- Status. It is used to retrieve the folder state such as the message count of the folder.
- Select. It is used to open an IMAP folder.
- Close. It is used to deselect an IMAP folder. The emails flagged as deleted in the folder will be purged automatically.
- Create. It is used to create a new IMAP folder (or a subfolder under another IMAP folder).

- Rename. It is used to rename an IMAP folder (or subfolder).
- Delete. It is used to delete an IMAP folder (or subfolder).

In [6], all 13 verbs are implemented in Java that conforms to a common Verb interface.

To facilitate consistent replay after an undo and repair, a verb must also implement two interfaces, one is related to user-interaction timeline management, and the other is related to consistent management:

- Sequencing interface. This interface includes three test methods and they all take another verb as the only argument:

  - Commutativity test. The test returns true if the two verbs are commutative (*i.e.*, the outcome of the execution of either verb is independent of their relative ordering in execution).

  - Independence test. The test returns true if the two verbs can be executed concurrently (*e.g.*, no race condition will be resulted in the concurrent execution of the two verbs).

  - Preferred-order test. If the two verbs are not commutative, this test returns the preferred execution order of the two verbs.

  These tests are necessary because the Undo Proxy does not control the execution order when the end-user requests are first executed at the application server, and the order in which the verbs are logged might not match that of the execution. During the replay, the Undo Manager can reinforce a semantically correct execution order with the same degree of concurrency level as that of the original execution.

- Consistency-management interface. This interface also includes three methods used to handle externally visitable inconstancy:

  - Consistency test. This test compares the external output of the original execution of the verb and that of the replay. A straightforward test would be to compare the hash valued of the two outputs. However, such tests might produce unnecessary false positives because of cosmetic differences in the outputs. That is why the application developers are tasked to provide the consistency test implementation so that they can determine application-specific rules for the comparison.

– Compensation. This method applies application-specific compensation action regarding the inconsistency visible to the external users. This method is invoked when the consistency test fails.

– Squash. This method is invoked by the Undo Manager on a verb that does not commute with a previous verb that causes externally visible inconsistency. As the method name suggests, squash turns the verb to nearly as a no-action verb except that it should inform the user properly that the original verb is not executed due to prior inconsistency. This happens most often to verbs that delete or overwrite part of the state.

EXAMPLE 3.12

For the verbs defined in the email system [6], a portion of the sequencing rule is provided as follows:

- Any two Deliver verbs are independent of each other and are commutative.
- Any two IMAP verbs that belong to different users are independent and commutative.
- The Deliver verb is commutative with any IMAP verb except Fetch for the Inbox.
- Expunge and Fetch are not commutative if they operate on the same target folder.
- Store and Copy are not commutative if they operate on the same target folder.

The consistency-management interface for the email system verbs is implemented based on an external consistency model [6]. On the SMTP side, the only scenario that an externally visible inconsistency could occur is that an email delivery failed in the original execution, but the same email can be delivered successfully during replay. The consistency rule is that the email is not delivered if the standard bounce message regarding the failure of delivery has already been sent back to the sender.

To increase the chance of delivery during replay, the bounce message is deferred.

On the IMAP side, the consistency test is based on the comparison of the externalized state as the result of a verb. The externalized state includes the following:

- The email message itself (the text and the attachments, if any) if one is fetched.
- The list of email headers, such as To, From, Cc, and Subject, for verbs that involve listing of emails.
- The list of folders for verbs that requested them.
- Execution status for verbs that modify the state of the email system.

The consistency test would declare inconsistency if any part of the externalized state is missing or different during replay compared with that of the original execution. For most verbs, when the consistency test fails, the compensation method inserts an explanatory message into the user's Inbox stating the reasons for the discrepancy.

REFERENCES

1. R. Bianchini, R. P. Martin, K. Nagaraja, T. D. Nguyen, and F. Oliveira. Human-aware computer system design. In *Proceedings of the 10th conference on Hot Topics in Operating Systems - Volume 10*, HOTOS'05, pages 13–13, Berkeley, CA, USA, 2005. USENIX Association.

2. D. M. Blough and A. Pelc. Diagnosis and repair in multiprocessor systems. *IEEE Trans. Comput.*, 42(2):205–217, Feb. 1993.

3. P. Bodík, A. Fox, M. I. Jordan, D. Patterson, A. Banerjee, R. Jagannathan, T. Su, S. Tenginakai, B. Turner, and J. Ingalls. Advanced tools for operators at amazon.com. In *Proceedings of the First international conference on Hot topics in autonomic computing*, HotACI'06, pages 1–1, Berkeley, CA, USA, 2006. USENIX Association.

4. A. Brown and D. Patterson. To err is human. In *Proceedings of the 2001 Worshop on Evaluating and Architecting System Dependability*, Gteborg, Sweden, 2001.

5. A. B. Brown and D. A. Patterson. Rewind, repair, replay: three r's to dependability. In *Proceedings of the 10th workshop on ACM SIGOPS European workshop*, EW 10, pages 70–77, New York, NY, USA, 2002. ACM.

6. A. B. Brown and D. A. Patterson. Undo for operators: building an undoable e-mail store. In *Proceedings of the annual conference on USENIX Annual*

Technical Conference, ATEC '03, pages 1–1, Berkeley, CA, USA, 2003. USENIX Association.

7. G. Candea, A. B. Brown, A. Fox, and D. Patterson. Recovery-oriented computing: Building multitier dependability. *Computer*, 37(11):60–67, Nov. 2004.

8. G. Candea, G. C, E. Kiciman, S. Zhang, A. Fox, P. Keyani, and O. Fox. Jagr: An autonomous self-recovering application server. In *Proceedings of the International Workshop on Active Middleware Services*, pages 168–178, 2003.

9. G. Candea, J. Cutler, and A. Fox. Improving availability with recursive microreboots: a soft-state system case study. *Perform. Eval.*, 56(1-4):213–248, Mar. 2004.

10. G. Candea, M. Delgado, M. Chen, and A. Fox. Automatic failure-path inference: A generic introspection technique for internet applications. In *Proceedings of the Third IEEE Workshop on Internet Applications*, WIAPP '03, pages 132–, Washington, DC, USA, 2003. IEEE Computer Society.

11. G. Candea, S. Kawamoto, Y. Fujiki, G. Friedman, and A. Fox. Microreboot - A technique for cheap recovery. In *Proceedings of the 6th Symposium on Operating Systems Design and Implementation*, San Francisco, CA, 2004.

12. Y. Chang, L. Lander, H.-S. Lu, and M.Wells. Bayesian analysis for fault location in homogenous distributed systems. In *Proc. of the 12th Symposium on Reliable Distributed Systems*, pages 44–53, 1993.

13. M. Y. Chen, A. Accardi, E. Kiciman, J. Lloyd, D. Patterson, A. Fox, and E. Brewer. Path-based faliure and evolution management. In *Proceedings of the 1st conference on Symposium on Networked Systems Design and Implementation - Volume 1*, NSDI'04, pages 23–23, Berkeley, CA, USA, 2004. USENIX Association.

14. M. Y. Chen, E. Kiciman, E. Fratkin, A. Fox, and E. Brewer. Pinpoint: Problem determination in large, dynamic internet services. In *Proceedings of the 2002 International Conference on Dependable Systems and Networks*, DSN '02, pages 595–604, Washington, DC, USA, 2002. IEEE Computer Society.

15. S. C. Geyik and B. K. Szymanski. Event recognition in sensor networks by means of grammatical inference. In *INFOCOM*, pages 900–908, 2009.

16. J. J. Horning, H. C. Lauer, P. M. Melliar-Smith, and B. Randell. A program structure for error detection and recovery. In *Operating Systems, Proceedings of an International Symposium*, pages 171–187, London, UK, UK, 1974. Springer-Verlag.

17. A. Hyvärinen and E. Oja. Independent component analysis: algorithms and applications. *Neural Netw.*, 13(4-5):411–430, May 2000.

18. R. Jain. *The Art of Computer Systems Performance Analysis: Techniques for Experimental Design, Measurement, Simulation, and Modeling*. John Wiley & Sons, 1991.

19. K. R. Joshi, W. H. Sanders, M. A. Hiltunen, and R. D. Schlichting. Automatic model-driven recovery in distributed systems. In *Proceedings of the 24th*

IEEE Symposium on Reliable Distributed Systems, SRDS '05, pages 25–38, Washington, DC, USA, 2005. IEEE Computer Society.

20. S. Kandula, R. Mahajan, P. Verkaik, S. Agarwal, J. Padhye, and P. Bahl. Detailed diagnosis in enterprise networks. *SIGCOMM Comput. Commun. Rev.*, 39(4):243–254, Aug. 2009.

21. D. Kaye. *Loosely Coupled: The Missing Pieces of Web Services*. RDS Press, 2003.

22. E. Kiciman and A. Fox. Detecting application-level failures in component-based internet services. *Trans. Neur. Netw.*, 16(5):1027–1041, Sept. 2005.

23. B. C. Ling, E. Kiciman, and A. Fox. Session state: beyond soft state. In *Proceedings of the 1st conference on Symposium on Networked Systems Design and Implementation - Volume 1*, NSDI'04, pages 22–22, Berkeley, CA, USA, 2004. USENIX Association.

24. D. Lymberopoulos, A. S. Ogale, A. Savvides, and Y. Aloimonos. A sensory grammar for inferring behaviors in sensor networks. In *Proceedings of the 5th international conference on Information processing in sensor networks*, IPSN '06, pages 251–259, New York, NY, USA, 2006. ACM.

25. C. D. Manning and H. Schutze. *Foundations of Statistical Natural Language Processing*. The MIT Press, 1999.

26. K. Nagaraja, F. Oliveira, R. Bianchini, R. P. Martin, and T. D. Nguyen. Understanding and dealing with operator mistakes in internet services. In *Proceedings of the 6th conference on Symposium on Operating Systems Design & Implementation - Volume 6*, OSDI'04, pages 5–5, Berkeley, CA, USA, 2004. USENIX Association.

27. F. Oliveira, K. Nagaraja, R. Bachwani, R. Bianchini, R. P. Martin, and T. D. Nguyen. Understanding and validating database system administration. In *Proceedings of the annual conference on USENIX '06 Annual Technical Conference*, ATEC '06, pages 19–19, Berkeley, CA, USA, 2006. USENIX Association.

28. F. Oliveira, A. Tjang, R. Bianchini, R. P. Martin, and T. D. Nguyen. Barricade: defending systems against operator mistakes. In *Proceedings of the 5th European conference on Computer systems*, EuroSys '10, pages 83–96, New York, NY, USA, 2010. ACM.

29. F. Preparata, G. Metze, and R. Chien. On the connection assignment problem of diagnosable systems. *IEEE Trans. on Electronic Comp.*, EC-16(6):848–854, December 1967.

30. A. O. Ramirez. Three-tier architecture. *Linux J.*, 2000(75es), July 2000.

31. Y.-Y. Su, M. Attariyan, and J. Flinn. Autobash: improving configuration management with operating system causality analysis. *SIGOPS Oper. Syst. Rev.*, 41(6):237–250, Oct. 2007.

32. A. S. Tanenbaum and M. V. Steen. *Distributed Systems: Principles and Paradigms*. Prentice Hall, 2nd edition, 2006.

33. W. Zheng, R. Bianchini, and T. D. Nguyen. Automatic configuration of internet services. *SIGOPS Oper. Syst. Rev.*, 41(3):219–229, Mar. 2007.

4

Data and Service Replication

Different from checkpointing/logging and recovery-oriented computing, which focus on the recovery of an application should a fault occur, the replication technique offers another way of achieving high availability of a distributed service by masking various hardware and software faults. The goal of the replication technique is to extend the mean time to failure of a distributed service. As the name suggests, the replication technique resorts to the use of space redundancy, *i.e.*, instead of running a single copy of the service, multiple copies are deployed across a group of physical nodes for fault isolation. For replication to work (*i.e.*, to be able to mask individual faults), it is important to ensure that faults occur independently at different replicas.

The most well-known approach to service replication is state-machine replication [26]. In this approach, each replica is modeled as a state machine that consists of a set of state variables and a set of interfaces accessible by the clients that operate on the state variables *deterministically*. With the presence of multiple copies of the state machine, the issue of consistency among the replicas becomes important. It is apparent that the access to the replicas must be coordinated by a replication algorithm so that they remain consistent at the end of each operation. More specifically, a replication algorithm must ensure that a client's request (that invokes on one of the interfaces defined by the state machine) reaches all non-faulty replicas, and all non-faulty replicas must deliver the requests (that potentially come from different clients) in exactly the same total order. It is important that the execution of a client's request is deterministic, *i.e.*, given the same request, the same response will be generated at all non-faulty replicas. If an application contains nondeterministic behavior, it must be *i.e.*, rendered deterministic by controlling such behavior, *e.g.*, by explicitly coordinating otherwise nondeterministic actions [34].

Even though data can be replicated using the service replication approach, the focus in data replication is in general different from that in service replication. In data replication, it is assumed that the data items that may be accessed are known, and the operations on the data items are limited to read or write. Furthermore, data replication is often discussed in the context of transactional processing systems, *i.e.*, each transaction consists of a group of read and/or write operations on a number of data items and these operations should be carried out atomically. As such, allowing concurrent access to data items from different transactions is essential in data replication. This is very different from service replication, which in general requires serial execution of all remote invocations on the replicas.

For many Internet based applications where data and service replication is needed, ensuring strict lock-step consistency among the replicas is often regarded as less desirable due to the runtime overhead incurred by doing so. Many optimistic data replication algorithms have been designed that offer weaker consistency guarantees.

The problem of balancing consistency and performance is made more complicated by the possibility of network partitions. Network partition is a fault (often caused by faulty network equipment) that separates the replicas into two or more groups. Within each group, the replicas can communicate. However, the replicas that belong to different groups can no longer communicate. When a network partition occurs, an important decision must be made by the replication algorithm, should the access to the replicas be suspended to ensure consistency of the replicas until the network partition is healed, which would sacrifice the availability of the data or service, or should some form of progress be allowed to be made by trading off the consistency of the replicas (referred to as partition tolerance)?

In 2000, Eric Brewer made a conjecture [6] that a distributed system can only guarantee at most two out of the three properties: consistency, availability, and partition tolerance (*i.e.*, it is impossible to build a system that meet all three requirements). The conjecture was proved by Seth Gilbert and Nancy Lynch two years later and becomes the CAP theorem [11]. For many practical systems, high availability and partition tolerance are considered more important than the risk of temporary inconsistency.

In this chapter, we first introduce the basic approaches for service and data replication that ensure strict replica consistency (often referred to as pessimistic replication), then we discuss the approaches and steps involved in optimistic replication. The chapter is concluded by a section on the CAP theorem.

4.1   Service Replication

In service replication, the client-server interaction model is typically used where one or more clients issue requests to the replicated server and wait for the corresponding responses synchronously. Multi-tiered interaction can be supported by super-imposing the client-server models. Service replication algorithms are often designed to operate in an asynchronous distributed computing environment, where there is no bound on processing time, no bound on message delays, and no bound on clock skews. Algorithms designed for asynchronous environment are more robust because their correctness does not depend on timing.

In service replication, each server replica is run as an application process. The server must export a set of interfaces for the clients to invoke remotely over a computer network or the Internet. However, the internal state of the server is fully encapsulated and not directly accessible by the clients. This model is drastically different from data replication. Furthermore, unlike data replication, the replicas in service replication might behave nondeterministically, *e.g.*, because of multithreading or the access of node-specific resources.

In service replication, a replication algorithm is typically implemented as part of a fault tolerance middleware framework, as shown in Figure 4.1. Such a framework often provides Application Programming Interfaces (APIs) to application developers to ease the complexity of achieving replication-based fault tolerance [8, 9] in the following ways:

- The client-side component facilitates the multicasting of a request from a client to all non-faulty replicas reliably. It is also responsible to filter out duplicate reply messages sent by the replicas, or to perform voting on the reply messages if necessary.
- The server-side component ensures the delivery of the requests in the same total order across all non-faulty replicas. It is also responsible of handling duplicate requests and the masking of faults.

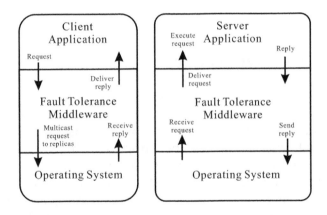

Figure 4.1   The replication algorithm is typically implemented in a fault tolerance middleware framework.

Some frameworks [21, 34, 38, 37] aim to provide transparent fault tolerance to applications by intercepting input/output related systems calls in lieu of offering APIs to application developers. On Unix/Linux based operation systems, the interception of system calls can be achieved via the dlsym() facility. Such a fault tolerance framework can be compiled to a dynamic library and be injected into the application process at launch time by pointing the LD_PRELOAD environment variable to the path that contains the dynamic library.

Transparent fault tolerance can also be accomplished by integrating with the middleware framework if the application is already using one [33, 35, 39]. For example, Web services applications are often built on top of extensive middleware libraries. Most of such libraries, such as Apache Axis (http://axis.apache.org/), offer plug-in APIs for developers to customize low level message processing and data communication. The fault tolerance components can be relatively easily plugged into the applications with minimum modifications required.

4.1.1   Replication Styles

As we mentioned before, the replicas must be coordinated in some way to ensure their consistency. There are a number of different schemes of coordinating the replicas. In the literature, we have seen the following replication styles being mentioned [36]:

- *Active replication.* As shown in Figure 4.2, in active replication, every replica delivers the requests in the same total order and executes them. Each replica plays the same role. Because every non-faulty replica would send a reply to the client, the duplicate replies must be filtered out. For active replication, it is often assumed that a reliable totally ordered multicast service is available to ensure the reliability and total ordering of the requests.

  To tolerate some non-failstop faults at the replicas, it is necessary to perform voting on the reply messages sent by the replicas. If less than half of the replicas may exhibit non-failstop faults, a majority voting at the client can ensure the delivery of the reply sent by a non-faulty replica.

- *Passive replication.* As shown in Figure 4.3, in passive replication, one of the replicas is designated as the primary and the remaining replicas as the backups. Only the primary executes the requests. Periodically, the primary transfers its state to the backups to bring them up to date. To ensure strong replica consistency, it is also necessary for the backups to receive and log incoming requests from the client.

- *Semi-active replication.* Semi-active replication was designed specifically to handle replica nondeterminism. In semi-active replication, similar to passive replication, one replica acts as the primary and the remaining as the backups,

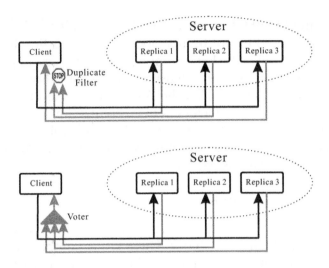

Figure 4.2   Active replication, without (top) and with (bottom) voting at the client.

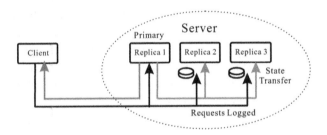

Figure 4.3   Passive replication.

as shown in Figure 4.4. The primary determines both the delivery order of the requests and the execution order of any potential nondeterministic operations. The primary then transfers the ordering information to the backups so that they deliver the requests in the same order and carry out the nondeterministic operations in the same order as that in the primary. Note that in semi-active replication, all replicas deliver and execute the requests. To tolerate fail-stop faults only, it is more efficient to disable the sending of replies from the backups (so that such messages do not compete against network and processing resources).

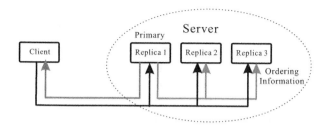

Figure 4.4   Semi-active replication.

- *Leader-follower replication.* The leader-follower replication encompasses both passive replication and semi-active replication. It simply refers to the fact that there is one leader (*i.e.,* the primary) among the replicas and the remaining replicas are followers.

4.1.2   Implementation of Service Replication

In pessimistic replication, the goal is to ensure that the fault at any replica is masked without disrupting the access to the data or service being replicated. For active replication, it means that the state of non-faulty replicas must be consistent at the end of execution of each and every client's request. For passive replication, it means that a backup must be prepared to take over the primary should it fail without losing any state changes or causing any inconsistency. Essentially, the replicas should be coordinated in a way that appears to be a single highly available copy of the server to the clients.

Assuming that the execution at the replica is deterministic, to ensure replica consistency, all requests must be delivered and *executed sequentially* at each replica in the same total order for active replication. For passive replication, all requests since the last state transfer from the primary to the backups must be logged at the backups with the execution ordering information recorded at the primary.

The requirements are often satisfied in one of three ways:

- Using a group communication system [5]. Such a system provides two services:
  - A membership service. The group communication system determines which replicas are available in

the current configuration (referred to as the current membership view) using an unreliable fault detector (often using heartbeat messages and a heuristic time-out). When a fault is detected, the system is reconfigured with a new membership view installed. Similarly, the membership service allows the addition of new replicas into the system, or planned removal of existing replicas from the current membership. For each membership change, every replica that is included in the new membership is informed of the membership change and formation.

- A reliable totally ordered multicast service. Such a service ensures that within each membership view, all replicas receive the same set of messages (possibly sent by different clients) with the same total order.

Furthermore, a group communication system ensures that membership changes are totally ordered with respect to regular messages to all surviving replicas, an important property of the virtual synchrony model [3]. The group communication system will be discussed in detail in Chapter 5.

- Using a consensus algorithm [8, 18, 39]. The total ordering and the reliable delivery of messages are ensured via the execution of a consensus algorithm among non-faulty replicas. Unlike the approach employed in the group communication system, which removes a faulty replica from the current membership, the consensus algorithm makes progress in the presence of faulty replicas by using quorums. Consensus algorithms and their application in building dependable systems will be discussed in detail in Chapter 6.

- Using transaction processing with atomic commit [2, 14]. This approach is most often adopted for data replication (for example, in replicated database systems). More details of the approach is provided in the subsection below.

The first two approaches are used typically for state machine replication (mostly for service replication, but sometimes for data replication as well). The last approach is often used for data replication.

4.2   Data Replication

Data replication is first studied extensively in the context of transaction processing systems [2, 14]. Transactional data replication is different from state-machine replication in that a transaction consists of a number of read and/or write operations on a set of data items while the granularity of operations in state-machine replication is on the replica in its entirety. While on the transaction-level, all transactions must be executed in a way that they appear to have been executed sequentially, similar to the sequential execution requirement of all requests on the server replicas in state-machine replication, the actually read/write operations (that may belong to different transactions) on different data items are always carried out concurrently. Hence, in transactional data replication, the replication algorithm not only has to ensure the consistency of the replicas, but also defines concurrency control as well.

A transactional data replication algorithm should ensure that the replicated data appears to the clients as a single copy, in particular, the interleaving of the execution of the transactions be equivalent to a sequential execution of those transactions on a single copy of the data. Such an execution is often referred to as one-copy serializable.

With data replication, in general, it is desirable to minimize the cost of read operations because (read-only) queries are much more prevalent than updates (transactions that consist of writes to some data items). We first highlight that it is nontrivial to design a sound data replication algorithm by examining two incorrect naive replications algorithms: write-all and write-all-available.

In the write-all data replication algorithm, as shown in Figure 4.5, a read operation on a data item x can be mapped to any replica of x and each write operation on a data item x would be applied to *all* replicas of x. As long as the nodes that manage the replicas do not fail, this replication algorithm satisfies the one-copy serializable requirement. This is because in any execution of a sequence of transaction, if a transaction writes to a data item x, it writes into all replicas of x, and if another transaction later reads data item x, regardless which replica it reads from, it reads the same value written by the most recent transaction that writes into x.

A problem occurs if a node or process that manages a replica becomes faulty (for convenience, we simply say that the replica

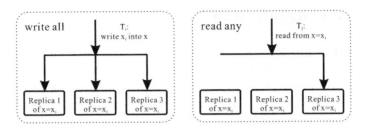

Figure 4.5   A write-all algorithm for data replication.

becomes faulty). The write-all algorithm would have to block until the faulty replica is repaired and fully recovered. This means that any single replica failure would render the entire system unavailable, which defeats the purpose of using replication in the first place.

To fix this problem of the write-all algorithm, one might attempt to use the write-all-available algorithm where a write operation on a data item x is simply translated to all *available* replicas of x while allowing the read operation to be applied to any copy of the replicas. This new algorithm fixes the blocking problem. However, it does not guarantee one-copy serializable execution because a transaction might read from a replica of certain data item not written to by the last transaction that writes to the same data item, *e.g.*, if the replica for the data item failed during the last transaction and recovered subsequently, as shown in Figure 4.6.

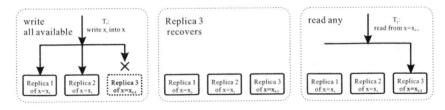

Figure 4.6   The problem of the write-all-available algorithm for data replication.

Apparently the above problem is caused by the accessing of a not-fully-recovered replica. Can we fix the problem by preventing a transaction from accessing the not-fully-recovered replicas? Unfortunately, this is not a viable solution either. To see why, consider the following example.

▣ EXAMPLE 4.1

Consider two transactions T_i, and T_j. T_i first issues a read operation on data x. It is mapped to replica 1 of x. Similarly, T_j first issues a read operation on data y. It is mapped to replica 2 of y. Subsequently, replica 1 of x and replica 2 of y, that is, the replica accessed by T_i, and that accessed by T_j, failed. Next, T_i issues a write operation on data y and concurrently, T_j issues a write operation on data x. T_i's write operation can only be mapped to replica 1 of y because the replica 2 of y is no longer available. Similarly, T_j's write operation can only be mapped to replica 2 of x because replica 1 of x is no longer available. The operations of the two transactions are illustrated in Figure 4.7.

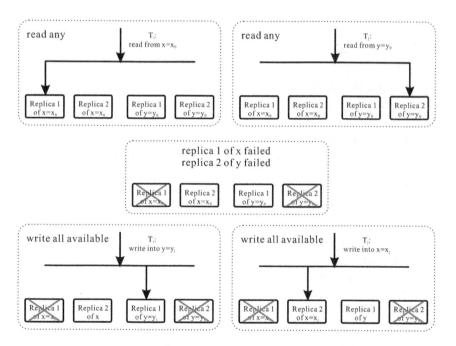

Figure 4.7   Preventing a transaction from accessing a not-fully-recovered replica is not sufficient to ensure one-copy serializable execution of transactions.

In this example, we cannot say T_i precedes T_j because T_j reads y before T_i writes to y. Unfortunately, we cannot say T_j precedes T_i either because T_i reads x before T_j writes to x. This violates the one-copy serializable execution of T_i and T_j.

As we can see from the above example, the problem is caused by the fact that conflicting operations are performed at difference replicas. A sound replication algorithm, therefore, must prevent this from happening. The quorum consensus replication algorithm [2] is one of such algorithms.

The quorum consensus replication algorithm achieves robustness against replica faults by write to a write quorum of replicas for each data item. As long as non-faulty replicas can form a write quorum, the write operation will succeed without blocking. The quorum consensus algorithm ensures one-copy serializable execution by read from a read quorum of replicas for each item. The read and write quorums are defined such as that a given read quorum must intersect any write quorum in at least one replica, and similarly any two write quorums must intersect in at least one replica.

Each replica is assigned a positive weight. A read quorum should have a minimum total weight of RT and a write quorum should have a minimum total weight of WT. Furthermore, $RT + WT$ and $2WT$ must be greater than the total weight of all replicas for each data item. This ensures the intersection requirement outline above. It is important to define RT to be the sum of weight of at least two replicas. For example, if each replica is assigned a weight of 1, then $RT = 2$. This is to ensure that the write quorum does not have to include all replicas (otherwise, the quorum consensus algorithm would reduce to the write-all algorithm, which is not fault tolerant).

Because a write operation would update only a quorum of replicas, different replicas may contain different values. To know which replica has the latest value, a version number is introduced and assigned to each replica. The version number would be increased by one for each subsequent write to a replica, if the replica is involved in all these write operations.

Rule for the read operation. For each read operation on a data item x, it is mapped to a read quorum of replicas of x. Each replica returns both the value of x and the corresponding version number. The client (or the transaction manager) selects the value that has the highest version number.

Rule for the write operation. For each write operation on a data item x, it is mapped to a write quorum of replicas of x. The write operation is carried out in two steps:

- Retrieve the version numbers from a write quorum of replicas. Set the new version number $v = v_{max} + 1$ for this write.
- Write to this quorum of replicas with the latest version number v. A replica overwrites both the value of the data item and the corresponding version number with the given values.

■ **EXAMPLE 4.2**

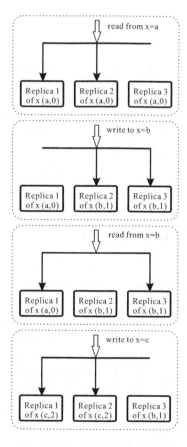

Figure 4.8 An example run of the quorum consensus algorithm on a single data item.

Figure 4.8 shows an example sequence of read/write operations on the replicas of a data item x. We assume that 3 replicas are used and the weight assigned for each replica is 1. The read quorum consists of 2 replicas (*i.e.*, $RT = 2$), and the write quorum also consists of 2 replicas (*i.e.*, $WT = 2$). Initially, all replicas contain a value of a with a version number 0 for x.

The first operation (read) is mapped to replica 1 and replica 2. Both replicas return a value a and a version of 0. Hence, the operation accepts the value a.

The second operation (write) is mapped to replica 2 and replica 3. Since both replicas return a version number 0, the new version number would be 1. Subsequently, the new value b and the new version number 1 are written to replicas 2 and 3. At the end of this operation, replica 1 contains older version of data.

The third operation (read) is mapped to replicas 1 and 3. Replica 1 returns a value a with version number 0, and replica 3 returns a value b with version 1. Hence, the operation accepts the value b because it has a higher version number.

The forth operation (write) is mapped to replicas 1 and 2. Replica 1 returns a version number 0 and replica 2 returns a version number 1. Hence, the new version number should be 2. Subsequently, the new value c with version number 2 are written to replicas 1 and 2. Note that replica 1 skips one update and catches up with the latest update.

4.3   Optimistic Replication

Research in optimistic replication is driven by the need of data replication over the Internet and data synchronization of mobile devices [25]. Traditional data replication algorithms described in the previous section often require frequent message exchanges among the replicas. Hence, they do not work well if the communication latency is large (such as over the Internet) or connectivity is not reliable (as in the wireless mobile environment). It is often desirable to allow the updates to be applied to the local copy immediately before the updates are propagated to all replicas. The immediate execution of updates might result in conflicts, in which case, the conflicts will be resolved either via pre-defined conflict resolution rules, or manually.

This approach is optimistic in that it is assumed that conflicts happen rarely, and they can be resolved when they are detected. Hence, the objective of optimistic data replication is to achieve eventual consistency among the replicas instead of one-copy serializable consistency. Here eventual consistency means that starting from the same initial state, replicas would reach the same final state if no new operations are submitted and after all existing operations submitted have been processed.

4.3.1   System Models

In optimistic data replication, we model the system as a set of objects that are replicated across N number of nodes, often referred to as sites [25]. The object is the smallest unit of replication and each object may define a set of operations for its local or remote clients to access the data encapsulated in the object. The operations may be as simple as read and write, but may be more sophisticated such as those defined using SQL [29].

The replicas are not necessarily equal in terms of update privileges. Some nodes might be designated as the master sites that have the privilege to update the replicas they manage, while others are restricted to allow read-only access for their clients. The most common configurations are:

- *Single-master replication.* Only a single node is granted the update privilege. All update operations must go through this single master site. The updates will be propagated to other replicas asynchronously.
- *Multi-master replication.* Every node is granted the update privilege. The updates then will be propagated from one replica to all other replicas. This is the most common configuration for optimistic data replication because it offers the highest data availability and convenience for the users. However, as a tradeoff, we must tackle the challenges of scheduling, conflict resolution, and commitment issues, to be explained shortly. Unless stated otherwise, we assume that multi-master replication is used in this section.

As shown in Figure 4.9, optimistic data replication often involves the following steps [25]:

- Operation submission. An operation is always submitted at the particular node chosen by a user. Different users may choose to submit their operations at different replicas.
- Local execution. An operation submitted locally is immediately executed.

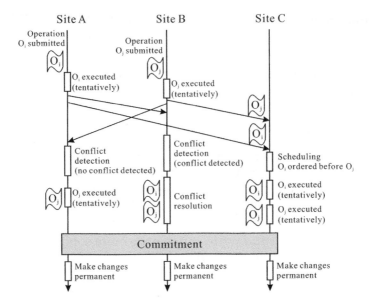

Figure 4.9   Basic steps for optimistic data replication for an operation-transfer system.

- Update propagation. The updates to the local replica may be propagated to other replicas in two alternative forms:

  - State transfer: the entire state of the local replica is transferred to other replicas. This form of update propagation is only applicable to systems that are limited to the use of read and write operations.

  - Operations transfer: Instead of transferring a copy of the state each time it is modified, other replicas can be brought up to date by logging the local operations and disseminating the logged operations to other replicas.

- Scheduling of operations. For multi-master replication, the arriving order of operations at each node is nondeterministic. The objective of scheduling is to impose a partial order on the operations to minimize conflicting execution of operations at different replicas, for example,

  - For operations that are causally related, the causal order must be respected when executing those operations.

  - For independent or commutative operations, they can be executed concurrently in arbitrary orders.

For example, in Figure 4.9, at site 3, operation O_i is executed ahead of O_j even though O_j is received first.

- Conflict resolution. Due to the nature of optimistic data replication, it is impossible to avoid conflicting execution orders carried out by different replicas. Such conflicting decisions would result in inconsistent replica states, which must be resolved.

- Update commitment. For both state transfer systems and operation transfer systems, an additional step is often needed for the following reasons:

  – It is desirable to know if an update made at a particular replica has been propagated to all other replicas. This knowledge would have two benefits: (1) all records regarding this update can now be garbage collected, and (2) the users can be assured that this update is now stable in that its effect will no longer be altered due to a conflict.

  – As a special case, in state transfer systems, deleted objects cannot be immediately removed from the system because of the possible delete/update conflicts. Hence, an additional step is necessary to garbage collect the deleted objects when the system has learned that all replicas have known the fact of deletion.

4.3.2   Establish Ordering among Operations

The foundation for optimistic data replication is to establish a partial ordering among all operations without excessive information exchanges among the replicas. The theory of event ordering and logical clocks [17] plays a big role to accomplish this.

The Happens-Before relationship. Given two operations O and O' submitted to node i and node j, respectively, we can say O happens before O', denoted as $O \rightarrow O'$, provided [17]:

- $i = j$ and O is submitted ahead of O', or,
- $i \neq j$, and O is propagated to node j and executed at j before O' is submitted.

The happens-before relationship is transitive, *i.e.*, if $O_a \rightarrow O_b$, and $O_b \rightarrow O_c$, then, $O_a \rightarrow O_c$. The happens-before relationship imposes a partial order on the operations. For those that cannot be qualified by the happens-before relationship, they are said to be concurrent, which implies that they do not have causal relationship.

Logical clocks can be used to capture the happens-before relationship among the operations [17]. A simple logical clock implementation is the Lamport clock [17]. To implement the Lamport clock, each replica maintains a counter variable, lc, representing the logical clock. The rules for using the Lamport clock for an operation-transfer system are defined as follows:

- On submission of a new operation O, the logical lock is incremented by 1, *i.e.,* $lc = lc + 1$.
- Then, the operation is assigned the current lc value as the timestamp of the operation, *i.e.,* $O.lc = lc$.
- When propagating the operation to other replicas, the assigned timestamp is piggybacked with the operation.
- On receiving an operation O, the receiving replica first adjusts its local logical clock, lc, to the timestamp piggybacked with the operation if the timestamp is bigger than its local clock value, then it increments its logical clock by 1, *i.e.,* $lc = max(lc, O.lc) + 1$.

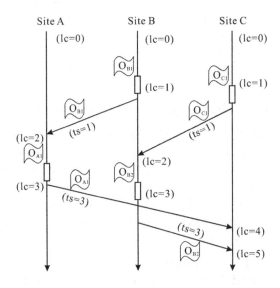

Figure 4.10   An example run of a system with three sites that uses Lamport clocks.

An example run of a system that uses the Lamport clocks is shown in Figure 4.10. The Lamport clock ensures that given two operations O and O', if O happens before O', then $O.lc < O'.lc$. For example, in Figure 4.10, O_{B1} happens before O_{A1}, and indeed

$O_{B1}.lc = 2 < O_{A1}.lc = 3$. However, the opposite is not true, i.e., one cannot conclude that O happens before O' simply because $O.lc < O'.lc$. For example, although O_{B2}'s Lamport timestamp is 3 and O_{A1}'s Lamport timestamp is 2, i.e., $O_{A1}.lc < O_{B2}$, we cannot conclude that $O_{A1} \rightarrow O_{B2}$. In fact, the two operations are concurrent. This observation precludes us from using the Lamport clock to generate timestamps for the purpose of causality identification because to determine if two operations are causally related, we want to simply compare their logical timestamps. Fortunately, a relatively simple extension of the Lamport clock, called vector clock [19], can satisfy this requirement.

For a system that consists of N nodes, each node maintains a vector clock, VC, in the form of an N-element array. We refer to the nodes in the system in terms of their indices, from 0 to N-1. For node i, the corresponding element in its vector clock, $VC_i[i]$, represents the number of events that have happened locally to node i. It learns the values for other elements from the timestamps piggybacked with the messages sent by other nodes to node i.

For data replication, the rules for using the vector clock by a system consisting of N master sites for an operation-transfer system are defined as follows:

- On submission of a new operation O at site i, where i ranges from 0 to $N - 1$, the element i of the vector clock at site i is incremented by 1, i.e., $VC_i[i] = VC_i[i] + 1$.
- Then, the operation is assigned the current VC_i value as the timestamp of the operation, i.e., $O.vc = VC_i$.
- When propagating the operation to other replicas, the assigned timestamp is piggybacked with the operation.
- On receiving an operation O at site j, the site j updates its vector clock in the following way:
  - For each element $k \neq j$ in the vector clock, $VC_j[k] = max(VC_j[k], O.vc[k])$

  Note that on receiving an operation from site i, site j might advance its vector clock at an element k other than i if site i receives an operation ahead of j. Site j might want to request a retransmission for that operation. If the communication channel between i and j does not ensure the first-in-first-out (FIFO) property, j might receive an old missing operation after an out-of-order operation from i, in which case, the vector clock is not advanced.

A site determines if an operation O^m happens before another operation O^n by comparing the vector clock timestamps piggybacked with the operations. O^m happens before O^n if $O^n.vc$ dominates $O^m.vc$, i.e., for any $k \in \{0...N\}$, $O^n.vc[k] \leq O^m.vc[k]$. If neither $O^n.vc$ dominates $O^m.vc$, nor $O^m.vc$ dominates $O^n.vc$, then, the two operations are concurrent and a conflict is detected.

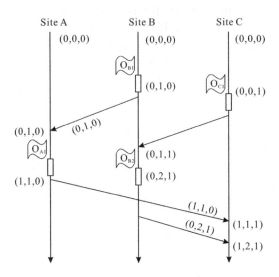

Figure 4.11   An example run of a system with three sites that uses vector clocks.

An example run of a system that uses vector clocks is shown in Figure 4.11. As can be seen, $O_{A1}.vc$ clearly dominates $O_{B1}.vc$, which indicates that $O_{A1} \to O_{B1}$. Furthermore, there is no ambiguity regarding the relationship between O_{B2} and O_{A1} because neither $O_{A1}.vc = (1,1,0)$ dominates $O_{B2}.vc = (0,2,1)$, nor $O_{B2}.vc$ dominates $O_{A1}.vc$.

4.3.3   State Transfer Systems

After an operation is submitted and applied locally, the update to the state needs to be propagated to other replicas. As we mentioned before, there are two distinct approaches to the update propagation from the master site to other replicas. In this subsection, we focus on the state transfer systems where the update is disseminated to other replicas via state transfer. The update propagation, conflict detection and reconciliation in operation transfer systems will be discussed in next subsection.

In a state transfer system, the replicas can become consistent with each other by applying the most up-to-date copy of the state assuming that no conflict is detected when different replicas synchronize with other each. This means that intermediate updates, if they exist, are effectively skipped at replicas other than those that have applied such updates. This property is often referred to as Thomas's write rule [30]. This rule was introduced in a (pessimistically) replicated database system that aims to preserve strong replica consistency by using only a scalar logical timestamps for updates and a majority consensus algorithm to ensure sequential updates [30]. In optimistic replication, vector clocks or their extensions are much more desirable:

- The use of vector clocks enables a replica to update its local copy regardless if it can communicates with other replicas, *i.e.*, the data is always available. This is very different from [30], which requires the majority of the replicas to form an agreement before an update. A replica would not be able to perform update on its data if the network partitions and it belongs to a minority partition.

- The vector clocks could be used to accurately capture the causality of different updates to the replicas for eventual replica consistency. The vector clocks also facilitates the detection of conflicting updates.

4.3.3.1 *Version Vectors*

The vector clocks used in this context are often referred to as version vectors (VV) [16] and discussed in the context replicated file systems. Each individual file (*i.e.*, object) is associated with a version vector. In practice, the version vector is typically represented with the site id explicitly spelled out instead of the compact form we have used in the previous section. For example, if a file is replicated at site A, B, and C, the version vector for the file would take the form of $(A : i, B : j, C : k)$, where i, j, and k, are the number of updates A, B, C, that have been applied to the file respectively. In fact, the version vector is represented as N number of (site-id, number-of-updates) pairs, where N is the number of replicas for the file. This format facilitates the addition of new replicas and the removal of existing replicas, *i.e.*, the version vector can be variable length instead of fixed ones.

Given two version vectors, VV_i and VV_j, if either one dominates the other, it is said that the two version vectors are compatible because one can make the replicas consistent by applying the Thomas's write rule. Otherwise, a conflict between the two replicas has been detected and it must be reconciled.

The general rule for using the version vector is rather similar to that described in section 4.3.2. In particular, for each update to the file at a site, the site increments the version count for that site in the version vector. However, the following additional rules are needed to handle cases not considered in section 4.3.2:

- When a file is renamed, it is treated as an update to the file. Hence, the version count will be incremented at the corresponding site element in the version vector.
- File deletion is also regarded as an update to the file. Furthermore, the file is not actually removed from the file system. Instead, the deletion operation would result in a version of the file with zero length (*i.e.*, essentially only the meta data for the file is retained). This mechanism is necessary for the simple reason that a site should always be prepared to detect possible conflicts on the updates made by different sites and reconcile them. Intuitively, only when all replicas have agreed to delete the file, could the file be completely removed from the file system. The garbage collection of deleted files can be achieved by a two-phase algorithm [15].
- After a conflict is detected and reconciled, it is important to assign a new version vector to the reconciled file at the site that initiated the reconciliation to ensure that the new version vector is compatible with all previous version vectors at all replicas of the file. To compute the new version vector, first, the version count for each element is set to the maximum of all its predecessors, then, the element that corresponds to the site that initiated the reconciliation is incremented by one.

EXAMPLE 4.3

In this example, we show how the new version vector is determined after a conflict is resolved. Consider a file that is replicated at three sites, A, B, and C, respectively, as shown in Figure 4.12. Assume that A creates the file and informs B and C, as this point, all three sites' version vectors are identical $(A : 1, B : 0, C : 0)$. Subsequently, B and C independent updates the file, which means that B's version vector is going to be changed to $(A : 1, B : 1, C : 0)$, and C's version vector is going to be changed to $(A : 1, B : 0, C : 1)$. When B sends its update to C, C then notices the conflict because B's and C's version vectors are not compatible (*i.e.*, neither dominates the other). When C reconciles the conflict, it assigns the reconciled file a new version vector by first taking the maximum of B's and C's version vector at each element $((A : 1, B : 1, C : 1))$, and subsequently increment C's version count by 1, which leads to a final new version vector of $(A : 1, B : 1, C : 2)$. This new version vector apparently dominates B's version vector $(A : 1, B : 1, C : 0)$, implying that the conflict has been resolved from this point on.

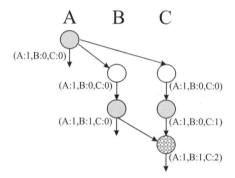

Figure 4.12   An example for the determination of the new version vector value after reconciling a conflict.

Once a conflict is detected, the next step is to reconcile the conflict. It is obvious that not all conflicts can be reconciled automatically in a generic manner because conflict reconciliation is inevitably application specific. Nevertheless, in some cases, conflicts can be reconciled automatically by exploiting application semantics. It has been reported in a number of systems that the majority of conflicts can in fact be reconciled automatically [16, 31].

For example, it is possible for two or more replicas to modify the same file in exactly the same way. Even though the version vectors for the updates at different replicas would report conflicts, the file in fact would be identical. A simple mechanism to reconcile the reported conflicts in this case is to compare the different versions of the file. If they turn out to be the same, the conflicts are reconciled effectively with a no-op operation.

As another example, in [31], conflicts on directories in a replicated file system are reconciled based on the fact that there are only two allowed operations: create a file or delete a file. As such, conflicts on directories can be reconciled by first merging all the files within the directory (from the conflicting replicas), and then by filtering out those that had been deleted.

4.3.4 Operation Transfer System

In an operation transfer system, each site must log the operations submitted as well as those received from other sites. The logged operations may be propagated to other sites via reliable multicast in a tightly-coupled system, or via point-to-point exchanges epidemically in loosely-coupled systems. In this subsection, we assume the latter approach is used because it might be more appearing to the Internet environment.

4.3.4.1 *Propagation Using Vector Clocks*

As we mentioned in section 4.3.2, operations must be properly timestamped so that the causality between different operations can be preserved when they are applied and vector clock is a powerful tool to enable this. For a vector clock VC_i maintained by site i:

- $VC_i[i]$ represents the number of operations submitted at site i locally.
- $VC_i[j]$ $(i \neq j)$ refers to what sites i knows about the number of operations submitted at a remote site j.

For two sites i and j to find out what operations are missing at each site, they exchange their vector clocks. Then, they propagate the operations needed by each other according to the following rules:

- For $\forall k \neq j$, if $VC_i[k] > VC_j[k]$, site i propagates all operations that were submitted originally at site k and carry timestamps larger than $VC_j[k]$ to site j.
- For $\forall k \neq i$, if $VC_j[k] > VC_i[k]$, site j propagates all operations that were submitted originally at site k and carry timestamps larger than $VC_j[k]$ to site i.

EXAMPLE 4.4

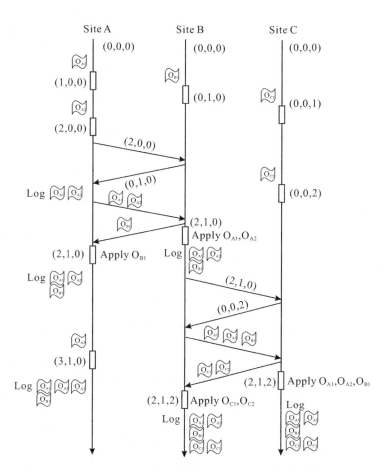

Figure 4.13   An example operation propagation using vector clocks in a system with three replicas.

We illustrate how the operation transfer using vector clocks works in a system with three replicas as shown in Figure 4.13. We assume that the index for site A is 0, the index for site B is 1, and the index for site C is 2, in the vector clocks.

Two operations O_{A1} and O_{A2} are submitted and processed at site A before site A initiates operation propagation with site B. Concurrently, site B has one operation O_{B1} submitted and processed locally. Site A's vector clock $VC_A = (2, 0, 0)$ and site B's vector clock $VC_B = (0, 1, 0)$. Because $VC_A[0] > VC_B[0]$, site A propagates its two operations O_{A1} and O_{A2} to site B. Similarly, because $VC_B[1] > VC_A[1]$, site B propagates its operation O_{B1} to site A. After site A applies the received operation O_{B1} (after having reconciled any conflict), it advances its vector clock to $(2, 1, 0)$. After site B applies the received operations O_{A1} and O_{A2} (again, after having reconciled any conflicts), it advances its vector clock to $(2, 1, 0)$ too.

Subsequently, site B engages an operations exchange with site C. Prior to the exchange, two operations O_{C1} and O_{C2} have been submitted and processed at site C. Hence, the vector clock is $(0, 0, 2)$ at the time of exchange. Because $VC_B[0] > VC_C[0]$, site B propagates operations O_{A1} and O_{A2} to site C. Similarly, because $VC_B[1] > VC_C[1]$, site B propagates operation O_{B1} to site C. Site C would propagate O_{C1} and O_{C2} to site B because $VC_C[2] > VC_B[2]$. After resolving any conflicts and applying the received operations, site B and site C advance their vector clock to $(2, 1, 2)$. In the meantime, one more operation O_{A3} is submitted and processed at site A.

4.3.4.2   Propagation Using Timestamp Matrices

Timestamp matrices [32] (also referred to as matrix clocks) can be used at each site to keep track of what it has learned about every other site's vector clock instead of only how many operations submitted at other sites. A row of a timestamp matrix at site i, $TM_i[j]$, corresponds to site i knowledge about the vector clock at site j. A cell in the timestamp matrix at site i, $TM_i[j][k]$, corresponds to site i knowledge about how many operations site j has received that are originated at site k. Using timestamp matrices eliminates the need for the round of exchanges on vector clocks prior to the sending of operations.

To use timestamp matrices, each site maintains timestamp matrix TM. On submitting a local operation at site i:

- The operation is assigned with the current self vector clock value, TM_i (i.e., the $i - th$ row of the time matrix).
- The corresponding cell of the matrix is incremented by one, i.e., , $TM_i[i][i] = TM_i[i][i] + 1$,

When a site i is ready to propagate operations to another site j, it does the following:

- Determine what operations are needed by site j from site i by comparing $TM_i[j][k]$ and $TM_i[i][k]$, for all $k \neq j$. If

$TM_i[j][k] > TM_i[i][k]$, it means site i has one or more operations originated at site k that are needed by site j. Hence, site i retrieves the operations from its log and sends them to site j, together with site i's timestamp matrix TM_i.

- Site i updates the row for site j in its timestamp matrix $TM_i[j]$ using the row that corresponds to its own vector time $TM_i[i]$, i.e., for all $k \neq j$, $TM_i[j][k] = max(TM_i[j][k], TM_i[i][k])$. The reason for doing this update is because once site j receives the operations and the timestamp matrix transmitted by site i, it would update the corresponding row in its timestamp matrix in exactly the same way.

When a site j receives the set of remote operations and the corresponding timestamp matrix from site i, it carries out the following:

- First, it makes sure that the operation received is not a duplicate because the row for site j in site i's timestamp matrix is inevitably an estimate - site j might have received operations from other sites without the knowledge of site i:

  - Accept a remote operation O_k (originated at site k) sent by site i, if $O_k.vc[k] > TM_j[j][k]$

- Apply operation O_k if it is in sequence. If site i sends the operation to site j via reliable ordered point-to-point protocol such as TCP, then, it is guaranteed that O_k will be in sequence. If there is a conflict, reconcile the conflict.
- Update the timestamp matrix.

  - $TM_j[j][k] = O_k.vc[k]$

  - For all other cells $m \neq k$, if $O_k.vc[m] > TM_j[j][m]$, it means that site j has not received some operations originated at site m. Site j then contacts the originating site for retransmission of the missing operations. Then, it updates the corresponding cells in its timestamp matrix: $TM_j[j][m] = O_k.vc[m]$.

- On receiving the timestamp matrix sent by site i, site j updates the cells of its timestamp matrix other than those in row j by applying the pairwise maximum operation.

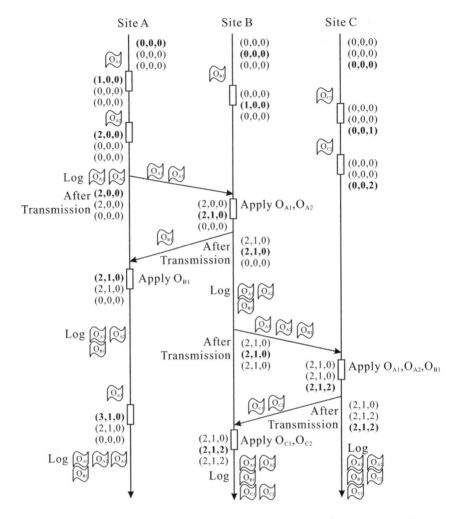

Figure 4.14 An example for operation propagation using timestamp matrices in a system with three replicas.

EXAMPLE 4.5

The scenario in this example is identical to that in Example 4.4, except that timestamp matrices are used instead of vector clocks. As can be seen, the round of message exchange prior to the operation transmission is omitted by using timestamp matrices.

When site A is ready propagates its logged operations to site B, it compares two rows in its timestamp matrix, $TM_A[0]$

and $TM_A[1]$. $TM_A[0]$ corresponds to its own vector clock, and $TM_A[0]$ corresponds to A's estimate on what B knows. Since $TM_A[0][0] = 2 > TM_A[1][0] = 0$, site A estimates that site B has not received the most recent two operations submitted at site A, O_{A1} and O_{A2}. Therefore, site A transmits the two operations to site B, followed by its timestamp matrix. Subsequently, site A updates the row in its timestamp matrix for site B, $TM_A[1]$, from $(0,0,0)$ to $(2,0,0)$.

On receiving each operation, site B checks to see if it is a duplicate by comparing the vector timestamp piggybacked with the operation and the corresponding cell in its timestamp matrix. For O_{A1}, because $O_{A1}.vc[0] = 1 > TM_B[1][0] = 0$, site B knows that O_{A1} is not a duplicate. Therefore, site B accepts the operation, applies it (after reconciling any conflict), and updates the corresponding cell in its timestamp matrix $TM_B[1][0] = 1$. Similarly, site B accepts O_{A2}, applies it, and updates its timestamp matrix $TM_B[1][0] = 2$.

Site B also takes this opportunity to propagates its operations to site A. By comparing $TM_B[0]$ and $TM_B[1]$, site B estimates that site A may need the operation O_{B1} because $TM_B[1][1] = 1 > TM_B[0][1] = 0$. After the transmission, site B updates its timestamp matrix to $TM_B[0] = (2,1,0)$ from $(2,0,0)$. On receiving O_{B1}, site A accepts it, applies it (after reconciling any conflict), and updates its timestamp matrix to $TM_A[0] = (2,1,0), TM_A[0] = (2,1,0)$. $TM_A[2]$ remains to be $(0,0,0)$.

The operation propagations from between site B and site C can be explained similarly. It is interesting to note that if site A subsequently wants to propagates its operations to site C, it would transmit all operations $(O_{A1}, O_{A2}, O_{A3}, O_{B1})$ in its log to site C because it would estimate that site C has received none of them based on the row for site C in its timestamp matrix, $TM_A[2] = (0,0,0)$. Site C would determine that O_{A1}, O_{A2}, and O_{B1} are duplicates and ignore them because $TM_C[2][0] = 2$ is larger than $O_{A1}.vc[0] = 1$ and equal to $O_{A2}.vc[0] = 2$, and $TM_C[2][1] = 1$ is the same as $O_{B1}.vc[0] = 1$. Site C would accept O_{A3} and updates its timestamp matrix accordingly.

4.3.5   Update Commitment

As we mentioned earlier in this section, an additional step is necessary in both state transfer and operation transfer systems. The primary objective for this step is to determine which update has been propagated to all replicas so that:

- Records regarding an update can be garbage collected once every replica has received and applied the update.
- The effect of the update to the system is now stable and the users can be assured that this update will not be altered due to conflict reconciliation. This is because:
  - Once the update has reached all replicas, all concurrent updates that might be in conflict with this update must have been reconciled.
  - This update would happen before any subsequently issued update by any replica, and the later update would bear a timestamp larger than the current update. Therefore, no later update could conflict with this update.

A number of algorithms and mechanisms have been developed to help determine if an update has been stabilized (*i.e.*, if all replicas have received and applied the update) for operation transfer systems. However, they should apply to state transfer systems else. Here we describe two of them. The first one is based on explicit acknowledgement, and the second one is based on timestamp matrices, which we have introduced in the context of operation propagation.

For state transfer systems, there is an additional challenge - to determine when deleted objects can be safely removed from the system. This is important because if the deleted objects cannot be removed from the system, sooner or later they would saturate the storage (in the context of replicated file systems, for example). Typically, a two-phase commit algorithm is used to ensure an object is garbage collected only after all replicas have agreed to delete the object [15, 24]. In the first phase, all replicas are queried regarding the deletion. If all replicas agree, the object is finally removed from the system in the second phase. The algorithm is complicated by the possible delete/update conflict and its reconciliation. The detailed description of the algorithm is outside the scope of this book.

4.3.5.1   Ack Vector

For systems that use vector clocks for operation propagation, scheduling, and conflict detection, an additional vector clock, called ack vector, is introduced to store acknowledgement information regarding the operations received at a site [13]. In particular, for site i, the $i - th$ element of its ack vector, $AV_i[i]$, stores the minimum timestamp among all elements of its vector clock, VC_i, i.e., $AV_i[i] = min(VC_i[0], VC_i[1], ..., VC_i[N-1])$, where N is the number of replicas in the system. $VC_i[i] = t$ means that site i has received the first t operations submitted at *every* site. For other elements, site i gradually learns about them when other sites share their ack vectors with site i. For example, when another site k shares its ack vector, VC_k to site i, site i learns that site k has received the first $VC_k[k]$ operations submitted at every site, including those at site i.

Hence, a site determines what operations have been stabilized by taking the minimum of all the elements in its ack vector. If $min(AV_i[0], AV_i[1], ..., AV_i[N-1]) = t$, then the first t operations submitted at *every* site have reached all replicas.

EXAMPLE 4.6

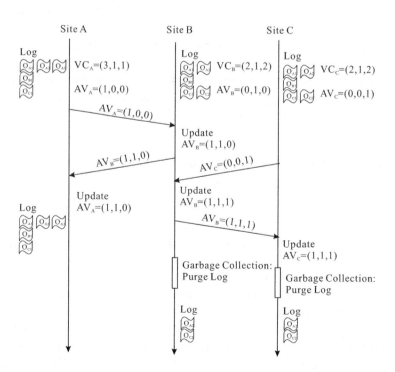

Figure 4.15   Update commit using ack vectors in a system with three replicas.

Consider a system with three replicas. Before the replicas exchange their ack vectors, site A's vector clock VC_A is $(3, 1, 1)$ with operations O_{A1}, O_{A2}, O_{A3}, O_{B1}, O_{C1} in its log, site B's vector clock VC_B is $(2, 1, 2)$ with operations O_{A1}, O_{A2}, O_{B1}, O_{C1}, O_{C2} in its log, site C's vector clock VC_C is $(2, 1, 2)$ as well with operations O_{A1}, O_{A2}, O_{B1}, O_{C1}, O_{C2} in its log.

Site A's ack vector AV_A can be calculated in the following:

- $AV_A[0]$ is calculated by taking the minimum of the elements in its vector clock, i.e., $AV_A[0] = min(VC_A[0], VC_A[1], VC_A[2]) = min(3, 1, 1) = 1$.
- Because site A has not received the ack vector from site B and site C yet, $AV_A[1] = AV_A[2] = 0$.

Similarly, site B's ack vector AV_B is $(0, 1, 0)$, and site C's ack vector AV_C is $(0, 0, 1)$. When site B receives site A's ack vector, it updates its ack vector AV_B to $(1, 1, 0)$. Site B subsequently sends its ack vector to site A. Site A then updates its ack vector to $(1, 1, 0)$. At this point, site A could not garbage collect any operations in its log because $min(AV_A[0], AV_A[1], AV_A[2]) = min(1, 1, 0) = 0$.

When site B receives C's ack vector $AV_C = (0, 0, 1)$, it updates its ack vector to $(1, 1, 1)$. At this point, site B can conclude that all replicas have received the first operation submitted at each site, because $min(1, 1, 1) = 1$. Therefore, site B can garbage collect these operations and the log has only two operations remaining: O_{A2} and O_{C2}.

Similarly, when site C receives B's ack vector, it updates its ack vector to $(1, 1, 1)$ as well. Site C can safely purge O_{A1}, O_{B1}, O_{C1}, from its log at this point.

Obviously, how quickly the system can garbage collect stable operations depends on how frequently the sites exchange their ack vectors. If a site is out of reach from other sites temporarily, no further garbage collection can be possibly done. This limitation is due to the intrinsic requirement that an operation is not stable (and hence can be garbage collected) until *all* sites have received it.

Another severe limitation of using ack vectors is that a site that has few operations submitted would prevent other sites from garbage collecting beyond the number of operations submitted at this site and those submitted at any other site. In the example scenario shown in Figure 4.15, because site B only submitted a single operation, O_{B1}, there is no chance for site A and site C to garbage collect O_{A2} and O_{C2}. In a worse situation, if a site has no operation submitted, then, no site in the system can garbage collect *any* operation.

4.3.5.2   Timestamp Matrix

For systems that use timestamp matrices, they can learn the stable operations without any additional message exchanges. At site i, a cell in its timestamp matrix, $TM_i[j][k] = t$, means that according to site i's conservative estimate, site j has received all operations originated from site k up to t. Hence, to find out what operations from site k that have become stable, all we need is to take the minimum of all rows at element k, *i.e.*, if $min(TM_i[0][k], TM_i[1][k], ..., TM_i[N-1][k]) = t$, all sites have received the first t operations submitted at site k.

■   EXAMPLE 4.7

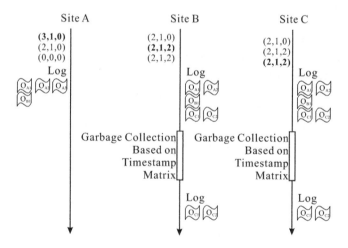

Figure 4.16   Update commit using timestamp matrices in a system with three replicas.

Consider a system shown in Figure 4.16. Site A's timestamp matrix is:

$$\begin{pmatrix} 3 & 1 & 0 \\ 2 & 1 & 0 \\ 0 & 0 & 0 \end{pmatrix}$$

Site B's timestamp matrix is:

$$\begin{pmatrix} 2 & 1 & 0 \\ 2 & 1 & 2 \\ 2 & 1 & 2 \end{pmatrix}$$

Site C's timestamp matrix is the same as that of site B:

$$\begin{pmatrix} 2 & 1 & 0 \\ 2 & 1 & 2 \\ 2 & 1 & 2 \end{pmatrix}$$

It is apparent that site A cannot garbage collect any operation because the third row in its timestamp matrix is $(0, 0, 0)$. For site B, the minimum of the first column (corresponding to the status of site A) is 2, the minimum of the second column (corresponding to the status of site B) is 1, and the minimum of the third column (corresponding to the status of site C) is 0. Then, site B can safely garbage collect the first two operations from site A: O_{A1} and O_{A2}, and the first operation from site B itself: O_{B1}. Similarly, site C can safely purge the three operations as well.

Even though the effectiveness of using timestamp matrices for update commit also depends on good connectivity of different sites, a site that has few or no operations submitted would not prevent other sites from committing updates and performing garbage collection.

4.4   CAP Theorem

The CAP theorem was introduced by Eric Brewer in 2000 [6] regarding what can be achieved in a practical distributed system. The theorem states that it is impossible to satisfy all three of the following guarantees:

- Consistency (C): the replicated data is always consistent with each other.
- Availability (A): the data is highly available to the users.
- Partition tolerance (P): the system can continue providing services to its users even when the network partitions.

The proof of the CAP theorem is straightforward [11] because in the presence of network partitions, replicas in different partitions could not communicate with each other. If the designer of a system favors replica consistency, then the availability may have to be sacrificed. Similarly, if the designer chooses to ensure high availability, there is no way strong consistency among the replicas in different partitions can be achieved - the replicas cannot communicate!

■ **EXAMPLE 4.8**

Similar to [11], we consider a network with only two nodes N_1, N_2. Assume that a network partitioning fault occurs and it isolates node N_1 from node N_2. We further assume that we are going to ensure P and A, which means the following could happen:

- A client that could reach N_1 issues an update W_1. The update is immediately applied at N_1. Due to the network partitioning fault, N_2 is not aware of the update W_1 at N_1.
- Another client that could reach N_2 also issues an update W_2. The update is immediately applied at N_2. Due to the network partitioning fault, N_1 is not aware of the update W_2 at N_2.
- It is apparent that the states of N_1 and N_2 have become inconsistent from now on.

Note that the states of the two nodes would become inconsistent only after different updates have applied at them. If one is an update operation W and the other is a read-only operation R, we cannot conclude that the states have become inconsistent. Indeed, even if the operation R on N_2 is issued significantly after the operation W on N_1 in real time, it does not necessarily mean that R is causally related to W and we should expect R to read the value written by W. Without some out-of-band channel that links the two operations, it is perfectly legal for R to read a value prior to the update operation W. If the system is repaired from the network partitioning fault, N_1 and N_2 could easily merge their history so that all operations are serializable (*e.g.*, R would be ordered prior to W after N_1 transfers its state or operations to N_2).

Since its inception, the CAP theorem has attracted extensive attentions and debates [1, 4, 7, 12, 23]. The CAP theorem highlighted the need to strike a good balance between consistency and availability in the presence of network partitioning faults when designing practical systems because many systems might face network partitioning faults [7]. Much debates lie on the reason for the use of reduced consistency models in favor of highly availability. As we have seen in the previous section on optimistic replication and rightly pointed out by a number of researchers [1], the adoption of reduced consistency models is often not due to concerns of network partitioning faults, but for better performance for applications running over wide-area networks.

Furthermore, the definitions of C, A, and P are quite unclear. For example, does requiring C means that all non-faulty replicas must be in sync all the time? On the other hand, if a quorum-based consensus algorithm (such as Paxos [18]) is used to coordinate the replicas, the system would make progress as long as the majority of the replicas agree with each and it is possible that the minority of replicas lag significantly behind or are in a confused state depending on the fault model used in the system. Can we call such a system as guaranteeing C? We probably should say that it does guarantee C based on common sense.

Whether or not a system guaranteeing A depends on the fault model used. For example, a system that provides high availability with a crash-fault-only model might not be able to ensure high availability in the presence of network partitioning faults or malicious faults. Without clarifying the fault model used, the scopes of availability and partition-tolerance would appear to overlap with each other:

- Partition tolerance implies that the system could ensure liveness in the presence of network partition faults.
- High availability, on the other hand, would require the tolerance of all types of faults, including network partition faults, *without specific qualification on the fault model used*.

In addition, the definition of A is vague. If the data is said to be available for a user, how long does the user has to wait for its request to be serviced? What is the relationship between A and the end-to-end latency (L) as experienced by a user? A is not absolute and neither is L. In [1], A and L are treated as different properties of a system, and thus, a PACELC model is proposed to replace CAP in system design:

If there is a network partition fault, how to balance the availability and consistency (A and C); else (E), during normal operation with a fully-connected network, how to balance the requirements on latency (L) and consistency (C)?

The meaning of partition tolerance is also unclear. First, what is considered as a network partitioning fault can be confusing. A straightforward interpretation of a network partitioning fault is that the network is partitioned into several disjoint partitions due to a fault at a router/switch or a communication link. However, normally there is no way for a replica to have such global knowledge and different replicas may have completely different views regarding whether or not the network has partitioned. If a replica could reach every node that it needs to communicate, then to its view, there is no network partitioning fault, even though the network has already been partitioned and that replica together with all other nodes it communicates with reside in one of the partitions. Furthermore, a replica could only detect a network partitioning fault by using a timeout when communicating with other nodes. *To a replica, a network partitioning fault has happened if it has timed out a request issued on another node.* That is why a network partitioning fault is often modeled as a message loss [11]. Obviously, if a network partitions and quickly recovers before the timeout, the partitioning fault might have no impact on the system.

4.4.1   2 out 3

The CAP theorem dictates that at the best, we could design a system that achieve 2 out of 3 properties, that is, a system that either ensures CA, CP, or PA, but not all three CAP, as shown in Figure 4.17.

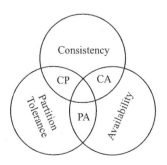

Figure 4.17   An illustration of the CAP theorem.

4.4.1.1   CA System

A CA system sacrifices partition tolerance for consistency and availability. This implies that the network partitioning fault is excluded from the fault model used in the system design. This type of systems can only be used in an environment that the network partitioning fault rarely happens, for example, a local area network or as big as a data center. Systems designed to achieve pessimistic replication are often CA systems.

4.4.1.2   CP System

Based on our previous argument, we cannot build a system that ensures strong consistency while tolerating all forms of network partitioning faults because it is bound that some replicas would not be able to reach other replicas by the definition of network partitioning. However, a CP system is possible under the following conditions:

- Consistency is achieved by a quorum-based algorithm. That is, as long as the majority of the replicas agree with each other, the system is considered consistent.
- The network partitioning fault results in a partition that consists of the majority of the replicas in the system.

In such a CP system, the replicas residing in the majority partition would proceed as usual (*i.e.*, as if there is no network partitioning fault), while the replicas in the minor partition (or partitions) would stop operating, hence losing the availability property. A number of partition-tolerant group communication systems [3, 20] are CP systems.

4.4.1.3   PA System

Many new cloud computing systems [1, 23], as well as systems that employ optimistic replication [25], are designed to ensure PA. As we discussed in section 4.3, the loss of consistency is only temporary - the replica states will eventually converge when the network partitions merge and when the system is quiescent.

4.4.2   Implications of Enabling Partition Tolerance

For a PA system, it should strive to detect and reconcile any consistency because users do expect eventual consistency even if they could tolerate temporary inconsistent states during period of network partitioning. In the absence of network partitioning, the system would behave as a CA system. When a replica realizes that it has difficulty in communicating with another node, it enters the partition mode, as shown in Figure 4.18. During the partition mode, a replica would trade consistency for better availability. However, when the partitions are merged, the replicas would reconcile their inconsistencies, similar to conflict reconciliation we have described in section 4.3 in the context of optimistic replication. Well-known methods for conflict reconciliation include:

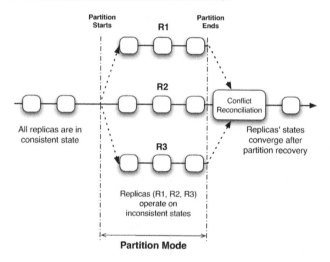

Figure 4.18   Partition mode and partition recovery.

- Compensation transactions/operations. In some systems, such as transaction processing systems, the effect of an operation can be reversed by applying a user-defined compensation operation [10]. Thus, the operations can be reordered as desired during the partition recovery.
- Operational transformation. For collaborative editing systems, operational transformation is often used to reconcile conflicting edits to a shared document [28]. Given two conflicting operations O_i applied at site i, and O_j applied at site j. O_i is transformed to O'_i, and O_j is transformed to O'_j such that given the same state at the beginning, the final state by applying O_i followed by O'_j at site i would be the same state by applying O_j followed by O'_i at site j.

- Commutative replicated data types (CRDTs). This approach was initially developed as an alternative solution to collaborative editing [22] and was recently expanded for use by potentially many other applications [27]. By using CRDTs to represent the state, all operations on the state are now commutative. Hence, concurrent operations are no longer in conflict with each other. A replica could apply an operation submitted locally immediately and propagates the update to other replicas asynchronously. A replica also orders deterministically a remote update sent by another replica as it is received *without* any inter-replica communication.

Detailed discussion on these methods are beyond the scope of this book.

To summarize this section, considering that the only way for a replica to detect that a network partitioning fault has happened is through a timeout and a user will have to wait a finite amount of time to see its request being serviced, what really matters are the following two parameters in system design:

- End-to-end latency. This parameter defines the end-to-end latency that a system can tolerate according to business requirement.

- Partition timeout value. This parameter defines the timeout value chosen by the system designer that a replica could use to enter the partition mode. Normally, the partition timeout value is significantly higher than the end-to-end latency.

For a system to be deployed over a wide area network, if the round trip latency between two remote replicas comes close to the partition timeout value, then the system would be operating in the partition mode most of time and hence, the system will basically operate as a PA system. Otherwise, the system would operate as a CA system until a network partitioning fault has happened. According to this interpretation, the PACELC model does not appear to be necessary (because the difference between A and C is undefined in the model).

REFERENCES

1. D. Abadi. Consistency tradeoffs in modern distributed database system design: Cap is only part of the story. *IEEE Computer*, 45(2):37–42, 2012.

2. P. A. Bernstein, V. Hadzilacos, and N. Goodman. *Concurrency control and recovery in database systems*. Addison-Wesley Longman Publishing Co., Inc., Boston, MA, USA, 1987.

3. K. Birman. A history of the virtual synchrony replication model. In B. Charron-Bost, F. Pedone, and A. Schiper, editors, *Replication*, pages 91–120. Springer-Verlag, Berlin, Heidelberg, 2010.

4. K. A. Birman, D. A. Freedman, Q. Huang, and P. Dowell. Overcoming cap with consistent soft-state replication. *IEEE Computer*, 45(2):50–58, 2012.

5. K. P. Birman. *Guide to Reliable Distributed Systems - Building High-Assurance Applications and Cloud-Hosted Services*. Texts in computer science. Springer, 2012.

6. E. A. Brewer. Towards robust distributed systems (abstract). In *Proceedings of the nineteenth annual ACM symposium on Principles of distributed computing*, PODC '00, pages 7–, New York, NY, USA, 2000. ACM.

7. E. A. Brewer. Pushing the cap: Strategies for consistency and availability. *IEEE Computer*, 45(2):23–29, 2012.

8. M. Castro and B. Liskov. Practical byzantine fault tolerance and proactive recovery. *ACM Transactions on Computer Systems*, 20(4):398–461, 2002.

9. P. Felber and R. Guerraoui. Programming with object groups in corba. *IEEE Concurrency*, 8(1):48–58, Jan. 2000.

10. H. Garcia-Molina and K. Salem. Sagas. In *Proceedings of the ACM SIGMOD Conference*, pages 249–259, San Francisco, CA, 1987.

11. S. Gilbert and N. Lynch. Brewer's conjecture and the feasibility of consistent, available, partition-tolerant web services. *SIGACT News*, 33(2):51–59, June 2002.

12. S. Gilbert and N. A. Lynch. Perspectives on the cap theorem. *IEEE Computer*, 45(2):30–36, 2012.

13. R. A. Golding and D. D. E. Long. Modeling replica divergence in a weak-consistency protocol for global-scale distributed data bases. Technical report, University of California, Santa Cruz, CA, USA, 1993.

14. J. Gray and A. Reuter. *Transaction Processing: Concepts and Techniques*. Morgan Kaufmann Publishers Inc., San Francisco, CA, USA, 1st edition, 1992.

15. R. G. Guy, G. J. Popek, T. W. Page, and Jr. Consistency algorithms for optimistic replication. In *In Proceedings of the First IEEE International Conference on Network Protocols*, 1993.

16. D. S. P. Jr., G. J. Popek, G. Rudisin, A. Stoughton, B. J. Walker, E. Walton, J. M. Chow, D. A. Edwards, S. Kiser, and C. S. Kline. Detection of mutual inconsistency in distributed systems. *IEEE Trans. Software Eng.*, 9(3):240–247, 1983.

17. L. Lamport. Time, clocks, and the ordering of events in a distributed system. *Commun. ACM*, 21(7):558–565, July 1978.

18. L. Lamport. Paxos made simple. *ACM SIGACT News (Distributed Computing Column)*, 32(4):18–25, December 2001.

19. F. Mattern. Virtual time and global states of distributed systems. In *Proceedings of the International Workshop on Parallel and Distributed Algorithms*, pages 216–226. Elsevier Science Publishers B.V. (North-Holland), 1989.

20. L. E. Moser, P. M. Melliar-Smith, D. A. Agarwal, R. K. Budhia, and C. A. Lingley-Papadopoulos. Totem: A fault-tolerant multicast group communication system. *Commun. ACM*, 39(4):54–63, 1996.

21. P. Narasimhan, L. E. Moser, and P. M. Melliar-Smith. Eternal: a component-based framework for transparent fault-tolerant corba. *Softw. Pract. Exper.*, 32(8):771–788, July 2002.

22. N. Preguica, J. M. Marques, M. Shapiro, and M. Letia. A commutative replicated data type for cooperative editing. In *Proceedings of the 2009 29th IEEE International Conference on Distributed Computing Systems*, ICDCS '09, pages 395–403, Washington, DC, USA, 2009. IEEE Computer Society.

23. R. Ramakrishnan. Cap and cloud data management. *IEEE Computer*, 45(2):43–49, 2012.

24. D. Ratner, P. Reiher, and G. J. Popek. Roam: a scalable replication system for mobility. *Mob. Netw. Appl.*, 9(5):537–544, Oct. 2004.

25. Y. Saito and M. Shapiro. Optimistic replication. *ACM Comput. Surv.*, 37(1):42–81, Mar. 2005.

26. F. Schneider. Implementing fault-tolerant services using the state machine approach: A tutorial. *ACM Computer Survey*, 22(4):299–319, 1990.

27. M. Shapiro, N. Preguiça, C. Baquero, and M. Zawirski. A comprehensive study of Convergent and Commutative Replicated Data Types. Technical Report 7506, INRIA, January 2011.

28. C. Sun, X. Jia, Y. Zhang, Y. Yang, and D. Chen. Achieving convergence, causality preservation, and intention preservation in real-time cooperative editing systems. *ACM Trans. Comput.-Hum. Interact.*, 5(1):63–108, Mar. 1998.

29. D. B. Terry, M. M. Theimer, K. Petersen, A. J. Demers, M. J. Spreitzer, and C. H. Hauser. Managing update conflicts in bayou, a weakly connected replicated storage system. In *Proceedings of the fifteenth ACM symposium on Operating systems principles*, SOSP '95, pages 172–182, New York, NY, USA, 1995. ACM.

30. R. H. Thomas. A majority consensus approach to concurrency control for multiple copy databases. *ACM Transactions on Database Systems*, 4:180–209, 1979.

31. B. Walker, G. Popek, R. English, C. Kline, and G. Thiel. The locus distributed operating system. In *Proceedings of the ninth ACM symposium on Operating systems principles*, SOSP '83, pages 49–70, New York, NY, USA, 1983. ACM.

32. G. T. Wuu and A. J. Bernstein. Efficient solutions to the replicated log and dictionary problems. In *Proceedings of the third annual ACM symposium on*

Principles of distributed computing, PODC '84, pages 233–242, New York, NY, USA, 1984. ACM.

33. W. Zhao. Design and implementation of a Byzantine fault tolerance framework for web services. *Journal of Systems and Software*, 82(6):1004–1015, June 2009.

34. W. Zhao, P. M. Melliar-Smith, and L. E. Moser. Low latency fault tolerance system. *The Computer Journal*, 2013. in press.

35. W. Zhao, L. E. Moser, and P. M. Melliar-Smith. Design and implementation of a pluggable fault-tolerant CORBA infrastructure. *Cluster Computing*, 7(4):317–330, 2004.

36. W. Zhao, L. E. Moser, and P. M. Melliar-Smith. Fault tolerance for distributed and networked systems. In *Encyclopedia of Information Science and Technology (II)*, pages 1190–1196. Idea Group, 2005.

37. W. Zhao, L. E. Moser, and P. M. Melliar-Smith. Unification of transactions and replication in three-tier architectures based on CORBA. *IEEE Transactions on Dependable and Secure Computing*, 2(1):20–33, 2005.

38. W. Zhao, L. E. Moser, and P. M. Melliar-Smith. End-to-end latency of a fault-tolerant corba infrastructure. *Perform. Eval.*, 63(4):341–363, May 2006.

39. W. Zhao, H. Zhang, and H. Chai. A lightweight fault tolerance framework for web services. *Web Intelligence and Agent Systems*, 7:255–268, 2009.

5

Group Communication Systems

The implementation of a state-machine based fault tolerance system can be made much easier with an underlying group communication system [3] that provides the following services:

- A totally ordered reliable multicast of messages. This ensures that all server replicas receive the same set of requests from clients in the same total order, which is essential to maintain replica consistency.

- A membership service. A fault tolerance system is designed to handle process and communication faults. When a replica is no longer reachable, the group communication system can automatically reconfigure the system. A membership service would inform the surviving server replicas and their clients about the configuration change and the list of members in the new configuration.

- A view synchrony service. To ensure replica consistency across different reconfigurations, a membership change notification must be totally ordered with respect to regular multicast messages before and after a reconfiguration change so that different replicas have consistent views regarding the configuration change and the messages that are multicast prior to and after the configuration change [4, 17]. Typically, the period between two consecutive reconfigurations are referred to as a view.

Group communication systems had been under intense study in 1980s and 1990s, and there are numerous publications on this subject (for example [3, 1, 12, 13, 18, 6]). We make no attempt to provide a survey on these publications. Instead, we focus on several group communication systems that are elegantly designed and are representatives of the respective approaches. Based on the mechanism used to achieve message total ordering, the most well-known approaches include [13]:

- Sequencer based. One of the nodes in the membership is designated the task of assigning a global sequence number (representing the total order) of each application message (may be multicast by any node in the membership). This special node acts as the sequencer for the entire system [12]. It is possible to stick to a particular node as the sequencer the entire time unless it becomes faulty, or to let the nodes in the membership to take turn to serve as the sequencer (often referred to as rotating sequencer). Regardless the strategies used, as long as the system allows only a single sequencer to operate at a time, message total ordering can be guaranteed.

- Sender based. If the system ensures that the nodes in the membership take turn to multicast, then all multicast messages are naturally totally ordered. The sender based approach also uses a global sequence number to represent the total order of each request sent. When a node takes its turn to multicast, it must know the global sequence number assigned to the last message sent. This requirement can be satisfied by passing a virtual token across different nodes [3, 18]. A node obtains the privilege to send when it receives the token, which carries the history information such as the sequence number of the last message sent. When a node is done sending, it completes its turn by passing the token to the next node in the membership list.

- Vector clock based. The causal relationship among different messages can be captured using vector clocks. In this approach, each message that is multicast is piggybacked with a vector timestamp. A receiver can deduce the causal relationship of the messages from the timestamps. A very efficient causally ordered reliable multicast service has been implemented using this approach [6]. It is possible to construct a totally ordered reliable multicast service using vector clocks. However, additional constraints must be imposed to the system so that a total order can be established, for example, a receiver must receive at least one message from each sender in the system before it can be certain of the total order of the messages it has received. Hence, in Isis [7], a dedicated sequencer node is used to establish the total order on top of the causally ordered multicast service.

Since the publication of the Paxos consensus algorithm in late 1990s [15], attention has been switched to rely on the Paxos family of algorithms, which will be introduced in the next chapter, to ensure message total ordering via distributed consensus [2, 5, 8, 11, 10, 19]. In fact, regardless of the approaches used to achieve message total ordering, distributed consensus is needed for membership changes. As we will explain in details later in this chapter, the membership change (or reconfiguration) protocols introduced in older generations of group communication systems often contain weaknesses compared with the Paxos family of algorithms.

5.1   System Model

We assume an asynchronous system with N nodes that communicate with each other directly by sending and receiving messages. A node may become faulty and stop participating the group communication protocol (*i.e.*, a fail-stop fault model is used). A failed node might recover. However, it must rejoin the system via a membership change protocol. Some protocols (such as Totem) requires the availability of stable storage that can survive crash failures.

We assume that the N nodes in the system form a single broadcast domain. During normal operation, when a node in the current membership multicasts a message, the message is broadcast to all nodes in that membership. Hence, we use the terms multicast and broadcast interchangeably. Furthermore, a node ignores messages sent by nodes that do not belong to the current membership (often referred to as foreign messages), unless they are membership-change related messages (such as the rejoin request). This means that we assume a closed, single group system.

A group communication system must define two protocols, one for normal operation when all nodes in the current membership can communicate with each other in a timely fashion, and the other for membership change when one or more nodes are suspected as failed, or when the failed nodes are restarted. These protocols work together to ensure the safety properties and the liveness property of the group communication system.

We define two levels of safety properties for total ordering [13]:

- *Uniform total ordering*: Given any message that is broadcast, if it is delivered by a node according to some total order, then it is delivered in every node in the same total order unless the node has failed.
- *Nonuniform total ordering*: Given a set of messages that have been broadcast and totally ordered, no node delivers any of them out of the total order. However, there is no guarantee that if a node delivers a message, then all other nodes deliver the same message.

Figure 5.1 highlights the differences between uniform total ordering and nonuniform total ordering. In uniform total ordering, if a message is delivered by any node, it is delivered by all nodes in the current membership except for those that have failed (such as $N1$). Hence, the messages delivered by the nodes that failed subsequently after joining the membership would form a prefix of those delivered by the nodes that remain operating, assuming that the nodes initially joined the system (*i.e.*, the current or a previous membership view) at the same time. For example, the messages delivered by $N1$, $m1$ $m2$ $m3$ form a prefix of the messages ($m1$ $m2$ $m3$ $m4$ $m5$ $m6$) delivered by $N2$ $N3$ and $N4$. Note that $N5$ joined after $N1$ failed, and therefore, the messages delivered by $N1$ do not form a prefix of the messages delivered by $N5$.

In nonuniform total ordering, however, this might not be the case. For example, as shown in Figure 5.1, $N1$ broadcasts message $m4$ and delivers it, and only $N2$ receives and delivers the message $m4$ and none of the other nodes. $N1$ and $N2$ subsequently failed

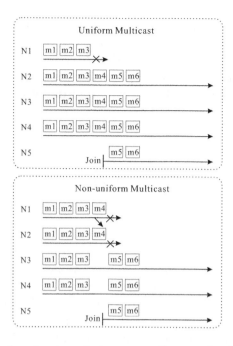

Figure 5.1   Examples of systems that ensure uniform total ordering and nonuniform total ordering.

before other nodes learn about $m4$. Hence, the messages delivered by $N1$ and $N2$, which are $m1$ $m2$ $m3$ $m4$, do not form a prefix of the messages delivered at $N3$ and $N4$, which are $m1$ $m2$ $m3$ $m5$ $m6$.

The uniform total ordering safety property is a strong property. It may be needed for applications that expose their state to components that are not part of the group communication system. For example, a replicated database system would require the uniform total ordering safety property to ensure replica consistency. However, for many applications, the nonuniform total ordering safety property would suffice. The only scenario that the uniform delivery cannot be ensured is when both the sender and the receivers (a portion of the N nodes in the system) of a message fail before other nodes learn about the message. If a node loses its state after it fails, or does not expose its state to other components of the system, such nonuniformity would not cause any negative side effect. In general, nonuniform total ordering can be achieved much faster than uniform total ordering.

The liveness of a group communication system means that if a nonfaulty node multicasts a message, it will eventually be delivered in a total order at other nodes. Liveness is ensured by fault tolerance mechanisms. For a message loss, it is addressed by retransmission. Node failures, extended delay in processing, and message propagations, are addressed by membership reconfigurations (*i.e.*, view changes).

5.2   Sequencer Based Group Communication System

Ensuring reliable broadcast is challenging because a protocol must support multiple senders broadcasting to multiple receivers. Guaranteeing totally ordered reliable broadcast is even more so. The first practical approach to ensuring reliable and total ordering of broadcast messages is introduced in [12]. In this approach, as shown in Figure 5.2, a general system is structured into a combination of two much simpler subsystems:

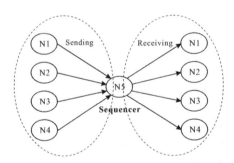

Figure 5.2   In the sequencer based approach, a general system is structured into a combination of two subsystems, one with a single receiver and the other with a single sender of broadcast messages.

- Multiple senders with a single receiver.
- A single sender with multiple receivers.

The single receiver and the single sender of broadcast messages are in fact served by a single node. Therefore, all broadcast messages sent by the multiple senders are effectively funneled through this special node, which is often referred to as the sequencer. This sequencer is responsible to assign a global sequence number for each broadcast message, thereby ensuring total ordering.

The simplest implementation of the sequencer based approach is to use a dedicated node, sometimes referred to as static sequencer. A node delivers a message that has been assigned a global sequence number if it has received and delivered all messages that carry smaller sequence numbers. Obviously, the sequencer constitutes a single point of failure. To ensure liveness, the sequencer is expected to periodically broadcast sequencing messages, even if no broadcast message is sent, and the other nodes would time out the sequencer if they do not receive sequencing messages for a number of times. Subsequently, the surviving nodes elect another node to act as the sequencer. This approach is used in [14]. It is apparent that only the nonuniform safety property is guaranteed. Furthermore, it is not clear whether or not the system is designed to offer view synchrony.

A more robust sequencer based group communication system was described in [12]. To achieve uniform total ordering, the nodes in the system take turn to serve as the sequencer, and a node does not deliver a message until it has received several sequencing messages from different sequencers. Given a failure resiliency of f (*i.e.*, at most f nodes may become faulty), the total number of nodes N in the system must satisfy $N > 2f$. This approach is often referred to as rotating sequencer based approach. In this section, we describe the rotating sequencer based approach in detail. In the original paper, the sequencer is referred to as the token site because the rotation of the sequencer role among the nodes resembles a token circulation among the nodes in the system (*i.e.*, the node that has the token becomes the sequencer). In this section, we choose not to use the term "token" to avoid confusion with another approach that uses the token differently (to be described in Section 5.3).

5.2.1 Normal Operation

During normal operation, we assume that a membership has been formed. Each node in the current membership maintains the following data structures:

- A view number v for the current membership and the corresponding list of node identifier in the current view. For convenience, we assume that each node is assigned an index and we use the node's index number to refer to the node.

- A local sequence number vector $M[]$ with each element representing the expected local sequence number for the corresponding node in view v. For example, $M[i]$ refers to the expected local sequence number carried by the next message sent by node i. Initially, every element is set to 0.
- The expected global sequence number s that is carried in the next sequencing message sent by the sequencer node.

After the formation of a membership, one of the nodes is designated as the initial sequencer. The membership also dictates the rank of each node so that a node knows when it should take over as the next sequencer.

The normal operation protocol involves three phases for each message to be totally ordered:

- Transmitting phase. A node broadcasts a message to all nodes in the current membership and waits for a sequencing message from the sequencer for the broadcast message. A broadcast message is denoted as $B(v, i, n)$, where v is the current view number, i is the sending node index number, and n is the local sequence number n for the message. The local sequence number is initially set to 0. For each new broadcast message, the local sequence number is incremented by 1. This mechanism is needed to ensure the reliability of message delivery. The sending node retransmits the same message if it does not receive the sequencing message in a timely fashion. When a node j receives the broadcast message $B(v, i, n)$, it accepts the message if it is in the same view and stores the message in its message queue Q_B.
- Sequencing phase. When the sequencer receives a broadcast message $B(v, i, n)$, it verifies that the message is the next expected message from node i, i.e., $M[i] = n$. The sequencer then assigns the current global sequencer value s to message $B(v, i, n)$ and broadcasts a sequencing message in the form $SEQ(s, v, [i, n])$, where $[i, n]$ is the identifier for the broadcast message $B(v, i, n)$. When a node j receives a sequencing message, it accepts the message provided that:
  - The global sequence number in the message matching its expected global sequence number, and

- It has the message that is being sequenced in its message queue. If the message is not in its queue, the node requests a retransmission from the current sequencing node.

The node then updates its data structures. Namely, the expected global sequence number s is incremented by 1, and the expected local sequence number from node i is incremented by 1. Note that for the sending node i of the broadcast message $B(v, i, n)$, the sequencing message $SEQ(s, v, [i, n]))$ would serve as the positive acknowledgement as well.

- Committing phase. To ensure uniform total ordering, a node does not deliver a broadcast message $B(v, i, n)$ when it receives the first sequencing message for B. To tolerate up to f faulty nodes, a node postpone the delivery of a broadcast message B until it receives f additional sequencing messages (for other broadcast messages) since it receives the sequencing message for B. Doing so would ensure that at least one node would join the new membership and pass on the binding of the global sequence number s to the broadcast message B to the new membership. It is said that a node commits a broadcast message B when it has collected $f + 1$ sequencing messages (the oldest of which is for B). A node does not deliver a broadcast message until it commits the message.

So far we have not described the mechanism on how the nodes take turn to serve as the sequencer. By default, each node sequences a single broadcast message at a time (although this can be parameterized). We assume that each node is ranked in a membership view such that a node knows deterministically when it is its turn to sequence a broadcast message (the original publication [12] did not describe any specific mechanism for the rotation of the sequencer). For example, a node i is responsible to sequence any broadcast message that is to be assigned a global sequence number s where $s\%N = i$, where N is the number of nodes in the current membership. The rotation of the sequencer does not involve any additional control message if the node that would serve as the next sequencer has received new broadcast messages to be ordered, *i.e.*, the transfer of the sequencer role can be achieved implicitly by the sending of a new sequencing message.

The next sequencer assumes its sequencer role when it receives a sequencing message that it can accept and the expected global sequence number indicates that it should sequence the next broadcast message. Furthermore, it has received all previous sequencing messages and the broadcast messages that have been ordered. On receiving a new broadcast message, the node then broadcasts a sequencing message, which will implicitly pass the sequencer role to the next node in the membership.

To ensure continuous rotation of the sequencer when there are uncommitted broadcast messages, a sequencer node would broadcast a sequencing message for a null broadcast message if it does not receive any new broadcast message with some predefined time period (the acceptance criteria for the sequencing message for a null broadcast message is similar to that for a regular sequencing message except that a node omits the check on receipt of the null message). If there is no uncommitted broadcast message and no new broadcast messages received, a sequencer would explicitly send the previous sequencer an acknowledgment message. This is because to ensure reliable message passing, a node that has just served as the sequencer must keep retransmitting the last sequencing message it generated until it receives a form of acknowledgment: it could be a new sequencing message (for a null or regular broadcast message), or an explicit acknowledgment for accepting the sequencer role from the next node. Furthermore, before the node receives some form of acknowledgment, it continues responding to retransmission requests for broadcast messages.

◼ EXAMPLE 5.1

Figure 5.3 shows an example rotating sequencer based group communication system in action during normal operation. The system consists of 5 nodes and all 5 nodes belong to membership view v. In step (a), node $N4$ broadcast a message $B(v, 4, 20)$ to all other nodes, where 4 is the sender id, 20 is the local sequence number at node $N4$. For this message, node $N1$ serves as the sequencer. In step (b), $N1$ responds with a sequencing message $SEQ(100, v, [4, 20])$ indicating that the global sequence number for $B(v, 4, 20)$ is 100 upon receiving the broadcast message from $N4$. When node $N4$ receives the sequencing message, it learns that the sequencer has received its message and stops retransmitting the message. At this point, none of

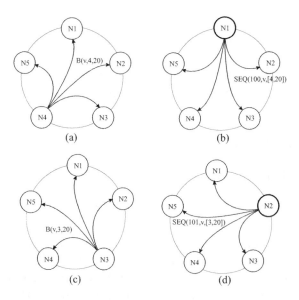

Figure 5.3   An example rotation sequencer based system in normal operation.

the nodes is allowed to deliver $B(v, 4, 20)$ because only one sequencing message has been received. Furthermore, node $N2$ would serve as the sequencer for the next broadcast message.

Subsequently, in step (c) another node $N3$ broadcasts a message $B(v, 3, 20)$ to all other nodes. the sequencer for this broadcast message is moved to node $N2$. After verifying that it has received all previous sequencing messages, and broadcast messages that have been sequenced, $N2$ broadcasts a sequencing message for $B(v, 3, 20)$ with a global sequence number 101 (*i.e.*, $SEQ(101, v, [3, 20])$) in step (d). By sending of a new sequencing message, node $N2$ acknowledges the previous sequencing message for sequencer rotation.

If the fault resiliency is set to 1, *i.e.*, only a single fault is tolerated, upon receiving both $SEQ(100, v[4, 20])$ and $SEQ(101, v, [2, 20])$ sequencing messages, a node is ready to deliver the broadcast message $B(v, 4, 20)$, but it must wait for one more sequencing message to deliver the next broadcast message.

5.2.2   Membership Change

A membership change is triggered by two types of events:

- The detection of a failure. A node retransmits a message for a pre-defined number of times. If it fails to receive the corresponding acknowledgment message, a failure is said to have occurred. The failed node that is detected this way is typically the current sequencer node, or next sequencer node.
- The recovery of a failed node. When a node recovers from a crash failure, it tries to rejoin the system.

The membership change protocol has the following objectives:

- Only one valid membership view can be formed by the nodes in the system.
- If a broadcast message is committed at some nodes in a membership view, then all nodes that belong to the new membership view must commit the broadcast message in the same way (*i.e.*, the same global sequence number is assigned to the message).

The membership change protocol operates in three phases. It is assumed that one node initiates the membership view change and this node is referred to as the originator. As shown in Figure 5.4, the protocol runs in three phases.

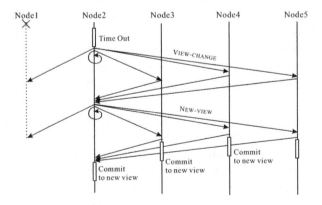

Figure 5.4   Normal operation of the membership view change protocol.

In phase I, the originator (Node2 in Figure 5.4) timed out the sequencer (Node1 in Figure 5.4), sets the new membership view number to be the current view number plus one, and broadcasts an invitation message to all nodes in the system for a new membership view. The invitation message carries the proposed new membership view number. Upon receiving an invitation message, a node accepts the invitation and sends a positive response to the originator provided that it has not accepted an invitation for a competing membership view (*i.e.*, a node joins the formation of at most one membership view at a time). Otherwise, the node sends a negative response. A positive response message carries the nodes' membership view number and the next expected global sequence number. A negative response message carries the membership view number that the node has joined. Note that once a node has accepted a membership view invitation, it joins that view and automatically abandons the previous membership view it has committed before.

In phase II, the originator collects responses to its invitation from other nodes in the system. It keeps collecting responses until either it has received a response from every node in the system, or it has collected at least $N - f$ responses from different nodes (including its own response) and a predefined timeout has occurred. Because we assume that at most f nodes may become faulty, the originator must be able to collect $N - f$ responses (including its own response). In the original publication [12], the criteria is set to be either the originator has received responses from every other node in the system or a predefined timeout has occurred. The latter criteria implicitly imposes a synchrony assumption that if a nonfaulty node will be able to respond within some predefined time period. In fact, this assumption is not necessary for the membership change protocol to work.

If the responses collected by the originator are all positive, the originator proceeds to build a node list for the new membership. The originator also learns the message ordering history of the previous membership view from the received next expected global sequence numbers reported by the nodes. Let the highest next expected global sequence number be s_{max}, and the expected global sequence number of the originator be s_o. It means that the originator is missing broadcast messages to be assigned global sequence numbers $s_o, s_o + 1, ..., s_{max} - 1$ if $s_{max} > s_o$. The originator then request retransmission for the missing broadcast messages from the node that reported s_{max}. It is possible that $s_{max} - 1$ is for an uncommitted broadcast message, and hence, greater than that of the last committed broadcast message. The originator would use s_{max} as the starting global sequence number for the new membership view as long as it has received the ordered broadcast message in the previous view, or after a retransmission. If the node that reported s_{max} fails before the originator could receive the ordered broadcast messages from that node, the originator chooses the second highest next expected global sequence number. The fault resilience assumption ensures that at least one nonfaulty node that has committed the last ordered message would join the new membership view. Therefore, s_{max} must be equal to or greater than that of the last committed message in the previous membership view.

The originator then broadcasts a new membership view message containing the node list, the view number, and the next expected global sequence number. When a node receives the new membership view message, it compares the received next expected global sequence number and its local expected global sequence number and detect whether or not it has missing broadcast messages. The node requests retransmission from the originator for the missing broadcast messages, if any. When the node has received all the missing broadcast messages, it commits to the new membership view.

If the originator receives one or more negative responses, it broadcasts a membership abort message. Subsequently, the originator sets the new view number to be the largest view number reported in the negative responses plus one, waits for a random period of time, and resends invitation messages.

A node other than the originator abandons the membership view it has accepted in one of two ways: (1) it receives a membership abort message for the view it has accepted, or (2) it has timed out the new membership view message. For the latter, a node starts a timer for the membership notification in phase II (new membership view or abort message) to ensure liveness.

In phase III, the originator collects responses to its new membership view message. If the node could manage to receive a positive response from every node in the membership node list, it commits to the new membership and serves as the first sequencer of the new membership view. If the node receives one or more negative responses from some nodes or timed out one or more nodes, it aborts the membership formation, broadcasts a membership abort message, waits for a random amount time, and retries with a larger view number.

It is possible that a node commits to a membership view while the originator (and possibly some other nodes as well) has decided to abort the membership. This would not lead to any problem because the nodes that have committed to an aborted membership view will either receive the abort announcement, or will eventually time out the membership view it has committed (and initiate a new membership view).

It is also possible that multiple nodes initiate membership view changes concurrently, in which case, none of the instances will be successful. That is why a node must wait a random amount of time before trying to reform a membership view again. This scenario, and a number of others, are discussed further in the examples below.

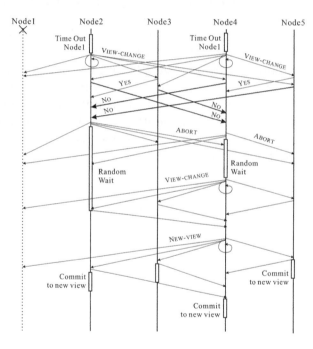

Figure 5.5   Membership change scenario: competing originators.

■ **EXAMPLE 5.2**

Competing originators. In the presence of (concurrent) competing originators, at most one of them may successfully install a new membership view. If the nodes can communicate promptly with each other, chances are none of the competing originators would succeed. In this example, we describe a scenario with two competing originators that timed out $Node1$ concurrently. As shown in Figure 5.5, $Node2$ and $Node4$ concurrently initiated a membership view change by broadcasting an invitation for a new view (referred to as VIEW-CHANGE in the figure). $Node3$ receives the invitation sent by $Node2$ first and accepts it. Hence, when $Node4$'s invitation arrives, $Node3$ rejects it and responds with a NO message. Similarly, $Node5$ receives and accepts the invitation sent by $Node4$ first, and rejects the invitation sent by $Node2$. Hence, both $Node2$ and $Node4$ would decide to abort their rounds of membership view change and wait for a random amount time before they each would initiate a new round of membership view change.

$Node4$ completes the random wait first and broadcast a new round of membership view change invitation. This time, the invitation arrives at $Node2$ before the node completes its random wait. $Node2$ terminates its random wait upon receiving the invitation from $Node4$, accepts the invitation, and responds with a YES message. Consequently, $Node4$ is able to collect positive responses from $Node2$, $Node3$, and $Node4$, and proceed to commit to the new view.

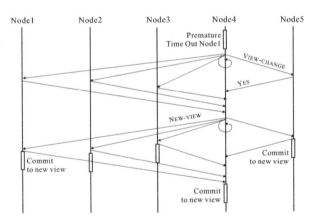

Figure 5.6   Membership change scenario: premature timeout.

EXAMPLE 5.3

Premature timeout. Due to the asynchrony of the system, a node might timeout the sequencer prematurely and initiate a membership view change. This scenario is shown in Figure 5.6, in which $Node4$ prematurely times out $Node1$ when in fact $Node1$ is operating fine. When $Node4$ broadcasts the invitation message for the new membership view, all other nodes, including $Node1$, receive the invitation and respond positively to $Node4$. Consequently, the new membership view will consists the same set of nodes as the previous view does.

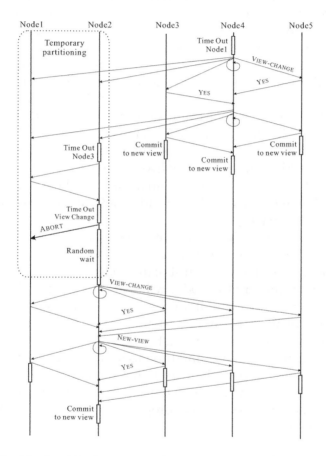

Figure 5.7   Membership change scenario: temporary network partitioning.

EXAMPLE 5.4

Temporary network partitioning. It is possible for a subset of the nodes in the system to be able to communicate with each other, but not other nodes due to a temporary network portioning fault. Figure 5.7 shows such a scenario where $Node1$ and $Node2$ are temporarily partitioned out of the rest of the nodes.

Due to the partitioning, some node outside the $Node1$ and $Node2$ partition will timeout $Node1$ or $Node2$. As shown in Figure 5.7, $Node4$ times out $Node1$ and initiates a new membership view. Assume that the system is designed with a failure resilience of 2, $Node4$ is able to collect sufficient number of positive responses from $Node3$ and $Node5$, and commit to the new membership view. $Node3$, $Node4$, and $Node5$ may order and commit more broadcast messages in this new view.

Eventually, $Node1$ and $Node2$ will timeout some other node outside their partition because according to the membership view they operates in, $Node3$, $Node4$, and $Node5$ should serve as sequencer eventually. For example, $Node2$ initiates a new membership view in Figure 5.7. However, $Node2$ is not able to collect sufficient number of positive responses to form a valid membership view (it needs at least 3 out of 5 positive responses, it could only get 2). Consequently, $Node2$ will have to abort the round of membership change and wait for a random amount of time before trying again.

Assume that when $Node2$ completes the random wait, the network partitioning is healed, *i.e.*, $Node1$ and $Node2$ are able to communicate with the rest of the nodes in the system. Hence, the invitation sent by $Node2$ will reach all other nodes. $Node2$ will be able to commit to the new membership view that consists of all nodes in the system.

During the temporary network partitioning, $Node1$ and $Node2$ cannot commit any broadcast messages sent since the partitioning happens. However, they could commit one broadcast message that is sent before the partitioning fault. This would not violate the safety property of the protocol. There can be only two scenarios:

- In the scenario shown in Figure 5.7, at least one of the nodes in $Node3$, $Node4$, and $Node5$ must have received the same broadcast message, together with the corresponding sequencing message. When the three nodes form a new membership, this node will carry such history information forward to the new view.

- If one of the nodes in $Node3$, $Node4$, and $Node5$ fails, they could not form a new membership view during the temporary network partitioning. The surviving nodes must wait until the network partitioning fault is healed. Based on the failure resilience assumption, either $Node1$ or $Node2$ must be nonfaulty, and this node would carry the history information to the new membership view when the partitions are merged eventually.

5.2.3   Proof of Correctness

Theorem 5.1 *The membership change protocol ensures that at any given time in the history of the system there exist at most one valid membership view.*

Proof: We prove by contradiction. Any valid membership view must consist of at least $N - f$ nodes, where f is the failure resiliency of the system and $N > 2f$ is the total number of nodes in the system. Furthermore, a valid membership view is not formed until the originator has committed to the view after receiving positive responses from all nodes that belong to its proposed node list. Assume that the nodes in the system form two valid membership views concurrently. The first view consists of a set $R1$ of nodes, and the second view consists of a set $R2$ of nodes. Then $R1$ and $R2$ must intersect in at least $2N - 2f - N = N - 2f \geq 1$ node. This is impossible because the membership change protocol dictates that a node can join at most one membership view at a time. More specifically:

- Once a node accepts an invitation for a new membership view, it abandons the previous view that it has committed before. If the originator can commit the new membership view, it means that at least $N - f$ nodes have committed the view. Therefore, the previous view can no longer be active (*i.e.*, no more broadcast messages will be committed, even if the sequencer was wrongly suspected).
- The node will not accept another invitation for a competing membership view unless it abandons the view it has joined in phase via either receiving an abort notification or a timeout. The node either eventually commits to the first invitation, or abandons the first membership view and joins the second one, but not both.

■

Theorem 5.2 *The normal operation protocol and the membership change protocol together ensure uniform total ordering of broadcast messages.*

Proof: We prove that if a broadcast message is delivered at a node in some total order, then the message will eventually be delivered at all nonfaulty nodes according to the same total order. To deliver a broadcast message, a node must first commit the message, which implies that the node has received the sequencing message for the broadcast message and f additional sequencing messages. This means that at least $f + 1$ nodes have received the broadcast message as well as the corresponding sequencing message. Because at most f nodes may be faulty, at least one of the nodes will survive any failures of the system. This node will be able to retransmit the broadcast message to all nodes that have missed the message, and pass on the information regarding the global sequence number assigned to the message in a future membership view.   ■

5.3   Sender Based Group Communication System

Similar to the rotating sequencer based approach, the sender based approach also imposes a logical ring structure on the nodes in the membership and each node takes turn to serve in a privileged role. The difference between the two approaches is that in the rotating sequencer based approach, when a node becomes privileged, it determines the total order of a broadcast message and sends a sequencing message, while in the sender based approach, when a node becomes privileged, it is allowed to broadcast messages directly in total order without an additional sequencing step, the total order of a broadcast message is determined by the original sender instead of some other node. As a tradeoff, a special message that carries a logical token must be passed from node to node in the ring.

The sender based scheme not only reduces the cost of achieving total ordering of messages, it facilitates the implementation of a windows-based flow control mechanism, hence, a sender based group communication system, such as Totem [3, 18], can achieve high system throughput under heavy messaging load. In this section, we describe in detail the design of the Totem (single-ring) group communication system.

Totem consists of the following protocols and the flow control mechanism to ensure high throughput under heavy load:

- Total ordering protocol: This protocol is used to totally order broadcast messages and ensure reliable delivery of these messages during normal operation.
- Membership protocol: This protocol is used to handle the failure of nodes and the addition of new nodes to the system. The outcome of the membership protocol is a new logical ring imposed on the nodes in the membership and a distinct leader.
- Recovery protocol: This protocol is used to deliver as many messages as possible in a total order while ensuring virtual synchrony during recovery.
- The flow control mechanism: This mechanism controls the number of messages that a node can send during each token possession such that no node is overwhelmed by the messages broadcast.

5.3.1   Total Ordering Protocol

The total ordering protocol provides two types of message delivery services:

- Agreed delivery: This is a form of nonuniform total ordering. A node can deliver a broadcast message as soon as it has delivered all messages that are ordered ahead of the message. At the time of the delivery, there is no guarantee that other nodes have received the message.
- Safe delivery: Safe delivery ensures uniform total ordering. A node can deliver a broadcast message only if it has learned that all other nodes in the membership has received the same message and all previously ordered messages.

The total ordering protocol involves two types of messages: regular message that contains the application payload to be reliably totally ordered, and a regular token message that contains important control information for total ordering.

In Totem, a node gains the privilege for broadcasting messages with a sender determined total order when it receives a special control message that carries a logical regular token. For convenience, we simply refer to the special control message as regular token, or token for short if it is clear from the context. The member-ship protocol also relies on similar form of control messages, and it is referred to as commit token.

A regular message takes the form $<type, v, s, i, m>$, where $type$ is either AGREED indicating the agreed delivery order, or SAFE indi-cating the safe delivery order, v is a view number (it is referred to as $ring\text{-}id$ in Totem [3]), s is the (global) sequence number for the message, i is the sender node id, and m is the message payload.

A   regular   token   message   takes   the   form $<$REGULAR$, v, token\_seq, seq, aru, aru\_id, rtr>$, where $token\_seq$ is the sequence number of the token (this is needed for the receiving node to tell whether it is the original token, or a retransmitted one), seq is the high watermark of the sequence number, $i.e.$, the largest sequence number that has been assigned to a broadcast message in the view, aru and aru_id indicate all received up to sequence number as reported by a node with id aru_id, and finally, rtr is a retransmission list.

Each node maintains two message queues, one for the regular messages received ($received\_message\_queue$), and the other for the messages that are originated at the node and are to be broadcast to other nodes ($new\_message\_queue$) The latter queue is not for the purpose of retransmission, but rather to store messages prior to the receiving of the regular token. Once the node receives a regular token and broadcasts a message in the new message queue, it trans-fer the message to the received message queue. A node will not delete a message in the received message queue unless it knows that the message is safe ($i.e.$, the message has been received by all nodes in the view). A node also keeps a copy of the last regu-lar token it has forwarded to the next node in the logical ring for retransmission and for determining whether or not a message is safe.

In addition, each node maintains the following local variables for the total ordering protocol:

- my_aru: it stores the highest sequence number for the regular messages the node has received without a gap.

- my_aru_count: it stores the number of times that the node has received the regular token with the same obsolete aru field ($i.e.$, aru is smaller than the high watermark seq in the regular token).

- *last_aru*: it stores the *aru* value of the token the last time a node receives the token. This variable is needed to facilitate the update on *my_aru_count* and to determine if it is time to deliver a message in safe order.

5.3.1.1   Rules on receiving a regular token

On receiving a regular token, a node converts the message into a temporary local variable referred to as *token* in its memory and performs the following main actions:

- Retransmits messages requested by the token if it has them. The token contains a retransmission request list *rtr* including the sequence numbers for the messages that some node or nodes have failed to receive. A node fetches the requested messages from its *received_message_queue* and retransmits them if they are found. Upon retransmitting a message, the node removes the corresponding sequence number in the retransmission list *token.rtr*.
- Broadcasts regular messages if the *new_message_queue* is not empty. For each new regular message, the node assign the value indicated in the *token.seq* field and subsequently increment the *token.seq* field. Once the node transmits a new regular message, it transfers the message from *new_message_queue* to *received_message_queue*. Furthermore, if *token.seq* is equal to *my_aru* (it implies that the node has received all regular messages that has been broadcast), it sets *my_aru* and *token.aru* to the new *token.seq* each time it broadcasts a new regular message. Furthermore, the node set *token.aru_id* to *null*.
- Updates the token.
    - A node add missing messages to *token.rtr* if *my_aru* < *token.seq* and if the messages (*i.e.,* out-of-ordered messages) are not buffered in the received message queue.
    - If *my_aru* < *token.aru*, the node sets *token.aru* to *my_aru* and *token.aru_id* to *my_id*.
    - If *token.aru* < *token.seq* and the *aru* field of the last token transmitted (denoted as *last_token.aru*) is the same as *token.aru*, the node increments *my_aru_count*. If *my_aru_count* exceeds a predefined threshold value,

the node assumes that the node that has id *token.aru_id* has failed and it initiates a view change.

- Deliver messages in safe order, if any. A regular message that should be delivered in safe order is always queued to meet the safe delivery order criteria. A node can deliver a message in safe order provided that the message's sequence number is smaller or equal to both *last_token.aru* and *token.aru* (*i.e.*, it takes two token rotations to deliver a message in safe order). Furthermore, the message is removed from the received message queue because no node would request for a retransmission of the message any more.

- Transmits the token to the next node in the logical ring, and keeps a copy of the token for retransmission and record keeping.

5.3.1.2   Rules on receiving a regular message

Upon receiving a regular message, a node stores the message in the received message queue unless the node has already received the message. If the message's sequence number is one higher than *my_aru*, then the message can be delivered in agreed order if all previously ordered messages have been delivered, and *my_aru* is incremented by one. If there are buffered messages in the received message queue and the newly received message completely fills a hole, additional messages may be delivered in agreed order and *my_aru* may be continuously incremented until all messages received have been delivered, or another hole in the received message queue is encountered. There are other scenarios when a node receives a regular message and they will be discussed in the examples in Section 5.3.1.4. Note that if a previously ordered message is a safe message and has not been delivered yet, the newly received message cannot be delivered even if it is an agreed message.

5.3.1.3   Rules on regular token retransmission

To minimize the likelihood of triggering a view change (which is expensive) due to the loss of the regular token message, a token retransmission timer is started every time a node passes on a regular token to the next node. On a token retransmission timeout, a node retransmits the token to the next node (this implies that the node must keep a copy of the last token it has transmitted).

To make it possible to distinguish the expected regular token from a retransmitted one, the token includes the filed *token_seq* and each node uses a local variable *my_token_seq*. For each new regular message sent, a node increments the *token.token_seq* field by one and sets *my_token_seq* to *token.token_seq* (if a node has no new message to send, it nevertheless still increments *token.token_seq* and sets *my_token_seq* to *token.token_seq* before forwarding the token to the next node). Therefore, *if the token is not lost*, when a node receives a new regular token, *token.token_seq* must be greater than *my_token_seq*, and when it receives a retransmitted token, *token.token_seq* must be smaller or equal to *my_token_seq*. Hence, a node discards a regular token received if *token.token_seq* is smaller or equal to *my_token_seq*.

5.3.1.4 *Examples*

Here we show several examples on how a node updates its *my_aru* low watermark, and how the *aru* field may be changed during a token rotation. These issues are critical to understand when a message can be delivered in safe order, and hence, can be garbage collected.

■ EXAMPLE 5.5

Receiving an originally transmitted regular message. If the message is a first transmission by the message's originator, there are two scenarios:

- The most straightforward scenario is when a node has received all previously broadcast messages and just received the next expected regular message. For example, if the last message that the node received carries a sequence number 100, the local variable at the node *my_aru* is set to 100. When a message with sequence number 101 arrives at the node, it is the next expected message and hence, the node updates its *my_aru* variable to 101.
- The node has a hole in its received message queue, *i.e.*, the sequence number of the message is not equal to *my_aru* + 1. The message is an out-of-ordered message and stored in the received message queue. The local variable *my_aru* is

not changed. For example, the node has received messages with sequence numbers 99 and 101 when a message with sequence number 102 arrives, the node cannot increment its my_aru variable due to the missing message with sequence number 100. It is also possible that the node has received messages with sequence numbers 99 and 100 when a message with sequence number 102 arrives, the node cannot increment its my_aru variable either due to the same reason.

EXAMPLE 5.6

Receiving a retransmitted regular message. There are several scenarios when a node receives a retransmitted regular message:

- The node has already received the message, *i.e.,* the message is already in the received message queue. In this case, the message is discarded and my_aru is not changed.
- The message is new to the node, however, its sequence number of the message is greater than $my\_aru + 1$, in which case, the message is buffered in the received message queue, but my_aru is not changed. For example, the node has already received messages with sequence numbers 99, 102 when a message with sequence number 101 is received, the node cannot change my_aru because it is still waiting for the message with sequence number 100.
- The message is new to the node, and its sequence number s is equal to $my\_aru + 1$, Furthermore, the message with sequence number $my\_aru + 2$ is still missing. The node increments my_aru by one and stores the message in its received message queue. If the node has already delivered all messages with a sequence number up to my_aru prior to the receiving of this message, it may deliver this message in agreed order. For example, the node has already received message with sequence numbers 99, 102 when a message with sequence number 100 arrives, the node would update its my_aru to 100, but not any further because it is still waiting for the message with sequence number 101.
- The message is new to the node with sequence number $s = my\_aru + 1$, and the node has received a message

with sequence number $s = my\_aru + 2$, we say that the message fills a hole and my_aru will be updated accordingly. For example, the node has already received messages with sequence numbers 99, 101, 102 when the message with sequence number 100 arrives, the node would update my_aru to 102.

EXAMPLE 5.7

We provide a number of examples to illustrate *how the aru field in the regular token is updated during a token rotation*. We assume a logical ring with 5 nodes $N1$, $N2$, $N3$, $N4$, and $N5$, and the token is passed from $N1$ to $N2$, from $N2$ to $N3$, from $N3$ to $N4$, from $N4$ to $N5$, and $N5$ back to $N1$. We further assume that $N1$ has just received the token. Before $N1$ transmits any new messages, $N1.my\_aru = 100$, $N2.my\_aru = 100$, $N3.my\_aru = 100$, $N4.my\_aru = 100$, and $N5.my\_aru = 99$. We know $token.aru$ must be set to 99 and $token.aru\_id$ must be set to 5 (representing $N5$) because $N5$'s $my\_aru = 99$ is smaller than $token.aru = 100$ when it receives the token.

$N1$ retransmits the message with sequence number 100 ($N5$ must have requested this message in the $token.rtr$ field) and sends 3 new regular messages with sequence numbers 101, 102, and 103, respectively, during this token visit. At the end of the token visit, $N1.my\_aru = 103$.

In one scenario, we assume that all nodes received all four messages transmitted by $N1$ during this token visit. It is easy to see that all other nodes will update their my_aru to 103 as well. Consequently, when $N1$ receives the token again, $token.aru$ must be set to 103 (if none of the other nodes sends any new message) or higher (if some of them transmitted one or more messages).

In another scenario, if $N5$ does not receive the retransmitted message with sequence number 100, or missed some of the new messages, its my_aru will be smaller than 103. Hence, $N5$ will lower $token.aru$ to its my_aru value and sets $token.aru\_id$ to 5 during the next token visit. Hence, when $N1$ receives the token again, it will notice that $token.aru$ is lowered than that when it forwards the token the last time. In this scenario, however,

$token.aru$ is the same or higher than that when it receives the token the last time.

In yet another scenario, we show that it is possible for a node to see a lower $token.aru$ value in a token visit than that in the previous token visit. Continue from the previous scenario, when $N2$ receives the token after $N1$ sends messages with sequence numbers 101, 102, and 103, respectively, $token.aru =$ 103 which is set by $N1$. Assume that $N2$ sends a new message with sequence number 104 (note that $N2$ does not retransmit the message with sequence number 100 because the message is removed from $token.rtr$ by $N1$ after it has retransmitted the message). Before passing the token to $N3$, $N2$ sets the $token.aru$ to 104. Assume that $N5$ does manage to receive the retransmitted message with sequence number 100, but missed another message with sequence number 101, it would set $token.aru$ to 100 and set $token.aru\_id = 5$ assuming that $N3$ and $N4$ have received all the broadcast messages by $N1$ and $N2$. Hence, when $N2$ receives the token again, it will notice that $token.aru = 100$, which is lower than the value (which is 103) the last time the token visits. That is why a node must wait for two consecutive token visits before it is certain if a message is safe. In this case, $N2$ knows that any message with a sequence number 100 or smaller is safe.

5.3.2   Membership Change Protocol

Totem is designed to operate in four different states. During normal operation, the total ordering protocol operates in the Operational state. When any of the predefined set of events happens, a node leaves the Operational state trying to form a new membership. First, a node enters a Gather state aiming to build a consensus on the membership. When it receives indication that a consensus on the membership has reached, it switches to the Commit state. While in the Commit state, nodes in the membership exchange additional control information in preparation for recovery. Once a node is certain that the information exchange has completed, it enters the Recovery state to execute the Recovery Protocol to ensure the virtual synchrony of the system. At the completion of the Recovery Protocol, a node switches to the Operational state. A node may switch to the Gather state (*i.e.*, initiates a membership change) while in `Operational`, `Commit`, or `Recovery` state if it fails to execute the protocol defined for each state. A simplified finite state machine specification for the Totem operation is shown in Figure 5.8.

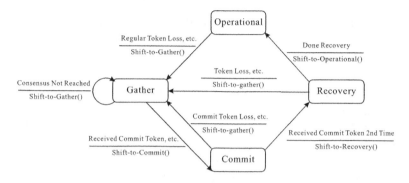

Figure 5.8   A simplified finite state machine specification for Totem.

The Membership Protocol is defined primarily for the `Gather` and `Commit` states, and transitions between different states. To execute the Membership Change Protocol, a node uses the following local variables:

- *my_view*: The view number of the most recent view that the node is involved in.
- *my_proc_set*: The set of ids for all the nodes in the system according to this node's knowledge.
- *my_fail_set*: The set of ids for the nodes that have failed according to this node's knowledge.
- *my_members*: The set of ids for the nodes in the current view.
- *my_new_members*: The set of ids for the nodes in the new view to be installed.
- *consensus*: The array that stores information whether or not any of the nodes in the new view has committed to the membership formation (*i.e.*, *my_proc_set* and *my_fail_set*).

Furthermore, each node maintains two timers, a `Join` timer and a `Consensus` timer. The `Consensus` timeout value is much larger than that for the `Join` timer. The `Join` timer is created whenever a node sends a `Join` message, and the `Consensus` timer is created when the node receives the first event that triggers a transition to the `Gather` state.

5.3.2.1 *Events and actions on transition from* `Operational` *state to* `Gather` *state*

While in the `Operational` state, a node may enter the `Gather` state when any of the following events happens:

- When a node determines that the regular token is lost. A node defines two timers for the regular token, one for retransmission of the token, and the other with longer time-out value for the loss of the token. When the latter timer (referred to as the token loss timer) expires, a node enters the `Gather` state.
- When a node determines that another node has repeatedly failed to receive broadcast messages, as exhibited by the fact that *token.aru* is stuck at a value smaller than *token.seq* due to a particular node as indicated in the *token.aru_id* field. Even though the problematic node is still operational because it is receiving and forwarding the regular token, it has to be removed from the current membership to enable safe delivery of messages and proper garbage collection.
- When a node receives a foreign message, *i.e.,* the message is originated by a node outside the current membership. This foreign node will be added to the membership list.
- When a node receives a membership change message (referred to as `Join` message) from another node in its membership. A node joins a membership change even if it has not encountered any of the previous events to ensure liveness of the system.

In response to any of the above events, a common group of actions, referred to as a function `Shift-to-Gather()`, are taken. The `Shift-to-Gather()` function is called when a node transits from the `Commit` and `Recovery` states to the `Gather` state, and sometimes when a node has to start all over again to form a new membership in the `Gather` state. These group of actions defined in the `Shift-to-Gather()` include:

- Prepare and broadcast a `Join` message, which takes the form <JOIN, $v, i, proc\_set, fail\_set$>, where the fields in the message are explained below:
  - v is the view number (referred to as the *ring_id.seq* in [3]). When a node first transition from the

Operational state to the Gather state, v is the view where the node was operating in. However, v may represent the view number of the last unsuccessful view change if the node switches from other states.

- i is the sending node id.

- *proc_set* is the set of ids for the nodes that the sending node is aware of in the entire system, including those it believes that have failed.

- *fail_set* is the set of ids for the nodes that the sending node believes that have failed.

- Cancel the regular/commit token loss/retransmission timer, if one is running.
- Launch a Join timer and a Consensus timer. If such a timer is already running, cancel it first.
- Initialize the *consensus* array so that every element is false except the one corresponding to the node itself, which is set to true.
- Finally, set the state to Gather.

5.3.2.2   *Operations in the* Gather *state*

When the Join timer expires, a node resends the Join message. When the Consensus timer expires, the node puts all nodes that have not reached an agreement with the node itself (as indicated in the *Consensus* array) to the *my_fail_set*, and call the Shift-to-Gather() function to retry a new membership formation.

According to the Membership Change Protocol, *my_proc_set* and *my_fail_set* can never shrink until the new view is installed. It is easy to understand the possible expansion of *my_proc_set* because new nodes might join the system. The do-not-shrink *my_fail_set* requirement means that if any node labels some node as failed, all other nodes follow suit to put the node in the *my_fail_set*, even if it is the result of a premature timeout. This also means that once a node is wrongly suspected, it will have to wait until a new view is installed before it can rejoin the system (which will cause another view change). Eventually, this wrongly suspected node will initiate a membership change and send a Join message. This Join message will be ignored by those nodes that have put the node in their *my_fail_set*.

Upon receiving a Join message sent by node i, a node compares the *proc_set* and *fail_set* in the Join message with its *my_proc_set* and *my_fail_set*, and takes the following actions depending on the comparison outcome:

- If the two sets in the Join message are identical to its own, the node sets *consensus*[i] to *true*.
- If the node finds one or more nodes in the *proc_set* or the *fail_set* that are not present in its own local variables, it adds the ids of the nodes other than itself to its own *my_proc_set* and *my_fail_set*, and rebroadcasts a Join message based on the updated local variables.
- If the node finds out that node i has included itself in the *fail_set*, the node includes node i in its *my_fail_set* reciprocally and rebroadcasts a Join message.
- If both the *proc_set* and *fail_set* are subsets of *my_proc_set* and *my_fail_set*, the Join message is ignored.
- Finally, as we mentioned before, if the sending node i is in *my_fail_set*, the Join message is also ignored.

When all elements of the *consensus* array become true at a node, an agreement on a new membership has reached for the node. If the node is the representative of the new logical ring, it will proceed to shift to the Commit state (more details to follow). If the node is not the representative, it expects to receive a commit token soon. Hence, it creates a token loss timer and cancels the consensus timer. If a node fails to receive the commit token before the token loss timer expires, it retries to form a new membership by calling the Shift-to-Gather() function. Once an agreement has been reached at a node, the node stops responding to Join messages while in the Gather state (only applicable to the non-representative nodes because the representative node would switch to the Commit state).

5.3.2.3   *Events and actions on transition from* Gather *to* Commit *state*

On reaching an agreement on the new membership, a node checks to see if its node id is the smallest one in the set of nodes of the new membership, if true, it becomes the representative of the new logical ring, prepares a commit token, and forwards the commit token to the next node in the new membership list (and thereby switching to the `Commit` state). The commit token message take the form $<\text{COMMIT}, v, memb\_list, memb\_index>$, where the fields are determined in the following way:

- The view number v is set to the maximum view number in the `Join` message received plus 4.
- The field $memb\_list$ contains the list of nodes for the new membership. For each node, the following set of fields are included:
  - The node IP address.
  - The old view number.
  - The my_aru value in the old view.
  - The sequence number of the largest message delivered at the node, denoted as $high\_delivered$.
  - A flag ($received\_flg$) indicating whether or not the node has received all messages that are known to the nodes that belong to both the old view and the new view and that are deliverable in a temporary transitional configuration that consists of only the nodes that belong to both the old view and the new view (more on this in Section 5.3.3).
- The field $memb\_index$ indicates the index of the node that last forwarded the commit token.

For a node that is not the representative of the new logical ring (regardless if the node has reached an agreement on the membership), the only way to switch to the `Commit` state is to receive a commit token whose $memb\_list$ field are consistent with its own record ($my\_proc\_set - my\_fail\_set$). When the condition is met, a node performs a group of actions that are referred to as the `Shift-to-Commit()` function:

- Populates the entry corresponding to the node itself in the $memb\_list$
- Increments the $memb\_index$ field of the commit token
- Forwards the token (with the updated information) to the next node in the new logical ring.
- Cancel the `Join` and `Commit` timers, if one is running.
- Restart the `Commit Token Loss` and `Retransmission` timers.

- Finally, set the state to Commit.

When a node receives a commit token with an inconsistent membership list, the node ignores the commit token.

5.3.2.4   Operations in the Commit state

The representative of the new logical ring waits for the commit token to rotate back to itself. If the Token Loss timer expires before it receives the commit token, it shifts to the Gather state.

While in the Commit state, a non-representative node waits for the commit token to visit the second time. If the Token Loss timer expires before it receives the commit token, it shifts to the Gather state.

Assuming that the commit token is not lost, each node in the new logical ring would wait for one full rotation of the commit token.

5.3.2.5   Events and actions on transition from Commit or Recovery to Gather state

In either the Commit state or the Recovery state, a node transitions to the Gather state when any of the following events happens:

- The Token Loss timer expires. The node takes the actions defined in the Shift-to-Gather() function.
- When the node receives a Join message with a view number that is equal to or larger than the current view and the sending node is in the *my_new_members* list (another node in the Commit or Recovery state could have sent this Join message when its Token Loss timer expires due to the loss of the token). The Join message is handled the same way as if the node is in the Gather state, and takes the actions defined in the Shift-to-Gather() function.

5.3.2.6   Examples

We show several examples to illustrate how the Membership Protocol works under different scenarios.

EXAMPLE 5.8

Figure 5.9 shows a successful run of the Membership Protocol. Initially, there are five nodes in the membership. Then $N1$ failed. $N2$ first times out $N1$ and initiates a membership change.

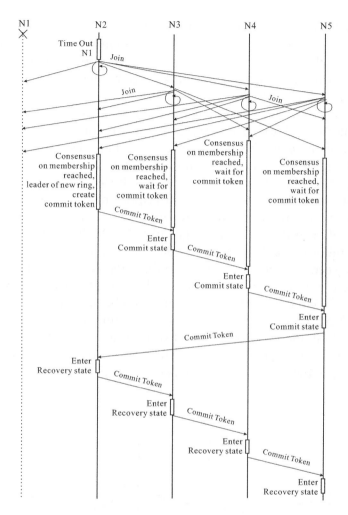

Figure 5.9 A successful run of the Totem Membership Protocol.

$N2$ broadcasts a Join message with $N1$, $N2$, $N3$, $N4$, and $N5$ in the *proc_set*, and $N1$ as the only node in the *fail_set*. $N3$, $N4$, and $N5$, each broadcasts a Join message with identical *proc_set* and *fail_set*. After the exchange of Join messages, $N2$, $N3$, $N4$, and $N5$ reach an agreement on the membership formation for the new view (*i.e.*, new logical ring).

Assume that $N2$ is the leader of the new logical ring, it generates a commit token, forwards the token to the next node, which is $N3$, and enters the Commit state. The remaining nodes wait for the commit token after they finds that an agreement on the membership has reached. When a node receives the commit token the first time, it fills the entry corresponding to itself in the commit token, forwards the token to the next node, and enters the `Commit` state too.

When $N2$ receives the commit token the second time, it has collected all the necessary information for recovery because every node in the new logical ring has provided necessary information. Hence, $N2$ updates its local variables and the commit token accordingly, forwards the token again to $N3$, and enters the `Recovery` state. An important step is to determine the view number for the new view, which the maximum view number in the `Join` messages plus 4. $N2$ also writes the view number to stable storage. When $N3$ receives the commit token the second time, it performs similar steps as $N2$, and forwards the commit token to $N4$. Similarly, $N4$ forwards the token to $N5$. $N5$ in turn will forward the token back to $N2$.

Note that even though we have assumed that $N2$ times out $N1$ first, the view change will still be successful if two or more nodes time out $N1$ concurrently and send `Join` messages as long as they all use the same *proc_set* and *fail_set*.

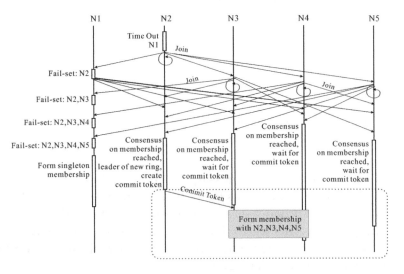

Figure 5.10   Membership changes due to a premature timeout by $N2$.

Figure 5.10 shows an example membership change due to a premature timeout by $N2$ on $N1$. When $N3$, $N4$, and $N5$ receive the Join message sent by $N2$, which has $N1$ in the $failset$, they all follow suit and put $N1$ in their my_fail_set. Eventually, $N2$, $N3$, $N4$, and $N5$ will form a new logical ring.

When $N1$ receives the Join message broadcast by $N2$, it finds that itself is included in the $fail\_set$. According to the Membership Protocol, $N1$ reciprocally put $N2$ in its my_fail_set, and broadcasts a Join message. Similarly, when $N1$ receives the Join messages sent by $N3$, $N4$, and $N5$, it puts $N3$, $N4$, and $N5$ in its my_fail_set too. Hence, $N1$ realizes that it can only form a singleton membership.

As we can see, the Totem Membership Protocol works very differently from the Membership Protocol for the rotating sequencer protocol, which does not allow the presence of multiple concurrent memberships.

5.3.3   Recovery Protocol

The Recovery Protocol dictates the actions taken while transitioning from the Commit state to the Recovery state, while in the Recovery state, and while transitioning from the Recovery state to the Operational state. During recovery, the nodes that belong to both the old view and the new view will try to deliver as many messages that were originated in the old view as possible according to the old view, then they will attempt to deliver messages that are not deliverable according to the old view, but deliverable according to the transitional configuration formed by only those nodes. Note that not all messages that were originated in the old view may be delivered. For example, if there is a gap in sequence number, the messages ordered after the gap cannot be delivered because doing so might violate causality.

The Recovery Protocol uses a regular token with one additional field activated:

- $retrans\_flg$: A boolean variable indicating whether or not there are additional messages that were originated in the old view that must be retransmitted in the transitional configuration (consists of nodes that belong to both the old view and the new view).

Furthermore, the protocol uses the following local variables at each node:

- *my_new_members*: The set of ids for the nodes in the new view.
- *my_trans_members*: The set of ids for the nodes that belong to both the old view and the new view.
- *low_ring_aru*: The smallest *my_aru* value among the nodes in the *my_trans_members* list in the old view.
- *high_ring_delivered*: The largest sequence number among the messages that have been delivered at some node that belongs to the transitional configuration (*i.e.*, in the *my_trans_members* list).
- *my_install_seq*: The largest sequence number among the messages that were sent in the old view and that were known to the new view.
- *retrans_msg_queue*: A queue of regular messages sent in the old view that should be retransmitted such that all the nodes in the transitional configuration would receive the same set of messages.
- *my_retrans_count*: The number of successive token visits in which the *retrans_flg* is false. It is initially set to 0.

5.3.3.1   *Event and actions on transition from* Commit *to* Recovery *state*

When a non-representative node receives the commit token the first time, it adds information in the token that is necessary to ensure total ordering and virtual synchrony. Once the commit token rotates back to the representative of the logical ring, the representative node would have compiled sufficient information to proceed to the Recovery state. Likewise, when a non-representative node receives the commit token the second time, it receives the information necessary to perform recovery. Hence, the receiving of the commit the second time is the event that triggers a node to transit from the Commit state to the Recovery state.

A node would perform the following actions collectively referred to as the Shift-to-Recovery() function:

- Assign the $my\_new\_members$ local variable based on the information provided in the $memb\_list$ field of the commit token.
- Assign the $my\_trans\_members$ local variable based on the membership information included in the commit token. They are nodes that belong to both the old view and the new view.
- Derive the value for $low_r ing\_aru$ and the value of $high\_ring\_delivered$. Transfer all messages from the old view with sequence number greater than low_ring_aru to $retrans\_msg\_queue$.
- Set my_aru to 0, and set my_aru_count to 0.
- Write the current view number to stable storage.
- Restart the `Token Loss` and `Token Retransmission` timers.
- Finally, set the state to `Recovery`.

5.3.3.2   Operation in the `Recovery` state

When the representative of the new logical ring receives the commit token the first time in the `Recovery` state, it converts the commit token to the regular token. Furthermore, it sets the $retrans\_flg$ field in the token to $true$ if its $retrans\_msg\_queue$ is not empty. Otherwise, it sets the $retrans\_flg$ field to $false$.

When a node receives the regular token, it operates the same way as in the `Operation` state except that it takes messages from $retrans\_msg\_queue$ to broadcast instead of new_msg_queue. Furthermore, the node does the following before it forwards the token to the next node:

- The node sets the $retrans\_flg$ field in the token to $true$ if its $retrans\_msg\_queue$ is not empty. Otherwise, it sets the $retrans\_flg$ field to $false$.
- If $retrans\_flg$ is $false$, increment $my\_retrans\_flg\_count$.
- If $my\_retrans\_flg\_count = 2$, set $my\_install\_seq$ to $token.seq$.
- If $my\_retrans\_flg\_count \geq 2$ and $token.aru \geq my\_install\_seq$ and $my\_received\_flg = false$, set $my\_received\_flg$ to $true$.
- If $my\_retrans\_flg\_count \geq 3$ and $token.aru \geq my\_install\_seq$ on the last two token visits, transition to the `Operation` state by calling `Shift-to-Operational`.

When a node receives a regular message, it adds the message to *receive_msg_queue* and updates *my_aru*. If the message was originated from the old view, the node transfers the message to the *receive_msg_queue* for the old view and remove it from *retrans_msg_queue*.

5.3.3.3   Actions on transition from Recovery to Operational *state*

A node takes following actions in Shift-to-Operational():

- For nodes in the *my_trans_members* list, deliver all messages that are deliverable according to the old view. Messages that have sequence number from *low_ring_aru* up to *high_ring_delivered* can be delivered at every node that belongs to *my_trans_members* regardless of delivery order types. A node might be able to deliver more messages if they are agreed messages and the node has delivered all messages that carry a smaller sequence number. Note that the set of messages received by nodes in *my_trans_members* is identical, and the decision on which message is deliverable is deterministic. Hence, all such nodes deliver the same set of messages in the same total order.
- For nodes in the *my_trans_members* list, deliver a membership change message for the transitional configuration.
- For nodes in the *my_trans_members* list, try to deliver more messages that are not deliverable according to the old view, but are deliverable in the transitional configuration as if the logical ring consists of only nodes in the *my_trans_members* list. A safe message would be deliverable according to the old view if the nodes in the *my_trans_members* list do not have evidence that all nodes in the old view have received the message (because some of the nodes have failed). Furthermore, any agreed messages that have a higher sequence number than that of the safe message would be deliverable either according to the old view. However, in the transitional configuration, such safe messages could be delivered if all messages that carry a smaller sequence number have been delivered, and any agreed messages that are ordered after the safe message can also be delivered in the transitional configuration.

- All all nodes, deliver a membership change notification for the new view (*i.e.*, the new logical ring).
- Set *my_memb* to *my_new_members*, set *my_proc_set* to *my_memb*, set *my_fail_set* to empty.
- Set the state to Operational.

5.3.3.4   Examples

We here show how to determine which messages can be delivered according to the old view and which messages can only be delivered in a transitional configuration under a couple of example scenarios.

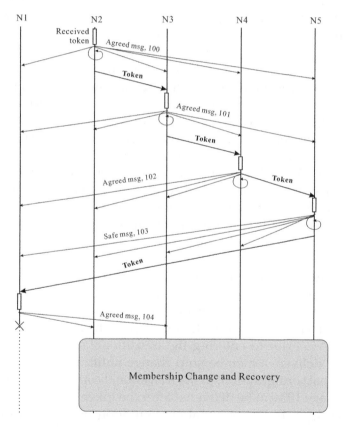

Figure 5.11   Messages sent before $N1$ fails in an example scenario.

Figure 5.12   Messages delivered during recovery for the example scenario.

Figure 5.11 shows an example scenario on the messages sent prior to $N1$ fails. When $N2$ receives the regular token, it broadcasts an agreed message with sequence number 100 and forwards the token to $N3$. $N3$ then broadcasts an agreed message with sequence number 101 and forwards the token to $N4$. $N4$ then broadcasts an agreed message with sequence number 102 and forwards the token to $N5$. Unlike $N2$, $N3$, and $N4$, $N5$ broadcasts a safe message with sequence number 103 before it forwards the token to $N1$. Subsequently, $N1$ broadcasts an agreed message with sequence number 104. However, $N1$ crashes right after it broadcasts the agreed message and the message is only received by $N2$ and $N3$.

A membership change would occur after $N1$ crashes. The new membership would consist of $N2$, $N3$, $N4$, and $N5$. Because $N2$ and $N3$ belong to the new membership, they would retransmit the agreed message 104 to $N4$ and $N5$. As shown in Figure 5.12, all four nodes would be able to deliver the agreed messages 100, 101, and 102 according to the old view. However, none of the four nodes can deliver the safe message sent by $N5$ because they have no evidence that all nodes (including $N1$) have received the message.

To deliver as many messages as possible during recovery, the nodes would enter a transitional configuration that consists of the surviving nodes in the old view, which are $N2$, $N3$, $N4$, and $N5$. Prior to entering the transitional configuration, each node delivers a membership change notification for the transactional configuration. In the transitional configuration, the safe message 103 can be delivered after the token circulates the logical ring in the transitional configuration twice. Subsequently, the agreed message 104 can also be delivered after the safe message. Finally, each node delivers a membership change notification for a regular configuration declaring that all future messages will be delivered according to the new view from now on. Note that in this example, because no new node joins the membership, the membership for the transitional configuration and the new regular configuration are identical.

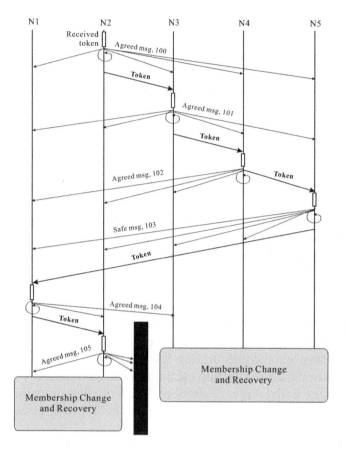

Figure 5.13   Message sent before the network partitions into two groups, one with $\{N1, N2\}$, and the other with $\{N3, N4, N5\}$.

EXAMPLE 5.11

In this example, we show the messages delivered during different stages of the recovery in a scenario illustrated in Figure 5.13. The 5 nodes in the system are communicating fine right before $N2$ broadcasts an agreed message with sequence number 105 when the newtork partitions the system into two groups. One group consists of $N1$ and $N2$, and the other group consists of $N3$, $N4$, and $N5$. Hence, the message broadcast by $N2$ cannot

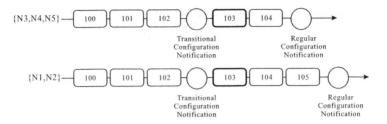

Figure 5.14   Messages delivered during recovery in the two different partitions for the example scenario.

reach $N3$, $N4$, and $N5$, and neither the token forwarded by $N2$. Hence, $N3$ would soon timeout the token and initiates a membership change. Eventually, $N1$ would also time out the token because it is not possible for $N1$ to receive the token from $N5$ before the network partitioning fault is healed. This would result in two concurrent memberships being formed coincide with the two network partitions.

As shown in Figure 5.14, all nodes in the partion of $\{N3, N4, N5\}$ can deliver the agreed messages with sequence numbers 100, 101, and 102 according to the old view during recovery. However, becasue of the safe message with sequence number 103, none of the nodes could deliver it until they enter the transitional configuration formed by $N3$, $N4$, and $N5$. In the transitional configuration each node can also deliver the agreed message with sequence number 104. Note that even though the message initially is received by $N3$ only, $N3$ will retransmit the message to $N4$ and $N5$.

During recovery, the nodes in the partition of $\{N1, N2\}$ can deliver an additional message, the agreed message with sequence number 105, which is broadcast by $N2$ after the network partitions, in the transitional configuration, as shown in Figure 5.14. The nodes in the other partition are not aware of this message, as can be seen in Figure 5.13.

5.3.4   The Flow Control Mechanism

The objective of the flow control mechanism is to ensure that the transmission rate of broadcasting messages in the system does not exceed the rate at which the slowest node delivers the messages. To achieve this objective, Totem uses a windows based control mechanism resembles that used in TCP. The window size restricts the maximum number of messages that may be transmitted in one token rotation, which determines the rate of transmission of broadcasting messages. The windows size is initially determined heuristically and dynamically adjusted.

The flow control mechanism introduces two additional fields in the regular token:

- *total_retrans_round*: This field denotes the total number of messages retransmitted during the last token rotation. The total number of messages transmitted (*i.e.*, new messages plus retransmitted messages) during the last token rotation, referred to as fcc, can be calculated by summing up *total_retrans_round* and the difference in the *seq* field of the current token and the value in the last token visit.
- *total_backlog_round*: This field denotes the sum of the number of messages waiting to be transmitted by each node when the token visits during the last token rotation on the logical ring.

Each node maintains the following local variables for flow control:

- *windows_size*: It defines the maximum number of messages that the nodes in the logical ring can broadcast during a token rotation (including both new messages and retransmitted messages).
- *max_msgs*: It defines the maximum number of messages that any single node can broadcast for each token visit (including both new messages and retransmitted messages).
- *my_trc*: It is short for my this rotation count. The variable denotes the number of messages the node may send during the current token visit.
- *my_pbl*: It is short for my previous backlog. The variable denotes the number of new messages waiting to be transmitted (*i.e.*, the size of the *new_msg_queue*) during the last token visit.
- *my_tbl*: It is short for my this backlog. The variable denotes the number of new message waiting to be transmitted during the current token visit.

The flow control mechanism limits how many messages that a node can send during the current token visit (*i.e.*, *my_trc*) in the following way:

- $my\_trc \leq max\_msgs$: The number of messages cannot exceed the predefined limit imposed by max_msgs for any single node. This is to prevent any single node from exhausting the quota for each token rotation.
- $my\_trc \leq windows\_size - fcc$: The number of messages cannot exceed the remaining quota for this token rotation.
- $my\_trc \leq window\_size \times my\_tbl/(total\_backlog\_round + my\_tbl - my\_pbl)$: This is to ensure a node does not send more messages than its fair share [9].

The window size is dynamically adjusted in the following way:

- If $token.total\_retrans\_round = 0$ and $fcc \geq window\_size/2$, it implies we might have more room to send, hence, we increment the window size by 1, *i.e.*, $window\_size = window\_size + 1$.
- If $token.total\_retrans\_round = R$ is greater than 0, it means that the nodes sent R too many messages during the last token rotation, hence, the window size should be reduced by R, *i.e.*, $window\_size = window\_size - token.total\_retrans\_round$.
- For practicality, we want to send a minimum number of messages during each token rotation, $window\_size\_min$, hence, if $window\_size < window\_size\_min$, we set $window\_size$ to $window\_size\_min$.

5.4   Vector Clock Based Group Communication System

Using a vector clock at each node in the system can track the causal relationship between different messages accurately [16]. As such, vector clocks have been used to achieve causal ordering in group communication system such as Isis [6]. The causal ordering protocol in Isis is referred to as CBAST. Similar to previous sections, we assume the system forms a single broadcast domain (*i.e.*, we do not consider the multiple process group case as in [6]). The total ordering service is provided in Isis by using a sequencer based protocol similar to what is described in Section 5.2.

In CBAST, a node N_i maintains a N-element vector clock, $VT(N_i)$, where each element is indexed by the node identifier (from 0 to $N-1$). Initially, all elements of $VT(N_i)$ are set to 0. The rule for broadcasting a message using the vector clock is defined below:

- When a node N_i broadcasts a message m, it increments the i-th element of its vector clock, i.e., $VT(N_i)[i] = VT(N_i)[i] + 1$, and piggyback a vector timestamp, referred to as $VT(m)$, using the current value of $VT(N_i)$ with m.

This rule ensures that given two broadcast events $broadcast(m)$ and $broadcast(m')$, $broadcast(m)$ happens before $broadcast(m')$, if and only if $VT(m) < VT(m')$, i.e., vector timestamps can be used to capture causality precisely. It is straightforward to compare two vector timestamps:

- $VT(m) \leq VT(m')$ if and only if for any i: $VT(m)[i] \leq VT(m')[i]$
- $VT(m) < VT(m')$ if $VT(m) \leq VT(m')$ and there exists an i such that $VT(m)[i] < VT(m')[i]$

On receiving the message m broadcast by N_i containing a vector timestamp $VT(m)$, node $N_j \neq N_i$ can deliver the message provided the following condition is met:

1. $VT(m)[i] = VT(N_j)[i] + 1$
2. For any $k \neq i$: $VT(m)[k] \leq VT(N_j)[k]$

The first condition means that node N_j has received all messages previously sent by node N_i. The second condition means that node N_j has *delivered* all messages that node N_i has delivered. Note that a node does not update its vector clock until it is ready to deliver a message (i.e., it does not update its vector clock as soon as it receives a message). When a node N_j *delivers* the message m from N_i containing $VT(m)$, it updates its vector clock in the following way:

- For any k in $[0, ..., N - 1]$: $VT(N_j)[k] = max(VT(N_j)[k], VT(m)[k])$.

The above rules ensure that all messages broadcast are delivered in causal order. For reliability, positive or negative feedbacks can be used to facilitate the retransmission of lost messages. Note that a node would block indefinitely if a lost message is not retransmitted.

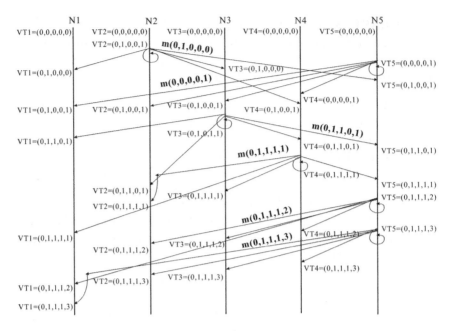

Figure 5.15   Causal ordering using vector clocks.

⬛ EXAMPLE 5.12

We show how the vector clock based causal delivery protocol works with an example illustrated in Figure 5.15. There are 5 nodes in the system ($N1$ to $N5$). The vector clock of each node is initialized to $(0, 0, 0, 0, 0)$. First $N2$ broadcasts a message containing a vector timestamp of $(0, 1, 0, 0, 0)$. Concurrently, $N5$ also broadcasts a message containing a vector timestamp of $(0, 0, 0, 0, 1)$. All nodes can deliver both messages in arbitrary order because they are not causally related, *i.e.*, $(0, 1, 0, 0, 0) \not> (0, 0, 0, 0, 1)$ and $(0, 1, 0, 0, 0) \not< (0, 0, 0, 0, 1)$, and it is apparent that there does not exist any message that is broadcast causally before either message (*i.e.*, the message delivery conditions are met). It is interesting to see that the delivery order of the two messages depends on the receiving order. At nodes $N1$, $N2$, $N3$, $m(0, 1, 0, 0, 0)$ is delivered ahead of $m(0, 0, 0, 0, 1)$. At nodes $N4$ and $N5$, however, $m(0, 1, 0, 0, 0)$ is delivered after $m(0, 0, 0, 0, 1)$. Upon the delivery of each message, a node updates its vector clock based on the updating rule. After the delivery of both messages, every node has vector clock value

$(0, 1, 0, 0, 1)$ indicating that $N2$ and $N5$ each has broadcast one message.

Subsequently, $N3$ broadcasts a message containing a vector timestamp $(0, 1, 1, 0, 1)$. When $N4$ receives this message, it delivers the message immediately because the delivery conditions are met and updates its vector clock to $(0, 1, 1, 0, 1)$. Subsequently, $N4$ broadcasts a message containing a vector timestamp $(0, 1, 1, 1, 1)$. At nodes $N1$, $N3$, and $N5$, $m(0, 1, 1, 0, 1)$ arrives before $m(0, 1, 1, 1, 1)$. Because the receiving order happens to conform to the causal order of the two messages, and the delivery conditions are met, these nodes deliver the two messages immediately in that order. However, it is not the case at $N2$, which receives $m(0, 1, 1, 1, 1)$ ahead of $m(0, 1, 1, 0, 1)$. At the time of receiving $m(0, 1, 1, 1, 1)$, node $N2$'s vector clock is $(0, 1, 0, 0, 1)$. We show that the second delivery condition is not met (*i.e.*, for any $k \neq i$: $VT(m)[k] \leq VT(N_j)[k]$). Because the sending node for $m(0, 1, 1, 1, 1)$ is $N4$, $i = 3$. Even though for $k = 0, 1, 4$, $VT(m)[k] = VT(N_2)[k]$, it is not the case for $k = 2$, where $VT(m)[2] = 1$ is greater than $VT(N_2)[2] = 0$. Therefore, $N2$ must delay $m(0, 1, 1, 1, 1)$ until it receives $m(0, 1, 1, 0, 1)$.

Then, node $N5$ broadcasts back-to-back two messages $m(0, 1, 1, 1, 2)$ and $m(0, 1, 1, 1, 3)$. All nodes receive the two messages in their sending order, which conforms to the causal order, except node $N1$. When $N1$ receives $m(0, 1, 1, 1, 3)$ before $m(0, 1, 1, 1, 2)$, it can see that the first delivery condition is not met (*i.e.*, $VT(m)[i] = VT(N_j)[i]+1$) because $VT(m)[4] = 3$ while $VT(N_1)[4] = 1$. Hence, node $N1$ delays $m(0, 1, 1, 1, 3)$ until it receives $m(0, 1, 1, 1, 2)$.

So far we have only considered static membership without failures. We now discuss how to adapt the vector clock based causal ordering protocol when the membership changes. We define additional mechanisms to cope with the addition of new nodes in the membership, and to cope with the failures of nodes in the current membership. The mechanisms assume the availability of a first-in-first-out (FIFO) reliable communication channel for broadcast messages among the nodes in the system. Although physical broadcast such as UDP broadcast or IP multicast does not ensure FIFO reliable delivery of broadcast messages, it is relatively easy to implement such service.

A key mechanism is the flushing mechanism. At the beginning of a new membership formation (*i.e.*, a new view), every node in the membership broadcasts a flush message and waits to collect flush messages from every other node in the new membership. Before a node has collected a flush message from every other node, it cannot broadcast new messages, but is allowed to receive and deliver messages sent in the previous view. Because the communication channel is FIFO and reliable, when a node i receives the flush message from another node j, it is certain that it has received all messages sent previously by node j. Therefore, when a node has collected the flush message from every other node, it is certain that it has received all messages broadcast in the previous view.

For addition of new nodes into the membership, the use of the flushing mechanism is straightforward. When a node has completed the flushing task, it expands its vector clock and can start broadcasting messages in the new view using a bigger sized vector timestamp. In the vector clock for the new view, the elements corresponding to the old nodes keep the old value at the end of the flushing. The elements corresponding to the new nodes are initialized to 0.

The mechanisms to handle failures of nodes are more complicated and include the following steps:

- When a node suspects that another node j has failed, it stops accepting regular messages from that node.
- The node re-broadcasts all messages that belong to an unterminated broadcast that it has received. A broadcast is said to be unterminated when a node is not certain that all nodes have received that broadcast message. A node can determine the condition from the vector timestamps it has received.
- The node then broadcasts a flush message.
- When a node has collected a flush message from every other node except the one from the failed node, it checks to see if it has received all messages sent by the failed node prior to its failure based on the vector timestamps in the retransmitted messages. If true, the node pretends that it has received a flush message from the failed node as well. This would lead to the termination of the flushing task.
- Discard any message that is delayed due to the missing of a message from the failed node.

- Remove the element corresponding to the failed node from the vector clock.

REFERENCES

1. Y. Amir, C. Danilov, and J. R. Stanton. A low latency, loss tolerant architecture and protocol for wide area group communication. In *Proceedings of the 2000 International Conference on Dependable Systems and Networks (formerly FTCS-30 and DCCA-8)*, DSN '00, pages 327–336, Washington, DC, USA, 2000. IEEE Computer Society.

2. Y. Amir and J. Kirsch. Paxos for system builders: An overview. In *Proceedings of the Workshop on Large-Scale Distributed Systems and Middleware*, Yorktown, NY, September 2008.

3. Y. Amir, L. E. Moser, P. M. Melliar-Smith, D. A. Agarwal, and P. Ciarfella. The totem single-ring ordering and membership protocol. *ACM Trans. Comput. Syst.*, 13(4):311–342, Nov. 1995.

4. K. Birman. A history of the virtual synchrony replication model. In B. Charron-Bost, F. Pedone, and A. Schiper, editors, *Replication*, pages 91–120. Springer-Verlag, Berlin, Heidelberg, 2010.

5. K. Birman, D. Freedman, Q. Huang, and P. Dowell. Overcoming cap with consistent soft-state replication. *Computer*, 45(2):50–58, 2012.

6. K. Birman, A. Schiper, and P. Stephenson. Fast causal multicast. Technical Report TR90-1105, Cornell University Computer Science Department, 1990.

7. K. P. Birman and R. V. Renesse. *Reliable Distributed Computing with the ISIS Toolkit*. IEEE Computer Society Press, Los Alamitos, CA, USA, 1994.

8. W. J. Bolosky, D. Bradshaw, R. B. Haagens, N. P. Kusters, and P. Li. Paxos replicated state machines as the basis of a high-performance data store. In *Proceedings of the 8th USENIX Symposium on Networked Systems Design and Implementation*, 2011.

9. O. J. Boxma, H. Levy, and J. A. Westrate. Optimization of polling systems. In *Proceedings of the 14th IFIP WG 7.3 International Symposium on Computer Performance Modelling, Measurement and Evaluation*, Performance '90, pages 349–361, Amsterdam, The Netherlands, The Netherlands, 1990. North-Holland Publishing Co.

10. M. Burrows. The chubby lock service for loosely-coupled distributed systems. In *Proceedings of the 7th symposium on Operating systems design and implementation*, OSDI '06, pages 335–350, Berkeley, CA, USA, 2006. USENIX Association.

11. T. D. Chandra, R. Griesemer, and J. Redstone. Paxos made live: an engineering perspective. In *Proceedings of the twenty-sixth annual ACM symposium on Principles of distributed computing*, PODC '07, pages 398–407, New York, NY, USA, 2007. ACM.

12. J.-M. Chang and N. F. Maxemchuk. Reliable broadcast protocols. *ACM Trans. Comput. Syst.*, 2(3):251–273, Aug. 1984.

13. X. Défago, A. Schiper, and P. Urbán. Total order broadcast and multicast algorithms: Taxonomy and survey. *ACM Comput. Surv.*, 36(4):372–421, Dec. 2004.

14. M. F. Kaashoek and A. S. Tanenbaum. An evaluation of the amoeba group communication system. In *Proceedings of the 16th International Conference on Distributed Computing Systems*, pages 436–447, Washington, DC, USA, 1996. IEEE Computer Society.

15. L. Lamport. Paxos made simple. *ACM SIGACT News (Distributed Computing Column)*, 32(4):18–25, December 2001.

16. F. Mattern. Virtual time and global states of distributed systems. In *Proceedings of the International Workshop on Parallel and Distributed Algorithms*, pages 216–226. Elsevier Science Publishers B.V. (North-Holland), 1989.

17. L. E. Moser, Y. Amir, P. M. Melliar-Smith, and D. A. Agarwal. Extended virtual synchrony. In *Proceedings of the 14th International Conference on Distributed Computing Systems*, pages 56–65, 1994.

18. L. E. Moser, P. M. Melliar-Smith, D. A. Agarwal, R. K. Budhia, and C. A. Lingley-Papadopoulos. Totem: a fault-tolerant multicast group communication system. *Commun. ACM*, 39(4):54–63, Apr. 1996.

19. W. Zhao, H. Zhang, and H. Chai. A lightweight fault tolerance framework for web services. *Web Intelligence and Agent Systems*, 7:255–268, 2009.

6

Consensus and the Paxos Algorithms

Distributed consensus has been studied in the past several decades because it is a fundamental problem in distributed computing. Consensus is particularly important in building a fault tolerant distributed system because it is essential to ensure the replica consistency (pessimistically or eventually in optimistic replication). One of the most important work in the research on distributed consensus is the impossibility result [6]. The impossibility result states that in an asynchronous distributed system, it is impossible for processes in a system to reach an agreement even if one of them might crash. Intuitively, the impossibility result is due to the fact that a process cannot distinguish a slow process from a failed one. Because of the impossibility result, older generations of consensus algorithms rely on the use of an unreliable failure detector to exclude the failed processes from the consensus consideration. Such an approach essentially mix together the safety property of the consensus requirement and the liveness property.

Consequently, they are less intuitive to understand and harder to prove for correctness.

The horizon on distributed consensus research has completely changed since Lamport published the now well-known Paxos algorithm. According to Lamport himself, the Paxos algorithm "is among the simplest and most obvious of distributed algorithms" [10]. Indeed this is the case. The Paxos algorithm approaches the distributed consensus problem by separating the safety and liveness properties. Roughly speaking, the safety property dictates that only a single value will be agreed upon by the processes in the system. Due to the impossibility result, it is possible that no consensus can be reached if the system is very asynchronous. However, a consensus will be reached (*i.e.*, liveness is achieved) during periods when the system is sufficiently synchronous.

Since the publication of the Paxos algorithm, a family of algorithms derived from the Paxos has been developed [14, 12, 11, 13]. Practical fault tolerant systems, such as Google's Chubby locking service [3, 5], have also been built based on the Paxos algorithm. In this chapter, we introduce the original Paxos algorithm and its derivative algorithms. We also incorporate recent work on Paxos-based fault tolerant systems [2, 8, 9, 16, 17].

6.1   The Consensus Problem

In a distributed system with a number of processes, any one of them may propose a value. For the processes to reach an agreement on a particular value proposed by a process, a consensus algorithm is required because otherwise different processes might choose different values. A sound consensus algorithm should ensure the following two properties:

- *Safety* property. The consensus algorithm should guarantee:
- (S1) If a value is chosen by a process, then the same value must be chosen by any other process that has chosen a value.
- (S2) The value chosen must have been proposed by one of the processes in the system.
- (S3) If a process learns a value, then the value must have been chosen by some process.

- *Liveness* property. Eventually, one of the values proposed is chosen. Furthermore, if a value has been chosen, then a process in the system can eventually learn that value.

The safety requirement S1 ensures that the same value is chosen by all processes. The requirements S2 and S3 are to rule out trivial solution such as all processes choose a pre-defined value.

More specifically, the processes in the system may assume different roles. Some processes may propose values to be chosen and learned by others. Such a process is referred to as a *proposer*. Some processes may participate in the agreement negotiation (*i.e.*, it is not necessary for every process in the system to participate). Such a process is referred to as an *acceptor*. Yet some processes might simply want to learn the value that has been chosen. Such a process is called a *learner*. Note that the roles are logical and a process can assume multiple roles (such as being a proposer and an acceptor).

We assume that the consensus algorithm will operate in an asynchronous environment with no malicious faults. This means that it may take a process arbitrary long time to complete a local task, and a message may take arbitrarily long time to be delivered at the intended destination process, possibly after many retransmissions.

A process may crash and stop operating. In the original Paxos algorithm, process restart is explicitly allowed [10]. However, allowing process restart would require each process to flush its state to stable storage pessimistically after every state change before sending out a message that reflects the latest state change. We prefer to drop this assumption for the following reasons:

- Flushing to stable storage after every state change could significantly increase the runtime overhead of the algorithm because the bandwidth of stable storage is much smaller than that of volatile memory.
- Not requiring stable storage may enable the use of the Paxos algorithm in diskless embedded devices.

Removing this assumption will not change the Paxos algorithm operation in anyway. The only downside may be a temporary lower number of processes operating in the system. Because to reach a consensus using the Paxos algorithm, the majority of the processes must be operating, this may temporarily reduce the resiliency of the system. If half or more processes fails concurrently, the system as a whole would fail. As long as this corner case does not happen, restarted processes could always rejoin the system as a new member. The membership change can be treated as a distributed consensus problem, *i.e.*, the value chosen will be the membership formation of the system when a process rejoins [17].

The original Paxos algorithm also assumes that messages are not corrupted [10]. We should clarify that messages can very well be corrupted by the network as long as the corruption can be detected. Once the corruption of a message is detected, the message is discarded by the receiving process, making this equivalent to a message loss, which can be resolved by a simple retransmission.

6.2   The Paxos Algorithm

In this section, we first describe the Paxos algorithm. Then we provide a sketch of proof of correctness. We also explain how the idea in the Paxos algorithm is developed as documented in [10] in details.

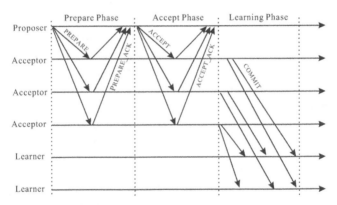

Figure 6.1   Normal operation of the Paxos algorithm.

6.2.1   Algorithm for Choosing a Value

The algorithm for choosing a value operates in two phases, the prepare phase and the accept phase, respectively, as shown in Figure 6.1. The prepare phase is initiated by a proposer sending a *prepare* request $P1a(n)$ to the acceptors in the system, where n is the proposal number selected by the proposer. At this stage, no value is included in the prepare request. This may appear to be counter-intuitive, but it is critical to limit the freedom of the proposer on what value it may propose. This is because some acceptors might have accepted a value proposed by a competing proposer. Allowing a proposer to propose an arbitrary value at all times may lead to multiple values to be accepted.

In the prepare phase, when an acceptor receives a *prepare* request $P1a(n)$, it does the following:

- If the acceptor has not responded to any *prepare* request, it records the proposal number n, and sends its acknowledgment $P1b(n)$ to the proposer.
- If the acceptor has already responded to another *prepare* request with a proposal number m, and $m < n$, there are two scenarios:
  - The acceptor has not received any *accept* request, which is sent by a proposer during the accept phase, it records the higher proposal number n and sends its acknowledgement $P1b(n)$ to the proposer.
  - The acceptor has already received an *accept* request with a proposal number k, it must have received a value proposed by some proposer in the past. This full proposal $[k, v]$ is included in the acknowledgment $P1b(n, [k, v])$ to the proposer. Obviously, k must be smaller than n.

The second phase (*i.e.*, the accept phase) starts when the proposer could manage to collect responses from the majority of acceptors. The proposer determines the value to be included in the accept request in the following way:

- If the proposer received one or more $P1b$ messages with full proposals. It selects the value v in the proposal that has the highest proposal number.
- If none of the $P1b$ messages received by the proposer contains a full proposal, the proposer has freedom to propose any value.

Then the proposer multicasts an *accept* request $P2a(n, v)$ to the acceptors. Note that the *accept* request contains a full proposal with a value v.

When an acceptor receives an *accept* request $P2a(n, v)$, it accepts the proposal $[n, v]$ only if it has responded to the corresponding *prepare* request $P(n)$ for the same proposal number n. The acceptor sends an acknowledgement message $P2b(n)$ if it accepts the proposal.

Note that accepting an accept request by an acceptor does not mean that the value contained in the proposal included in the accept request has been chosen. Only after the majority of acceptors have accepted the same accept request does the value is considered chosen. It is possible that no value is chosen or another value is eventually chosen after a minority of acceptors have accepted an accept request.

6.2.2   Algorithm for Learning a Value

There are many alternative methods for a learner to find out the value that has been chosen. The most straightforward method is for an acceptor to multicast a message containing the value that has been chosen, $L(n, v)$, to all learners whenever it has accepted a proposal (*i.e.*, it has accepted an accept request), as shown in Figure 6.1. When a learner has collected the confirmation messages for the same proposal from the majority of acceptors, it will be rest assured that the value has been chosen.

As an alternative, if the number of learners is large, a small group of learners can be selected to receive the multicasts from the acceptors and they can relay the chosen value to the remaining learners. Yet another alternative is for each learner to periodically poll the acceptors to see if they have chosen a value.

If a learner wants to make sure that the value it has learned is indeed the value that has been chosen, it can ask a proposer to issue a new proposal. The result of this proposal would confirm whether or not the value is chosen.

6.2.3   Proof of Correctness

In this section, we provide a sketch of proof of correctness for the safety property of the Paxos algorithm. For the liveness property of the Paxos, we provide a discussion on the condition when the liveness holds and scenarios that prevent a value from being chosen.

The safety property S2 and S3 are obviously satisfied by the Paxos algorithm because the value chosen is not pre-defined. We prove that the Paxos algorithm satisfies the safety property S1 by contradiction. Assume that two different values, $v1$ and $v2$ are chosen. According to the Paxos algorithm, the only way for a value to be chosen is for the majority of acceptors to accept the same accept request from a proposer. Hence, a set of majority of acceptors $A1$ must have accepted an accept request with a proposal $[n1, v1]$, and similarly a set of majority of acceptors $A2$ must have accepted an accept request with a proposal $[n2, v2]$.

If the two proposal numbers are the same, *i.e.*, $n1 = n2$, considering that the two sets $A1$ and $A2$ must intersect in least one acceptor, this acceptor must have accepted two different proposals with the same proposal number. This is impossible because according to the Paxos algorithm, an acceptor would ignore the prepare and accept requests with a proposal number identical to that of the prepare and/or accept requests that it has accepted.

If $n1 \neq n2$, without loss of generality, assume that $n1 < n2$. We first further assume that $n1$ and $n2$ are for consecutive proposal rounds. A set of majority acceptor $A1$ must have accepted the accept request with a proposal number $n1$ *before* another set of majority acceptor $A2$ accepted the accept request with a proposal number $n2$ because an acceptor would ignore the prepare or accept request if it contains a proposal number smaller than the one it has acknowledged in response to a prepare request. Furthermore, according to the Paxos algorithm, the value selected by a proposer for the accept request must either come from an earlier proposal with the highest proposal number or a value of its own if no earlier proposal is included in the acknowledgement messages. Because $A1$ and $A2$ must intersect in at least one acceptor, and this acceptor must have accepted the accept request for the proposal $[n1, v1]$ *and* the accept request for the proposal $[n2, v2]$. This is impossible because that acceptor would have included the proposal $[n1, v1]$ in its acknowledgement to the prepare request for the proposal with proposal number $n2$, and the proposer must have selected the value $v1$ instead of $v2$.

If $n1$ and $n2$ are not consecutive proposals, any intermediate proposals must also select $v1$ as the value according to the above argument. This concludes the proof of correctness for the safety property S1.

The liveness of the Paxos algorithm cannot be guaranteed when two or more proposers propose concurrently. Consider the scenario illustrated in Figure 6.2. Assume that there are two competing proposers $P1$ and $P2$. $P1$ first completes the prepare phase and multicasts an accept request to the acceptors including a proposal $[n, v]$. In the mean time, before the majority of acceptors accept the accept request, $P2$ multicasts a prepare request with a larger proposal number $n + 1$. If $P2's$ prepare request reaches the majority of acceptors prior to the accept request sent by $P1$, these acceptors would reject $P1's$ accept requests (as indicated by the red dots in Figure 6.2), preventing $P1$ from collecting the number of acknowledgement messages to choose the value v. Note that it is possible for a minority of acceptors to accept $P1's$ proposal, as shown in Figure 6.2 where acceptor 1 accepts the accept request $P2a(n, v)$ and sends the proposer 1 ($P1$) an acknowledgment $P2b(n)$.

A red dot signifies that the message received will be rejected.

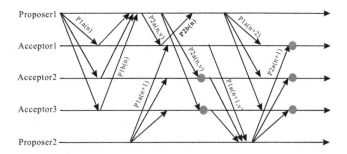

Figure 6.2   A deadlock scenario with two competing proposers in the Paxos algorithm.

Assume that $P1$ realizes that its proposal for round n will not succeed (*e.g.*, either via a timeout, or by receiving sufficient number of rejection messages from the acceptors), it launches a new round with proposal number $n+2$. If $P1's$ prepare request with a proposal number $n + 2$ is received by the majority of acceptors before they receive the accept request from $P2$ for proposal $n+1$, $P2$ would not be able to choose a value either.

This competition can go on and no value can be chosen by either $P1$ or $P2$.

6.2.4   Reasoning of the Paxos Algorithm

Instead of describing the complete Paxos algorithm alone, in [10], Lamport provides a detailed reasoning on how the Paxos algorithm is derived starting with the most simple and intuitive idea. This is tremendously helpful in understanding the Paxos algorithm.

To ensure consensus, the most simple and intuitive approach is to designate a single acceptor as the decision maker. If a proposer proposes a value, it has to send its proposal containing the value to that acceptor for approval. A consensus can be ensured if we mandate that the acceptor must choose the value contained in the *first* proposal it receives. Apparently, this solution is not fault tolerant - the system would cease operating when the acceptor fails.

Therefore, we should use a group of acceptors instead of a single one. To tolerate up to f number of faulty acceptors, we need to use a set of at least $2f + 1$ acceptors. Now with a group of acceptors, an acceptor is not allowed to *choose* the value for the system (*i.e.*, decides on the value for consensus) unilaterally anymore because different acceptors may choose different values. Hence, an acceptor may only *accept* a value initially. Then an additional mechanism is needed for the system to find out if a value can be chosen. It is easy to see that as long as an acceptor can accept at most one value, all we need is a simple majority of the acceptors to accept the same value for the system to reach a consensus on that value. Therefore, it is intuitive to enact the following requirement:

P1 An acceptor accepts and only accepts the first proposal that it receives.

Unfortunately the requirement P1 is too restrictive. It is safe to ensure that at most one value is chosen by the group of acceptors (*i.e.*, when the majority of them have accepted the same value). Unfortunately, in the presence of multiple proposals, different subsets of the acceptors may accept different proposals and none of the subsets forms the majority of the acceptors, which would prevent a value from being chosen.

Therefore, P1 must be modified such that an acceptor should be allowed to accept another proposal if it is newer than the one it has accepted. For an acceptor to tell if a proposal is newer, each proposal must be assigned a monotonically increasing proposal number. The acceptor may accept a proposal if its proposal number is greater than the one that the acceptor has accepted. Obviously, for the scheme to work, different proposers should try to find out the highest proposal number that has been used and use a larger one for its next proposal. Using an obsolete proposal number would lead to the rejection of the proposal by the acceptors.

Once we open the door for an acceptor to accept multiple proposals, we cannot avoid the possibility for multiple proposals to be chosen by the system because as long as the majority of acceptors accept a proposal (and its value), that proposal is chosen. This is not necessarily a problem if we ensure that the proposals that are chosen contain the *same* value. Therefore, we need to add the following requirement:

P2 After the first proposal (with value v) is chosen, then all newer proposals (with higher proposal numbers) that are chosen must have the same value v.

To satisfy requirement P2, it is sufficient to ensure that all higher-numbered proposals contain the same value that has been chosen earlier:

P2a After the first proposal (with value v) is chosen, then all higher numbered proposals must contain the same value v.

Our next task is to reason about how to satisfy requirement P2a. It is apparent that allowing an arbitrary value to be included in a proposal each time a proposer disseminates a new proposal would endanger the requirement P2a. Hence, we must put certain restriction on the proposer regarding what value it is to include in its proposal. To figure out what restriction to use, we need to consider the actions of the acceptors. Once a proposal is chosen, it implies that the majority of the acceptors have accepted the same proposal. We want to be sure that any proposer that wants to publish a new proposal learns the value that has been chosen by the acceptors and uses that value in its new proposal. This can be accomplished by requiring the proposer to solicit information regarding the accepted values from the *majority* of acceptors in a separate phase. This communication phase is referred to as the prepare phase, and the request sent by the proposer soliciting information from the acceptors is referred to as the prepare request. Because the two majority sets (the one that has accepted the same proposal, and the set that provides information to the proposer) must intersect in at least one acceptor, this acceptor would pass on the value it has accepted to the proposer to be included in the new proposal.

Is it possible for different acceptors to accept proposals with different values? The answer is yes if the system has not chosen any proposal yet. Accepting different values at the acceptors prior to the chosen of the first proposal would not endanger the safety requirement for consensus. Nevertheless, an acceptor should inform the proposer regarding the value it has accepted together with the proposal number when it is contacted by the proposer. When a proposer has collected information from a majority of acceptors, it may find different values that have been accepted by the acceptors. The proposer always selects the value contained in the most recent proposal (*i.e.*, the one with the highest proposal number). This would guarantee that if a proposal has been chosen, the value in that proposal is selected.

It is also possible that at the time a proposal is issued, no acceptor has accepted any value yet, in which case, the proposer would have the freedom to choose any value.

Unfortunately, learning the past accepted values (if any) alone is *not* sufficient to ensure the requirement P2a because before the proposer finishes collecting information from some majority of acceptors, the acceptors might have accepted *other* proposals sent concurrently by other proposers. That is, the proposer might never learn the *latest* status of the acceptors. To prevent this from happening, the proposer also asks the acceptors to *promise* that they would not accept any proposal that has the same or lower proposal numbers. The role played by this requirement is further explained via two scenarios in Example 6.1.

To summarize, for a value to be chosen, two phases of communication must be involved. During the first phase (*i.e.*, the prepare phase), the proposer sends a prepare request to the acceptors and waits until it has collected responses from the majority of acceptors, which would trigger the start of the second phase (*i.e.*, the accept phase). At the beginning of the second phase, the proposer selects the value in the following ways:

- If there are earlier proposals included in the responses to its prepare request, the value contained in the highest numbered proposal is selected.
- Otherwise, the proposer is free to use any value.

The proposer then sends an accept request containing its proposal (with a value) to the acceptors.

An acceptor would respond to a prepare request if and only if (iff for short) it has not responded to another prepare request with the same or a higher proposal number. Furthermore, an acceptor would accept an accept request (*i.e.*, accepting the proposal) iff (1) it has responded to the corresponding prepare request; and (2) it has not responded to a prepare request with a higher proposal number.

EXAMPLE 6.1

In this example, we study the role of the promise-not-to-accept-older-proposal requirement on the safety property for consensus. If the system has already chosen a value before a competing proposer proposes, the safety property for consensus would hold even without the promise-not-to-accept-older-proposal requirement, as shown in Figure 6.3. For the system to choose a value, the majority of acceptors must accept a proposal (proposal $P(n, v)$ in Figure 6.3). When another proposer (proposer 2) wants to send a proposal (proposal $P(n+1)$ in Figure 6.3), it must collect information from the majority of acceptors regarding if they have accepted any proposal. Therefore, in this case, at least one acceptor that has accepted the proposal $P(n, v)$ would pass on the fact that it has accepted proposal $P(n, v)$. Therefore, proposer 2 must use v as the value for the new proposal $P(n + 1)$. However, the promise-not-to-accept-older-proposal requirement is essential to ensure only a single value is chosen if the system has two or more competing proposers to start with.

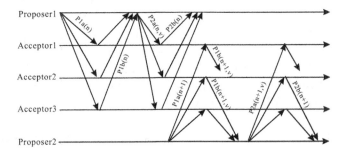

Figure 6.3   If the system has already chosen a value, the safety property for consensus would hold even without the promise-not-to-accept-older-proposal requirement.

As shown in Figure 6.4, before proposer 1 completes the accept phase for proposal $P(n)$, proposer 2 may have completed the prepare phase. Despite the fact that acceptor 1 has accepted $P(n, v)$ before it receives the prepare request $P(n+1)$, its response might not reach proposer 2 soon enough before proposer 2 concludes that no value has been chosen in the past and proposes a new value v' in its proposal $P(n + 1)$. Without the promise-not-to-accept-older-proposal requirement, acceptor 2 and acceptor 3 would still accept $P(n, v)$ after they have responded to proposer 2's accept request for $P(n + 1)$. This would lead the system to choose v. Subsequently, the acceptors would accept the accept request for $P(n + 1)$ because it is a newer proposal. Unfortunately, at this point, the system has chosen two different values, violating the safety property for consensus.

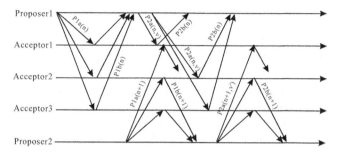

Figure 6.4   If two competing proposers propose concurrently, the system might end up choosing two different values without the promise-not-to-accept-older-proposal requirement.

With the promise-not-to-accept-older-proposal requirement in place, acceptor 2 and acceptor 3 would have rejected the accept requests for $P(n)$ that arrive later than the prepare request for $P(n+1)$, which would prevent value v being chosen by the system. If the accept phase for $P(n + 1, v')$ can be completed before a newer proposal is issued, the system would choose v'.

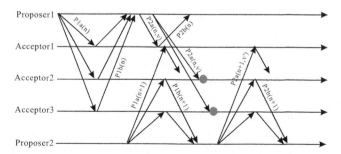

Figure 6.5   With the promise-not-to-accept-older-proposal requirement in place, even if two competing proposers propose concurrently, only a single value may be chosen by the system.

6.3   Multi-Paxos

An immediate application of the Paxos algorithm is to enable state machine replication where a set of server replicas provide services for the clients by executing the requests sent by the clients and returning the corresponding replies to the clients. In this context, a client partially assumes the role of a proposer, and all the server replicas are acceptors. At the highest level, the value to be agreed on by the server replicas (*i.e.*, acceptors) is the total ordering of the requests sent by the clients. The total ordering determination is accomplished by running a sequence of instances of the Paxos algorithm. Each instance is assigned a sequence number, representing the total ordering of the request that is chosen. For each instance, the value to be chosen is the particular request that should be assigned to this instance.

The reason why a client only partially assumes the role of a proposer is because it is only capable of proposing a value (which is the request it sends), but without the corresponding proposal number. One of the server replicas must assume essentially the other half of the proposer role. This special replica is referred to as the coordinator [14], the leader [10], or simply the primary [16, 17]. We could argue that the primary is essentially the proposer as it is described in the Paxos algorithm [10] and it is the primary that selects the value, which is supplied by the clients. Furthermore, the primary propagates the chosen value to the remaining replicas (often referred to as backups) so that they can learn the value as well. Obviously, the primary is the first to know that a value is chosen for each instance of the Paxos algorithm, and usually the first to send the reply to the client. The backups can suppress their replies unless they have suspected the primary because the client needs only a single reply for each of its requests.

Normally, one of the server replicas is designated as the primary at the beginning of the system deployment. Only when the primary becomes faulty, which is rare, or being suspected of being faulty by other replicas, another replica will be elected as the new primary. As long as there is a sole primary in the system, it is guaranteed that no replica would report having accepted any proposal to the primary, which would enable the primary to select any value (*i.e.*, any request). Therefore, the first phase (*i.e.*, the prepare phase) can be omitted during normal operation (*i.e.*, when there is only a single primary in the system). The full Paxos algorithm is needed to elect a new primary and it is needed to run only once right after a new primary is elected. In essence, this run would execute the first phase of all instances of the Paxos as long as the current primary is operating.

The above scheme of applying the Paxos algorithm for state machine replication is first proposed in [10] and the term "Multi-Paxos" was first introduced in [5]. The Multi-Paxos during normal operation is illustrated in Figure 6.6. Note that the primary can execute the request as soon as it receives the *P2b* messages from a quorum of replicas. As shown in Figure 6.6, the primary does so prior to the receiving of the *P2b* message from replica 2.

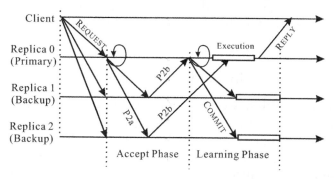

Figure 6.6   Normal operation of Multi-Paxos in a client-server system with 3 server replicas and a single client.

6.3.1   Checkpointing and Garbage Collection

The Paxos algorithm is open-ended in that it never terminates – a proposer is allowed to initiate a new proposal even if every acceptor has accepted a proposal. As such, an acceptor must remember the latest proposal that it has accepted and the latest proposal number it has acknowledged. Because the Multi-Paxos is derived from Paxos, all server replicas must remember such information for *every* instance of the Paxos algorithm that it has participated in, even after it has long executed the request chosen by this instance. This would require infinite amount of memory space, which is obviously not desirable for practical systems.

The problem can be eliminated by performing periodic checkpointing at each replica [16, 17]. A replica takes a checkpoint after the n-th request has been executed, where n is the checkpointing period in terms of the number of requests executed. When $f + 1$ or more replicas have taken a checkpoint at the same logic point, the checkpoint becomes stable. When a checkpoint has become stable, a replica can subsequently garbage collect all logged information and messages pertinent to the last n messages (including the clients' requests).

A slow replica might lag behind and need either to find out which request is chosen for an instance, or need a copy of the request itself. Such information might no longer be available for a Paxos instance older than the most recent stable checkpoint, in which case, the replica should contact the primary for a state transfer. Upon a state transfer request, the primary would send a copy of its latest checkpoint to the slow replica. The slow replica then roll-forwards its state by restoring its state using the checkpoint received.

6.3.2   Leader Election and View Change

Earlier in this section, we mentioned that upon the primary failure, a new leader would be elected (using the Paxos algorithm itself), and the new primary would need to execute a full two-phase Paxos algorithm to establish whether or not a request has been or might be chosen for each incomplete instance of the Paxos algorithm. In fact, the two steps can be combined to eliminate the extra message delays, as first shown in a Byzantine fault tolerance algorithm [4] and later was adapted for the non-Byzantine environment [16, 17], as shown in Figure 6.7. Such an algorithm is referred to as a view change algorithm [4].

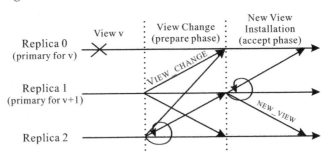

Figure 6.7   View change algorithm for Multi-Paxos.

The view change algorithm assumes that each replica is assigned a unique integer identifier, starting from 0. Given a set of $2f + 1$

replicas, the identifiers used would be $0, 1, ..., 2f$, one for each replica. The history of the system would consists of a sequence of views. Within each view, there is one and only one primary, ensured by the view change algorithm. Initially, the replica with identifier 0 would assume the primary role. If this primary is suspected, then the replica with identifier 1 would be a candidate for the primary of the next consecutive view. It is possible that the view change does not complete in time due to the asynchrony of the system, or due to the failure of the next primary in line, the next replica in line will be selected as the candidate for the primary role in a round-robin fashion.

To ensure the liveness of the system, a replica starts a view change timer on the initiation of each instance of the Paxos algorithm. If the replica does not learn the request chosen for an instance before the timer expires, it suspects that the current primary has become faulty. On suspecting the failure of the primary for the current view, a replica multicasts a view change message to all other replicas, including the primary that has been suspected. The reason why the current primary is also informed is to minimize the probability of having two or more replicas believing that they all are the primary for the system. Recall that in an asynchronous system, a process cannot distinguish a crashed process from a slow one. If the current primary is simply slow instead of crashed, upon receiving a new view message (for a view greater than the current view), it would stop acting as a primary and join the view change instead.

To expedite the advancement to a new view, a backup replica also suspects the primary and joins the view change upon receiving a view change message for a view greater than the current view from another replica. Once it suspects the primary, a replica stops participating activities in the current view, except for checkpointing and for view change, until a new view is installed.

Because the view change algorithm combines both leader election and a full round of Paxos for message ordering, the view change message contains a new view number (from which the identifier of the new primary can be inferred) as well as the following information to ensure that if a request has been chosen or might have been chosen, such a request will be known to the new primary (to ensure it is chosen as well in the new view):

- The sequence number of the last stable checkpoint.

- A set of accepted records since the last stable checkpoint. Each record consists of the view number, sequence number, and the request message. As an optimization, the hash value of the request can be included instead of the message itself. The message can be retransmitted to a replica that needs it.

When the primary in the proposed new view has collected view change messages from the majority of replicas (including itself), it installs the new view and notifies the backups with a new view message. In the new view message, the primary includes a set of accept requests that are typically sent at the accept phase of the Paxos algorithm. The accept requests are determined in the following way:

- If the primary (in the new view) received an accepted record from one of the view change message, it includes the record in the accept requests set.
- It is possible for the primary to see a gap between the last checkpoint sequence number and the smallest sequence number of the accepted records, or a gap between the sequence numbers of two accepted records, in which case, the primary creates an accept request with a no-op for each missing sequence number.

A replica accepts the new view message if it has not installed a newer view, and starts responding to the accept requests included in the new view message in the context of the new view. If a request is a no-op or if it has been executed in the old view, it is simply skipped in the new view.

6.4 Dynamic Paxos

In the previous sections, we assumed that the set of replicas are fixed. This may not be the case in practice because when a replica fails, it may be replaced by another spare replica, which would require a reconfiguration of the system. In [14], the Paxos algorithm is extended to enable the reconfiguration of the system. Such an algorithm is referred to as Dynamic Paxos because the membership formation of the replicas can now be dynamically changed via an administrative command. Furthermore, a special instance of

Dynamic Paxos is provided, referred to as Cheap Paxos, in which the spare replicas are involved *only* during a reconfiguration.

In addition, for all the algorithms described so far, we have required the majority of the replica to agree on a decision as a core step of reaching consensus. This notion of majority can be extended as a *quorum*. A quorum in a system is defined to be a set of processes such that any two quorums of the system intersect in at least one process. Obviously, a majority of replicas would form a quorum. Any two such quorums would always intersect in at least one replica. However, a quorum does not necessarily the majority of the replicas. Some quorum might consist of more than the majority, while some quorum might consist of less than the majority. In the extreme case, a single replica can constitute a quorum, in which case, all other quorums must include this replica as well. Hence, we can conclude that we have used a static quorum size (and quorum formation) in the algorithms described. As we will see later, in Cheap Paxos, dynamic quorum is used to further reduce the resource requirement for fault tolerance.

6.4.1   Dynamic Paxos

As pointed out in [14], by using spare replicas and reconfiguration upon failures, fewer replicas are required to tolerate the same number of faults, provided that no other replica becomes faulty during the reconfiguration. For example, for a system with $2f + 1$ active replicas, and f spare replicas, the system can keep operating correctly after a sequence of reconfigurations even when there are only a single active replica and a single spare replica left, *i.e.*, the system can manage to tolerate as many as $3f - 1$ faults provided that one replica becomes faulty at a time and no replica becomes faulty during each reconfiguration. Without reconfiguration, a system with $3f + 1$ total replicas can only tolerate up to $\lfloor 3f/2 \rfloor$ faults.

■   EXAMPLE 6.2

In this example, we show how reconfiguration can help a system tolerate more number of single faults. The system initially has 5 active replicas and 2 spare replicas. Therefore, the active replicas are configured to tolerate up to 2 faults (without reconfiguration), *i.e.*, $f = 2$. Accordingly, the quorum size is 3.

If we were to use both the 5 active replicas and the 2 spare replicas together, then we could tolerate up to 3 faults. In Figure 6.8, we show how the system can tolerate up to 5 single faults with proper reconfigurations:

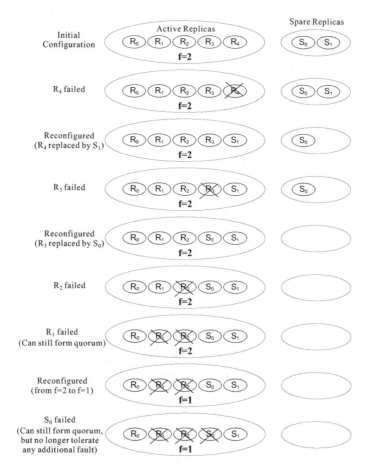

Total Number of Faults Tolerated with Reconfiguration: 5
(Total Number of Faults Tolerated without Reconfiguration: 3)

Figure 6.8   With reconfigurations, a group of 7 replicas (initially 5 active and 2 spare replicas) can tolerate up to 5 single faults (without reconfigurations, only up to 3 faults can be tolerated).

- When one of the active replicas, say R_4, becomes faulty and is detected by the system, it is replaced by a spare replica, S_1

during the reconfiguration. After the reconfiguration, there are still 5 active replicas with $f = 2$.

- A while later, another active replica, R_3, becomes faulty. When the fault is detected, a reconfiguration request is generated to replace R_3 by the last spare replica S_0. After this configuration, there are still 5 active replicas with $f = 2$, but there is no longer any spare replica available.

- When one more active replica, R_2, becomes faulty, no more spare replica is available to replace it. It is important to know that the quorum size should not be reduced if a reconfiguration takes place (to inform the surviving replicas about the loss of R_2). In fact, the membership change notification can be delayed until another replica becomes faulty because this fault has no impact on the operations of surviving replicas. The reason why we should not reduce the quorum size is because there are 4 active replicas remaining after R_2 becomes faulty. Reducing the quorum size from 3 to 2 (*i.e.*, reducing from $f = 2$ to $f = 1$) at this stage might result in two artificial partitions, with each partition (consisting of 2 replicas) agreeing on a different value.

- When yet one more active replica, R_1, becomes faulty, the system has only 3 replicas remaining. Without reconfiguration, the system would not be able to tolerate another fault because no quorum would be able to form for $f = 2$. Therefore, a reconfiguration is carried out by the system to reduce f from 2 to 1 and reduce the quorum size from 3 to 2. It is safe to do so now because 2 replicas are a clear majority in a 3-replica system.

- If another replica, S_0, becomes faulty, the system has only 2 replicas remaining. Even though the system can still form a quorum for $f = 1$, it can no longer tolerate any subsequently fault. Neither could the system perform further reconfiguration because there are simply not enough replicas left.

The sole extension to the basic Paxos algorithm is the facilitation of reconfiguration. In Dynamic Paxos, the membership formation and the quorum size are determined by the system dynamically via the execution of a reconfiguration request. Such a request can be issued by a system administrator or injected by a built-in failure detection mechanism upon the detection of a failed replica. The request will be totally ordered with respect to normal requests from the clients of the system using Multi-Paxos.

Whether or not the reconfiguration should take place immediately after the execution of the reconfiguration request may be application dependent. Hence, in [14], an integer constant, α, was introduced to allow this flexibility. If the reconfiguration command is executed at instance i of the Paxos algorithm, the reconfiguration will take place when the system executes the instance $i + \alpha$ of the Paxos algorithm. This scheme is useful for planned reconfigurations. However, in case of the failure of an active replica, it is reasonable to assume that the reconfiguration should take place immediately (for the next request) because if more replicas become faulty prior to the reconfiguration, the system might not be able to form a quorum according to the current configuration.

A reconfiguration request should include both a complete set of membership and a quorum definition. The membership includes the identifiers of the replicas that are considered operating correctly. In a straightforward implementation of Dynamic Paxos, the quorum definition for each configuration can be as simple as the size of the quorum, *i.e.*, as long as a replica receives support from this many replicas, it would proceed to the next step. As we will show in a special instance of Dynamic Paxos in the following subsection, the quorum definition might not always assume the form of a size definition.

After a reconfiguration, it is essential for the replicas in the membership to not accept messages *unrelated* to reconfigurations from replicas that have been deemed as faulty and excluded from the membership. In particular, such external replicas should not be allowed to participate in the consensus step for obvious reasons. A replica that has been mistakenly excluded from the current membership, or that has recovered from a fault, is allowed to join the system by sending a reconfiguration request, in which case, the primary should transfer its state to the joining replica to bring that replica up-to-date.

6.4.2 Cheap Paxos

Cheap Paxos is a special instance of Dynamic Paxos that aims to minimize the involvement of spare replicas. The objective of Cheap Paxos is to reduce the hardware redundancy needed by a fault tolerant system. By minimizing the involvement of spare replicas, existing nodes that are performing other functionalities can be used as spares instead of acquiring more dedicated nodes, or cheaper hardware with less computing power may be used as spares.

Cheap Paxos enables the use of $f + 1$ active replicas to tolerate f faults, provided that sufficient number of spares are available (f or more). As such, the design of Cheap Paxos is in a way drastically different from other Paxos algorithms:

- All other Paxos algorithms rely on the use of a uniform quorum. That is, a quorum used by any replica consists of the majority replicas of the current membership, and each replica has the same role in forming a quorum (*i.e.*, no replica has a special to role within a quorum).
- This is not the case for Cheap Paxos. In Cheap Paxos, only $f + 1$ active replicas are used to tolerate up to f faults in the active replicas. These $f + 1$ active replicas form a primary quorum. During normal operation, an active replica would always try to build the primary quorum consisting of *all* $f + 1$ active replicas. Because of this design, the active replicas are referred to as *main* replicas, and the spare replicas are referred to as *auxiliary* replicas, to differentiate them from the roles played by the replicas in the original Dynamic Paxos.
- In Cheap Paxos, a secondary quorum can be formed by a majority of the combined replicas (main and auxiliary replicas) provided that at least one of them is a main replica, as shown in Figure 6.9. The secondary quorum is used when a main replica finds that it has timed out the formation of the primary quorum consisting of all main replicas.
- A fault detection mechanism is assumed in Cheap Paxos that would inject a reconfiguration request to the replicas as soon as it has detected that one of the main replicas has become faulty. The reconfiguration request is totally ordered with respect to the regular clients' requests.
- When the reconfiguration request is executed by the replicas (main replicas and auxiliary replicas), the main replica that has been suspected of failure is removed from the membership. Furthermore, the primary quorum is reconfigured to consist all surviving main replicas. The secondary quorum definition may also be redefined depending on the number of surviving replicas, as shown in Figure 6.10. If

there is only one main replica left, it forms the primary quorum on its own, and a secondary quorum must include this sole main replica.

- Once the reconfiguration request is executed, the system will switch back to the new configuration and new quorum definitions. If a grace period parameter α is used as suggested in [14], all replicas will switch to using the new configuration at α rounds later. As we have argued earlier, there seems to be no reason why the system should not switch to the new configuration immediately after the removal of a replica.

- During normal operation when the high priority quorum is used, the auxiliary replicas do not participate in any instance of the Paxos algorithm for request total ordering. An auxiliary replica is contacted only when a main replica could not form a high priority quorum, until a new configuration is installed at all main replicas.

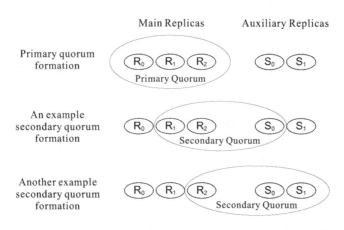

Figure 6.9   The Primary and secondary quorums formation for a system with 3 main replicas and 2 auxiliary replicas.

So far, we have implicitly assumed that the main replica that becomes faulty is not the primary. If the primary becomes faulty, a view change will take place. The view change algorithm is slightly different from that we have described in section 6.3.2 because the quorum definition is changed:

- Instead of simply collecting from a majority of the replicas (main plus the auxiliary replicas) on the chosen or possibly

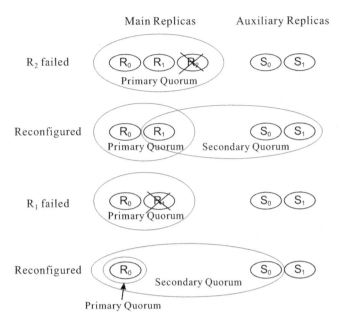

Figure 6.10   The Primary and secondary quorums formation as the system reconfigures due to the failures of main replicas.

chosen values, the primary for the new view must receive the required information from *every* main replica except the one that is suspected as failed because the auxiliary replicas would not be able to provide any useful information to the new primary – they are not participating in the consensus step during normal operation.

- The new primary should rely on a secondary quorum that consists of all surviving main replicas and one or more auxiliary replicas for approval of its new role.
- The new primary then uses this secondary quorum to complete all Paxos instances that were started by the previous primary, but not yet completed.
- The reconfiguration request will have to be ordered after all Paxos instances started by the previous primary.

As we mentioned earlier, once the reconfiguration request is executed by a secondary quorum, the system will switch to using the new primary quorum formation. To alleviate the burden of requiring the auxiliary replicas to keep all the clients requests and control messages, Cheap Paxos requires that the replicas in the secondary quorum propagate their knowledge to all other replicas (main and auxiliary replicas) prior to moving back to the primary quorum. How exactly this is carried out is not defined in [14]. A simple way of implementing the requirement is outlined below.

- The primary notifies its latest state (the most recent Paxos instance number) to all replicas that are not in the secondary quorum (that enabled the reconfiguration).
- On receiving such a message, a main replica examines its state to see if it is missing any messages. If yes, it would ask for retransmissions from the primary to bring itself up to date. After receiving all missing messages, the replica sends the primary an acknowledgement message.
- On receiving such a message, an auxiliary replica simply remembers the fact provided by the primary, and garbage collect all logged messages. The auxiliary replica then sends the primary an acknowledgement.
- The primary resumes ordering the next request (*i.e.,* launching a new instance of the Paxos algorithm) using the primary quorum once it receives acknowledgement from every replica.

Obviously, the above requirement (and hence its implementation) is not fault tolerant. The primary would be stuck if one of the replicas becomes faulty before the primary receives the acknowledgement from that replica. When this happens, the fault detection mechanism in place would issue a reconfiguration request to the replicas. The primary should abandon the effort of collecting acknowledgement from every replica and engage in the new reconfiguration instead. Abandoning such an effort is harmless in case of failures because the safety property of the operation is not affected. Of course, the primary itself might become faulty in the mean time, in which case, a view change will follow so that a new primary can be elected.

Note that the selection of the primary or a secondary quorum is determined by the primary, if the system has a unique primary. When the current primary becomes faulty, the system will be forced to use a secondary quorum for view changes.

■ **EXAMPLE 6.3**

In this example, we show how Cheap Paxos works both during normal operation and when one of the main replicas becomes faulty in a system with 3 main replicas and 1 auxiliary replica. In this system, the primary quorum consists of all 3 main replicas, and a secondary quorum consists of 2 of the main replicas and the 1 auxiliary replica.

As shown in Figure 6.11, during the normal operation, the primary sends the accept request (the $P2a$ message in the figure) to the primary quorum (*i.e.*, all the main replicas) and must wait until it has received the corresponding acknowledge messages from all the main replicas before it is convinced that the request is chosen. Then the primary sends a commit notification to the other main replicas so that they can learn the request that is chosen. All main replicas would execute the request that is chosen provided that all previously ordered requests have been executed. Only the primary sends the reply to the client that issued the request.

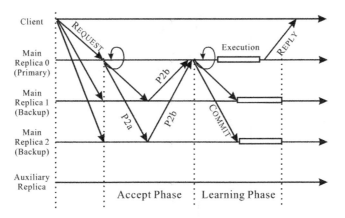

Figure 6.11   Normal operation of Cheap Paxos in a system with 3 main replicas and 1 auxiliary replica.

Now lets consider a different scenario when one of the main replicas becomes faulty, as shown in Figure 6.12. In this case, the primary could not receive an acknowledgement message in response to its accept request. Eventually, the primary would time out building the primary quorum and switch to using a secondary quorum. For the particular configuration we have assumed in this example, there is only one secondary quorum consisting all surviving 2 main replicas and the auxiliary replica. Hence, the primary would send the accept request to the auxiliary replica. When the auxiliary replica has responded,

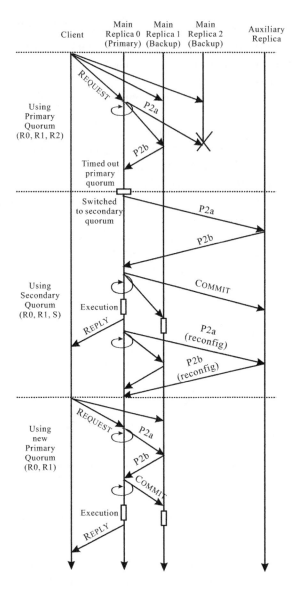

Figure 6.12   The Primary and secondary quorums formation for a system with 3 main replicas and 2 auxiliary replicas.

the primary could finally choose the request and subsequently notifies the other main replica and the auxiliary replica, and executes the request chosen.

After it is done handling all ongoing instances of the Paxos algorithm (in our case, only one instance), the primary initiates a reconfiguration. The value to be chosen is the new membership of the system with the faulty main replica excluded. The primary sends an accept request for the new membership to the other main replica and the auxiliary replica. When they both have responded, the primary knows that the new configuration has been accepted by the system.

Due to the particular configuration used in this example, the primary does not need to do anything extra to alleviate the burden of the auxiliary because the secondary quorum used by the primary consists of *all* surviving replicas. The primary can then switch to using the new primary quorum consisting of two main replicas for future requests.

6.5   Fast Paxos

The objective of Fast Paxos [12] is to reduce the end-to-end latency of reaching a consensus in scenarios where the clients are responsible to propose values to be chosen by the acceptors. In Multi-Paxos, we have shown that the first phase of the Paxos algorithm can be run once for all instances of the Paxos algorithm provided that initially there is a single leader. Hence, in Multi-Paxos (and later variants of the Paxos algorithm we introduced so far), the cost of reaching agreement is the second phase of the Paxos algorithm. Fast Paxos aims to further reduce the cost of reaching consensus by enabling the running of one phase 2a message for *all* instances of Fast Paxos in a client-server system where the server is replicated. This would enable an acceptor to select a value (provided by a client) unilaterally and sends the phase 2b message to the leader (or a learner) immediately, thereby reducing the end-to-end latency.

Because the original Paxos algorithm is proven to be optimal, to reduce the latency, we must sacrifice something else. In Fast Paxos, to tolerate f faults, more than $2f + 1$ replicas are required. We will develop the criteria on the minimum number of replicas to tolerate f faults for Fast Paxos to work in this section. Furthermore, because an acceptors (*i.e.*, a server replica) unilaterally selects a value (*i.e.*, a request message sent by a client), different acceptors might select different values. This scenario is referred to as a collision (in choosing the same value) in [12]. Collision avoidance and collision recovery are new problems exist in Fast Paxos and not other variants of the Paxos algorithm previously introduced.

In this section, we first describe the basic steps of the Fast Paxos algorithm, then we discuss collision recovery, the quorum requirement, and the value selection rule for the coordinator.

6.5.1   The Basic Steps

The basic steps of the Fast Paxos algorithm are rather similar to those of the original Paxos (from now on referred to as Classic Paxos to differentiate it from other variants of the Paxos algorithms). Fast Paxos also operates in rounds (the round number corresponds to the proposal number in Classic Paxos) and each round has two phases. The first phase is a prepare phase to enable the coordinator (originally the proposer in Classic Paxos) to solicit the status and promises from the acceptors. The second phase is for the coordinator to select a value to be voted on by the acceptors. When an acceptor has responded to a phase 1a ($P1a$) message in a round i, it is said that the acceptor has participated in round i. When an acceptor has sent to the coordinator a phase 2b ($P2b$) message in response to the phase 2a ($P2a$) message from the coordinator, it is said that the acceptor has casted its vote for that round.

Fast Paxos has a number of differences from Classic Paxos:

- In Fast Paxos, a round may be either a fast round or a classic round. A fast round may use a quorum of different size from that of a classic round. We refer to the quorum used in a fast round as fast quorum, and the quorum used in a classic round as classic quorum.
- The value selection rule at the coordinator is different from that of the Classic Paxos due to the presence of the fast round.
- In a classic round, the coordinator always selects the value to be voted on, similar to that of Classic Paxos.
- In a fast round, if the new value selection rule allows the coordinator to select its own value, it may send a special phase 2a message to the acceptors without any value selected. This special phase 2a message (referred to as *any* message in [12]) enables an acceptor to select its own value (proposed by a client) to vote on.

Assuming that there has been a unique coordinator since the server is turned on, the first time a fast round is run will always allow the coordinator to send an *any* message in phase 2. In a typical state-machine replicated system, this would allow the running of a single phase 2a message for all instances of Fast Paxos, which would eliminate one communication step, as shown in Figure 6.13. This is the sole advantage of Fast Paxos, hence, whenever possible, a fast round is run and a classic round is used only when a consensus cannot be reached in the fast round due to the failure of the coordinator or due to a collision.

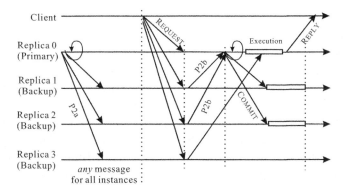

Figure 6.13 Normal operation of (Multi-) Fast Paxos in a client-server system.

6.5.2 Collision Recovery, Quorum Requirement, and Value Selection Rule

In this subsection, we elaborate on the issues that we have ignored so far, including collision recovery, quorum requirement, and value selection rules. All these issues are rooted at the possible collision in a fast round.

During a fast round, if the coordinator issues an *any* phase 2a message, the acceptors would have freedom to select its only values. If there are several clients proposing different values concurrently (*i.e.*, they issue requests to the server replicas concurrently), it is likely that different acceptors could select different values, which would cause a collision. When this happens, the coordinator might see different values in the quorum of votes it has collected, which would prevent the consensus from being accomplished in this fast round.

Note that it is not an option for the coordinator to block waiting until it has collected votes with the same value from a quorum of acceptors because it may never be able to build a quorum if less than a quorum of acceptors have voted for the same value. Therefore, on detecting a collision, the coordinator should initiate recovery by starting a new, classic round. In this new classic round, it is apparent that the coordinator would receive the same, or similar information from a quorum of acceptors in the first phase of the new round. Therefore, the first phase can be omitted and the coordinator can proceed to determine a value to be voted on in the second phase.

With a quorum of votes containing different values, the coordinator must be careful in selecting a value that has chosen in a previous round (just like Classic Paxos, Fast Paxos does not terminate, and hence, once a value is chosen, the same value must also be chosen in any future round), or might be chosen. A value is chosen or might be chosen if a quorum of acceptors have voted the same value. Choosing any other value might cause two or more values be chosen, which would violate the safety property for consensus. However, it is not straightforward for the coordinator to determine if a value in the quorum of votes has been chosen or might be chosen.

Before we delve further on the value selection rule, we first show that the simple-majority based quorum formation in Classic Paxos is no longer valid in Fast Paxos. In Classic Paxos, to tolerate f faulty acceptors, a total of $2f + 1$ acceptors are required and the quorum size is a simple majority ($f + 1$). With a quorum size of $f + 1$, two quorums may intersect in as few as a single acceptor. Therefore, with this quorum formation, a coordinator cannot rule out the possibility that a value might have been chosen even if it has collected a single vote with that value. As such, the coordinator would not be able to determine which value to select if it sees different values in the quorum of votes it has collected. Note that only one of the different values could have been chosen because it is impossible for the acceptors to form two quorums each with a different value in the same round.

It should be apparent now that a bigger quorum than the simple majority must be used in Fast Paxos. Intuitively, given a fast quorum R_f (with a size $|R_f|$) and a classic quorum R_c (with a size $|R_c|$), a value that has been or might have been chosen will be present in the majority of the votes the coordinator has collected provided that:

- Any two fast quorums must intersect in at least $\lceil |R_f|/2 \rceil$ acceptors, and
- Any fast quorum and any classic quorum must intersect in at least $\lceil |R_c|/2 \rceil$ acceptors.

Hence, it is safe for the coordinator to select the value contained in the majority of the votes it has collected, if such a value exists [15]. We should note the following related facts:

- By the basic quorum definition, there can be at most one value be chosen in a fast round, even if collision occurs.
- A value that is contained in a minority of votes in the quorum R_c cannot possibly have been chosen due to the above quorum requirement.
- The presence of a common value from the majority of votes in the quorum R_c does not necessarily mean that the value has been chosen.

To summarize, we have the following quorum requirements:

1. Any two classic quorum must intersect in at least one acceptor.
2. Any two fast quorum must intersect in at least $\lceil |R_f|/2 \rceil$ acceptors.
3. Any fast quorum R_f (with a size $|R_f|$) and any classic quorum R_c (with a size $|R_c|$) must intersect in at least $\lceil |R_c|/2 \rceil$ acceptors.

With the list of quorum requirements in place, we are now ready to derive the quorum sizes. Let the total number of acceptors be n, the number of faulty acceptors that can be tolerated in a classic round be f, and the number of faulty acceptors that can be tolerated in a fast round be e. Intuitively, $f \geq e$. Hence, the size of a classic quorum is $n - f$, and the size of a fast quorum is $n - e$. The three quorum requirements can now be translated to the following:

$$(1) : n - f + n - f - n > 0$$
$$(2) : n - e + n - e - n > (n - e)/2$$
$$(3) : n - f + n - e - n > (n - f)/2$$

The requirements can be further reduced to:

$$(1) : n > 2f$$
$$(2) : n > 3e$$
$$(3) : n > 2e + f$$

Because the quorum requirement 2 is superseded by the quorum requirement 3. We end up with only the following two quorum requirements:

$$n > 2f \tag{6.1}$$

$$n > 2e + f \tag{6.2}$$

We can have two different quorum formations by maximizing e or f.

- Because $f \geq e$, to maximize e, we have $e = f$ and $n > 3f$. Hence, a classic quorum would be the same size of a fast quorum: $|R_c| = n - f > 3f - f = 2f$. For all practical purposes, the total number of acceptors would be set to $n = 3f + 1$ and the quorum size (both classic and fast) would be $2f + 1$. For example, if we choose $f = 1$, we would need a total of 4 acceptors, and the quorum size would be 3.
- To maximize f, we can use the upper bound given in Equation 6.1 for f, therefore:

$$f < n/2$$

We can derive the requirement on e from Equation 6.2:

$$e < (n - f)/2$$

By replacing f with $n/2$ (i.e., f's upper bound), we have:

$$e \leq (n - n/2)/2$$

Finally, we have:

$$e \leq n/4$$

Therefore, the size of a classic quorum must be greater than $n/2$ (i.e., a simple majority), and the size of a fast quorum must be greater than $3n/4$. For example, if use the smallest e possible, i.e., $e = 1$, we need a minimum of 4 acceptors. The size of a fast quorum would happen to be the same as that of a classic quorum, which is 3. Note that $f = 1$ too in this case. Furthermore, a classic quorum does not always have the same size of a fast quorum. Consider the case when $e = 2$. We need 8 acceptors, which means a classic quorum can consists of 5 acceptors while we would need 6 acceptors to form a fast quorum. Hence, $f = 3$ in this case.

Having fully defined the classic and fast quorums for Fast Paxos, lets come back to the value selection rule at the coordinator. We have already argued that in case of different values are present in the votes the coordinator has collected, the coordinator should choose the value contained in the majority of the votes in the (classic) quorum, if such a value exists. If no such majority votes exist in the quorum, the coordinator is free to choose any value because no value could have been chosen in a previous round due to our quorum requirement 3. Hence, the value selection rule is defined below:

1. If no acceptor has casted any vote, then the coordinator is free to select any value for phase 2.
2. If only a single value is present in all the votes, then the coordinator must select that value.
3. If the votes contain different values, a value must be selected if the majority of acceptors in the quorum have casted a vote for that value. Otherwise, the coordinator is free to select any value.

Rule 1 and rule 2 are the same as those for Classic Paxos. The rule 3 is specific for Fast Paxos.

EXAMPLE 6.4

In this example, we demonstrate a collision scenario and the corresponding collision recovery in a system with 2 concurrent clients and 4 server replicas. In this system, the number of faults tolerated is 1 for both a classic round and a fast round (*i.e.*, $f = e = 1$). The quorum size for both a classic round and a fast round is 3.

As shown in Figure 6.14, the two clients send simultaneously request 1 ($r1$) and request 2 ($r2$) to the replicas. We assume that the replicas (*i.e.*, the acceptors) would use a fast round trying to order a request. Replica 0 (*i.e.*, the coordinator) and replica 1 receive $r1$ ahead of $r2$, and thus vote to order $r1$ in this round. Replica 2 and replica 3 receive $r2$ ahead of $r1$, and thus vote to order $r2$ in this round.

The coordinator (*i.e.*, the primary) finds two different values (2 $r1$ and 1 $r2$) in the quorum of votes it has collected. Hence, a collision is detected. The coordinator subsequently starts a new classic round to recover from the collision. According to the value selection rule introduced earlier, the coordinator chooses $r1$ and include the value in its phase 2a message. When a quorum of replicas has voted, $r1$ is chosen and the coordinator informs the other replicas, after which, the request $r1$ is executed and the corresponding reply is returned.

As we can see in this example, the presence of a common value from the majority of the votes ($r1$ in our example) does not necessarily mean that the value has been chosen in an earlier round.

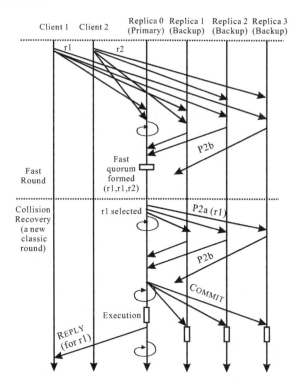

Figure 6.14   Collision recovery in an example system.

6.6   Implementations of the Paxos Family Algorithms

The original Paxos algorithm and several of its derivative algorithms have been implemented in a number of open-source projects, including:

- libPaxos. This project consists the implementations for both the original Paxos and Fast Paxos in C/C++, and a Paxos algorithm simulator in Erlang. More information for the project can be found at: http://libpaxos.sourceforge.net/.
- Paxos for System Builders [1]. It is an implementation of the Paxos algorithm in C with a number of optimizations. More information for the project can be found at: http://www.dsn.jhu.edu/Paxos-SB.html.
- OpenReplica. OpenReplica is an implementation of the Paxos algorithm for state machine replication in Python. More information for the project can be found at: http://openreplica.org/.
- Plain Paxos. It is another implementation of the Paxos algoirthm in Python. More information for the project can be found at: https://github.com/cocagne/paxos.
- JPaxos. It is an implementation of the Paxos algorithm for state machine replication in Java. More information for the project can be found at: http://www.it-soa.eu/en/resp/jpaxos/. The source code is available for download at: https://github.com/JPaxos/JPaxos.
- Java-Paxos. It is another implementation of the Paxos algorithm in Java. More information for the project can be found at: http://java-paxos.sourceforge.net/.

The Paxos algorithm has also been used in production systems. The most well known system perhaps is Chubby at Google [5]. Chubby provides a fault tolerant distributed locking service for various clients such as Google File Systems and Bigtable clients. In Chubby, an implementation of the Paxos algorithm (Multi-Paxos to be specific) is used to provide a fault tolerant logging service. In this section, we introduce a number of challenges that arise in the production system as reported in [5].

6.6.1   Hard Drive Failures

Paxos assumes the availability of persistent storage locally to each acceptor so that if it makes a promise in the phase 1b message, it won't forget about it after recovering from a crash failure. In Chubby, a replica logs its promise to the local hard drive for more robust crash recovery. Unfortunately, hard drive failures do occur and in particular, a disk may be corrupted and the log file may be accidentally deleted due to operator errors. When a replica recovers from a crash fault, it may not have access to the log file that recorded its promises prior to the crash fault, in which case, the safety property of Paxos might be violated.

As we elaborated in the beginning of this chapter, one approach to handle this challenge is to require the recovering replica to rejoin the system instead of continuing as usual. To reinforce this policy in practice, there must be a way to preventing a recovering replica from continuing operating as if the crash did not occur. In Chubby, this is achieved by requiring a replica to register a marker file with the Google File System each time it starts/restarts. When a replica restarts after a crash fault, it is reminded that it should not participate in any Paxos instances in the system until it has gone through a catch-up procedure. Basically, the replica must observe a full instance of Paxos that is started after its recovery before it participates in voting again.

In [5], there is also an discussion on skipping flushing the log (for the promises made and votes casted by a replica) synchronously to disk as an optimization, which is consistent with our argument on the need for writing to persistent storage in the beginning of this chapter.

6.6.2   Multiple Coordinators

When the current coordinator is disconnected or crashed, the system would elect a new coordinator. When the disconnected replica reconnects, or restarts after a crash, it may not realize that it is no longer serve as the coordinator role. Furthermore, some clients might not know that the coordinator has changed and they would still issue their requests to the old coordinator. In this case, the old coordinator would attempt to proceed to launch new instances of the Paxos algorithm. This might cause rapid changes of the coordinator in the system, which is apparently not desirable.

To prevent this from happening, in Chubby, the coordinator periodically starts a new round of Paxos algorithm even if no client's request is received. This mechanism can minimize the chance that a reconnected or restarted replica from successfully getting the coordinator role back. Implicitly, the coordinator is granted a master lease [7] each time it successfully runs an instance of the Paxos algorithm. As long as the coordinator has a valid master lease, it is guaranteed that it has the latest state of the system. When the coordinator receives read-only requests, it can execute them immediately without the need of totally ordering them.

In Chubby, when a client issues a request to the coordinator for processing, if the replica has lost its coordinator role either at the time of submission of the request, or prior to the execution of the request, the request should be aborted. The most tricky scenario is when the coordinator fails and quickly restarted, in which case, the requests submitted before the crash but not yet fully executed should be aborted. To distinguish this scenario from normal operation, an epoch number is introduced such that requests received by the coordinator while it is continuously serving as the coordinator role are assigned the same epoch number. The epoch number is stored in the database for persistency.

Even though the above mechanisms apparently work in Chubby (it is a product system), it is unclear why the more elegant approach, *i.e.*, the view change mechanism [16, 17], is not adopted. If the view change mechanism as we described in section 6.3.2 is used, the reconnected or restarted replica cannot possibly run a successful instance of the Paxos because the instance would possess an obsolete view number. The use of view number also eliminates the need for the epoch number.

6.6.3 Membership Changes

The Paxos algorithm (and most of its variants) assumes a static membership on the acceptors. In Cheap Paxos [14], a mechanism is provided to cope with configuration changes. However, it was reported in [5] that handling membership changes is not straightforward, although the details were not provided. Hence, in this section, we discuss the caveat in handling membership changes as reported in [17]

6.6.3.1 Rejoin and Replacement

Because processes fail over time, it is important to repair or replace replicas that have become faulty to ensure the long running of a fault tolerance system. As we have argued before, when a replica rejoins the system, it must first obtain the latest state of the system before it can participate in the Paxos algorithm again. This mechanism negates the need of logging Paxos-related information (promises and votes, etc.) on persistent storage. As reported in Chubby [5], local hard drives cannot be used as true persistent storage and hence, a rejoining replica is not allowed to immediately take part in the Paxos algorithm. A replacement replica would assume the replica id of the replaced one, and it joins the system by first requesting a state transfer, exactly the same as a rejoining replica.

6.6.3.2 Membership Expansion

When expanding the membership, two replicas should be added at a time. Assuming the current membership consists of $2f + 1$ replicas, after adding the two replicas, the new membership would be able to tolerate $f + 1$ faulty replicas, thereby, increasing the failure resiliency of the system. To join the system, a replica multicasts a join request to all existing members of the system. The join request is totally ordered with respect to all other application requests. The execution of the join request is a membership change.

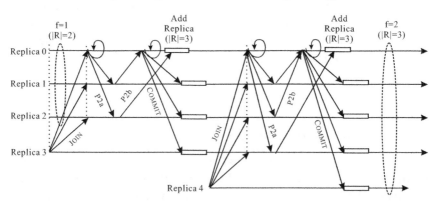

Figure 6.15 Expansion of the membership by adding two replicas in method 1.

Care must be taken on adding the first of the replicas. There can be two alternative approaches:

1. Immediately change the quorum size from $f + 1$ to $f + 2$ after adding the first replica to the system, as shown in Figure 6.15. Note that the bigger quorum does not mean higher failure resiliency at this stage because the system can only tolerate f faulty replicas. The bigger quorum ($f + 2$) must be used when adding the second replica. Not enlarging the quorum size might result in two different values be chosen.

2. As shown in Figure 6.16, after the first replica is added to the system, it is not allowed to participate in any Paxos instance until the second replica is also added. At this stage, the new member is only marked. The quorum size remains to be $f + 1$ after the first replica is added. Only original group of replicas participate in the Paxos instance to add the second replica into the system. Immediately after the second replica is added, the quorum is changed to $f + 2$.

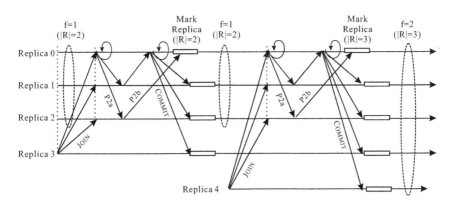

Figure 6.16   Expansion of the membership by adding two replicas in method 2.

6.6.3.3   Membership Reduction

Similar to membership expansion, if the replication degree is to be reduced, two replicas must be removed from the membership at a time. To leave the current membership, a replica multicast a leave request to all other members and the leave request is totally ordered with respect to all other requests.

Membership reduction is more subtle than membership expansion due to the fact that other replicas might become faulty in due course. For example, if after the decision of reducing the membership size is made, another replica becomes faulty, the system should remove only one more replica from the system. If on the other hand, two replicas become faulty, no other replicas should be removed from the membership. This observation calls for the following conservative approach in removing replicas.

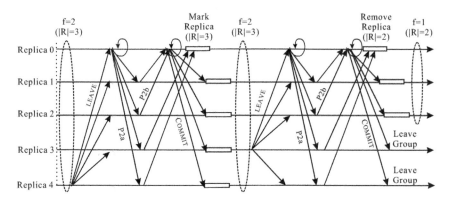

Figure 6.17   Reduction of the membership by removing two replicas one after another.

As shown in Figure 6.17, when a leave request is executed, the replica is only marked for removal and the quorum size is not changed. That replica should continue participating the Paxos algorithm as usual. Only when the second leave request is executed, do both replicas be removed from the membership, and the quorum size is reduced by one. If before the second leave request is executed, another replica becomes faulty, the faulty replica together with the first marked replica are removed. Furthermore, the system administrator is alerted regarding the failure. If two other replicas become faulty, the originally marked replica is unmarked and again, the system administrator is alerted.

If the replica that issued the leave request is the primary, a planned view change would take place when the leave request is executed. Because it is the primary that initiates the view change, the current primary can pass on its latest status to the new primary without engaging a round message exchange. The new view can be installed immediately after the new primary is informed of the need for the new view.

The above discussion assumes that replicas themselves initiate the leave process. As an alternative, a system administrator could issue one request to remove two replicas at the same time, in which case, both replicas are removed after the request is totally ordered and executed.

6.6.4   Limited Disk Space for Logging

The Paxos algorithm did not provide any mechanism to truncate the logs. Because each acceptor must log its promises it has made and votes it has casted, the log might eventually saturate the disk without an appropriate log truncation mechanism. In Chubby, each replica periodically takes a snapshot (*i.e.*, a checkpoint) of the application state and when the snapshot is fully recorded on local disk, the logged entries prior to the snapshot are truncated. The following mechanism is used so that the application layer and the fault tolerance framework layer are in sync when taking a snapshot:

- A snapshot handle is used to record the Paxos-specific information regarding a snapshot. Hence, the snapshot handle is always stored together with the actual snapshot.
- The application must first request a snapshot handle from the fault tolerance framework layer prior to taking a snapshot.
- While the application is taking a snapshot, the system does not stop processing new requests. To accomplish this, Chubby uses a shadow data structure to track the changes to the application's state to ensure the state recorded in the application snapshot corresponds to the framework state as reflected in the snapshot handle.
- When the application finishes taking a snapshot, it informs the framework layer, using the snapshot handler as the identifier for the snapshot. The framework layer then can truncate the log according to the information contained in the handler.

The truncation of logs could lead to the inability for a replica to supply a log entry for a slow replica, in which case, the slow replica must recover via a state transfer by using the latest snapshot of another replica in the leading quorum, as we have described in Section 6.3.1. After applying the snapshot, the slow replica must also obtain all entries logged since that the snapshot. If another snapshot is taken and the log is truncated accordingly while the slow replica is applying the snapshot, it would have to request a new state transfer.

REFERENCES

1. Y. Amir and J. Kirsch. Paxos for system builders: An overview. In *Proceedings of the Workshop on Large-Scale Distributed Systems and Middleware*, Yorktown, NY, September 2008.

2. W. J. Bolosky, D. Bradshaw, R. B. Haagens, N. P. Kusters, and P. Li. Paxos replicated state machines as the basis of a high-performance data store. In *Proceedings of the 8th USENIX Symposium on Networked Systems Design and Implementation*, 2011.

3. M. Burrows. The chubby lock service for loosely-coupled distributed systems. In *Proceedings of the 7th symposium on Operating systems design and implementation*, OSDI '06, pages 335–350, Berkeley, CA, USA, 2006. USENIX Association.

4. M. Castro and B. Liskov. Practical byzantine fault tolerance and proactive recovery. *ACM Transactions on Computer Systems*, 20(4):398–461, 2002.

5. T. D. Chandra, R. Griesemer, and J. Redstone. Paxos made live: an engineering perspective. In *Proceedings of the twenty-sixth annual ACM symposium on Principles of distributed computing*, PODC '07, pages 398–407, New York, NY, USA, 2007. ACM.

6. M. J. Fischer, N. A. Lynch, and M. S. Paterson. Impossibility of distributed consensus with one faulty process. *J. ACM*, 32(2):374–382, Apr. 1985.

7. C. Gray and D. Cheriton. Leases: an efficient fault-tolerant mechanism for distributed file cache consistency. In *Proceedings of the twelfth ACM symposium on Operating systems principles*, SOSP '89, pages 202–210, New York, NY, USA, 1989. ACM.

8. Z. Guo, C. Hong, M. Yang, D. Zhou, L. Zhou, and L. Zhuang. Paxos made parallel. Technical report, Microsoft Research, 2012.

9. F. Junqueira, Y. Mao, and K. Marzullo. Classic paxos vs. fast paxos: caveat emptor. In *Proceedings of the 3rd workshop on on Hot Topics in System Dependability*, HotDep'07, Berkeley, CA, USA, 2007. USENIX Association.

10. L. Lamport. Paxos made simple. *ACM SIGACT News (Distributed Computing Column)*, 32(4):18–25, December 2001.

11. L. Lamport. Generalized consensus and paxos. Technical report, Microsoft Research, March 2005.

12. L. Lamport. Fast paxos. *Distributed Computing*, 19(2):79–193, 2006.

13. L. Lamport, D. Malkhi, and L. Zhou. Vertical paxos and primary-backup replication. In *Proceedings of the 28th ACM symposium on Principles of distributed computing*, PODC '09, pages 312–313, New York, NY, USA, 2009. ACM.

14. L. Lamport and M. Massa. Cheap paxos. In *Proceedings of the 2004 International Conference on Dependable Systems and Networks*, DSN '04, pages 307–314, Washington, DC, USA, 2004. IEEE Computer Society.

15. G. M. D. Vieira and L. E. Buzato. On the coordinator's rule for fast paxos. *Inf. Process. Lett.*, 107(5):183–187, Aug. 2008.

16. W. Zhao. A lightweight fault tolerance framework for web services. In *Proceedings of the IEEE/WIC/ACM International Conference on Web Intelligence, WI '07*, pages 542–548, Washington, DC, USA, 2007. IEEE Computer Society.

17. W. Zhao, H. Zhang, and H. Chai. A lightweight fault tolerance framework for web services. *Web Intelligence and Agent Systems*, 7:255–268, 2009.

7

Byzantine Fault Tolerance

The fault tolerance approaches we have discussed in previous chapters all adopt a non-malicious fault model. In many cases, tolerating non-malicious faults, such as those caused by power outages and node failures, are sufficient for the dependability required for a system. However, it is reasonable to expect an increasing demand for systems that can tolerate both non-malicious faults as well as malicious faults for two reasons:

- Our dependency on services provided via distributed systems (often referred to as cloud services, Web services, or Internet services) has increased to the extent that such services have become essential necessities of our everyday life.
- Unfortunately, cyber attacks and cyber espionage activities have also been increasing rapidly and they may inject malicious faults into a system which may disrupt the services in a number of ways:
  - Denial of service. Some or all clients are prevented from accessing the service.

- Compromise the integrity of the service. A client's request might not be executed as it should be and the response generated might not be correct.
- The leak of confidential information (either confidential to the client, or confidential to the business owner).

An arbitrary (encompassing both malicious and non-malicious) fault is often referred to as a Byzantine fault. The term Byzantine fault is first coined in [26] by Lamport *et al.* It highlights the following specific malicious faulty behavior:

- A faulty process might disseminate conflicting information to other processes. For example, a Byzantine faulty client might send different requests to different server replicas, and a faulty primary replica might propose different orders for a request to other replicas.

Because a Byzantine faulty process can choose to behave as a non-malicious fault such as a crash fault, we can refer an arbitrary fault as a Byzantine fault. In the presence of Byzantine faults, the problem of reaching a consensus by a group of processes is referred to as Byzantine agreement [26].

Byzantine agreement and Byzantine fault tolerance have been studied over the past three decades [26, 25, 5, 6]. Early generations of algorithms for reaching Byzantine agreement and Byzantine fault tolerance are very expensive in that they incur prohibitively high runtime overhead. In 1999, Castro and Liskov published a seminal paper on a practical Byzantine fault tolerance (PBFT) algorithm [5]. PBFT significantly reduced the runtime overhead during normal operation (when the primary is not faulty). Their work revitalized this research area and we have seen (at least) hundreds of papers published subsequently.

7.1   The Byzantine Generals Problem

In [26], Lamport *et al.* pointed out the need to cope with faulty components that disseminate inconsistent information to different parts of the system. For example, in a distributed system that requires periodic clock synchronization, one of the processes, process k, is faulty in the following ways:

- When process i queries k for the current time at local time 2:40pm, process k reports 2:50pm.

- Concurrently process j queries k at local time 2:30pm, process k reports 2:20pm.

If process i and process j were to adjust their local clocks based on the information provided by the faulty process k, their clocks would diverge even further (*e.g.*, 2:45pm for process i and 2:25pm for process j).

7.1.1 System Model

The distributed consensus problem in the presence of this type of faults is framed as a Byzantine generals problem in which a group of generals of the Byzantine army encircles an enemy city and decides whether to attack the city together or withdraw. One or more generals may be traitors. The only way for the Byzantine army to win the battle and conquer the enemy city is for all the loyal generals and their troops attack the enemy city together. Otherwise, the army would lose.

The generals communicate with each other by using messengers. The messengers are trustworthy in that they will deliver a command issued by a general in a timely manner and without any alteration. In a computer system, each general is modeled as a process, and the processes communicate via plain messages that satisfy the following requirements:

- A message sent is delivered reliably and promptly.
- The message carries the identifier of its sender and the identifier cannot be forged or altered by the network or any other processes.
- A process can detect the missing of a message that is supposed to be sent by another process.

To tolerate f number of traitorous generals, $3f + 1$ total generals are needed, one of which is a commander, and the remaining generals are lieutenants. The commander observes the enemy city and makes a decision regarding whether to attack or retreat. To make the problem and its solution more general, we expand the scope of the command issued by the commander process to contain an arbitrary value proposed by the commander (*i.e.*, the value is not restricted to attack or retreat). A solution of the Byzantine generals problem should ensure the following interactive consistency requirements:

IC1 All non-faulty processes (*i.e.*, loyal generals) agree on the same value (*i.e.*, decision).

IC2 If the commander process is not faulty, then the value proposed by the commander must be the value that has been agreed upon by non-faulty processes.

Intuitively, a solution to the Byzantine generals problem would contain the following steps:

- The commander issues a command to all its lieutenants.
- The lieutenants exchange the commands they have received with each other.
- Each lieutenant applies a deterministic function, such as the majority function, on the commands it has collected to derive a final decision.

A big concern for the solution is that the set of commands collected by different loyal generals might not be the same for two reasons:

- The commander may send different commands to different lieutenants.
- A traitorous general might lie about the command it has received from the commander.

A solution to the Byzantine generals problem must ensure that the set of commands received by loyal lieutenants be the same. Apparently the total number of generals needed to tolerate f traitorous generals has to be greater than $2f+1$ because a lieutenant could not know which decision is the right one if f commands are "Attack" and the other f commands it has collected are "Retreat". Defaulting to "Retreat" or "Attack" in this case might result in loyal generals making different decisions, as shown in the following example.

◘ EXAMPLE 7.1

Assume that there are three generals, G0, G1, and G2, and one of them might be traitorous. We consider two scenarios. In the first scenario, lieutenant 2, G2, is traitorous, and in the second scenario, the commander, G0, is a traitor. As shown in Figure 7.1, in the first scenario, the commander issues an "Attack" command to both lieutenants (G1 and G2), but the traitorous lieutenant (G2) (circled in Figure 7.1) tells lieutenant 1 (G1) that the command it has received from the commander (G0) is "Retreat". In the second scenario, the commander (G0) issues an "Attack" to lieutenant 1 (G1), but a "Retreat" command to lieutenant 2 (G2). The two lieutenants (G1 and G2) inform each other the commands they have received.

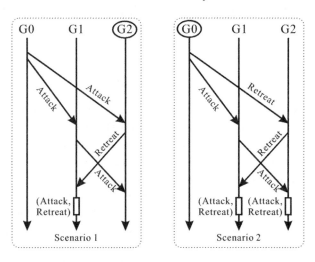

Figure 7.1   Two scenarios that highlight why it is impossible to use 3 generals to solve the Byzantine generals problem.

In both scenarios, lieutenant 1 (G1) receives two conflicting commands. If a lieutenant defaults to "Retreat" in case of receiving conflicting commands, the final decision would happen to be consistent among loyal generals (G1 and G2) in scenario 2 because lieutenant 2 (G2) would also decide to retreat. However, in scenario 1, lieutenant 1 (G1) would decide to retreat, which is different from the command issued by the loyal commander, thereby violating the interactive consistency requirement.

Note that from the scenarios shown in Figure 7.1, it may appear that if all loyal lieutenants default to "Attack" in case of receiving conflicting commands, both G1 and G2 would reach consistent decision in scenario 2, and G1 would also reach a consistent decision (*i.e.*, "Attack") with the commander G0. Unfortunately, defaulting to "Attack" will not work if the loyal commander G0 issues a "Retreat" command instead of "Attack".

As shown in the above example, it is impossible to ensure that loyal generals reach the same decision if there are only 3 generals total and one of them might be traitorous. This observation can be generalized for the case when more than one general is traitorous. Let f be the number of traitorous generals we want to tolerate. By having each general in the 3-general example simulate f generals, it is easy to see that there is no solution if we use only $3f$ total number of generals. Therefore, the optimal number of generals needed to tolerate f traitorous generals is $3f + 1$.

7.1.2   The Oral Message Algorithms

A solution to the Byzantine generals problem is the Oral Message algorithms [26]. The oral message algorithms are defined inductively. The solution starts by running an instance of the Oral Message algorithms $OM(f)$ with n generals, where f is the number of traitors tolerated, and $n \geq 3f + 1$. One of the generals is designated as the commander and the remaining generals are lieutenants. Each general is assigned an integer id, with the commander assigned 0, and the lieutenants assigned $1,...,n-1$, respectively.

$OM(f)$ would trigger $n-1$ instances of the $OM(f-1)$ algorithm (one per lieutenant), and each instance of the $OM(f-1)$ algorithm involves $n-1$ generals (i.e., all the lieutenants). Each instance of $OM(f-1)$ would in turn triggers $n-2$ instances of the $OM(f-2)$ algorithm (each involves $n-2$ generals), until the base case $OM(0)$ is reached (each $OM(0)$ instance involves $n-f$ generals).

Because of the recursive nature of the Oral Message algorithms, a lieutenant for $OM(f)$ would serve as the commander for $OM(f-1)$, and so on. Each lieutenant i uses a scalar variable v_i to store the decision value received from the commander, where i is an integer ranges from 1 to $n-1$. Furthermore, a lieutenant also uses a variable v_j to store the value received from lieutenant j $(j \neq i)$.

Algorithm $OM(0)$:

1. The commander multicasts a message containing a decision (for wider applicability of the solution, the decision could be any value) to all the lieutenants in the current instance of the algorithm.
2. For each i, lieutenant i set v_i to the value received from the commander. If it does not receive any value from the

commander, it defaults to a predefined decision (such as "retreat").

Algorithm $OM(f)$:

1. The commander multicasts a decision to all the lieutenants in the current instance of the algorithm.
2. For each i, lieutenant i sets v_i to the value received from the commander. If it does not receive any value from the commander, it defaults to a predefined decision. Subsequently, lieutenant i launches an instance of the $OM(f - 1)$ algorithm by acting as the commander for $OM(f-1)$. The $n-1$ generals involved in the instance of the OM(f-1) algorithm consists of all lieutenants in the OM(f,n) instance.
3. For each i and $j \neq i$, lieutenant i sets v_j to the value received from lieutenant $j \neq i$ in step (2). If it does not receive any value from lieutenant j, it sets v_j to the predefined default value. When all instances of the $OM(f - 1)$ algorithm have been completed, lieutenant i chooses the value returned by the majority function on the set $[v_1, ..., v_{n-1}]$.

Before further discussion on the OM algorithms, we need to define a notation for the messages in the algorithms. Due to the recursive nature of the OM algorithms, a general may receive multiple messages that belong to different recursion levels. To distinguish these messages and to identify the recession level in which a message belongs, we denote a message received at a lieutenant i at recursion level k as $M_i^{s0,...,sk}$, where k ranges from 0 to f, and $s0, ..., sk$ records the hierarchy of the set of OM algorithms from recursion level 0 to the level k, *i.e.*, the commander $s0$ initiates the $OM(f)$ algorithm, lieutenant $s1$ then invokes an instance of the $OM(f - 1)$ algorithm upon receiving the message sent by the commander, and at the lowest recursion level lieutenant sk invokes an instance of the $OM(f - k)$ algorithm. We may also denote the receiver id because a traitorous general might send conflicting messages to different lieutenants.

■ **EXAMPLE 7.2**

In this example, we show how the Oral Message algorithms work with $f = 1$ and $n = 4$. The basic steps and the message flow of the $OM(1)$ algorithms are shown in Figure 7.2. In the first step, the commander, G0, multicasts a message to the three lieutenants, G1, G2, and G3. In step 2, upon receiving a message M_i^0 from the commander, lieutenant i invokes an instance of the $OM(0)$ algorithm and multicasts a message M^{0i} to all other lieutenants. Because there are 3 lieutenants, three instances of the $OM(0)$ algorithm are launched.

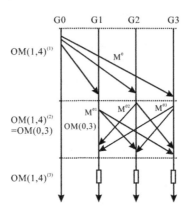

Figure 7.2 The message flow and the basic steps of the $OM(1)$ algorithms.

In step 3, each lieutenant calculates the final decision based on the three messages it has received, one message from the commander in $OM(1)$, and two messages in the two instances of the $OM(0)$ algorithm. More specifically, lieutenant 1 (G1) receives M_1^0, M_1^{02}, M_1^{03}, lieutenant 2 (G2) receives M_2^0, M_1^{01}, M_1^{03}, and lieutenant 3 (G3) receives M_3^0, M_3^{01}, M_3^{02}.

We consider two cases. In the first case, G0 is a traitor and it sends different values to the three lieutenants, *i.e.*, $M_1^0 = x$, $M_2^0 = y$, $M_3^0 = z$, where $x \neq y \neq z$. All three lieutenants are loyal, hence, $M_2^{01} = M_3^{01} = x$, $M_1^{02} = M_3^{02} = y$, and $M_1^{03} = M_2^{03} = z$. Therefore, G1's decision is $majority(x, y, z)$, G2's decision is also $majority(x, y, z)$, and the same is true for G3. G1, G2, and G3 all uses the predefined default decision.

In the second case, let G1 be the traitor (G0 then must be loyal) and the messages it sends to G2 and G3 contain different values (x and y). Hence, $M_1^0 = M_2^0 = M_3^0 = v$, $M_2^{01} = x$, $M_3^{01} = y$, $M_1^{02} = M_3^{02} = v$, and $M_1^{03} = M_2^{03} = v$. Therefore, G2's decision is $majority(x, v, v) = v$, and G3's decision is $majority(x, v, v) = v$.

	Messages Collected	Case 1: G0 Traitor	Case 2: G1 Traitor
G1	M_1^0, M_1^{02}, M_1^{03}	$majority(x, y, z)$="Retreat"	n/a
G2	M_2^{01}, M_2^0, M_2^{03}	$majority(x, y, z)$="Retreat"	$majority(x, v, v) = v$
G3	M_3^{01}, M_3^{02}, M_3^0	$majority(x, y, z)$="Retreat"	$majority(y, v, v) = v$

Table 7.1   Messages received and final decisions in two cases for OM(1,4).

For clarity, the results for these two cases are summarized in Table 7.1.

As can be seen in Example 7.2, the algorithm descriptions for the OM algorithms are very clear when applied to the $f = 1$ case. It is apparent that the step (3) in the $OM(f)$ algorithm is expressed implicitly for $f = 1$ (for only two levels of recursion). If 3 or more recursion levels are involved (*i.e.*, $f \geq 2$), the rules outlined for step (3) have the following two issues:

1. A lieutenant i would receive more than one message from each $j \neq i$ in step (2). In fact, for an integer k between 1 and f inclusive, there will be $(n - 1) \cdots (n - k)$ instances of the $OM(m - k)$ algorithm executed. Hence, there will be $1 + (\sum_{k=2}^{f} (n - 1) \cdots (n - k + 1) - 1)$ such messages for each j. It is vague as to exactly which value lieutenant i should set for v_j.

2. For an intermediate instance of the algorithm, $OM(f - k)$, where $1 \leq k < f$, it is unclear what it means by choosing a decision based on the majority function, and especially what the implication is for this operation on the enclosing instance of the OM algorithm.

We can augment the rules for step (3) in the following ways:

- We start by proposing a fix to issue 2. At lieutenant i, in step (3) of the $OM(f - k)$ instance started by lieutenant $j \neq i$, v_j is set to the value returned by the majority function. This is what means by choosing the decision stated in the original rule.
- Except for $OM(1)$ and $OM(0)$, a lieutenant only sets the v variable corresponding to itself based on the message received from its commander (there is only one such

message). For the v variables corresponding to other lieutenants, a lieutenant uses the values set in step (3) of the
immediate lower level recursion instance it has started.

To illustrate how the augmented rules for step (3) works,
consider the following example with $f = 2$.

■ EXAMPLE 7.3

In this example, we show how the $OM(2)$ algorithm works
with 7 generals. The basic steps are highlighted in Figure 7.3.
As can be seen, $OM(2)$ will trigger three levels of recursion,
from $OM(2)$ to 6 instances of $OM(1)$, and $6 \times 5 = 30$ instances
of $OM(0)$ (to avoid cluttering, we only included 6 instances of
$OM(0)$ in Figure 7.3).

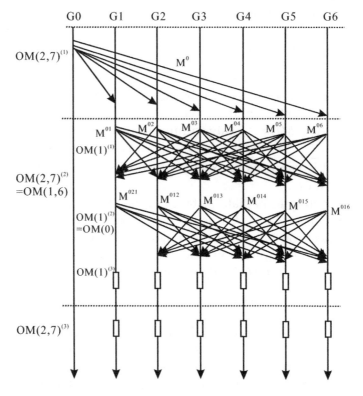

Figure 7.3   The message flow and the basic steps of the $OM(2)$ algorithms.

At the end of step (2) of the $OM(1)$ instance that is started by
lieutenant i, a lieutenant $j \neq i$ receives 4 messages sent in the

$OM(0)$ instances invoked by this $OM(1)$ instance (one for each other lieutenant that participates in this instance of $OM(1)$), and one message sent by lieutenant i in $OM(1)$. Lieutenant j then sets its variables according to the messages received. In step (3) of the $OM(1)$ instance, because this is an intermediate OM instance, instead of choosing a value by applying the majority function on the set of v variables (doing so would make no sense), lieutenant j sets v_i to the value returned by the majority function.

Because there are 6 instances of $OM(1)$, all the v variables at a lieutenant j except v_j would have been reset once all these $OM(1)$ instances have been completed. As shown in Figure 7.3, step (3) of $OM(2)$ will be executed next. In this step, the reset v variables will be used to calculate the majority value for the final decision. To differentiate different instances of the $OM(1, 6)$ algorithm, we use Gi-$OM(1)$ to refer to the $OM(1)$ instance launched by lieutenant i. In the following, we consider two cases: (1) G0 and G6 are traitors, and (2) G5 and G6 are traitors:

- In case (1), we assume that:
  - G0 sends a value x to G1, G2, and G3, and a different value y to G4, G5, and G6 in $OM(2)$.
  - In G6-$OM(1)$, we assume that G6 sends $s1$ to G1, $s2$ to G2, $s3$ to G3, $s4$ to G4, and $s5$ to G5, i.e., $M_1^{06} = s1, M_2^{06} = s2, M_3^{06} = s3, M_4^{06} = s4, M_5^{06} = s5$.
  - Because G1, G2, G3, G4, and G5 are loyal, $M^{061} = s1$, $M^{062} = s2, M^{063} = s3, M^{064} = s4, M^{065} = s5$, for all receivers.

- In case (2), we assume that:
  - G0 sends a value v to all lieutenants $OM(2)$.
  - G5 (a traitor) sends $t1, t2, t3, t4, t6$ to G1, G2, G3, G4, and G6 respectively, i.e., $M_1^{05} = t1, M_2^{05} = t2, M_3^{05} = t3, M_4^{06} = t4, M_6^{06} = t6$.
  - G6 (a traitor) sends $u1, u2, u3, u4, u5$ to G1, G2, G3, G4, and G5 respectively, i.e., $M_1^{06} = u1, M_2^{06} = u2, M_3^{06} = u3, M_4^{06} = u4, M_5^{06} = u5$.
  - Because G1, G2, G3, and G4 are loyal, $M^{051} = t1, M^{052} = t2, M^{053} = t3, M^{054} = t4, M^{061} = u1, M^{062} = u2, M^{063} = u3, M^{064} = u4$, for all receivers.

G1	Msgs Collected	Case 1: G0 and G6 are traitors	Case 2: G5 and G6 are traitors
G2-$OM(1)$	$M^{02}, M^{023}, M^{024},$ M^{025}, M^{026}	$m(x,x,x,x,?) = x$	$m(v,v,v,?,?) = v$
G3-$OM(1)$	$M^{03}, M^{032}, M^{034},$ M^{035}, M^{036}	$m(x,x,x,x,?) = x$	$m(v,v,v,?,?) = v$
G4-$OM(1)$	$M^{04}, M^{042}, M^{043},$ M^{045}, M^{046}	$m(y,y,y,y,?) = y$	$m(v,v,v,?,?) = v$
G5-$OM(1)$	$M^{05}, M^{052}, M^{053},$ M^{054}, M^{056}	$m(y,y,y,y,?) = y$	$m(t1,t2,t3,t4,?)$
G6-$OM(1)$	$M^{06}, M^{062}, M^{063},$ M^{064}, M^{065}	$m(s1,s2,s3,s4,s5) = s$	$m(u1,u2,u3,u4,?)$

Table 7.2   Messages received and step (3) calculation in two cases for instances of $OM(1)$ at G1.

The messages received and the calculations performed in step (3) of $OM(1)$ are provided in 5 separated tables for G1, G2, G3, G4, and G5 (from Table 7.2 to Table 7.6). The table for G6 is omitted because we assume G6 is a traitor in both cases. Because each table is for a specific lieutenant, we omit the receiver subscript in the messages received. To limit the size of the table, we use $m()$ to refer the majority function.

In the tables, a question mark (?) is used to represent an arbitrary value sent by a traitorous lieutenant that is not important for the final outcome. As can be seen, this value is filtered out by the majority function for all $OM(1)$ instances except the OM instances started by the traitorous lieutenant.

Note that for G6-$OM(1)$, despite the fact that G6 (acting as the commander) is a traitor, all loyal lieutenants still agree on the same set of values,

i.e., $majority(s1, s2, s3, s4, s5)$. We denote this value as s.

We explain the calculations shown in Table 7.2 in detail. The calculations shown in the other 4 tables are straightforward once Table 7.2 is understood. In case 1, G0 sends G1, G2, and G3 a value x, but sends G4, and G5 a value y in $OM(2)$. However, in the $OM(0)$ instance started by a loyal lieutenant i upon receiving a message M_i^{0j} from lieutenant $j \neq i$, lieutenant i multicasts the value contained in M_i^{0j} instead of M^0 received from G0.

G2	Messages Collected	Case 1: G0 and G6 are traitors	Case 2: G5 and G6 are traitors
G1-$OM(1)$	$M^{01}, M^{013}, M^{014},$ M^{015}, M^{016}	$m(x, x, x, x, ?) = x$	$m(v, v, v, ?, ?) = v$
G3-$OM(1)$	$M^{03}, M^{031}, M^{034},$ M^{035}, M^{036}	$m(x, x, x, x, ?) = x$	$m(v, v, v, ?, ?) = v$
G4-$OM(1)$	$M^{04}, M^{041}, M^{043},$ M^{045}, M^{046}	$m(y, y, y, y, ?) = y$	$m(v, v, v, ?, ?) = v$
G5-$OM(1)$	$M^{05}, M^{051}, M^{053},$ M^{054}, M^{056}	$m(y, y, y, y, ?) = y$	$m(t2, t1, t3, t4, ?)$
G6-$OM(1)$	$M^{06}, M^{061}, M^{063},$ M^{064}, M^{065}	$m(s2, s1, s3, s4, s5) = s$	$m(u2, u1, u3, u4, ?)$

Table 7.3 Messages received and step (3) calculation in two cases for instances of $OM(1)$ at G2.

For example, G1 multicasts a message containing y instead of x in the G4-$OM(1)$ instance, and the G5-$OM(1)$ instance. Similarly, G4 multicasts a message containing x instead of y in the G2-$OM(1)$ instance, and the G3-$OM(1)$ instance.

In step (3) of the G2-$OM(1)$ instance, G1 overrides the v variable for G2, v_2, using the value returned by the majority function on the messages it has collected, i.e., $v_2 = majority(x, x, x, x, ?) = x$. Note that the previous value for v_2 happens to be x as well because G2 is loyal. However, the step is still necessary because G1 does not know whether or not G2 is a traitor in advance.

Similarly, G1 resets the v variables for G3, G4, G5, and G6 to the values returned by the corresponding $OM(1)$ instances:

- $v_3 = majority(x, x, x, x, ?) = x$.
- $v_4 = majority(y, y, y, y, ?) = y$.
- $v_5 = majority(y, y, y, y, ?) = y$.
- $v_6 = majority(s1, s2, s3, s4, s5) = s$. Note that previously, $v_6 = s1$.

Once all instances of $OM(1)$ have completed, step (3) of $OM(2)$ is carried out at each lieutenant. The calculations for this step at G1, G2, G3, G4, and G5 are summarized in Table 7.7. As can be seen in Table 7.7, all loyal lieutenants reach the same decision. In case 1, the decision is $majority(x, x, x, y, y, s)$, and

G3	Msgs Collected	Case 1: G0 and G6 are traitors	Case 2: G5 and G6 are traitors
G1-$OM(1)$	$M^{01}, M^{012}, M^{014},$ M^{015}, M^{016}	$m(x,x,x,x,?) = x$	$m(v,v,v,?,?) = v$
G2-$OM(1)$	$M^{02}, M^{021}, M^{024},$ M^{025}, M^{026}	$m(x,x,x,x,?) = x$	$m(v,v,v,?,?) = v$
G4-$OM(1)$	$M^{04}, M^{041}, M^{042},$ M^{045}, M^{046}	$m(y,y,y,y,?) = y$	$m(v,v,v,?,?) = v$
G5-$OM(1)$	$M^{05}, M^{051}, M^{052},$ M^{054}, M^{056}	$m(y,y,y,y,?) = y$	$m(t3,t1,t2,t4,?)$
G6-$OM(1)$	$M^{06}, M^{061}, M^{062},$ M^{064}, M^{065}	$m(s3,s1,s2,s4,s5) = s$	$m(u3,u1,u2,u4,?)$

Table 7.4   Messages received and step (3) calculation in two cases for instances of $OM(1)$ at G3.

G4	Msgs Collected	Case 1: G0 and G6 are traitors	Case 2: G5 and G6 are traitors
G1-$OM(1)$	$M^{01}, M^{012}, M^{013},$ M^{015}, M^{016}	$m(x,x,x,x,?) = x$	$m(v,v,v,?,?) = v$
G2-$OM(1)$	$M^{02}, M^{021}, M^{024},$ M^{025}, M^{026}	$m(x,x,x,x,?) = x$	$m(v,v,v,?,?) = v$
G3-$OM(1)$	$M^{03}, M^{031}, M^{032},$ M^{035}, M^{036}	$m(x,x,x,x,?) = x$	$m(v,v,v,?,?) = v$
G5-$OM(1)$	$M^{05}, M^{051}, M^{052},$ M^{053}, M^{056}	$m(y,y,y,y,?) = y$	$m(t4,t1,t2,t3,?)$
G6-$OM(1)$	$M^{06}, M^{061}, M^{062},$ M^{063}, M^{065}	$m(s4,s1,s2,s3,s5) = s$	$m(u4,u1,u2,u3,?)$

Table 7.5   Messages received and step (3) calculation in two cases for instances of $OM(1)$ at G4.

G5	Msgs Collected	Case 1: G0 and G6 are traitors	Case 2: G5 and G6 are traitors
G1-$OM(1)$	$M^{01}, M^{012}, M^{013}, M^{014}, M^{016}$	$m(x,x,x,x,?) = x$	n/a
G2-$OM(1)$	$M^{02}, M^{021}, M^{023}, M^{024}, M^{026}$	$m(x,x,x,x,?) = x$	n/a
G3-$OM(1)$	$M^{03}, M^{031}, M^{032}, M^{035}, M^{036}$	$m(x,x,x,x,?) = x$	n/a
G4-$OM(1)$	$M^{04}, M^{041}, M^{042}, M^{043}, M^{046}$	$m(y,y,y,y,?) = y$	n/a
G6-$OM(1)$	$M^{06}, M^{061}, M^{062}, M^{063}, M^{064}$	$m(s5, s1, s2, s3, s4) = s$	n/a

Table 7.6   Messages received and step (3) calculation in two cases for instances of $OM(1)$ at G5.

Lieutenant	Case 1: G0 and G6 are traitors	Case 2: G5 and G6 are traitors
G1	$m(x,x,x,y,y,s)$	$m(v,v,v,v,?,?) = v$
G2	$m(x,x,x,y,y,s)$	$m(v,v,v,v,?,?) = v$
G3	$m(x,x,x,y,y,s)$	$m(v,v,v,v,?,?) = v$
G4	$m(x,x,x,y,y,s)$	$m(v,v,v,v,?,?) = v$
G5	$m(x,x,x,y,y,s)$	n/a

Table 7.7   Final decision made at each lieutenant in step (3) of $OM(2)$.

in case 2, the decision is clearly v, the same value sent by the loyal commander G0.

Recall that the v variables for remote lieutenants have all been reset in step (3) of the $OM(1)$ instances at each lieutenant. In case 1, only the value for v_6 is changed to s for all loyal lieutenants.

In case 2, the new values for the v variables of loyal lieutenants remain the same because G0 is assumed loyal. The values for v_5 and v_6 may have changed. However, the values for v_5 and v_6 are not important in the final decision because the v variables for the four loyal lieutenants (G1, G2, G3, and G4) have the same value v.

7.1.3   Proof of Correctness for the Oral Message Algorithms

We first prove the following lemma.

Lemma 7.1 *For any f and $0 \le k \le f$, Algorithm $OM(k)$ satisfies the interactive consistency IC2 requirement provided that the total number of generals is greater than $3f$.*

Proof: The interactive consistency IC2 requirement is applicable to the case when the commander is loyal. It is easy to see that when $k = 0$, Algorithm $OM(0)$ satisfies the IC2 requirement (and therefore Lemma 7.1 is correct for $k = f$. Because all lieutenants in $OM(0)$ receive the same value from the loyal commander, all loyal lieutenants would use the same value sent by the commander.

Next, we prove that if the lemma is true for $k - 1, 1 \le k \le f$, then the lemma must be true for k. In the $OM(k)$ instance, there are $n - (f - k) - 1$ lieutenants. Because the commander for $OM(k)$ is loyal, it sends the same value v to all these lieutenants in the instance. Each loyal lieutenant then executes an $OM(k-1)$ instance involving $n - (f - k) - 2$ lieutenants. Per the induction hypothesis, the commander and all loyal lieutenants in an $OM(k - 1)$ instance agree on the same value sent by the commander, which means that given a loyal lieutenant i in $OM(k)$ that receives a value v, all its lieutenants must also agree on v. That is, at each such lieutenant j, its v variable for i is set to v ($v_i = v$) at the end of $OM(k - 1)$.

Next, we show that the majority of the lieutenants in $OM(k)$ is loyal. Because there are $n - (f - k) - 1$ lieutenants, $n > 3f$, and $k \ge 1$, we get $n - (f - k) - 1 > 3f - f + k - 1 \ge 2f$. This means that at each loyal lieutenant, the majority of its v variables have value v. Therefore, the value returned by the majority function on the set of v variables must be v in step (3). Hence, $OM(k)$ satisfies the IC2 requirement. This proves the lemma. ∎

Now, we prove the following theorem using the above lemma.

Theorem 7.1 *For any f, Algorithm $OM(f)$ satisfies the interactive consistency requirements IC1 and IC2 provided that the total number of generals is greater than $3f$.*

Proof: Similar to the proof of the Lemma 7.1, we prove the theorem by induction. If $f = 0$ (no traitor), it is trivial to see that $OM(0)$ satisfies IC1 and IC2. We assume that the theorem is correct for $f - 1$

and prove that it is correct for f ($f \geq 1$). There are only two cases: (1) the commander in $OM(f)$ is loyal, and (2) the commander is a traitor.

For case (1), we can prove that the theorem satisfies IC2 by applying Lemma 7.1 and set $k = f$. Because the commander is loyal, IC1 is automatically satisfied as well.

For case (2), since the commander is a traitor in $OM(f)$, at most $f - 1$ lieutenants are traitors. Furthermore, there are at least $3f - 1$ lieutenants in $OM(f)$, and each of these lieutenants would invokes an instance of the $OM(f-1)$ participated by all lieutenants. Because $3f - 1 > 3(f - 1)$, we can safely apply the induction hypothesis for $f - 1$ and apply the Lemma 7.1. Therefore, for all $OM(f - 1)$ instances launched by loyal lieutenants, they return the same value v_{loyal} in step (3) of $OM(f - 1)$. Because the majority of lieutenants are loyal ($3f - 1 - (f - 1) > f - 1$), the majority function on the set of v variables would return v_{loyal} as well in step (3) of $OM(f)$. Therefore, Algorithm $OM(f)$ satisfies IC1. Hence, the theorem is correct. ∎

7.2 Practical Byzantine Fault Tolerance

The Oral Message Algorithms solve the Byzantine consensus problem. Unfortunately the solution is not practical for primarily two reasons:

- The Oral Message Algorithms only work in a synchronous environment where there is a predefined bound on message delivery and processing, and the clocks of different processors are synchronized as well. Practical systems often exhibit some degree of asynchrony caused by resource contentions. The use of a synchronous model is especially a concern in the presence of malicious faults because an adversary could break the synchrony assumptions, for example, by launching a denial of service attack on a nonfaulty process to delay message delivery.
- Except for $f = 1$, the Oral Message Algorithms incur too much runtime overhead for reaching a Byzantine agreement.

More efficient Byzantine fault tolerance protocols, such as SecureRing [16] and Rampart [30], were developed and they were designed to operate in asynchronous distributed systems. However, they rely on the use of timeout-based unreliable fault detectors to remove suspected processes from the membership, as a way to overcome the impossibility result. Because the correctness of such protocol rely on the dynamic formation of membership, which in turn depends on the synchrony of the system. This is particularly dangerous in the presence malicious adversaries, as pointed out in [5].

In 1999, Castro and Liskov published a seminal paper on practical Byzantine fault tolerance (PBFT) [5] with an algorithm that is not only efficient, but does not depend on the synchrony for safety. The design of the PBFT algorithm is rather similar to that of the Paxos algorithm. Hence, the PBFT algorithm is sometimes referred to as Byzantine Paxos [23, 24].

7.2.1 System Model

The PBFT algorithm is designed to operate in an asynchronous distributed system connected by a network. Hence there is no bound on message delivery and processing time, and there is no requirement on clock synchronization. The PBFT algorithm tolerates Byzantine faults with certain restrictions and assumes that the faults happen independently.

To ensure fault independence in the presence of malicious faults, replicas must be made diverse. One way to satisfy this requirement is via the N-version programming where different versions of a program with the same specification are developed [1]. However, the disadvantage for N-version programming is the high cost of software development as well as maintenance. It is also possible to utilize existing software packages that offer similar functionalities to achieve diversified replication, such as file systems and database systems [7, 30]. This approach requires the use of wrappers to encapsulate the differences in the implementations. A more promising approach to achieving diversity is via program transformation [2, 3, 10, 11, 12, 16, 17, 19, 29, 32], for example, by randomizing the location of heap and stack memory [3, 16, 32].

To ensure that a replica can authenticate a message sent by another replica, cryptographic techniques are employed. In the PBFT algorithm description, we assume that each message is protected by a public-key digital signature. Later in this section, we discuss an optimization by replacing the digital signature, which is computationally expensive, with a message authentication code (MAC) [4]. The use of digital signatures or MACs also enables a replica to detect corrupted or altered messages.

The restrictions assumed for an adversary is that it has limited computation power so that it cannot break the cryptography techniques used to spoof a message (*i.e.*, to produce a valid digital signature of a nonfaulty replica). It is also assumed that an adversary cannot delay a message delivery at a nonfaulty replica indefinitely.

7.2.2   Overview of the PBFT Algorithm

The PBFT algorithm is used to implement state machine replication where a client issues a request to the replicated server and blocks waiting for the corresponding reply. To tolerate f faulty replicas, $3f + 1$ or more server replicas are needed. The PBFT algorithm has the following two properties:

- Safety. Requests received by the replicated server are executed atomically in a sequential total order. More specifically, all nonfaulty server replicas execute the requests in the same total order.
- Liveness. A client eventually receives the reply to its request provided that the message delivery delay does not grow faster than the time itself indefinitely.

The minimal number of replicas, $n = 3f + 1$, to tolerate f faulty replicas are optimal for any asynchronous system that ensures the safety and liveness properties. Because up to f replicas may be faulty and not respond, a replica must proceed to the next step once it has collected $n - f$ messages from different replicas. Among the $n - f$ messages, up to f of them might actually be sent by faulty replicas. To have any hope of reaching an agreement among the nonfaulty replicas, the number of messages from nonfaulty replicas must be greater than f (*i.e.*, among the $n - f$ messages collected, the number of messages from nonfaulty replicas must be the majority). Hence, $n - 2f > f$, which means the optimal number of replicas $n = 3f + 1$.

In the presence of faulty clients, the PBFT algorithm can only ensure the consistency of the state of nonfaulty replicas. Furthermore, the algorithm itself does not prevent the leaking of confidential information from the replicated server to an adversary.

We assume that the optimal number of replicas $n = 3f + 1$ are used, and each replica is referred to by an index number ranges from 0, 1, ..., up to $3f$. One of the replicas is designated as the primary, and the remaining ones are backups. The primary is responsible to assign a sequence number to each request received and initiates a new round of protocol to establish the total ordering of the request at all nonfaulty replicas. The sequence number binds a request to its total order relative to all other requests. Initially, the replica 0 assumes the primary role. When replica 0 is suspected as failed, replica 1 will be elected as the new primary. Each primary change is referred to as a view change and each view is identified by a view number v (from 0 to 1, and so on). Hence, for a view v, replica $p = v \bmod n$ would serve as the primary for that view.

The PBFT algorithm works in the following steps:

- A client multicasts a request to all server replicas. A request has the form $<\text{REQUEST}, o, t, c>_{\sigma_c}$, where o is the operation to be executed at the server replica, t is a timestamp, c is the identifier of the client, and σ_c is the client's digital signature for the request. The client must ensure that a later request bears a larger timestamp. The timestamp t is used by the replicas to detect duplicates. If a duplicate request is detected, the replica would return the logged reply to the client instead of reordering them.
- The server replicas exchange control messages to establish and agree on the total order for the request. The complexity of the PBFT algorithm lies in this step.
- The server replicas execute the request according to the total order established and send the corresponding reply to the client. A replica may have to delay the execution of the request until all requests that are ordered ahead of the request have been executed.
- The client would not accept a reply until it has collected consistent replies to its request from $f + 1$ server replicas. This is to ensure that at least one of them comes from a nonfaulty replica. A reply has the form $<\text{REPLY}, v, t, c, i, r>_{\sigma_i}$, where v is the current view number, t is the timestamp of the corresponding request, i is the replica identifier, and r is the application response as the result of the execution of the operation o. The client verifies consistency by comparing the r component in the reply message.

7.2.3   Normal Operation of PBFT

During normal operation, *i.e.*, when the primary is not faulty, the server replicas can establish and agree on the total order of each request in three phases (referred to as pre-prepare, prepare, and commit phases), as shown in Figure 7.4. PBFT also requires each replica to log both application messages (requests received and reply generated), and control messages that sent during the three phases to achieve Byzantine agreement on the total order of messages.

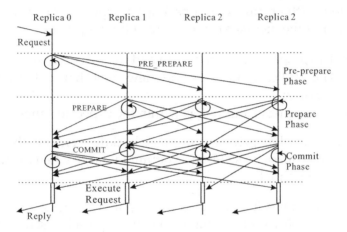

Figure 7.4   Normal operation of the PBFT algorithm.

During the first phase, *i.e.*, the pre-prepare phase, when the primary receives a new request m, it assigns the next available sequence number s to the request and multicasts a pre-prepare message to the backups. The pre-prepare message has the form $<\text{PRE-PREPARE}, v, s, d>_{\sigma_p}$, where d is the digest for the request m.

A backup verifies a pre-prepare message in the following way before it accepts the message:

- The pre-prepare message has a valid digital signature.
- The backup is in view v and it has not accepted a pre-prepare message with sequence number s.
- Furthermore, the sequence number is within the expected range bounded by a low water mark h and a high water mark H. This is to prevent a faulty primary to exhaust the address space of the sequence number (to avoid the sequence number wrap-around problem).

The backup would need to search its message log for the request associated with the pre-prepare message based on the received message digest. If no request is found, the backup should ask the primary to retransmit that request. On accepting a pre-prepare message, the backup logs the pre-prepare message, creates a prepare message, saves a copy of the prepare message in its message log, and starts the second phase (*i.e.*, the prepare phase) by multicasting the prepare message to all other replicas. The prepare message has the form $<\text{PREPARE}, v, s, d, i>_{\sigma_i}$, where i is the identifier of the sending backup.

A replica (the primary or a backup) accepts a prepare message and logs it if the message can pass the following checks:

- The prepare message has a valid digital signature.
- The replica is in the same view v as that in the prepare message.
- The sequence number is within the expected range.

A replica (the primary or the backup) enters the third (*i.e.*, commit) phase by sending a commit message when the following condition is met:

- The replica has collected $2f$ prepare messages from different replicas (including the one the replica has sent) and the matching pre-prepare message.

When this condition is met at replica i, it is said that $prepared(m, v, s, i)$ is true. The commit message has the form $<\text{COMMIT}, v, s, d, i>_{\sigma_i}$.

A replica verifies a commit message in the same way as for a prepare message. The replica accepts the commit message if the verification is successful and logs the message. When a replica i has sent a commit message and has collected $2f + 1$ commit messages (including the one it has sent) that match the pre-prepare message from different replicas, it is said that $committed\text{-}local(m, v, s, i)$ is true. If $prepared(m, v, s, i)$ is true for all replicas i in some set of $f+1$ nonfaulty replicas, it is said that the predicate $committed(m, v, s)$ is true. A replica i proceeds to execute the request m when $commit\text{-}local(m, v, s, i)$ becomes true and if it has already executed all message ordered before m (*i.e.*, requests that are assigned a smaller sequence number than s).

The PBFT algorithm ensures the following two invariance.

1. If the predicate $prepared(m, v, s, i)$ is true for a nonfaulty replica i, and the predicate $prepared(m', v, s, j)$ is true for another nonfaulty replica j, then $m = m'$.
2. If $committed\text{-}local(m, v, s, i)$ is true for a non-faulty replica i, then the predicate $committed(m, v, s)$ is true.

The first invariance shows that the first two phases (*i.e.*, pre-prepare and prepare) of the PBFT algorithm ensures that all nonfaulty replicas that can complete the two phases in the same view agree on the total order of the messages. The proof of this invariance is straightforward. Given any two nonfaulty replicas i and j, if $prepared(m, v, s, i)$ and $prepared(m', v, s, j)$ are true, then a set of $2f + 1$ replicas $R1$ must have voted for m (in the pre-prepare and prepare messages), and similarly, a set of $2f + 1$ replicas $R2$ must have voted m'. Because there are $3f + 1$ replicas, $R1$ and $R2$ must intersect in at least $f + 1$ replicas, and one of these $f + 1$ replicas is nonfaulty. This nonfaulty replica would have voted for two different messages for the same sequence number s, which is impossible.

It is easy to see why the second invariance is true. When $committed\text{-}local(m, v, s, i)$ is true for replica i, the replica i must have received the commit messages from $2f$ other replicas. This implies that the predicate $prepared(m, v, s, i)$ must be true for replica i, and $prepared(m, v, s, j)$ is true if all the $2f$ other replicas j. Because there are at most f faulty replicas, there must be at least $f + 1$ nonfaulty replicas among these $2f + 1$ replica, which means the predicate $committed(m, v, s)$ is true.

The second invariance together with the view change protocol guarantee that all nonfaulty replicas agree on the same total order for messages, even if they reach the *committed-local* state for the messages in different views.

7.2.4 Garbage Collection

Because PBFT requires that all messages are logged at each replica, the message log would grow indefinitely. This obviously is not practical. To limit the size of the message log, each replica periodically takes a checkpoint of its state (the application state as well as the fault tolerance infrastructure state) and informs other replicas about the checkpoint. If a replica learns that $2f + 1$ replicas (including itself) have taken a checkpoint and the checkpoints are consistent, the checkpoint becomes stable and all previously logged messages can be garbage collected. This mechanism ensures that the majority of nonfaulty replicas have advanced to the same state, and they can bring some other nonfaulty replica up to date if needed.

To ensure that all nonfaulty replicas take checkpoints at the same synchronization points, the best way is to predefine the checkpoint period in terms of a constant c, and each replica takes a checkpoint whenever it has executed a request with a sequence number that is multiple of c. A replica i multicasts a checkpoint message once it has taken a checkpoint. The checkpoint message has the form $<\text{CHECKPOINT}, s, d, i>_{\sigma_i}$, where s must be multiple of c, and d is the digest of the checkpoint. When a replica receives $2f + 1$ valid checkpoint messages for the same s with the same digest d, the set of $2f + 1$ messages become the proof that this checkpoint has become stable. The proof is logged together with the checkpoint, before the replica garbage-collects all logged messages that bear a sequence number less than or equal to s.

Previously we mentioned that each replica maintains a low and a high water marks to define the range of sequence numbers that may be accepted. The low watermark h is set to the sequence number of the most recent stable checkpoint. The range of acceptable sequence numbers is specified in a constant k so that the high watermark $H = h + k$. As suggested in [5], k is often set to be $2c$ (twice the checkpoint period).

A direct consequence of truncating the log after a stable checkpoint is that when a replica requests a retransmission for a request or a control message (such as pre-prepare), the message might have been garbage-collected. In this case, the most recent stable checkpoint is transferred to the replica that needs the missing message.

7.2.5   View Change

Because PBFT relies on the primary to initiate the 3-phase Byzantine agreement protocol on the total order of each request, a faulty primary could prevent any progress being made by simply not responding, or by sending conflicting control messages to backups. Hence, a faulty primary should be removed of the primary role and another replica would be elected as the new primary to ensure liveness of the system.

Because in an asynchronous system, a replica cannot tell a slow replica from a crashed one. It has to depend on a heuristic view-change timeout parameter to *suspect* the primary. A backup does this by starting a view-change timer whenever it receives a request. If the view-change timer expires before *committed-local* is true for a replica i in view v, the replica suspects the primary and initiates a view change by doing the following:

- The replica multicasts a view-change message to *all* replicas (including the suspected primary so that the primary can learn that it has been suspected).
- The replica stops participating operations in view v, *i.e.*, it would ignore all messages sent in view v except the checkpoint, view-change, and new-view messages.

The view-change message has the form $<$VIEW-CHANGE$, v + 1, s, C, P, i>_{\sigma_i}$, where s is the sequence number for the most recent stable checkpoint known to replica i, C is the proof for the stable checkpoint (*i.e.*, the $2f + 1$ checkpoint messages for the checkpoint with sequence number s), P is a set of prepared certificates, one for each sequence number $ss > s$ for which the predicate $prepared(m, v', ss, i)$ is true. Each prepared certificate contains a valid pre-prepare message for request m that is assigned a sequence number ss in view $v' \leq v$, and $2f$ matching valid prepare messages from different backups.

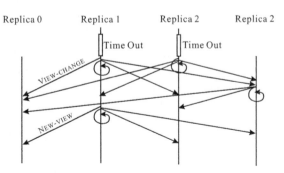

Figure 7.5   PBFT view change protocol.

As shown in Figure 7.5, when the primary for view $v+1$ receives $2f$ matching view-change messages for view $v + 1$ from other replicas, it is ready to install the new view and multicasts a new-view message to all other replicas (including the primary that has been suspected in v to minimize the chance of two or more replicas believe that they are the primary). The new-view message has the form $<\text{NEW-VIEW}, v + 1, V, O>_{\sigma_p}$, where V is proof for the new view consisting of $2f + 1$ matching view-change messages ($2f$ from other replicas and the view-change sent or would have sent by the primary in view $v + 1$), and O is a set of pre-prepare messages to be handled in view $v + 1$, which is determined as follows:

- First, the primary in the new view $v + 1$ computes the range of sequence numbers for which the 3-phase Byzantine agreement protocol was launched in the previous view v. The lower bound $min - s$ is set to be the smallest sequence number s (for stable checkpoint) included in a view-change message included in V. The higher bound $max - s$ is set to be the largest sequence number contained in a prepared certificate included in V.

- For each sequence number s between $min - s$ and $max - s$ (inclusive), the primary in view $v + 1$ creates a pre-prepare message. Similar to the Paxos algorithm, the primary (acting as the role of the proposer) must determine which message m should be assigned to the sequence number s (analogous to the proposal number in Paxos) based on the collected history information in the previous view v.

- If there exists a set of prepared certificates in V containing the sequence number s, the message m contained in the certificate with the highest view number is selected for the pre-prepare message in view $v + 1$.

- If no prepared certificate is found for a sequence number within the range, the primary creates a pre-prepare message with a null request. The execution of the null request is a no-op, similar to the strategy employed in Paxos.

Upon receiving the new-view message, in addition to checking on the signature of the message, a backup verifies the O component of the message by going through the same steps outlined above. The backup accepts a pre-prepare message contained in O if the validation is successful, and subsequently multicasts the corresponding prepare message. Thereafter, backup resumes normal operation in view $v + 1$.

Because the primary in view $v + 1$ reorders all requests since the last stable checkpoint, the predicate *commit-local* might be already true for some of the messages reordered. The replica would nevertheless participate in the ordering phases by multicasting prepare and commit messages. It is also possible that a replica has already executed a request, in which case, the request is not re-executed.

Another detail is that $min - s$ might be greater than the sequence number of the latest stable checkpoint at the primary for view $v + 1$. In this case, the primary labels the checkpoint for $min - s$ as stable if it has taken such a checkpoint, and logs the proof for this stable checkpoint (included in the view-change message received at the primary). If the primary lags so far behind and has not taken a checkpoint with sequence number $min - s$, it would need to request a copy of the stable checkpoint from some other replica.

Finally, to facilitate faster view change, a nonfaulty replica joins a view change as soon as it receives $f + 1$ valid view-change messages from other replicas before its view-change timer expires. Figure 7.5 shows this case for Replica 3.

7.2.6   Proof of Correctness

Theorem 7.2 *Safety property. All nonfaulty replicas execute the requests they receive in the same total order.*

Proof: We have already proved in Section 7.2.3 that if two nonfaulty replicas commit locally for a sequence number s in the same view v, then both must bind s to the same request m. What is remaining to prove is that if two nonfaulty replicas commit locally for a sequence number s in different views, then both must bind s to the same request m. More specifically, if the predicate *commit-local*(m, v, s, i) is true for replica i, and *commit-local*(m', v', s, j) is true for replica j, we show that $m = m'$.

Assume that $m \neq m'$ and without loss of generality $v' > v$. Because *commit-local*(m, v, s, i) is true for replica i, the predicate *prepared*(m, v, s, i) must be true for a set $R1$ of at least $2f + 1$ replicas. For the replica j to install view v', it must have received the proof for the new view, which consists of a set $R2$ of $2f + 1$ view-change messages from different replicas. Because there are $3f + 1$ replicas in the system, $R1$ and $R2$ must intersect in at least $f + 1$ replicas, which means at least one of them is not faulty. This nonfaulty replica must have included a prepared certificate containing the binding of s to m in its view-change message. According to the view change protocol, the new primary in view

v' must have selected m in the pre-prepare message with sequence number s. This ensures that $m = m'$.

It is possible that by the time the view change takes place, replica i has taken a stable checkpoint for sequence number equal or greater than s, in which case, no nonfaulty replica would accept a pre-prepare message with sequence number s.

∎

Theorem 7.3 *Liveness property. A client eventually receives the reply to its request provided that the message delivery delay does not grow faster than the time itself indefinitely.*

Proof: It is easy to see that if the primary is Byzantine faulty, it may temporarily delay progress. However, it cannot prevent the system from making progress indefinitely because every nonfaulty replica maintains a view-change timer. A replica starts the timer when it receives a request if the timer is not running yet. If it fails to execute the request before the timer expires, the replica suspects the primary and multicasts to other replicas a VIEW-CHANGE message. When $f + 1$ replicas suspect the primary, all nonfaulty replicas join the view change, even if their timers have not expired yet. This would lead to a view change.

Next, we show that as long as the message delivery delay does not grow faster than the time itself indefinitely, a new view will be installed at nonfaulty replicas. This is guaranteed by the adaption of the timeout value for unsuccessful view changes. If the view-change timer expires before a replica receives a valid NEW-VIEW message for the expected new view, it doubles the timeout value and restart the view-change timer.

There is also a legitimate concern that a Byzantine faulty replica may attempt to stall the system by forcing frequent view changes. This concern is addressed by the mechanism that only when a nonfaulty replica receives at least $f + 1$ VIEW-CHANGE messages does it join the view change. Because there are at most f faulty replicas, they cannot force a view change if all nonfaulty replicas are making progress.

∎

7.2.7 Optimizations

Reducing the cost of cryptographic operations. The most significant optimization in PBFT is to replace digital signatures by message authentication code for all control messages except the checkpoint, view-change and new-view messages. According to [4], message authentication code (MAC) based authentication can be more than two orders of magnitude faster than that using digital signatures with similar strength of security.

The main reason that MAC-based authentication is much faster than that digital signature based authentication is that MACs use symmetric cryptography while digital signatures are based on public-key cryptography. To use MAC, two communication parties would need to establish a shared secret session key (or a pair of keys, one for each communication direction). A MAC is computed by applying a secure hash function on the message to be sent and the shared secret key. Then the computed MAC is appended to the message. The receiver would then authenticate the message by recompute the MAC based on the received message and its secret key and compare with the received MAC. The message is authenticated if the recomputed MAC is identical to the received MAC.

For a message to be physically multicast (using UDP or IP multicast) to several receivers, a vector of MACs is attached to the message. The vector of MACs is referred to as an authenticator. In an authenticator, there is one MAC for each intended receiver.

The purpose of using digital signatures in pre-prepare, prepare, and commit messages is to prevent spoofing. Using MACs instead of digital signatures could achieve the same objective. To see why, consider the following example. Replica i is faulty, and Replicas j and k are not faulty. We show that replica i cannot forge a message sent to replica j preventing that replica j sent it. Even though replica i has a shared secret key with replica j, it does not know the shared secret key between replica j and replica k. Therefore, if replica i were to forge a message from replica j to replica k, the MAC cannot be possibly correct and replica k would deem the message invalid. Therefore, during normal operation, the pre-prepare, prepare, and commit messages can be protected by MACs instead of digital signatures without any other changes to the PBFT algorithm.

For the checkpoint message, even though it is possible to use MACs instead of digital signatures during normal operation, when the proof for a stable checkpoint is needed, a new control message, called check-sign message, which is protected by a digital signature, must be exchange among the replicas to assemble the proof. Considering that checkpoints are taken periodically (say one for every 100 requests executed), it is more beneficial to use digital signatures in the first place for simplicity of the algorithm and faster recovery (because the proof is needed during view changes and when to recover a slow replica).

The use of MACs in pre-prepare and prepare messages does have some impact on the view change protocol because a faulty replica could in fact forge the proof that it has collected a pre-prepare message with $2f$ matching prepare messages. Hence, during a view change, a replica that has prepared a message m with sequence number s must build the proof by going through a round message exchange with other replicas.

For each request m that has prepared with a sequence number s at replica i, the replica digitally signs any pre-prepare and prepare messages it has sent and multicasts a prepare-sign message in the form $<\text{PREPARE-SIGN}, v, s, d, i>_{\sigma_i}$ to other replicas, where d is the digest of m. Upon receiving a valid prepare-sign message, a non faulty replica j responds with its own prepare-sign message for the same m and s, if it has not produced a stable checkpoint with a sequence number equal or greater than s. Replica i waits to collect $f + 1$ valid prepare-sign messages (including the one it has sent) to build the proof. The reason why replica i has to stop waiting when it receives $f + 1$ prepare-sign messages is because in the worst case, up to f faulty replicas that responded during normal operation may choose not to respond at all or respond with a valid prepare-sign message.

Theoretically, it is possible for the primary in the new view to receive valid view-change messages that conflict with each other because there are only $f + 1$ signed prepared certificates in the proof for a prepared message. For example, replica i's proof contains $f + 1$ prepared certificates for a message m with sequence number s, whereas replica j's proof contains $f + 1$ prepared certificates for a message m' with the same sequence number. If this happens, the primary for the new view might not know which message to choose for sequence number s.

It turns out that the proofs from nonfaulty replicas for the same prepared message will never conflict due to the invariance that if a message m is prepared with a sequence number s at a nonfaulty replica, all nonfaulty replicas that prepared message m would agree with the same sequence number s.

Therefore, if the primary for the new view always waits until it has collected $2f + 1$ view-change messages with no conflict before it issues the new-view message. One consequence for doing this is that in the worst case, the primary for the new view must wait until all nonfaulty replicas have advanced to the same stage if the f faulty replicas initially participated in the 3-phase Byzantine agreement protocol but refused to help build the proof for prepared requests.

Tentative execution. To reduce the end-to-end latency, a replica tentatively executes a request as soon as it is prepared and all requests that are ordered before it have been committed locally and executed. With tentative execution enabled, the client must collect $2f + 1$ matching replies from different replicas instead of $f + 1$. If $2f + 1$ have prepared and tentatively executed a message, it is guaranteed that the message will eventually committed locally, possibly after one or more view changes. To see why this is the case, let $R1$ be the set of $2f+1$ replicas that have prepared and tentatively executed a message m. If a view change has occurred subsequently, the primary for the new view must collect valid view-change messages from a set $R2$ of $2f + 1$ replicas. Because there are $3f + 1$ replicas in the system, $R1$ and $R2$ must intersect in $f + 1$ replicas, which means at least one of the replicas is not faulty. This nonfaulty replica must have included the prepared certificate for m in its view-change message, which ensures that the primary in the new view would assign the same sequence number in the prepared certificate for m.

If the primary fails before $2f+1$ replicas have prepared a message m, the primary for the new view might not be able to find a prepared certificate for m in the $2f + 1$ view-change messages it would collect, hence, there is no guarantee that the primary in the new view would assign m the same sequence number as that for the tentative execution.

▉ EXAMPLE 7.4

In this example, we show that even if the client collects $2f$ matching replies, there is no guarantee that the tentative

execution would succeed if the primary fails, as illustrated in
Figure 7.6. We assume that $2f$ replicas have prepared and tentatively executed m with a sequence number s. In the worst case,
f of the replicas that have tentatively executed m are faulty
and the $f + 1$ remaining nonfaulty replicas have not prepared
m yet. In the ensuing view change, the f faulty replicas may
decide not to include their prepared certificates in their view-
change messages. If the view change messages from the $f + 1$
nonfaulty replicas that have not prepared m and the f faulty
replicas form the $2f + 1$ view-change messages that the primary
in the new view would collect, the primary would not find a
prepared certificate for m, and hence, might assign m a different
sequence number than s.

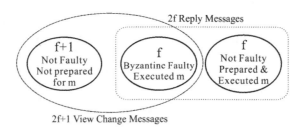

Figure 7.6   A worst case scenario for tentative execution.

To avoid the potential inconsistency in requests ordering highlighted in the above example, replicas rollback to the most recent
checkpoint if a view change happens and there exists at least
one request that has been tentatively executed. To facilitate this
mechanism, each of the prepared certificates in the view-change
messages must indicate whether or not a request has been tentatively executed. Because all nonfaulty replicas would receive the
view-change messages that enabled the new view, they all should
be able to determine whether or not a request has been tentatively
executed and decides whether or not to rollback its state.

Read-only requests. If operations that do not modify the system
state are predefined, it is desirable to avoid totally ordering read-
only requests so that the client can receive a reply faster. Since
a read-only request does not change the system state, a replica
can immediately execute a read-only request as soon as it receives
one without risking the divergence of the state at different replicas provided that all tentative executions have been committed.

However, the downside for immediate execution of read-only requests is that different replicas may return different states to the client if there are concurrent modifications to the state accessed by the read-only request.

Without tentative execution, a client waits for $f + 1$ matching replies from different replicas to ensure that at least one of them is from a nonfaulty replica. If tentative execution is enabled, the client must wait until it has collected $2f + 1$ matching replies. It is possible that the client is unable to collect $f + 1$ or $2f + 1$ matching replies, in which case, the client has to resubmit the request as a regular request.

7.3 Fast Byzantine Agreement

Similar to Fast Paxos [22], faster Byzantine agreement can be achieved by using more replicas. By using a quorum size of $4f + 1$ (total number of acceptors needed is $5f + 1$), a Byzantine agreement can be achieved in two communication steps instead of three in normal operation where there is a unique proposer [28]. Figure 7.7 shows the normal operation in a state-machine Byzantine fault tolerance system. The view change algorithm for PBFT can be used for new leader election in case of the primary failures. Similarly, the optimizations introduced in PBFT [7] such as read-only operations and speculative execution can be applied to Fast Byzantine fault tolerance system as well.

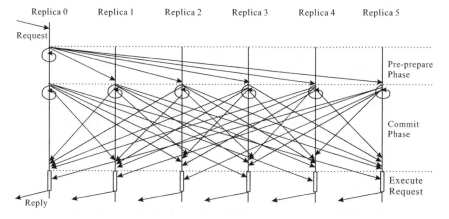

Figure 7.7 Normal operation of Fast Byzantine fault tolerance.

7.4   Speculative Byzantine Fault Tolerance

Because faults are rare, it is reasonable to expect that the performance of a Byzantine fault tolerance system can be improved by speculative execution. If a speculative execution is wrong due to the presence of faulty replicas, the speculative execution must be rolled back. Speculative execution in the context of state-machine Byzantine faulty tolerance is first introduced in PBFT [5] where replicas can tentatively execute a request as soon as it is prepared and all requests that are ordered before it have been delivered and executed. Server-side speculative execution is pushed to the limit in Zyzzyva [20] where replicas can speculatively execute a request as soon as a request is assigned a sequence number (by the primary). In [31], client-side speculative execution is introduced to primarily reduce the end-to-end latency of a remote method invocation, where the client speculatively accepts the first reply received and carries on with its operation.

Client-side speculative execution is relatively straightforward. To avoid cascading rollbacks in case of wrong speculation, a client must not externalize its speculative state. A client that has speculatively accepted a reply keeps tracks of additional replies received. When a client has received sufficient number of matching replies, the speculative execution related to the request and reply will be labeled as stable.

In this section, we focus on the server-side speculative execution as described in Zyzzyva [20]. Zyzzyva employs the following main mechanisms:

- A replica speculatively executes a request as soon as it receives a valid pre-prepare message from the primary.
- The commitment of a request is moved to the client. A request is said to have *completed* (instead of committed) at the issuing client if the corresponding reply can be safely delivered to the client application according to Zyzzyva. Zyzzyva ensures that if a request completes at a client, then the request will eventually be committed at the server replicas.
- The all-to-all prepare and commit phases are reduced to a single phase. As a trade-off, an additional phase is introduced in view change.

- A history hash is used to help the client determine if its request has been ordered appropriately. A server replica maintains a history hash for each request ordered and appends the history hash $h_s = H(h_{s-1}, d_s)$ to the reply for the request that is assigned a sequence number s, where $H()$ is the secure hash function, and d_s is the digest for the request that is assigned the sequence number s. h_{si} is a prefix of h_{sj} if $sj > si$ and there exist a set of requests with sequence numbers $si + 1, si + 2, ..., sj - 1$ with digests $d_{si+1}, d_{si+2}, ..., d_{sj-1}$ such that $h_{si+1} = H(h_{si}, d_{si+1}), h_{si+2} = H(h_{si+1}, d_{si+2}), ..., h_{sj} = H(h_{sj-1}, dsj)$.

The system model used in Zyzzyva is identical to that in PBFT. Similar to PBFT, Zyzzyva employs three protocols: the agreement protocol for normal operation, the view change protocol for new primary election, and the checkpointing protocol for garbage collection.

Zyzzyva ensure the following safety and liveness properties:

Safety: Given any two requests that have completed, they must have been assigned two different sequence numbers. Furthermore, if the two sequence numbers are i and j and $i < j$, the history hash h_i must be a prefix of h_j.

Liveness: If a nonfaulty client issues a request, the request eventually completes.

7.4.1   The Agreement Protocol

A client maintains a complete timer after issuing each request. A request may complete at the issuing client in one of the following ways:

Case 1: The client receives $3f + 1$ matching replies from different replicas before the complete timer expires. This means that *all* replicas have executed the request in exactly the same total order.

Case 2: The client receives at least $2f + 1$ matching replies when the complete timer expires. In this case, the client would initiate another round of message exchanges with the server replicas before the request is declared as complete.

The main steps for case 1 and case 2 are shown in Figure 7.8 and Figure 7.9, respectively. The client initially sends its request to the

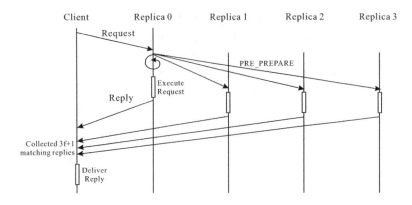

Figure 7.8   Zyzzyva agreement protocol (case 1).

primary and starts the complete timer for the request. The request has the form $<\text{REQUEST}, o, t, c>_{\sigma_c}$, where o is the operation to be executed at the server replica, t is a timestamp, c is the identifier of the client, and σ_c is the client's digital signature or authenticator for the request.

Upon receiving a valid request m from a client, the primary assigns the request a sequence number and multicasts a ORDER-REQ message and the request m to all backup replicas. The ORDER-REQ is similar to the pre-prepare request in PBFT and has the form $<\text{ORDER-REQ}, v, s, h_s, d, ND>_{\sigma_p}$, where v is the current view number, s is the sequence number assigned to request m, h_s is the history hash for the request, d is the digest of m, and ND is a set of values chosen by the primary for nondeterministic variables involved in the operation o.

When a replica receives an ORDER-REQ message from the primary, it verifies the message in the following way:

- The digest d is the correct digest for the request m.
- The sequence number s in ORDER-REQ is the next expected sequence number based on the replica's knowledge (*i.e.*, the replica maintains a max sequence number max_s, and in this case, $max_s = s - 1$), and the history hash received in the ORDER-REQ message, $h_s = H(h_{s-1}, d)$, where h_{s-1} is the history hash at the replica prior to receiving the ORDER-REQ message.
- The ORDER-REQ is properly signed by the primary.

If the ORDER-REQ message is valid, the replica accepts it and updates its history hash. Then it executes the request speculatively and sends a SPEC-RESPONSE message to the client. The SPEC-RESPONSE message includes the following components:

- A component signed by the replica: $<$SPEC-RESPONSE$, v, s, h_s, H(r), c, t, i>_{\sigma_i}$, where $H(r)$ is the digest of the reply r, c and t are the client id and the timestamp included in the request m, and i is the sending replica id. (In [20], i is outside the signed component. We believe it is more robust to include i in the signed component so that the client can be assured the identity of the sending replica, *i.e.*, a faulty replica cannot spoof a SPEC-RESPONSE message as one or more nonfaulty replicas.)
- The reply r.
- The original ORDER-REQ message received from the primary, *i.e.*, $<$ORDER-REQ$, v, s, h_s, d, ND>_{\sigma_p}$.

If the client receives matching SPEC-RESPONSE from all replicas (*i.e.*, $3f + 1$) before the complete timer expires, as described in case 1 and shown in Figure 7.8, the request completes and the client deliver the reply to the application layer for processing. Two SPEC-RESPONSE messages match provided that they have identical

- view number v,
- sequence number s,
- history hash h_s,
- client id c,
- timestamp t,
- reply r,
- digest of the reply $H(r)$.

When the complete timer expires, if the client manages to receive at least $2f + 1$ matching replies, but not from all replicas, as described in case 2 and shown in Figure 7.9, the client assembles a commit certificate CC using the $2f + 1$ or more matching replies, broadcasts to the replicas a $<$COMMIT$, c, CC>_{\sigma_c}$ message, and starts another timer for retransmission. A commit certificate contains the following components:

- A list of $2f + 1$ replica ids,
- The signed component of the SPEC-RESPONSE from each of the $2f + 1$ replicas.

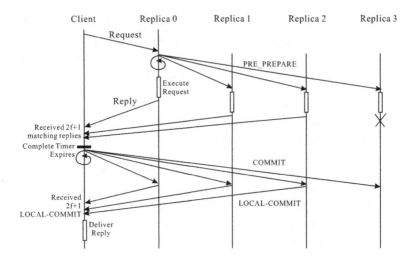

Figure 7.9   Zyzzyva agreement protocol (case 2).

Upon receiving a COMMIT message, a replica responds with a LOCAL-COMMIT message to the client. If the client could receive $2f + 1$ or more valid LOCAL-COMMIT messages before the retransmission timer expires, it knows that the request has completed and it is safe to deliver the reply.

When a replica receives a COMMIT message with a valid commit certificate, it further verifies that its local history hash is consistent with the certified history hash:

- If the replica has received a ORDER-REQ message for the request to be committed, the history hash for the request must be identical to that included in the commit certificate.
- If the replica has not received a ORDER-REQ message for the request to be committed, then the request must carry the next expected sequence number *i.e.*, $max_s + 1$.

If the verification on the history hash is successful, the replica performs the following operations:

- If the commit certificate's sequence number is higher than the stored maximum sequence number, it increments its local maximum sequence number max_{CC}.
- The replica sends the client a message <LOCAL-COMMIT, $v, d, h_s, i, c>_{\sigma_i}$.

When the client receives $2f + 1$ consistent LOCAL-COMMIT messages, it completes the request and delivers the corresponding reply.

If the client receives fewer than $2f + 1$ matching replies before the complete timer expires, or the additional of round of message exchanges in case 2 is not successful, it retries the request by broadcasting the request to all replicas.

7.4.2 The View Change Protocol

Because the primary is designated to assign sequence numbers to the requests and drive the agreement protocol, a faulty primary can easily stall the progress of the system. To ensure liveness, the current primary must be removed from the role if it is suspected of being faulty and another replica will be elected to serve as the primary. This is referred to as a view change. In Zyzzyva, a view change can be triggered in one of two ways:

1. Sufficient number of backups time out the current primary. This is identical to that in PBFT. On receiving a request from a client, a backup replica starts a view change timer and it expects that the request would be committed before the timer expires if the primary is not faulty.
2. In Zyzzyva, a client might receive two or more SPEC-RESPONSE messages for the same request in the same view, but different sequence numbers or history hash values, in which case, the client broadcasts a POM message to all replicas. The POM message contains the current view number and the set of conflicting ORDER-REQ messages that it has received. A replica initiates a view change when it receives a valid POM message. In addition, the replica also multicasts the POM message it has received to other replicas to speed up the view change.

The Zyzzyva view change protocol differs from the PBFT view change protocol in the following ways:

- In Zyzzyva, only one of the prepare and commit phases is effectively used (when the client receives at least $2f + 1$ but less than $3f + 1$ matching SPEC-RESPONSE messages, or none of them (when the client receives $3f + 1$ matching SPEC-RESPONSE messages). As a tradeoff, an additional "I hate the primary" phase is introduced in the beginning of the view change protocol.
- In the best case for Zyzzyva where the client receives $3f + 1$ matching SPEC-RESPONSE messages, the replicas would not

possess a commit certificate. As such, the condition for including a request in the NEW-VIEW message is weakened so that such requests will be present in the history.

In [20], the authors made an interesting observation regarding the dependencies between the agreement protocol and the view change protocol, and why in PBFT both the prepare and the commit phases are needed to ensure proper view changes. The latter is illustrated with the following counter example.

Assume that the primary and $f - 1$ other replicas are Byzantine faulty. The primary forces f nonfaulty replicas to suspect itself and not the remaining replicas. Recall that in PBFT, once a replica suspects the primary (*i.e.*, commits to a view change), it stops accepting messages in the current view except checkpoint and view change messages (and hence would not participate in the ordering and execution of requests in the current view). The remaining $f + 1$ nonfaulty replicas could still make progress with the help of the f faulty replicas. However, if one or more requests have been prepared since the f nonfaulty have suspected the primary, there is no guarantee that the corresponding prepared certificates would be seen at the primary for the new view *if the commit phase is omitted*.

Recall in PBFT, if a replica has committed locally a request, it is guaranteed that the replica would have secured a prepared certificate with $2f$ matching prepare messages and the corresponding pre-prepare message from the primary. If the commit phase is omitted and a replica "commits" a request as soon as it has prepared the request, the above guarantee would no longer hold. Assume that f nonfaulty replicas have "committed" a request this way. The $2f + 1$ view-change messages collected by the primary for the new view could have come from the remaining $2f + 1$ replicas, therefore, the primary for the new view would not know that a request has been committed at some replicas to a particular sequence number and hence, might order the request differently, thereby, violating the safety property. That is why the commit phase is necessary in PBFT. With the commit phase, if any replica has committed locally a request, then at least $2f + 1$ replica would have prepared the request, and therefore, the primary for the new view is assured to receive the prepared certificate for the request from at least one nonfaulty replica and the safety property would be preserved.

If the PBFT view change protocol is directly applied in Zyzzyva, the liveness will be lost (instead of safety violation) in similar cases.

Again, consider a Byzantine faulty primary that forces exactly f nonfaulty replicas to suspect it, thereby these f nonfaulty replicas would stop accepting new requests and the corresponding ORDER-REQ messages. If the f faulty replicas would not execute new requests either, the client would only receive the SPEC-RESPONSE messages from the $f + 1$ nonfaulty replicas that have not suspected the primary. As a result, the client cannot complete the request. In the meantime, no view change could take place because only f nonfaulty replicas suspect the primary.

For Zyzzyva, the problem is caused by the fact that a nonfaulty replica may commit to a view change without any assurance that a view change will take place according to the PBFT view change protocol. The solution, therefore, is to ensure that a nonfaulty replica does not abandon the current view unless all other nonfaulty replicas would agree to move to a new view too. This is achieved by introducing an additional phase on top of the PBFT view change protocol in Zyzzyva.

In Zyzzyva, when a replica suspects the primary, it broadcasts a no-confidence vote to all replicas in the form <I-HATE-THE-PRIMARY, $v, i>_{\sigma_i}$. Only when a replica receives $f + 1$ no-confidence votes in the same view, does it commit to a view change and broadcasts a VIEW-CHANGE message containing the $f + 1$ no-confidence votes it has collected as the proof. Because of this additional phase, a nonfaulty replica joins the view change even if it receives a single valid VIEW-CHANGE message.

Another significant difference between the PBFT view change protocol and the Zyzzyva view change protocol is the information included in the VIEW-CHANGE messages. In PBFT, a replica includes its prepared certificates, which is equivalent to the commit certificates in Zyzzyva. However, in Zyzzyva, a replica receives a commit certificate for a request only if the client receives between $2f + 1$ and $3f$ matching SPEC-RESPONSE messages. If the client could receive $3f + 1$ matching SPEC-RESPONSE messages for its request, no replica would receive commit certificate. To deal with this case, the Zyzzyva view change protocol makes the following changes:

- Instead of prepare (or commit) certificates, a replica includes all ORDER-REQ messages it has received since the latest stable checkpoint or the most recent commit certificate.

- The primary for the new view compute the request-sequence number binding for the new view in the following way:

  - The primary for the new view adopts the request-sequence number binding if there are at least $f + 1$ matching ORDER-REQ messages.

The above changes ensure that if a request has completed at a client, the total order (reflected by the sequence number) for the request is respected in the new view. However, the primary for the new view may find more than one set of $f + 1$ matching ORDER-REQ messages for different requests but with the same sequence number. This corner case turns out will not damage the safety property of the system because such requests could not have completed at any clients. The primary for the new view can choose to use either request-sequence number binding in the new view. Note that when a backup for the new view verifies the NEW-VIEW message, it may find a conflict in the request-sequence number binding for such requests. Being aware of this corner case, it should take the binding chosen by the primary. More details are discussed in the following example.

■ EXAMPLE 7.5

The corner case introduced above will not happen when $f = 1$, but it may happen when $f \geq 2$. In this example, we show a case when $f = 2$ as illustrated in Figure 7.10. There are $3f + 1 = 7$ replicas. We assume that the primary, Replica 0, for the current view is Byzantine faulty. For $Req1$, the primary assigns a sequence number $s1$ for Replicas 1, 2, and 3. But for Replicas 4, 5, and 6, $Req1$ is given a different sequence number $s2$. Similarly, for $Req2$, the primary assigns $s2$ for Replicas 1, 2, and 3, and $s1$ for Replicas 4, 5, and 6.

Assume $s1$ is the next expected sequence number at all backup replicas, and $s2 = s1 + 1$. Replicas 1, 2, and 3 would execute $Req1$ speculatively. However, the ORDER-REQ for $Req2$ will be rejected at Replicas 4, 5, and 6. When Replicas 1, 2, and 3 receives the ORDER-REQ for $Req2$ with sequence number $s2$, they will speculatively execute $Req2$ because $s2$ is now the next expected sequence number. Replicas 4, 5, and 6 will also

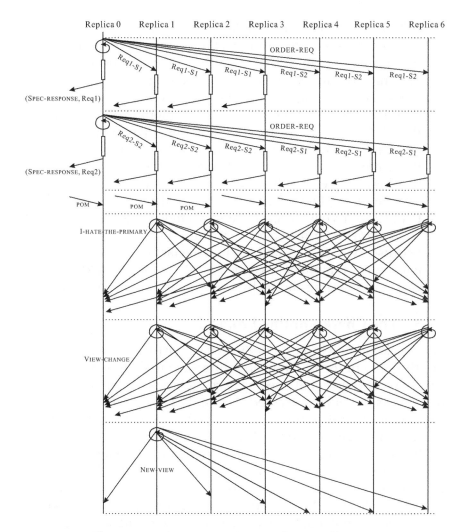

Figure 7.10   A corner case in view change in Zyzzyva.

accept the ORDER-REQ for $Req2$ because $s1$ is the next expected sequence number.

When the client that issues $Req2$ may detect that the primary is Byzantine faulty as soon as it receives one SPEC-RESPONSE message from the replicas group 1, 2, and 3, and one SPEC-RESPONSE message from the replicas group 4, 5, and 6. The client then broadcasts a POM message to all replicas.

Upon receiving the POM message, a replica broadcasts a I-HATE-THE-PRIMARY message to all replicas. When a replica collects $f + 1$ such no-confidence votes, it broadcasts a VIEW-CHANGE message. The primary at the new primary (Replica 1 in our example) would determine the request-sequence number bindings and multicast a NEW-VIEW message.

As shown in Figure 7.10, the primary of the new primary (Replica 1) would choose the $Req2 - s2$ binding because among the $2f + 1 = 5$ VIEW-CHANGE messages it has collected, there are $f + 1 = 3$ ORDER-REQ messages that indicate such binding (there are only 2 ORDER-REQ messages that contain the $Req1 - s1$ binding). However, when Replicas 4, 5, and 6 verify the NEW-VIEW message, they would detect a conflict because according to the $2f + 1$ VIEW-CHANGE messages they have collected, there are 3 ORDER-REQ messages that show the $Req2 - s1$ instead. Because Replicas 4, 5, and 6 know the fact there are two different sequence numbers assigned to $Req2$, they should take the $Req2 - s2$ binding chosen by the primary for the new view.

7.4.3   The Checkpointing Protocol

The checkpointing protocol in Zyzzyva in virtually identical to that in PBFT, except the BFT infrastructure state is slightly different. A core piece of state maintained by each replica is the ordered history of requests that it has executed. The replica also keeps track of the maximum commit certificate, which is the commit certificate with the largest sequence number (max_{CC}) that it has received (if any). In the history of the requests, those that carry a sequence number smaller or equal to max_{CC} are part of the committed history, and those with a sequence number larger than max_{CC} are part of the speculative history. The history is truncated using the checkpointing protocol. Similar to PBFT, each replica also maintains a response log.

7.4.4   Proof of Correctness

Theorem 7.4 *Safety property. Given any two requests that have completed, they must have been assigned two different sequence numbers. Furthermore, if the two sequence numbers are i and j and $i < j$, the history hash h_i must be a prefix of h_j.*

Proof: We first prove that the safety property holds if the two requests complete in the same view. It is easy to see why two requests cannot be completed with the same sequence number because a request completes only when (1) a client receives $3f + 1$ matching SPEC-RESPONSE messages, or (2) $2f + 1$ matching LOCAL-COMMIT messages. Because a nonfaulty replica accepts one ORDER-REQ message or sends one LOCAL-COMMIT for the same sequence number, if one request completes in case (1), no other request could have completed with the same sequence number, and if one request completes in case (2), any other request could at most amass $2f$ matching ORDER-SEQ or LOCAL-COMMIT messages and hence, cannot complete with the same sequence number.

Next, assume that $Req1$ completes with sequence number i, and $Req2$ completes with sequence number j. Without loss of generality, let $i < j$. For a request to complete, at least $2f + 1$ replicas have accepted the i for $Req1$ and at least $2f + 1$ replicas have accepted j for $Req2$. Because there are $3f + 1$ replicas, the two sets of replicas must intersect in at least $f + 1$ replicas and at least one of which is not faulty. This nonfaulty replica ordered both $Req1$ and $Req2$. This would ensure that h_i is a prefix of h_j.

If on the other hand, $Req1$ completes in view $v1$ with sequence number i and $Req2$ completes in view $v2$ with sequence number j. Without loss of generality, let $v1 < v2$. If $Req1$ completes when the client receives $3f + 1$ matching ORDER-REQ messages, then in the VIEW-CHANGE message, every nonfaulty replica must have included the corresponding ORDER-REQ message, which ensure that the primary for view $v2$ learns the sequence number i and history hash h_i for $Req1$. Therefore, the primary in view $v2$ cannot assign the same sequence to $Req2$, and h_i must be prefix for h_j. If $Req1$ completes when the client receives $2f + 1$ matching LOCAL-COMMIT messages, then at least $f + 1$ nonfaulty replicas must have included the corresponding commit certificate for i in the VIEW-CHANGE messages, and at least one of them must be included in the set of $2f + 1$ VIEW-CHANGE messages received by the primary in view $v2$. This nonfaulty replica would ensure the proper passing of history information from view $v1$ to view $v2$. ∎

Theorem 7.5 *Liveness property. If a nonfaulty client issues a request, the request eventually completes.*

Proof: We prove this property in two steps. First, we prove that if a nonfaulty client issues a request and the primary is not faulty, then the request will complete. Second, we prove that if a request does not complete, then a view change will occur.

If both the client and the primary are not faulty, then the agreement protocol guarantees that all nonfaulty replicas would accept the same ORDER-REQ message, execute the request, and send matching SPEC-RESPONSE to the client. Because there are at least $2f + 1$ nonfaulty replicas, the client would be able to receive at least $2f + 1$ matching SPEC-RESPONSE messages and subsequently $2f + 1$ matching LOCAL-COMMIT messages in the worst case, or $3f + 1$ matching SPEC-RESPONSE messages in the best case. In both cases, the request will complete at the client.

If a request did not complete at the client, then the client must not have received $3f + 1$ matching SPEC-RESPONSE messages and must not have received $2f + 1$ matching LOCAL-COMMIT messages. There can be only two types of scenarios:

1. The client did not receive conflicting SPEC-RESPONSE and LOCAL-COMMIT messages, if any, and the number of SPEC-RESPONSE messages received is fewer than $3f + 1$ and the number of LOCAL-COMMIT messages are fewer than $2f + 1$. In this case, the client retransmit the request to all replicas (possibly repeatedly until the request complete). This would ensure all nonfaulty replicas receive this request. If the primary refuses to send a ORDER-REQ message to all or some nonfaulty replicas, these replicas would suspect the primary. Since we assume that fewer than $2f + 1$ LOCAL-COMMIT messages have been received by the client, at least $f + 1$ nonfaulty replicas would suspect the primary, which would lead to a view change.

2. The client received conflicting SPEC-RESPONSE or LOCAL-COMMIT messages, in which case, the client would multicast a POM message to all replicas. This would lead to a view change.

∎

REFERENCES

1. A. Avizienis and L. Chen. On the implementation of n-version programming for software fault tolerance during execution. In *Proceedings of the IEEE International Computer Software and Applications Conference*, pages 149–155, 1977.

2. E. D. Berger and B. G. Zorn. Diehard: probabilistic memory safety for unsafe languages. In *Proceedings of the ACM SIGPLAN Conference on Programming Language Design and Implementation*, pages 158–168, 2006.

3. S. Bhatkar, D. C. DuVarney, and R. Sekar. Address obfuscation: an efficient approach to combat a board range of memory error exploits. In *Proceedings of the 12th conference on USENIX Security Symposium - Volume 12*, SSYM'03, pages 8–8, Berkeley, CA, USA, 2003. USENIX Association.

4. M. Castro and B. Liskov. Authenticated byzantine fault tolerance without public-key cryptography. Technical Report Technical Memo MIT/LCS/TM-589, MIT Laboratory for Computer Science, 1999.

5. M. Castro and B. Liskov. Practical byzantine fault tolerance. In *Proceedings of the third symposium on Operating systems design and implementation*, OSDI '99, pages 173–186, Berkeley, CA, USA, 1999. USENIX Association.

6. M. Castro and B. Liskov. Practical byzantine fault tolerance and proactive recovery. *ACM Transactions on Computer Systems*, 20(4):398–461, 2002.

7. M. Castro, R. Rodrigues, and B. Liskov. Base: Using abstraction to improve fault tolerance. *ACM Transactions on Computer Systems*, 21(3):236–269, 2003.

8. H. Chai, H. Zhang, W. Zhao, P. M. Melliar-Smith, and L. E. Moser. Toward trustworthy coordination for web service business activities. *IEEE Transactions on Services Computing*, 6(2):276–288, 2013.

9. H. Chai and W. Zhao. Interaction patterns for byzantine fault tolerance computing. In T.-h. Kim, S. Mohammed, C. Ramos, J. Abawajy, B.-H. Kang, and D. Slezak, editors, *Computer Applications for Web, Human Computer Interaction, Signal and Image Processing, and Pattern Recognition*, volume 342 of *Communications in Computer and Information Science*, pages 180–188. Springer Berlin Heidelberg, 2012.

10. B.-G. Chun, P. Maniatis, and S. Shenker. Diverse replication for single-machine byzantine-fault tolerance. In *USENIX 2008 Annual Technical Conference on Annual Technical Conference*, ATC'08, pages 287–292, Berkeley, CA, USA, 2008. USENIX Association.

11. F. Cohen. Operating system protection through program evolution. *Computers and Security*, 12(6):565–584, October 1993.

12. B. Cox, D. Evans, A. Filipi, J. Rowanhill, W. Hu, J. Davidson, J. Knight, A. Nguyen-Tuong, and J. Hiser. N-variant systems: A secretless framework for security through diversity. In *15th USENIX Security Symposium*, pages 105–120, 2006.

13. T. Distler and R. Kapitza. Increasing performance in byzantine fault-tolerant systems with on-demand replica consistency. In *Proceedings of the sixth Eurosys conference*, 2011.

14. H. Erven, H. Hicker, C. Huemer, and M. Zapletal. The Web Services-BusinessActivity-Initiator (WS-BA-I) protocol: An extension to the Web Services-BusinessActivity specification. In *Proceedings of the IEEE International Conference on Web Services*, pages 216–224, 2007.

15. M. Feingold and R. Jeyaraman. Web services coordination, version 1.1, OASIS standard, July 2007.

16. S. Forrest, A. Somayaji, and D. Ackley. Building diverse computer systems. In *Proceedings of the Sixth Workshop on Hot Topics in Operating Systems*, pages 67–72, Cape Cod, MA, 1997.

17. M. Franz. Understanding and countering insider threats in software development. In *Proceedings of the International MCETECH Conference on e-Technologies*, pages 81–90, January 2008.

18. T. Freund and M. Little. Web services business activity version 1.1, OASIS standard. http://docs.oasis-open.org/ws-tx/wstx-wsba-1.1-spec-os/wstx-wsba-1.1-spec-os.html, April 2007.

19. Z. M. Kedem, K. V. Palem, M. O. Rabin, and A. Raghunathan. Efficient program transformations for resilient parallel computation via randomization. In *Proceedings of the 24th Annual ACM Symposium on Theory of Computing*, pages 306–317, Victoria, British Columbia, Canada, 1992.

20. R. Kotla, L. Alvisi, M. Dahlin, A. Clement, and E. Wong. Zyzzyva: Speculative byzantine fault tolerance. In *Proceedings of 21st ACM Symposium on Operating Systems Principles*, 2007.

21. R. Kotla and M. Dahlin. High throughput byzantine fault tolerance. In *Proceedings of International Conference on Dependable Systems and Networks*, 2004.

22. L. Lamport. Fast paxos. *Distributed Computing*, 19(2):79–193, 2006.

23. L. Lamport. Brief announcement: leaderless byzantine paxos. In *Proceedings of the 25th international conference on Distributed computing*, DISC'11, pages 141–142, Berlin, Heidelberg, 2011. Springer-Verlag.

24. L. Lamport. Byzantizing paxos by refinement. In *Proceedings of the 25th international conference on Distributed computing*, DISC'11, pages 211–224, Berlin, Heidelberg, 2011. Springer-Verlag.

25. L. Lamport and P. M. Melliar-Smith. Byzantine clock synchronization. In *Proceedings of the third annual ACM symposium on Principles of distributed computing*, PODC '84, pages 68–74, New York, NY, USA, 1984. ACM.

26. L. Lamport, R. Shostak, and M. Pease. The byzantine generals problem. *ACM Transactions on Programming Languages and Systems*, 4:382–401, 1982.

27. M. Little and A. Wilkinson. Web services atomic transactions version 1.1, OASIS standard. http://docs.oasis-open.org/ws-tx/wstx-wsat-1.1-spec-os/wstx-wsat-1.1-spec-os.html, April 2007.

28. J. Martin and L. Alvisi. Fast byzantine consensus. *IEEE Transactions on Dependable and Secure Computing*, 3(3):202–215, 2006.

29. C. Pu, A. Black, C. Cowan, and J.Walpole. A specialization toolkit to increase the diversity of operating systems. In *Proceedings of the ICMAS Workshop on Immunity-Based Systems*, Nara, Japan, 1996.

30. B. Vandiver, H. Balakrishnan, B. Liskov, and S. Madden. Tolerating byzantine faults in database systems using commit barrier scheduling. In *Proceedings*

of the 21st ACM Symposium on Operating Systems Principles, Stevenson, WA, 2007.

31. B. Wester, J. Cowling, E. B. Nightingale, P. M. Chen, J. Flinn, and B. Liskov. Tolerating latency in replicated state machines. In *Proceedings of the Sixth Symposium on Networked Systems Design and Implementation (NSDI)*, Boston, Massachusetts, Apr. 2009.

32. J. Xu, Z. Kalbarczyk, and R. Iyer.   Transparent runtime randomization for security.   In *Proceedings of the 22nd International Symposium on Reliable Distributed Systems*, pages 260–269, 2003.

33. H. Zhang, H. Chai, W. Zhao, P. M. Melliar-Smith, and L. E. Moser. Trustworthy coordination for web service atomic transactions.   *IEEE Transactions on Parallel and Distributed Systems*, 23(8):1551–1565, 2012.

34. H. Zhang, W. Zhao, P. M. Melliar-Smith, and L. E. Moser. Design and implementation of a byzantine fault tolerance framework for non-deterministic applications. *IET Software*, 5:342–356, 2011.

35. W. Zhao, L. Moser, and P. M. Melliar-Smith.   Deterministic scheduling for multithreaded replicas.   In *Proceedings of the IEEE International Workshop on Object-oriented Real-time Dependable Systems*, pages 74–81, Sedona, AZ, 2005.

8

Cryptocurrency and Blockchain

This chapter provides an overview of cryptocurrency and the blockchain technology. We first introduce the history of cryptocurrency, then we describe the design principle and major components of the first cryptocurrency, Bitcoin [15]. Next, we outline the vision and key components of Ethereum [23], which was developed not aiming to compete directly with Bitcoin as a cryptocurrency, but instead, as a platform for developing decentralized applications based on its smart contract implementation, which is in turn powered by the blockchain technology. Finally, we present common attacks on the blockchain technology.

8.1 History of Cryptocurrency

A cryptocurrency that is powered by decentralized computer technology has long been a dream for some pioneers such as Nick Szabo. In his online post [21], Nick Szabo elaborated his idea of Bit Gold. He proposed to use a decentralized solution to replace a third party to establish trust in monetary transactions. He pointed out the issue of double-spending because unlike physical paper bills, digital money can be easily reproduced. Some publication claimed that Nick Szabo proposed the Bit God idea as early as 1998 [16]. Unfortunately, no hard evidence can be found. Nick Szabo's blog has a timestamp of December 27, 2008. In the blog itself, Nick Szabo stated that he "hit upon the idea of bit gold" "a long time ago" without citing any evidence.

Nick Szabo pointed out the value of precious metals such as gold. Gold was used historically as money "largely independent of any trusted third party." However, it is too cumbersome to directly use gold in conventional transactions. In the Internet age, obviously gold cannot be used to as a form of payment for online transactions. Hence, he proposed a bit gold concept, where the bit gold is represented as a bit string. The bit string contains solution to a particular challenge string, which is periodically published. A client who wishes to acquire bit gold would have to solve the puzzle by doing proof of work using a one-way function. The blog did not seem to explain how exactly to determine the value of a bit string, but it appears to be proportional to the work that is done to find the solution of the current puzzle. The envisaged bit gold system would depends on two sets of services: (1) a secure timestamp service, and (2) a distributed property title registry service. Apparently, the trustworthiness of these two services would determine the trustworthiness of the bit gold system. The bit gold concept, although quite visionary and indeed some of the characteristics of bit gold have passed on to Bitcoin, lacks too much details for anyone to implement this proposed system. As we will show a little later, Bitcoin provides a much more elegant method to implement the two services, and the mechanisms for challenge string generation, distribution, and proof of work (which is exactly part of the blockchain technology).

It is worth noting that some pioneers have worked on other aspects of digital cash, such as privacy protection for users of the digital cash. David Chaum introduced the blind signature concept as early as 1983 [7]. In a later paper, he elaborated in more details on how to launch a digital cash payment system worldwide [8]. As we will show later, again Bitcoin provides a much simpler and elegant solution to the privacy need of cryptocurrency.

Proof of work (PoW) as a fundamental concept was first proposed by Dwork and Naor in [11] in 1992. The basis of PoW is that the puzzles must be difficult to solve computationally but very easy to verify. The original design goal was to make every email include the solution to a predefined puzzle to reduce the amount of spam emails. A few years later, Adam Back made public via an email announcement his implementation of the scheme, which he called hashcash [3], in 1997. He further extended the PoW concept to counter denial of service attacks and published the theoretical framework in 2002 [4]. In 1998, Wei Dai posted an online article about the idea of using hashcash to create cryptocurrency [9], which follows the crypto-anarchy concept proposed by Tim May. The protocols rely on the use of a broadcast channel and required the network to be synchronous (*i.e.*, the network can ensure a message is delivered within some predefined bounded time). Hence, it was not practically implementable. This PoW idea was later adopted in Bitcoin but was transformed as the basis to solve the distributed consensus problem. One could argue that in Bitcoin, PoW also creates cryptocurrency because the node that solves the puzzle first would get a sizable monetary reward. However, the cryptocurrency in Bitcoin is not represented by the PoW bit-string in any way.

Another very important early idea related to cryptocurrency and the blockchain technology is about smart contract. Nick Szabo is the first person who proposed the concept of a software and algorithm powered smart contract [20]. He distilled the requirements for contract design into four properties: (1) observability; (2) verifiability; (3) privity; (4) enforceability.

- *Observability.* This requirement refers to the ability of stakeholders of a contract can observe the execution status so that early sign of contract breach can be detected to minimize loss.
- *Verifiability.* This requirement refers to the ability to determine whether or not the contract is performed according to specified, and if breached, whether it is intentionally breached or due to some good faith errors. In the article, Nick Szabo assumed the need for a trusted arbitrator.
- *Privity.* This requirement refers to the assignments and control on who gets to view and enforce which part of the contract, which is to protect the privacy and confidentiality of the contract to its stakeholders.
- *Enforceability.* This requirement is fairly obvious because any contract must be enforceable by definition. Paradoxically, the need for external enforcement

should be minimized. This goal can in fact be achieved by self-enforcing enabled by programming code and algorithms.

As we will show later, the smart contract as implemented in Ethereum ensures the observability property, and partially meets the other three requirements. In Ethereum, if a contract is executed successfully to the end, then the contract is guaranteed to have been fully fulfilled as designed. This is a form of verifiability. However, if the contract execution is aborted due to some reason, then the system cannot provide information regarding whether or not this is due to an intentional breach of contract. Regarding privity, because the contract is fully visible to the public, confidentiality is not fully protected. It is conceivable that some critical information can be encrypted and the party that is responsible to execute a particular part of the contract would have to possess the right security key. On surface, the smart contract in Ethereum appears to be fully self-enforceable. However, the platform cannot handle the case when external actions are needed, such as shipping a product ordered to its customer as specified in the contract [24].

Nick Szabo also expressed the concern on the binding of a private key with an identity [20]. It was assumed that one client would have a known identity, and somehow all the keys that belong to the person would have to be bound to this identity in someway. As we will show later, Bitcoin provided a much simpler solution to this problem by linking the balance of cryptocurrency to a pair of public-private keys. To mimic physical cash, the privacy of cryptocurrency must be protected anyway. Hence, there is no needed to bind the keys to a particular identity.

8.2   Bitcoin

In late 2008, a white paper was posted online with a pseudonym Satoshi Nakamoto regarding Bitcoin [15]. In January 2009, Bitcoin was launched as the first ever practical cryptocurrency in human history. Bitcoin is powered by the blockchain technology, which operates on a peer-to-peer network without any trusted entities. The central idea is to use a heavily replicated distributed ledger to store all transactions in the Bitcoin system. Mechanisms have been designed in such a way that the ledger is basically immutable, at least for transactions that have been placed on the ledger for some time. For scalability, transactions are grouped into a block structure. The biggest challenge and hence the most notable innovation in the blockchain technology is a mechanism that ensures the ledger grow consistently when there are many copies (*i.e.*, replicas) of the ledger across the Bitcoin network. This requires a practical distributed consensus algorithm that can operate on the large-scale peer-to-peer network without any notion that is imposed by classical consensus algorithms such as membership, leader election, and multi-round voting. Bitcoin also introduced several less prominent innovations so that the platform is self-contained without the reliance on any trusted third party. The design of Bitcoin reflected some vision proposed previously such as those in Bit Gold, where the cryptocurrency should be decentralized and the system should not be influenced by monetary policies (to avoid the too-big-to-fail nightmare as happened in 2008). Bitcoin has an upper-bound on the coins that can be minted. So, there will be no inflation risk in Bitcoin. Unfortunately, these idealistic design decisions also become the deficiencies for Bitcoin to compete with major currencies [24].

Bitcoin is not a conventional computer-based networked system that is controlled and funded by one company. Bitcoin is open to anyone to join the network. Hence, it is running on top of a public blockchain platform. Inevitably, Bitcoin must offer incentives for people who set up computing nodes to help maintain and grow the distributed ledger. Satoshi Nakamoto could have required that everyone who wishes to participate the network to help maintain and grow the ledger so that no additional incentive is needed. However, doing so would be detrimental to the acceptability of Bitcoin as a currency by the public because the PoW-based consensus scheme is highly computationally intensive. In Bitcoin, there are two different kinds of participants: (1) regular users, who usually must pay a transaction fee to use the network, similar to other types of electronic transactional networks such as Visa and Master credit card; (2) miners, who are dedicated to compete in the PoW consensus to help maintain and grow the distributed ledger.

This design decision has several consequences:

- Bitcoin could attract many regular users because they can use lightweight devices such as a smartphone to make purchases with Bitcoin at vendors who accept it.

- The miners are incentivized with a block reward. More specifically, the miner who solves the PoW puzzle first for a new block gets a block reward, and also gets the right to assemble the block and add the block to the existing blockchain. In a way, this is rather similar to a process of mining gold, where the lucky miner would find a pot of gold and get to keep it. That is why the owners of the nodes that compete to solve the PoW puzzle are referred to as miners.

- The miners are expected to invest in computing hardware and networking services to verify individual transactions, proporgate transactions, assemble transactions into blocks, verify blocks and disseminate them, keep a copy of the distributed ledger (*i.e.*, the blockchain), and participate in the PoW competition.

- Because the PoW competition is a stochastic process, it is possible for two or more miners concurrently solve the puzzle in the same round (*i.e.*, at the same block height, which will be explained later in this chapter), in which case, the miners must select the chain that has the most difficulty (*i.e.*, usually the longest chain) as the main chain to grow.

Bitcoin's block reward started with 50 Bitcoins (here Bitcoin is used as the unit of the cryptocurrency) and the reward is halved for every 210,000 blocks, which is roughly every 4 years. As of writing, the block reward is 6.25 Bitcoins, and it will be halved again in May 2024. The block reward will drop to 0 around year 2140. In Bitcoin, another inventive offered to miners is that miners get to collect transaction fees in the block that the miner assembled. Currently the block reward is significantly bigger than the transaction fees in the block, but when the block reward shrinks in the future, the transaction fees will become an important source of income for miners (many also anticipate that the price of Bitcoin will rise over time due to the limited supply).

Bitcoin follows the decentralized design principle set by pioneers such as Nick Szabo, Adam Back, Wei Dai. In fact, Bitcoin incorporated some important concepts proposed earlier such as PoW-based hashcash, which Satoshi Nakamoto acknowledged in his white paper on Bitcoin [15]. This principle is reflected consistently in every part of the Bitcoin system. We can roughly say Bitcoin has four building blocks [1]: (1) decentralized network and architecture; (2) decentralized data structure; (3) decentralized algorithms; (4) self-contained cryptography.

8.2.1   Decentralized network and architecture

Bitcoin operates on a peer-to-peer network, that is, the system does not rely on any centralized server for processing or data storage, nor does it rely on any trusted third party, such as a timestamp server or a public registry as mentioned in earlier work prior to Bitcoin, not even the public-key infrastructure, which is often needed for public-key distribution.

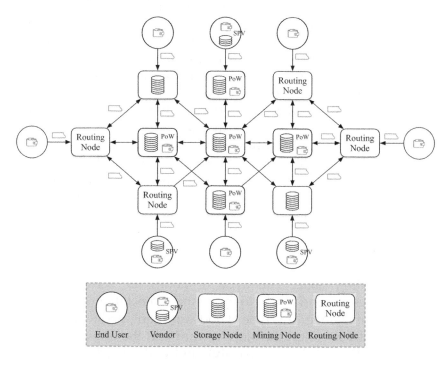

Figure 8.1   Bitcoin nodes.

A closer look at the nodes in the Bitcoin network will find four distinct functionalities: (1) wallet, (2) routing, (3) storage (of the distributed ledger, *i.e.,* the blockchain), (4) mining. The nodes in the Bitcoin network might have one or more these functionalities. Figure 8.1 shows a highly simplified Bitcoin network with five different types of nodes:

- End user. This type of nodes only include the wallet functionality, where the end user would use to purchase Bitcoin
  from an exchange or from a friend using traditional money,
  and use Bitcoin to pay for services or product (such as a
  Pizza). The digital wallet is used to generate private-public
  key pairs and addresses for transactions, as well as to keep
  track of the balance for the user.
- Vendor. For vendors who wish to take Bitcoin as a means
  of payment, their nodes normally would include a digital
  wallet and at least a lightweight-version of the blockchain,
  which consists of all the headers of the blocks in the
  blockchain, without the actual transactions. Such node is
  called SPV (short for simplified payment verification) node,
  or SPV wallet. As the name suggests, the purpose of this
  type of nodes is to facilitate the verification of payments
  tendered by end users. The task would be to verify a
  transaction provided by an end user is indeed part of the
  blockchain (*i.e.*, the distributed transaction ledger). In a
  way, this is similar to verifying that a large-value paper
  bill is genuine. We note that the information included in
  such nodes is not sufficient to verify a transaction. The SPV
  node would have to ask a node that has a full blockchain to
  provide a set of hashes to verify that indeed the tendered
  transaction belongs to a particular block in the blockchain
  by recomputing the Merkle root of the block of transactions.

- Storage node. This type of nodes are setup to store the full
  blockchain.
- Routing node. This type of nodes are setup to route
  messages and blocks to the connected neighboring nodes.
- Mining node. This type of nodes are equipped with a digital
  wallet to collect the block reward and the transaction fees,
  a full blockchain (typically), and dedicated hardware for
  performing the hashing operation for the PoW competition.

8.2.2 Self-contained cryptography

Cryptography provides the basic tools to protect an asset for
confidentiality, integrity, and availability. In a cryptocurrency like
Bitcoin, cryptography plays an even more important role. Because
the most important data in Bitcoin, *i.e.*, the distributed ledger in the

form of a blockchain, is public, confidentiality is not a consideration except the wallet software where the private keys must be kept
confidential and safe. Cryptographic hash function (*i.e.*, SHA256)
is pervasively used in Bitcoin operation. It is also referred to as
secure hash function or one-way hash function because one cannot
deduce the original value that is being hashed from the resulting
hash bit-string. In addition to the one-way transformation capability, cryptographic hash produces unpredictable result in that given
a hash value, it is computationally impossible to find a string that
would lead to exactly the same hash. This in fact is a fundamental requirement for cryptographic hash functions. The difficulty
of finding the preimage of a hash and the unpredictability of the
hashing operation form the basis for the PoW algorithm. The PoW
competition is a stochastic process and there is no better way of
finding a preimage than trying out different nonce one by one.
We will elaborate this further in the next chapter on blockchain
consensus.

Traditionally, the use of public-key cryptography typically
requires a certificate to bind the public key to its owner. Not doing
so could be vulnerable to the man-in-the-middle attack. The certificate must be certified by an authority (called certificate authority,
or CA) that vouches for the fact the the owner indeed owns the
public key presumably based on some legal documents, which is
verified offline. Of course, the question is why anyone should trust
the CA? Hence, in the end a public key infrastructure (PKI) is
established, where there is a hierarchical of authorities formed in
a tree structure. Any certificate received must be verified using a
chain of trust up to the root authority. Certification management is
highly complex due to the possibility of revocation and reinstate-
ment, expiration and renewal. PKI obviously must be considered
as a trusted third party, which is not compatible with the design
principle of Bitcoin.

Digital signature is another foundation for Bitcoin operation as
well as security. It is used to verify who has the right credential
to spend the fund received. Can Bitcoin operates without a PKI?
The answer is absolutely yes. The intrinsic reason for the need of
a PKI is the requirement on the association of an identity with
a public key. Interestingly, for a cryptocurrency that wanted to
mimic cash, which offers a large-degree of anonymity, such association is in fact not only not needed, but would be regarded as

undesirable because an easy linkage of an identity and the cryptocurrency received or spent would make the cryptocurrency lose its anonymity protection of its users. In Bitcoin, the fund received would be associated with an address, which is derived from the public key. Furthermore, one address is supposed to receive fund only one time for both security and for anonymity (or the privacy of the user) reasons. The digital wallet software would generate as many addresses as needed and manage the balance of unspent fund for the user. This model is called the unspent transaction output (UTXO) model [1].

A remaining question is how one could obtain a public key to verify a digital signature. The solution is easy. The one who wishes to spend the fund received on an address must present a public key corresponding to the address. As we will show next, this is implemented as the spending condition in the form of locking and unlocking scripts.

In Bitcoin (and many other cryptocurrencies), the elliptic-curve cryptograph (ECC) is used as the public-key cryptograph of choice because shorter keys can be used to achieve the same security strength as RSA [13], for example, a 256-bit EEC key would be equivalent to a 3072-bit RSA key in terms of security strength. ECC is based on the assumption that it is computationally infeasible to solve the elliptic curve discrete logarithm problem (until quantum computing becomes a reality). The elliptic curve digital signature algorithm (ECDSA) is recommended by the US National Institute of Standards and Technology for digital signature.

8.2.3 Decentralized data structure

In Bitcoin, there is no centralized server for storing the transaction records. Instead, the full ledger that contains all the transactions since the launch of the network are maintained by many nodes, most of which are mining nodes. This decentralized approach makes the system much more resilient to cyberattacks and hardware failures because the data are massively replicated and the loss or tampering with a few copies of the ledger will not impact the system in any significant way. Blocks and transactions are verified before they are passed on to other nodes (*i.e.*, invalid transactions and blocks will be discarded immediately), hence, invalid data are doomed to be short-lived.

The data structures used in Bitcoin are also carefully and cleverly designed. We can roughly categorize the data structures in Bitcoin into three levels: (1) Private-public key pairs and addresses; (2) Transactions; (3) Blocks. The key pairs are used to secure transactions and blocks. The addresses enables a Bitcoin user to receive cryptocurrency in a transaction.

8.2.3.1   Private key, public key, and address

The three items are actually closely related. As shown in Figure 8.2. The wallet software would first derive a private key based on a seed. The public key is derived from the private key using elliptic curve multiplication, which is a one-way operation (*i.e.*, from the public key, it is impossible to deduce the corresponding private key). The Bitcoin address is in turn derived from the public key via a sequence of cryptographic hash operations. Again, this is a one-way process meaning that from the address, no one can deduce the corresponding public key. The address itself is 20-byte long (*i.e.*, 160 bits). The actual address contains 5 extra bytes. The first byte indicates the network ID, which differentiates addresses used in the main Bitcoin network and other types of networks such as the test network for development. The last four bytes are checksum for the address to protect its integrity. The cryptocurrency one receives is tied to the address and if the address is wrong, then the person would not be able to access the cryptocurrency because the corresponding private key does not exist.

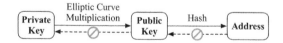

Figure 8.2   The relationship between private key, public key, and address in Bitcoin.

8.2.3.2   Transaction

In Bitcoin, a transaction is a double-entry record, as shown in Figure 8.3. A transaction consists of one or more inputs and one or more outputs. The transaction input has three main components: (1) the hash of the transaction in which this input is one of the outputs, which is referred to as the transaction id; (2) the index of the output in the original transaction, the first of which will be 0;

(3) an unlocking script provided by the creator of the current transaction. the transaction output consists of two main components: (1) the amount will be paid to a new owner, which could be another Bitcoin user or the user himself/herself; and (2) a locking script. In addition to inputs and outputs, the transaction also has a lock time field, indicating when the transaction outputs can be spent. Usually, this field has a value 0, which means the fund in the transaction outputs can be spent immediately. But sometimes one would have to wait at a future time or block height (the block height concept will be explained next) to spend.

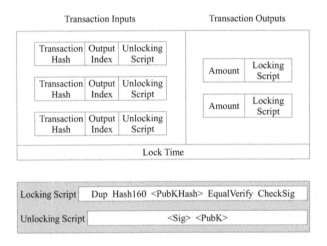

Figure 8.3   Bitcoin transaction structure.

Bitcoin intentionally offers very limited scripting capability to protect the security of the system, but it is sufficiently powerful to enable setting up the locking condition where a user would then be able to provide the corresponding unlocking information to spend the fund received in a transaction. The only data structure used to evaluate a script is a stack and the script is executed sequently (without any loop). Figure 8.3 shows the most common locking script format, which is referred to as pay-to-public-key-hash (P2PKH). The symbol $< PubKHash >$ is the address that receives the fund, and $Hash160$ is the algorithm to compute the address based on the public key. The symbols, Dup, $EqualVerify$, and $CheckSig$, are predefined operations to verify the information provided in the unlocking script. Dup means to duplicate an item and place it on the stack. $EqualVerify$ is to compare the top two items on the stack and see if the two are identical. If the result is false, the script is terminated immediately. $CheckSig$ is to verify the signature supplied as part of the unlocking script. The unlocking script is much simpler. It contains a signature and the corresponding public key. The public key must hash to the address (*i.e.*, $PubKHash$) the user wishes to spend fund from.

We next explain the digital signature. Unlike a physical signature, which can exist on its own. A digital signature is tied to both the signer's private key as well as the information it is applied on. In Bitcoin, one could sign on four different types of information [17]. For P2PKH locking script, typically the signature applies to all transaction inputs and outputs. Let the information to which the signature applies be P, to verify the signature, $Sig(P)$, one would use the supplied (and already verified) public key $PubK$ on the signature such that $PubK(Sig(P)) = P$.

One might wonder where is the field for the transaction fee. The answer is no, there is no such field in the transaction data structure. The transaction fee can be easily calculated by taking the difference between the total of the input fund and the total of the output fund in a transaction.

In Bitcoin, the miner who has successfully mined a new block (*i.e.*, the person who finds the solution to the puzzle first) gets to create a special transaction, called CoinBase transaction, to pay himself or herself the block reward and the transaction fees included in the block. Format-wise, this transaction looks the same as a typical transaction. However, this transaction does not have a real input because the fund is rewarded to the miner by the Bitcoin system. Hence, the transaction id field in the transaction input is set to all zeros, and the output number is set to all ones in binary presentation or all f's in hexadecimal presentation. The miner could then leave any text that he or she wishes to as the unlocking script. That is why the CoinBase transaction of the genesis block (*i.e.*, the very first Bitcoin block) contains the following phrase: "The Times 03/Jan/2009 Chancellor on brink of second bailout for banks" referring to the title of the cover story of *The London Times* on January 3, 2009. Another important feature for the CoinBase transaction is that the time lock is set to 100 blocks later so that the miner can only be spent 100 blocks later. What is the reason for imposing this lock time? It is not to force the miners to have longer-term interest in the Bitcoin network as one might have thought because 100 block-time is only about 16.6 hours. The real reason for this design decision is to make sure that only the block awards for the blocks included in the main blockchain can be spend. Because of the possibility of forking, a new block might appear to be on the main chain initially, but later becomes part of a side branch, and when this happens, the block is abandoned so should the corresponding block reward. The CoinBase transaction is drastically different from regular transactions because the CoinBase transaction is tied to a specific block, where a regular transaction can be easily included in another block again if it is initially included in a block that becomes part of a side branch.

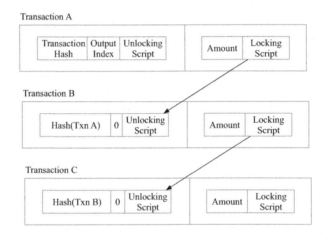

Figure 8.4   An example transaction chain in Bitcoin.

The double-entry transaction design in Bitcoin would create a chain of transactions from the output of one transaction to the input in a later transaction when the user spends the received cryptocurrency, as shown in Figure 8.4.

8.2.3.3   Block

In Bitcoin, transactions are assembled into blocks. Currently, the block is limited to 1MB. The size of the transactions varies depending on the number of inputs and outputs and the different types of payment methods used. According to an analysis of 2015 data posted online at `https://tradeblock.com/blog/analys` `is-of-bitcoin-transaction-size-trends/`, the size of the transactions is trending upward. The mean transaction size is almost 600 bytes in October 2015. The medium size, however, is significantly smaller. For the basic P2PKH type of transactions (which accounts for 89% of the all transactions), the median size is 274 bytes while the mean is 566 bytes in 2015. If we take the median (or mean) size as the transaction size, one block could accommodate roughly 3,737 (or 1,809) transactions. The actual number of transactions in a block started with a very low number (in single digit in 2010) and has been increasing rapidly, as shown in Figure 8.5. Currently it is around 2,000 transactions per block on average, getting close to the block size limit due to the popularity of Bitcoin.

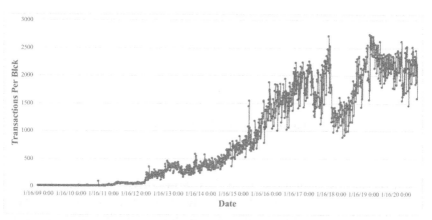

Figure 8.5   Bitcoin transactions per block data since its inception in 2009 through September 15, 2020. The data are downloaded from https://www.blockchain.com/charts/n-transactions-per-block.

The Bitcoin block structure is illustrated in Figure 8.6. Each block starts with a 4-byte long magic bytes, which is always $0xD9B4BEF9$ in hexadecimal representation. This is followed by a 4-byte long block size, indicating the total number of bytes in the block excluding the magic number field. Then, it is the block header, which is 80-byte long. After the block header is a field denoting the number of transactions in the block, which takes 1-9 bytes depending on the need. The last part of the block is the list of transactions in the block.

The block header contains six fields. It starts with a 4-byte long version field, which indicates the software version the mining node is using. This is followed by a 32-byte long field for the hash of the previous block (*i.e.*, the parent block). More specifically, this is the

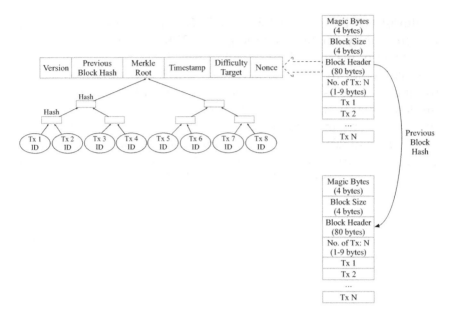

Figure 8.6   Bitcoin block structure.

hash of the block header of the previous block, which effectively chains the blocks together. The next field is the 32-byte long Merkle root. This is the hash of all the transactions included in the current block. Bitcoin construct a balanced Merkle tree to facilitate fast verification on whether or not a transaction is included in the block. The fourth field is the timestamp represented as the number of seconds that has passed since the start of January 1, 1970 UTC. This design, together with the consensus algorithm essentially make the Bitcoin network a self-contained timestamp server, which was envisaged prior to the creation of Bitcoin as a prerequisite for cryptocurrency. The last two fields are designed for PoW computation. The difficulty target is a 4-byte long field representing a value. The hash of the block header must be smaller than this difficulty target value. The last field is a 4-byte long nonce. In the original design, the miner would try different nonce values hoping to derive a hash that meets the difficulty target. Unfortunately, due to the arms race on the hashing power, this field alone is often not sufficient to find a solution to the PoW puzzle. Miners have resorted to the change of the timestamp, and the CoinBase transaction input to discover solutions.

Another term we quite often hear about is the block height. It is apparently not present in any part of the block. Instead, every node that manages the blockchain would keep track of such information. The block height refers to the block's position in the chain starting from the genesis block, which has a block height of 0. If we say a block has a block height n, then it means that there are n blocks preceding this block. The block height is similar to the floor number in the UK system. A block can be identified both by its block height and its hash (or more precisely it is the hash of the block header).

Figure 8.6 also shows how the Merkle root is computed. Using an 8-transaction block as an example, the transaction ids (*i.e.*, recall that the transaction id means the hash of a transaction) are lined up as the leaves of the tree at the bottom. The transaction ids are pair-wise hashed twice using SHA256. Then, the intermediate hash values are again pair-wise hashed to produce a higher-level node. This process will go on until the top node is produced, which is the root of the Merkle tree. The root node contains the information of all the leaf nodes. Any alternation of individual transactions in the block, the reordering of any transaction, deleting or inserting a transaction would all produce a completely different Merkle root. That is why when the blocks are chained together using the previous block hash field, the change of any transaction in a block would invalidate all later blocks that are chained to that block. This forms the foundation for the immutability of the ledger.

The Merkle tree computation requires that the number of transactions is power of 2 so that the tree is balanced at each step in the computation. What if the number of transactions in a block is not power of two? The last component is duplicated to form a pair for the hash calculation. In Figure 8.7, we show two examples. In the first example (the top figure), there are only 7 transactions in the block. To balance the tree, the last transaction is duplicated at the leaf-level. In the second example, there are 6 transactions and at the level just above the leaf-level, the hash of transaction 5 and transaction 6 $H56$ would have to be duplicated. Unfortunately, this strategy could enable one to construct multiple lists of transactions that have exactly the same Merkle tree, which could subvert the immutability property of the Bitcoin ledger! In the first example, $\{Tx1, Tx2, ..., Tx7\}$ and $\{Tx1, Tx2, ..., Tx7, Tx7\}$ would produce the same Merkle root. In the second example, $\{Tx1, Tx2, Tx3, Tx4, Tx5, Tx6\}$ and $\{Tx1, Tx2, Tx3, Tx4, Tx5, Tx6, Tx5, Tx6\}$ would produce identical Merkle root. Bitcoin

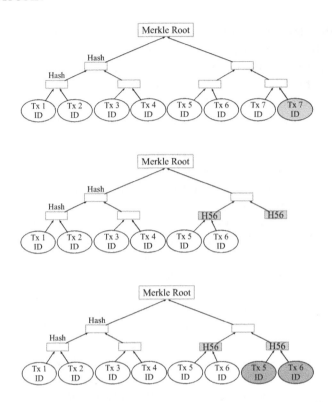

Figure 8.7   An issue with Bitcoin Merkle tree computation where different trees could produce the same Merkle root.

has a mechanism to detect duplicate transactions to prevent the double-spending attacks. Hence, the block that contains duplicate transactions would be labeled as invalid. It might appear the issue is a non-issue after all. However, a denial-of-service attack could be designed based on this vulnerability, as pointed out in the discussion at https://bitcointalk.org/?topic=102395. This vulnerability is referred to as CVE-2012-2459 (block merkle calculation exploit) and the full disclosure was made public on August 22, 2012.

To launch this denial-of-service attack, the adversary does not need to mine a block. One only need to listen for a new block, if the number of transactions in the block is not power of 2, the attacker would construct a new list of transactions that contain duplicates, and propagate to other nodes. If a node receives this mutated block ahead of the genuine one, the node would label the block as invalid and cache the invalid block. Even if the genuine block arrives a little later, the node would not accept it because the block has already been labeled as invalid by checking the block hash. The node would not ask for a retransmission of the block either because it is invalid. The issue was resolved by Gavin Andresen on April 30, 2020 (prior to the public release of the vulnerability) by immediately reject a block that contains duplicate transactions without caching so that when the genuine block arrives, it can be accepted.

8.2.4 Decentralized algorithms

As previously noted, classical distributed consensus algorithms require the participating nodes to know the current membership, rely on a leader (which is called often primary or coordinator), and many rounds of message exchanges among the current members [6, 14, 25, 27, 26, 28]. Such algorithms are not going to work well in the large-scale peer-to-peer network where cyberattacks could be prominent primarily for two reasons:

- The reliance on multi-round of broadcast-based message exchanges on leader election and on agreement is detrimental to the scalability of the system, and is also prone to denial-of-service attacks.
- The reliance on a particular node to carry additional responsibility will immediately make this node vulnerable to cyberattacks. Such attacks could essentially prevent the system from making any progress.

In Bitcoin, the PoW-based consensus algorithm does not assume any notion of membership and does not rely on any node to take any additional responsibility. Mining nodes would compete to solve a PoW-puzzle for the right to assemble the next block and collect a reward [29]. The algorithm is designed in such a way that the PoW competition is a stochastic process [22]. Although nodes with higher hashing power have greater probability to win the competition, they are not guaranteed to win. The puzzle design is amazingly simple: Given the predefined difficulty target D, the task is to build a block with a block header H such that $Hash(H) < D$. If a miner could assemble a block that satisfy the requirement, we say the block meets the target. The block header contains several fields, one of which is a nonce (4-byte long), which is designed for the miner to use to alter the block header with different nonce hoping to have $Hash(H) < D$. Unfortunately, with the availability of the application-specific-integrated-circuit (ASIC)-based hardware, this single field is no longer enough to guarantee to meet the difficulty target. Other means include the changing the timestamp field and changing the text in the CoinBase transaction. When a miner finds a way to make the block header meets the target, it will announce the new block to all the nodes that it connects to and eventually the new block will be propagated to the entire network. Due to the nature of the cryptographic hash, one cannot predict what kind of block header would meet the target. Hence, the only way to solve the puzzle is to try many many times until one is found. This PoW-puzzle design is formalized as a non-interactive zero-knowledge proof [22] where the verification does not involve any interrogation of the original solver of the puzzle.

In Bitcoin, the target difficulty is set to lead to a 10-minute block interval, *i.e.*, a new block will be added to the blockchain for every 10 minutes *on average*. This design is to ensure that the system is stable when growing the blockchain. In most cases, only a single miner would win the competition for each new block. As long as this is the case, all nodes would see exactly the same blockchain, which ensures the consensus of the entire system. However, because the puzzle-solving competition is a stochastic process, occasionally, two or more miners do find blocks that meet the target concurrently, in which case, the system would have a temporary inconsistency. Bitcoin specifies a conflict resolution mechanism: a miner should choose the top block of the branch that has the greatest cumulative difficulty as the parent. Typically, this means the longest chain would be selected.

▉ EXAMPLE 8.1

Figure 8.8 shows on example on how the blockchain grows and how a conflict is resolved. In this example, we assume that there are four mining nodes (labeled as A, B, C, and D) and the blockchain has three blocks. For the next block, we suppose that node C finds a block that meets the target first and immediately announce the new block to all other mining nodes. Because in this round, this is the only block announced, all mining nodes add this new block to their blockchain. Now the blockchain has four blocks and all mining nodes would see exactly the same blockchain. A mining node would stop working on the current block once it has received a new block for the same round (as indicated by the block height).

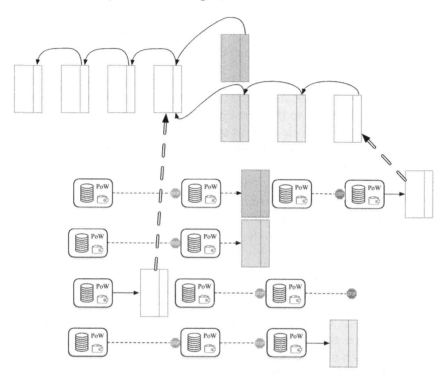

Figure 8.8 Bitcoin blockchain consensus and conflict resolution.

Roughly 10 minutes later, A and B each finds a block that meets the target concurrently. The block assembled by A is colored blue, and the one by B is colored green. Both A and B would announce their new blocks to the network. At this point, the system has an inconsistency and it is typically referred to as a *fork*. Node A obviously would add its own block (the blue-colored block) to the blockchain and proceed to mining for the next block, and B would do the same for its green-colored block. Let's assume that D receives B's new block ahead of A's block, add the green-colored block on its blockchain, and immediately starts to work on the next block, using the green-colored block as the parent block. Luckily, node D finds a new block, colored yellow in the Figure, before another mining node could find a new block, and announces it to the network. When node A receives the yellow-colored block from D, node A would now know that its own branch can no longer be considered as the main branch because the alternative branch has greater cumulative difficulty.

As can be seen, the PoW-based consensus algorithm is drastically different from classical consensus algorithm in several ways:

- No mining node carries any special responsibility. All mining nodes are equal in terms of responsibility and functionality to the consensus process.
- There is no notion about membership. A mining node only connects to a few other nodes in the Bitcoin network, and it has no knowledge how many other mining nodes there are in the network. The algorithms and the rules a mining node must follow are not altered in anyway with respect to the number of nodes in the network. The target difficulty, which will be adjusted periodically, will indirectly reflect the number of mining nodes in the network. If all mining nodes have equal hashing power, then the difficulty will arise proportionally with the number of nodes.
- There is no explicit voting. There is no additional messages sent or received for the purpose of reaching consensus. Hence, the notion of majority has no place in the execution of each mining node. The dissemination of a new block may be considered a form of voting, but it does not carry any additional overhead.
- There is no well-defined condition that anyone could say definitely that a consensus is reached on the formation of the blockchain. The consensus is achieved probabilistically instead of definitively in Bitcoin. Each node would simply proceed forward according to the PoW rule no matter what. Even if there is inconsistency where two or more blocks are found for the same round, a node would choose one of them as the parent based on the cumulative difficulty to resolve the fork. This obviously can be regarded as a drawback for the system because the user would have to wonder when she can be sure that her transaction is fully settled (*e.g.*, so that she can ship the product paid in the transaction). To cope with this uncertainty, heuristic rule has been used. In Bitcoin, high-value transaction would want to wait for 6 confirmations before it is considered immutable. In general, the deeper the block in the chain, the less likely

it can be replaced in an attack. Recently, several other cryptocurrencies have adopted a mechanism for checkpointing of stable blockchain so that no attacker could possibly alter the segment of blockchain that has been checkpointed.

Many regard the PoW consensus algorithm as a disruptive solution for building consensus and trust in a large-scale peer-to-peer network. Perhaps the best summary for the algorithm is given by Andreas M. Antonopoulos in [1]: *"Satoshi Nakamoto's main invention is the decentralized mechanism for emergent consensus. Emergent, because consensus is not achieved explicitly - there is no election or fixed moment when consensus occurs. Instead, consensus is an emergent artifact of the asynchronous interaction of thousands of independent nodes, all following simple rules."*

8.3 Ethereum

The creation of Ethereum was due to a much grander vision: to go beyond cryptocurrency and build decentralized applications that inherit similar characteristics of Bitcoin in terms of security and dependability without the need to trust any third party. The formation of the vision, design, and development was led by a young software developer named Vitalik Buterin. One key direction Vitalik wanted to go is to extend the scripting capability of Bitcoin to implement smart contracts. Initially, Vitalik attempted to introduce his idea to the Mastercoin development team. The Mastercoin runs an overlay protocol on top of Bitcoin to offer limited smart contract capability. When his attempt was rejected (as being too radical), Vitalik started to work on a new decentralized computing platform in 2013. With the help of Gavin Wood, Vitalik made the design for Ethereum, which provides a deterministic and secure computing environment for decentralized applications. The core invention is a method to power the execution of a Turing-complete scripting language with a built-in mechanism to deal with the halting problem, which is well-known for Turing-complete machines. In July 30, 2015, the Ethereum platform started to operate with the first block mined [2].

In addition to supporting Turing-complete computing, Ethereum attempted to address several shortcomings in Bitcoin, and adopted an account model on transaction processing and balance tracking in contrast to the UTXO model used in Bitcoin.

Each user may have multiple accounts of two different types. One type is called externally owned accounts (EOAs). Each EOA has a private key so that the user may spend the fund in the account. The other type is contract accounts, which do not have the corresponding private keys. In Ethereum, the account number is a 160-bit (or 20-byte) string. Ethereum also uses a SHA-3 variation of secure hash function that produces 256-bit string called Keccak hash function. Bitcoin uses the SHA2 hash function that produces the same fix-length bit string.

As a result of Ethereum's design decisions, the data structures used in Ethereum are significantly more complex than those in Bitcoin. Even though Ethereum consensus is based on PoW, it is also made much more sophisticated by making the PoW computation memory-limited instead of purely CPU limited as in Bitcoin. We note that despite that Ethereum has made it public for quite some time it intents to switch to Proof-of-Stake (PoS)-based consensus, the target date for making the switch has been extended multiple times due to technical difficulties of implementing a sound PoS algorithm.

With the support for the Turing-complete computing, Ethereum has an ambitious plan to develop decentralized applications (Dapps) or even decentralized autonomous organizations (DAOs). As part of the effort, Ethereum is a strong proponent to extending the coin construct introduced in Bitcoin to represent entities in physical world. This is called tokenization. The security and trustworthiness of cryptocurrency exchanges within the platform is fully guaranteed by the consensus algorithm and security mechanisms. However, that alone is far from sufficient to develop Dapp and DAOs. Smart contracts for the latter cases would inevitably interact with external entities and receive information from these external entities. The trustworthiness of these external entities will directly impact the trustworthiness of the entire smart contract execution. There have been arguments that currently it is lacking a distributed oracle that ensure such external entity trustworthiness [24].

8.3.1   Ethereum Computing Model

Alan Turing introduced the concept of Turing machine, which is a state machine that can manipulate the state by reading and writing a set of symbols on some unbounded sequential memory. If a programming language function as a Turing machine, then we say the language is Turing-complete. The scripting language introduced in Bitcoin is not Turing-complete because it does not support loops. The choice of Bitcoin is easy to understand because a Turing-complete system has the unsolvable halting problem (such as infinite loop) as Turing has proved. Since the goal of Ethereum is to become a platform for Turing-complete state machine, it must offer a Turing-complete programing language (which is called Solidity), and in the mean time, introduce mechanisms to prevent the halting problem from happening.

The solution in Ethereum is actually quite simple and elegant. All execution of instructions as part of the transaction and smart contract is done within a virtual machine called Ethereum Virtual Machine (EVM), and the issuer of the transaction or smart contract must pay for every single instruction executed at the EVM. In Ethereum, the cost to execute every instruction is defined in the Ethereum yellow paper [23]. For example, the cost of running every transaction itself would cost 21,000 units. In Ethereum, the fee unit is called gas, presumably analogous to driving a gasoline car - you will need to have gas in your car's tank to drive. When the user's provided gas has run out before the end of the smart contract execution, then the smart contract is terminated, thereby preventing the halting problem. It is also interesting to note that Ethereum asks the issuer of a transaction or a contract to set the price for the gas in terms of the cryptocurrency, Ether, used in Ethereum.

With the potential halting problem resolved, Ethereum is set to be used as a decentralized, secure and trustworthy state machine. In Ethereum, the state is defined as the collection of state maintained by each account address (of 20-byte long). For each address, the following state is maintained:

- The nonce for this address. For an EOA address, the nonce is the number of transactions that this address has issued. For a contract account address, the nonce is the number of contracts created under this account. Indeed, a contract may create one or more contracts if specified by the contract code.
- The balance of this account. For an EOA address, the balance refers to the amount of Ether that the account has. For a contract account, the balance refers to the amount of gas remaining for execution of the contract.

- The 256-bit Merkle Patricia tree root for the data stored for this account. The Patricia tree provides more flexibility than the Merkle tree, which must be balanced. The hash of each data item under this account (which is stored as key-value pairs) will be placed at the leaf nodes. The root is calculated in a rather similar fashion as that for the Merkle tree used in Bitcoin. The actual content of the data can be arbitrary based on the smart contract.
- The hash of the smart contract code, which has already been compiled into EVM byte-code. Unlike the first three types of state, this one is immutable in that once it is created, it should never be changed.

Both EOA and contract accounts have the nonce and the balance. For an EOA, the code is empty and so does the root for the data storage. The root hash for the data storage is for the data generated by the contract.

In Ethereum, the change of state is always initiated by a transaction. The so-called a smart contract is simply a piece of code defining one or more functions, which can be invoked. Once a function is invoked, the function will be executed at all full nodes, and the result will be deterministic so that outcome of the execution will be the same everywhere provided that the contract is adequately funded.

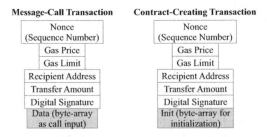

Figure 8.9   Structure of Ethereum transaction.

Due to the account-based design in Ethereum, the transaction structure is quite different from that in Bitcoin. In Bitcoin, a transaction contains a double-entry booking record, as well as the unlocking and unlocking scripts where digital signature is used to unlock the fund received (to prove ownership of the fund). In the Ethereum, every transaction is digitally signed by the issuer using the private key of the account. Please note that only an EOA can create a transaction. As shown in Figure 8.9, there are two different kinds of transactions, one is referred to as message-call transaction, and the other is called contract creating transaction. The only difference is the last field between the two types. For a message-call transaction, the last field is called data, which contains a byte-array as the input for the message-call. Apparently this is for the purpose of using a transaction to invoke contract. For a contract-creating transaction, the last field, Init, contains a byte-array containing the EVM byte-code for the initialization of the smart contract. Init is executed only once and it returns a body, which is a segment of EVM byte-code for the smart contract so that it can be invoked via message calls [23]. The common fields include the following fields:

- A nonce field, which is nothing but a sequence number to ensure each transaction issued by an account is processed exactly once and in the right order by the Ethereum mining nodes, *i.e.,* duplicate or reordered transaction can be detected. Similar approach has been used pervasively in networking protocols such as TCP.
- The gas price, which the issuer sets depending on how much the issuer is willing to pay per unit of gas in terms of the smallest unit of coin used by Ethereum called Wei.
- The gas limit, which is the amount of gas that the issuer sets to cover the cost of running the transaction. For a routine transaction that transfers certain amount of Ether from one account to another, the standard cost is 21,000 gas. If the gas limit is set lower than the required amount, the transaction (and the invoked smart contract) will be aborted.
- The recipient account address. If this address is an EOA address, then the transaction is a simple fund-transfer transaction. If this address is an existing contract account account, then the transaction is invoking the contract with the address. For smart contract creation, the address will be all 0s.
- The amount being transferred to the recipient account address. For a contract-creating transaction, this is the amount the issuer provided for the contract as the initial gas limit. For message-call transaction, this amount is transferred to the address, which could be an EOA account for a fund transfer, or a smart contract address to add more gas to the contract.

- The digital signature. Ethereum also uses ECC for digital signing. More accurately, this field contains both the digital signature and the public key.

The execution of a transaction in Ethereum is atomic. If a transaction fails, all states will be reverted back to their original values except that the gas used for the transaction will be consumed.

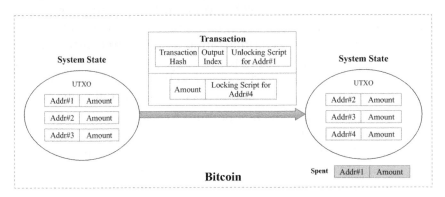

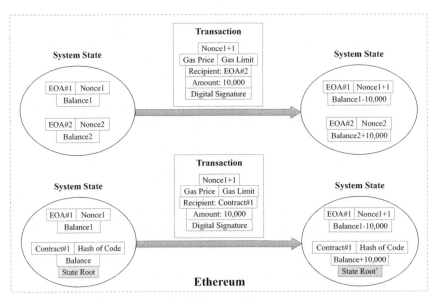

Figure 8.10   State transition via transaction in Bitcoin and Ethereum.

Even though Bitcoin does not support a Turing-complete computing, it can still be modeled as a limited state machine where the state consists of UTXO. The processing of a transaction would trigger a state change. In the example shown in the top scenario of Figure 8.10, the Bitcoin transaction would spend the fund received earlier on *Addr#1*, and pay the amount to *Addr#4*. Prior to the transaction, the system state consists of three UTXO on *Addr#1*, *Addr#2*, and *Addr#3*. After the transaction, the state is changed to having UTXO with *Addr#2*, *Addr#3*, and *Addr#4*.

In Ethereum, the transaction that transfers some fund from one EOA to another will trigger a state transition that is rather similar to that of Bitcoin, as shown in the middle scenario of Figure 8.10. Instead of UTXO changes, the account balances for the two EOA accounts are changed, in a way similar to the bank fund transfer. If the recipient is a contract account, in addition to the balance changes, the state root under the contract account could be changed as the result of the invocation, as shown in the bottom scenario shown in Figure 8.10. If an issuer of a transaction wanted to invoke a function defined in a contract, the function to be called will be specified in the data field.

The contract-creating transaction is similar to the bottom scenario in Figure 8.10 with two exceptions: (1) the recipient address is initially set to be $0x0$ (0 in hexadecimal) and a unique contract address will be assigned once the contract is deployed on the blockchain; (2) The contract code will be included as part of the transaction for deployment.

We have said that the contract is a piece of code, one might wonder what a smart contract looks like in Ethereum. Because the contract code will be compiled into byte-code to run in EVM, several programming languages are supported for writing the smart contract. The native programming language for writing smart contract in Ethereum is Solidity. Similar to Java, Solidity is an object-oriented programming language. In Solidity, a smart contract looks like a class definition with an optional constructor, one or more state variable, and one or more functions in it, as shown in Figure 8.11. There are four visibility attributes, external, public, internal, and private. External can only be used for functions, which means the function is part of the contract interface and it can be called via transactions or from other contracts. The remaining three can be used for both functions and state variables. Public means it can be invoked via a message call from another contract or internally within the contract. Internal means that it can only be called internally from within the contract and all the derivative contracts (*i.e.,* the contracts that this contract has created). `Private` means it can only be accessed in the current contract.

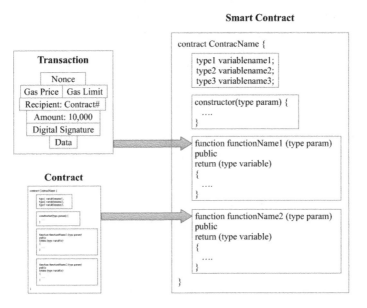

Figure 8.11   Ethereum smart contract structure.

It is important to emphasize that contract execution can only be initiated by a transaction issued by an EOA. Once a contract is invoked, it may create new contracts and call other contracts, but a contract will never run non-triggered on its own. We also note that the smart contract is designed to run absolutely deterministically, thereby the execution of a contract is strictly sequential. Furthermore, contract is executed one at a time. Hence, Ethereum can be thought of as a single-threaded state machine.

A smart contract cannot be altered once deployed on the blockchain. However, a contract may be deleted if the contract lays out a specific condition when the contract should be deleted with a special EVM opcode called `SELFDESTRUCT`. When a contract is deleted, all its storage space is released. However, all transactions related to this contract will still be part of the blockchain. When a contract is deleted, the issuer of the contract may get a refund of 24,000 gas. The contract may also decide to relinquish its storage space by setting the storage address to 0, which will result a refund of 15,000 gas.

So far, we have talked about the structures of transactions and contracts, and the state transitions triggered by transactions. However, we have not mentioned exactly when the contract will be executed. In Bitcoin, a transactions is *tentatively* "executed" every time it is being verified by a node because the unlocking scripts will run as part of the verification. However, only when a transaction is included in a block, and the block is placed on the main blockchain, would the state change be official (*i.e.*, the fund is changing hands at this point, for high-value transactions, one might want to wait to receive 6 confirmations before it is declared final). Naturally, the best time to execute the transaction and the smart contract if one is called will be at the block formation time (more precisely is when a transaction is being verified for inclusion in a block).

As there is a delay between the submission and the execution of a transaction, a Dapp issuing the transaction on a smart contract cannot depends on getting a synchronous answer from the contract execution (for example to display useful information on a user interface (UI)). To accommodate this application need, Ethereum introduced two mechanisms: (1) adding an event construct in the contract specification and providing a logging facility; (2) adding a transaction receipt construct, which contains the log and will be included as part of the block. When an event is generated by a contract, the supplied arguments to the event will be stored in the log for the transaction that initiated the contract execution. The Dapp may fetch the transaction receipt included in the block later to retrieve the logged event information.

The transaction receipt in fact carries much more responsibility than accommodating the need for UI display of contract execution information. Unlike Bitcoin transaction, where the transaction itself is the data to be stored and protected, Ethereum contract contains arbitrary code. How do we really know the contract has already been executed by the mining node? We need evidence for the execution and its outcome. The transaction receipt would include all relevant information to prove that the contract has been successfully executed.

According to the authoritative book on Ethereum (the co-author is the Ethereum co-founder Gavin Wood) [2], the transaction receipt contains four tuples: (1) the cumulative gas used right after this transaction was executed within the current block; (2) the set of logs produced by this transaction (via the invoked contract); (3) the Bloom filter that can be used to search for the corresponding logs; (4) the status code of the transaction. Figure 8.12 shows an actual transaction receipt obtained via the `eth_getTransactionReceipt()` call using JSON-RPC (taken from `https://infura.io/docs/ethereum/json-rpc /eth-getTransactionReceipt`), the actual JSON document contains slightly more information than specified, which we categorize into two types: (1) the gas used by this transaction alone; (2) identifier information for the transaction, the address of the contract created/invoked, the block hash and block number to which the transaction belongs. Note that the `contractAddress` is set to null for a message-call transaction that invokes an existing contract, and it contains the contract address for a contract-creating transaction. For the former case, the `to` element will contain the contract address. For the latter case, the `to` element will be set to null.

The Bloom filter is used in Bitcoin to add some privacy protection for lightweight clients when they ask for missing transactions. In Ethereum, it is used rather as an efficient way for searching for the presence of events in the log. Bloom filter uses a short string (256 bytes array in Ethereum, as `logsBloom`) to condense information regarding the events characteristics. When one queries for an event, the filter would provide two answers: (1) `maybe`, when there is a match, or (2) `no`, when there is no match.

Previously, we mentioned the events generated by a contract for allowing an Dapp to fetch information for display on the UI. Where can we find such information from the transaction receipt then? It is in the log. The events are encoded under the *topics* component as a list. More specifically, each topic is a 20-byte Keccak256 hash of the event name and the types of the event's parameters.

8.3.2   Block and Consensus

Due to several reasons, the Ethereum block structure is much more complex than that in Bitcoin. First, Ethereum supports smart contract with internal data storage, which is not present in Bitcoin. Second, Ethereum aims to facilitate much faster block confirmation time (or shorter block interval) than Bitcoin while preserving the system security and stability. A typical block interval in Ethereum is about 12 seconds while the target block interval is 10 minutes in Bitcoin. Third, Ethereum wanted to discourage centralization in mining. Fourth, Ethereum aims to minimize the ASIC-based

```
{
    "blockHash": "0xb3b20624f8f0f86eb50dd04688409e5cea4bd02d700bf6e79e9384d47d6a5a35",
    "blockNumber": "0x5bad55",
    "contractAddress": null,
    "cumulativeGasUsed": "0xb90b0",
    "from": "0x398137383b3d25c92898c656696e41950e473 16b",
    "gasUsed": "0x1383f",
    "logs": [
        {
            "address": "0x06012c8cf97bead5deae237070f9587f8e7a266d",
            "blockHash": "0xb3b20624f8f0f86eb50dd04688409e5cea4bd02d700bf6e79e9384d47d6a5a35",
            "blockNumber": "0x5bad55",
            "data":
"0x0000000000000000000000000398137383b3d25c92898c656696e41950e47316b00000000000000000000000000
0000000000000000000000000000000000000cee6100000000000000000000000000000000000000000000000000000000
000000ac3e1000000000000000000000000000000000000000000000000000000000000005baf35",
            "logIndex": "0x6",
            "removed": false,
            "topics": [
                "0x241ea03ca20251805084d27d4440371c34a0b85ff108f6bb5611248f73818b80"
            ],
            "transactionHash": "0xbb3a336e3f823ec18197f1e13ee875700f08f03e2cab75f0d0b118dabb44cba0",
            "transactionIndex": "0x11"
        }
    ],
    "logsBloom":
"0x00000000000000000000000000000000000000000000000000000000000000000000000000000000000000000000000
0000000000000000000000000000000000000000000000000001000000000000000000000000000000800000000
00000000000000000000000000000000000000000000000000000000000000000000000000000000000000000000
0000000000008000000000000000000000000000000000000000000000000000000080000000000000000
0000000000000000000000000000000000000000000000000000000000000000000000000000000000000000
00000000000000000000000080000020000000000000000000000000000000",
    "status": "0x1",
    "to": "0x06012c8cf97bead5deae237070f9587f8e7a266d",
    "transactionHash": "0xbb3a336e3f823ec18197f1e13ee875700f08f03e2cab75f0d0b118dabb44cba0",
    "transactionIndex": "0x11"
}
```

Figure 8.12   An example transaction receipt in the JSON format. The content is color-coded. The yellow blocks are identifier information for the transaction, the contract invoked, and the block in which the transaction reside. The blue block contains the cumulative gas used. The green block contains the logs. The red block contains the logs Bloom filter string. The purple block contains the status of the transaction (success or not). The pink block contains the gas used for this transaction alone.

hashing arms race by altering the PoW algorithm to make it a memory-bandwidth-limited process instead of a pure CPU-limited process.

In Ethereum, the contract data are stored as key-value pairs and they are organized in a more advanced Merkle Patricia tree than the plain balanced binary Merkle tree. A Merkle Patricia tree allows the insertion and deletion operations efficiently. The root of the tree is included in the block header. Because between two consequent blocks, the change of the tree is usually local, which means that only changes of the tree are recorded and the actual storage at each mining node is not overwhelming.

Ethereum follows the Greedy Heaviest Observed Subtree (GHOST) protocol for consensus [19]. The issue of allowing a faster confirmation time is a high stale rate, which refers to the fact that there will be many forks, *i.e.*, many blocks will be created concurrently in each block height and only one can be placed on the main chain. Not only this would lead to a lot of waste in computing (and energy consumption), the presence of large number of stale blocks would be detrimental to the security and stability of the network. Sompolinsky and Zohar proposed to include the entire subtree when choosing the main chain. More specifically, the total computation of the blocks in the subtree is compared. Effectively, instead of comparing different branch chains, GHOST compares different subtrees. This way, all concurrently created blocks in the same subtree would contribute to the security of the system. A direct consequence of considering the entire subtree is that the new block must not only include the hash of the parent block, but the information of the subtree as well, which makes the block structure considerably more complex. In Ethereum white paper [5], the blocks in the subtree, but not on the main chain are referred to as ommer blocks (ommer is a gender-neutral term to mean sibling of parent). In online forums as well as the Ethereum source code, the ommer block is referred to as an uncle block. An ommer block is in fact a stale block, in that the transactions in the block are not confirmed because they are not on the main blockchain. Some online forums claimed that ommer blocks are orphan blocks, which is incorrect. An orphan block is a block without a parent (temporarily), which could happen when a block is arrived ahead of its parent block at a mining node.

Despite early claims by the Ethereum white paper [5], whether or not GHOST protocol is implemented in Ethereum, and to what degree the protocol is implemented are rather confusing, as shown in the online forums at ethereum.stackexchange.com (such as `https://ethereum.stackexchange.com/questions/13378/what-is-the-exact-longest-chain-rule-implemented-in-the-ethereum-homestead-p` and `https://ethereum.stackexchange.com/questions/38121/why-did-ethereum-abandon-the-ghost-protocol`). The Ethereum source code at github (`https://github.com/ethereum/go-ethereum/blob/master/consensus/ethash/consensus.go`) as well as the Ethereum Beige Paper [10] show that currently Ethereum is indeed using a form of GHOST protocol, but it is implemented in a rather limited fashion. At most two ommers (called uncles in the source code) are counted instead of all stale blocks in a subtree when calculating the total difficulty of the subtree. There are additional restrictions on the ommer blocks, which will be discussed further in the next subsection.

The mechanism introduced in Ethereum for the third objective on minimizing centralization is closely related to the partial implementation of the GHOST protocol. The at-most-two ommer blocks included by each block for the difficulty calculation will also receive block rewards at a slightly reduced level. To incentivize miners to include ommer blocks, the reward for the new block that includes ommer blocks will be increased.

To make the PoW algorithm a memory-bandwidth-limited process, a very large dataset is built off some historical block data. First, a relatively small collection of data is generated, which is often called cache. The dataset is then derived based on the cache, and is arranged as a direct acyclic graph (DAG), which is often simply referred to as the DAG. Both the cache size and the DAG size keep increasing with more blocks mined. The current cache size is 48MB, and according to `https://investoon.com/tools/dag_size`, the current DAG size (as of writing on September 21, 2020) is 3.84GB (at the 363th epoch). This two-level design is to force the mining node to engage in memory-bandwidth-limited PoW while enabling other nodes to quickly verify the PoW result based on the cache only. A mining node would have to choose a nonce and then pseudorandomly sample the DAG 128 times to produce an intermediate hash. Then it must check if the intermediate hash would meet the difficulty target. This mechanism prevents a miner from trying out different nonce very quickly using ASCI hardware.

Later in this chapter, we will present the details on the above topics, including the ommer block verification and the block reward scheme for the ommer block and the new block, and the modified PoW algorithm, which is referred to as the Ethash algorithm.

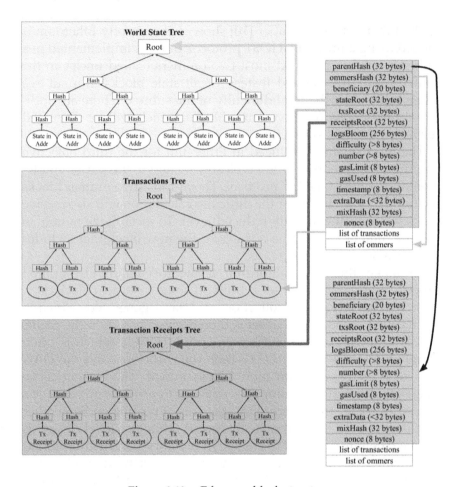

Figure 8.13   Ethereum block structure.

8.3.2.1   *Ethereum Block Structure*

The Ethereum block structure is shown in Figureu 8.13. As can be seen, the block structure is much more complex than Bitcoin block and its header is much larger than that of the Bitcoin block (which is only 80-byte long). The minimum Ethereum block header will be $32 + 32 + 20 + 32 + 32 + 32 + 256 + 8 + 8 + 8 + 8 + 8 + 32 + 8 = 516$ byte-long. Here we assume that the difficulty and number each takes 8 bytes, and there is no extraData. In addition to the root hash pointing to the list of transactions included in the current block, Ethereum has two additional root hashes that point to a state tree and a transaction receipts tree. Both are necessary because

Ethereum maintains arbitrary state for each account address, and the execution results of transactions (which in turn may call smart contracts) must be preserved and made immutable. Due to its design choices, Ethereum allows each block to include up to two ommer blocks, which are stale blocks not on the main blockchain.

Now we go over the meaning of each component in the block. The `parentHash` is the hash of the parent block, or more accurately the 32-byte hash of the header of the parent block. The `ommersHash` is the hash of the up-to-two ommer block's headers. Because there are only up to two ommer blocks allowed for each block, the blocks are simply concatenated for hashing. The `beneficary` is the 20-byte EOA address for the miner who mined this block. The block reward will be provided in the CoinBase transaction for this block, which is similar to Bitcoin. Because Ethereum uses the account model, the address is explicitly stated in the block header instead of as part of the CoinBase transaction like Bitcoin.

The `stateRoot` is the root hash for the world state as explained earlier. In Ethereum, the state under each account is put as the leaf nodes in the tree and a hash tree is computed using what is referred to as the Merkle Patricia tree (also called trie). This tree is more reflexible that the classical Merkle tree and it does not require the tree being balanced. The `txsRoot` (short for `transactionsRoot`) is the root hash for the transactions, also organized as a Merkle Patricia tree. Similarly, the `receiptsRoot` is the root hash for the transaction receipts.

As mentioned earlier, it is impossible for a frontend process that issues a transaction to communicate with a smart contract directly because the smart contract will be executed until the transaction is about to be placed on the blockchain. Ethereum solves this issue by providing a logging facility. Hence, the logs are important to retrieve informations. Recall that each transaction receipt has a logsBloom component. The `logsBloom` in the block header is a union (*i.e.*, by using the binary OR operation) of all the `logsBloom` in the receipts of the transactions included in this block. This enable anyone to quickly search if the needed events are likely to be present in the block.

The `difficulty` denotes the difficulty target in the PoW calculation, similar to that in Bitcoin. The `number` is the height of the current block. In Bitcoin, the block height is not explicitly included in the block header. In the reference implementation of Ethereum (using the `Go` programming language), both components are represented as a Big integer, which uses at least 8-byte space, but could take much more space for really large number). Presumably this is designed for the future when the difficulty target and the block height grew many orders of magnitude larger. The `gasLimit` is the upper bound on the total gas used by the transactions included in the current block. This effectively limits the number of transactions that can be included in a block. The `gasUsed` denotes the actual total gas used in the transactions in the current block.

The `timestamp` represents when the block is mined. The `extraData` provides the miner of the block an opportunity to add any phrase to the block (without costing any gas) up to 32 bytes, in a way similar to what the Bitcoin miner could do in the CoinBase transaction. The `mixHash` is the final hash after many rounds of hashing of randomly selected portion of the huge dataset called DAG. The mixHash is then used together with the nonce to see if they have met the difficulty target. This is to ensure that the miner actually did the work.

The final components of the Ethereum block are the list of transactions and the list of (up to two) ommer block headers included in this block.

8.3.2.2   Ommer Block

The original GHOST protocol has too much flexibility on ommer block selection because every single subtree would have to be considered. That could lead to the inclusion of a large number of stale blocks, and the subtree could go very deep close to the genesis block level, which is apparently not implementable. It took quite some time before Ethereum actually incorporated the basic idea of the GHOST protocol. Currently, there is a severe lack of documentation on how the modified protocol works. We aim to fill this gap here.

In addition to imposing a limit on the number of ommer blocks to 2 instead of an arbitrary number from the GHOST protocol, Ethereum applied two more restrictions as outlined in the Ethereum white paper [5]: (1) An ommer block that is considered must have an ancestor block that is on the main chain within 7-generations. (2) Once an ommer block has been included as an uncle block for a block that has been placed on the main chain, that particular ommer block cannot be included by any other block as an uncle block any more. The first restriction is for the efficiency and for the stability of Ethereum so that a mining node does not have to search from the genesis block and this also eliminates the possibility of forking from the bottom of the blockchain. The second restriction is to prevent a stale block from being included multiple times. Obviously, a mining node is not allowed to select a sibling block at the same level. An ommer block must be at least one generation older than the new block. Another obvious restriction that is mentioned in the Ethereum white paper [5] is that the ommer block should not be an ancestor of the new block.

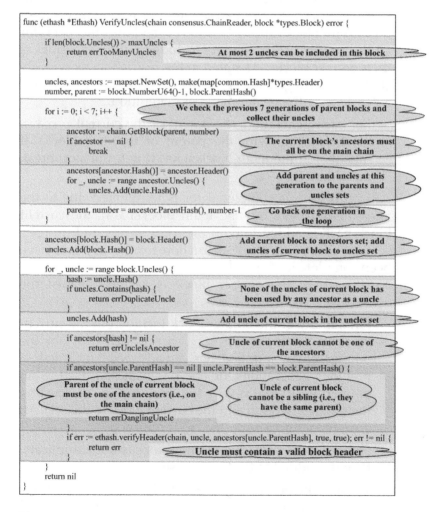

Figure 8.14   The annotated source code on verification of an ommer block.

The restrictions outline above still leave some room for ambiguity. For example, would a stale block that is a child block of another stale block be eligible as an ommer block? According to the GHOST protocol, it is. To find out a definitive answer, we studied the source code (the `Go` reference implementation of Ethereum). The annotated source code is shown in Figure 8.14. We elaborate the `VerifyUncles` function from the beginning to the end.

- The first check is to make sure that at most two ommer blocks are included in the block. An error is returned immediately if more than two ommer blocks are supplied.
- The next task is to build two sets, one set for the ancestors of the current block called `ancestors`, and the other set is for all the ommer blocks that are included by the ancestors as their ommer blocks. As stated in the restrictions previously stated, this will go back 7 generations. The source code uses a `for` loop with one iteration per generation.
  - For each generation, the parent of the current `parent` block (starting with the parent of the new block), it must be on the main blockchain. If not, the loop break immediately.
- After this loop is completed (or is terminated due to the ancestor not being on the main blockchain), the current block hash is added to both the `ancestprs` and `uncles` sets. At this point, the construction for the two sets have been completed.
- Next, each of the ommer block is verified against the `ancestors` and `uncles` sets.
  - First, if any of the ommer block included in the current block is already in the `uncles` set, then it means the ommer block supplied has already been included in previous generations, or one has included itself as an ommer block (that is why the final step in constructing the `uncles` set is to add the current block to the set). An error (`errDuplicateUncle`) is returned.
  - Second, if the provided ommer block is not a duplicate, then it is added to the `uncles` set.
  - Third, if the provided ommer block is in fact an ancestor block (on the main blockchain), then an error is returned (`errUnclesIsAncestor`).

- Forth, two error conditions are checked in this step. If the ommer block's parent is not one of the ancestors, then it means that the ommer block's parent is also a stale block (*i.e.*, there are two stale blocks linked together). Furthermore, if the ommer block and the current block share the same parent, then the ommer block is in fact a sibling block in the same generation of the current block, which is not allowed. In both cases, an `errDanglingUncle` error is returned.

- The final step is to verify that the ommer block's header is valid.

While not explicitly programmed, it is a concern when the first loop is broken due to the ancestor not being on the main blockchain. First, if the current block's parent is not on the main blockchain (could happen during the very first iteration when `i=0`). The loop is terminated without throwing an error at this stage. Please note that in this case, the `ancestors` set contains only the current block itself. Assume that at least one ommer block is provided by the current block. During the ommer block verification, the check for dangling uncle would fail because the current block cannot possibly be the parent of the ommer block provided (*i.e.*, `ancestors[uncle.ParentHash] == nil` would be evaluated to true). The only scenario that the parent of some ancestor in certain generation is not on the main blockchain is the loop has gone back to the genesis block and that ancestor is the genesis block itself. In this case, there is no error. Put it another way, it is impossible for a block that is on the main blockchain that has a parent that is not on the main blockchain (*i.e.*, being a stale block).

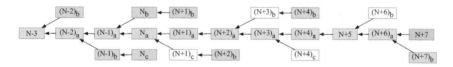

Figure 8.15   An example on what kind of stale blocks may be chosen as an ommer block.

EXAMPLE 8.2

We illustrate what kind of stale blocks are eligible to be selected as an ommer block using an example shown in Figure 8.15.

In this example, we assume that the block numbered $N + 7$ is the new block that would select ommer blocks. The blocks on the main blockchain are colored in light green. There are also several stale blocks, which will be examined one by one for the possibility of being a candidate for inclusion as an ommer block. The ineligible blocks are colored in light red, and the eligible ones are colored in white.

We start with the oldest block labeled as $(N - 2)_b$. According to the rules implemented in the source code in Figure 8.14, the parent of an ommer block must have an ancestor on the main blockchain within the previous 7 generations. This would go from block height $N + 6$ back to N. The parent block of $(N - 2)_b$ is $N - 3$, which is too old. Hence, $(N - 2)_b$ is not an eligible ommer block. The next oldest block is $(N - 1)_b$. Again, it is not eligible because its parent $(N - 2)_a$ is older than block height N. Next, we consider blocks N_b and N_c. Both have a parent that is in the $N - 1$ generation, which makes them ineligible. By the way, the parent of block N_c is also a stale block. Hence, block N_c is in fact a dangling block.

At the $N + 1$ generation, $(N + 1)_b$ is not eligible because it is a dangling block (*i.e.*, its parent N_b is a stale block), but $(N + 1)_c$ is the oldest eligible block for an ommer block because its parent is N_a. At the $N + 2$ generation, $(N + 2)_b$ is not eligible because it is also a dangling block (*i.e.*, its parent $(N + 1)_c$ is a stale block). At the $N + 3$ generation, $(N + 3)_b$ is eligible because its parent $(N + 2)_a$ is on the main blockchain. At the $N + 4$ generation, $(N + 4)_c$ is eligible because its parent $(N + 3)_a$ is on the main blockchain. However, $(N + 4)_b$ is not eligible because it is again a dangling block (*i.e.*, its parent $(N + 3)_b$ is a stale block).

The $(N + 6)_b$ block is eligible for an ommer block because its parent $N + 5$ is on the main blockchain. The $(N + 7)_b$ block is not eligible because it is a sibling of the current block (*i.e.*, they share the same parent $(N + 6)_a$).

Another important mechanism related to ommer blocks is the block reward scheme in Ethereum. This is another source of confusion, presumably Ethereum has been changing its scheme over the years. The Ethereum white paper [5] stated that each ommer block would receive 93.75% of the standard CoinBase reward, and the block would receive 3.125% of the standard block reward for each ommer block it includes. However, the source code shown

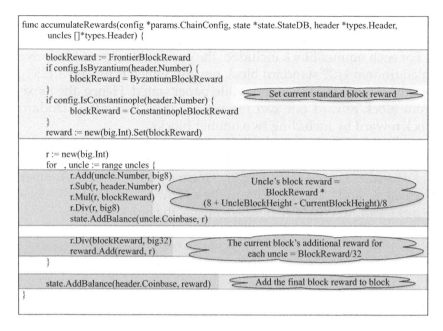

```
func accumulateRewards(config *params.ChainConfig, state *state.StateDB, header *types.Header,
    uncles []*types.Header) {

    blockReward := FrontierBlockReward
    if config.IsByzantium(header.Number) {
        blockReward = ByzantiumBlockReward
    }
    if config.IsConstantinople(header.Number) {                    Set current standard block reward
        blockReward = ConstantinopleBlockReward
    }
    reward := new(big.Int).Set(blockReward)

    r := new(big.Int)
    for _, uncle := range uncles {
        r.Add(uncle.Number, big8)                       Uncle's block reward =
        r.Sub(r, header.Number)                         BlockReward *
        r.Mul(r, blockReward)                   (8 + UncleBlockHeight - CurrentBlockHeight)/8
        r.Div(r, big8)
        state.AddBalance(uncle.Coinbase, r)

        r.Div(blockReward, big32)               The current block's additional reward for
        reward.Add(reward, r)                        each uncle = BlockReward/32
    }

    state.AddBalance(header.Coinbase, reward)       Add the final block reward to block
}
```

Figure 8.16   The annotated source code on the block reward scheme in Ethereum.

in Figure 8.16 revealed that the actual implementation is slightly different. As can be seen, the ommer block's rewards is set to be $(8 + UncleBlockHeight - CurrentBlockHeight)/8$. Because $CurrentBlockHeigh >= UncleBlockHeight + 1$, the more generation apart between the current block and the ommer block, the smaller the block rewards is going to be. Let's consider two extreme situations for the boundary of the reward. The smallest gap in generations between the ommer block and the current block is 1. Hence, the maximum reward would be $(8 - 1)/8 = 87.5\%$ of the standard block reward. The largest gap is 6 (because the oldest ancestor for the ommer block has to be within 7 generations before the current block). Hence, the smallest reward would be $(8 - 6)/8 = 25\%$ of the standard block reward. While this might appear to be a scheme to discourage the inclusion of older stale blocks because the block reward for older block is much smaller than the one that is only one generation apart, it actually plays no part on what kind of blocks one would select as an ommer block because the selecting miner would get a block rewards that is linearly increasing based on the number of ommer blocks, but not only how many generation apart between the current block and the ommer block.

For each ommer block included, the current block would receive an additional 1/32 standard block reward, which is indeed 3.125%, exactly as what the Ethereum white paper stated. Hence, the maximum block reward one can receive is 1.0625 times the standard block reward by including two ommer blocks.

We note that the source code (written in the Go programming language) can be confusing to read. In particular, `r.Add(uncle.Nubmer, big8)` means `r = uncle.Number + big8` and `r.Div(blockReward, r)` means `r = blockReward/r` (where `Number` means the block height).

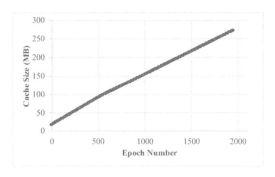

Figure 8.17   The cache size vs. the epoch number.

8.3.2.3   Ethash

A major change Ethereum introduced to the PoW algorithm is to make the process a memory-bandwidth-limited process. First, a cache is calculated based on the current block height. Both the cache size and the cache content are functions of the current block height. The cache size and the cache content actually do not change with every block. They are changed for every epoch, which is defined as 30,000 blocks in Ethereum. Considering that the block interval in Ethereum is set at 12 seconds, each epoch is exactly 100 hours. From the cache, a huge dataset in the form of a directed acyclic graph (DAG) is constructed.

The size and content of the dataset are also a function of the current block number. The cache size and the dataset size with respect to the epoch number are shown in Figure 8.17 and Figure 8.18 respectively. More specifically, because the cache and

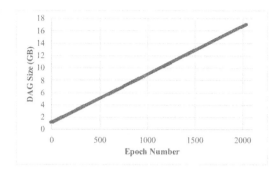

Figure 8.18 The dataset size vs. the epoch number.

the dataset change every epoch, the current block height is first converted into an epoch number by dividing the block height by the epoch length. For example, for any block that has a block height 1-29,999, it will be converted into epoch 0, and for a block that has a block height 30,000 - 59,999, it will be converted to epoch 1, etc. Ethereum has two large mapping tables for the first 2,048 epochs, one to map an epoch number to the corresponding cache size and the other to map an epoch number to the corresponding dataset size. At the time of writing of this book, the dataset size is close to 4GB.

One would have expected that the cache would be somehow calculated by sampling blocks in the main blockchain after reading the Ethereum white paper. In fact, this is not the case. The cache content is only related to the current epoch number and has nothing to do with the blocks already in the blockchain. The dataset is also deterministically generated based on the given cache for the current epoch. The Ethereum yellow paper has great details on the cache and dataset generation process [23].

As shown in Figure 8.19, during the Ethash PoW calculation (or mining), the dataset is sampled based on a mix byte array. First, a seed is derived using the Keccak512 hash function based on the nonce and the current block header without the nonce (referred to as the sealhash) and the mixHash fields. Then, the very first 128-byte mix is derived from the the seed. For each round, the seed (more specifically it is the seedHead instead of the seed. The seedHead is converted from the seed with the little endian binary presentation) and the current mix is fed into a function called $fnv()$, which performs a non-associative operation similar to the

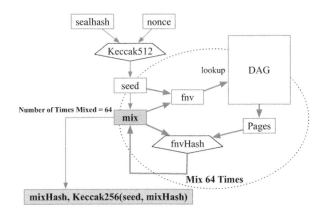

Figure 8.19   The Ethash algorithm.

exclusive OR on the two inputs. The definition of the $fnv()$ function is actually quite simple: $fnv(a,b) = a \times 0x01000193^b$. The output from the $fnv()$ is used to determine which part of the dataset to fetch using a lookup function. The fetched pages are fed into a mixing function called $fnvHash()$, which produces the output of the current round of mixing. The definition of $fnvHash()$ is almost the same as that for $fnv()$ except that $fnvHash$ operate on an array of a and an array of b. The output becomes the `mix` for the next round of mixing. A total of 64-rounds of sampling of the dataset is carried out.

After the final round, the final `mix` is compacted into 32-byte `mixHash` (from 128 bytes), which is referred to as the `digest` in the source code. The digest is then concatenated with the `nonce`, the `sealhash`, and then hashed with `Keccak256` hash function. The hash result is compared against the difficulty target. If the target is met, then the block is mined successfully. Otherwise, the nonce is incremented and the whole process is restarted.

8.3.3   Tokenization

In addition to smart contract, Ethereum is a big proponent for tokenization [5]. Prior to the creation of cryptocurrency, we were already quite familiar with tokens, such as the tokens used for playing arcade games and tokens for using laundry machines. Although such tokens are not currency and cannot be used elsewhere, people would have to use actual money to pay for them.

Such tokens represent some specific value in a restricted environment. Blockchain systems such as Bitcoin typically refer to their cryptocurrency some kind of coin, and the coins essentially carries exactly the same role of the physical tokens in these cases. Blockchain tokens are meaningful only in their own designated platform. Although blockchain tokens are originally designed to be a form of cryptocurrency (as is the case for Bitcoin), their meaning can be expanded to represent the right to some asset in the digital or physical world. This token-asset association is referred to as tokenization. The digital form of tokenization could open the door for many more application of the blockchain technology [5].

There are two types of assets represented by tokens in blockchains [23]: (1) digital assets that can be entirely represented and used in the blockchain platform; and (2) other assets that corresponds to assets in the real world. The former is referred to as intrinsic to the blockchain, while the latter is extrinsic to the blockchain. An example of the former could be a token used for game playing in a Dapp. There are many more examples for the latter. For example, the blockchain token can be used to facilitate voting when a token represents the voting right in an organization, to facilitate identity management when a token is used to represent an individual, to enable attestation services when a token represents a certificate for an academic degree or marriage certificate etc. Interestingly, a particular form of tokenization is to use a token to peg with a real-world currency such that the exchange rate is always one-to-one, which could solve the issue of wide fluctuation in cryptocurrency prices.

We should note that tokenization for extrinsic assets necessitates the involvement of trusted third parties to guarantee the bond between the token and the real-world asset. This is to mitigate the counterparty risk. If a transaction is trading some tokens representing some physical asset, there is a risk that the owner of the physical asset would not honor the trade described in the transaction. This is why a trusted third party would be needed to counter the risk.

Except the built-in coin in a blockchain (*e.g.*, Satoshi in Bitcoin, and Ether in Ethereum), all other blockchain tokens must be programmed explicitly. In Ethereum, these blockchain tokens are created and handled by smart contracts. To facilitate the development of Dapps that use such tokens, Ethereum introduced a standard, initially proposed by Fabian Vogelsteller in November

2015 as Ethereum Request for Comment 20 (ERC20). ERC20 defines a standard interface for implementing the token in smart contract.

8.4 Attacks on Blockchain

In this section, we go over several possible attacks on the blockchain system. The most well-known attack is the double-spending attack. For physical cash or gold, once someone spent the money, the person would no longer have possession of the money. However, because cryptocurrency exists in a digital form only, one could still possess a copy of the digital money even after it has been spent. This imposes a grave concern that one could spend the money again, which is referred to as the double-spending attack. How to prevent the doubles-spending attack is therefore the primary concern on designing a cryptocurrency. The solution adopted by the blockchain-based cryptocurrency systems is to maintain a secure distributed ledger for all transactions that have ever taken place. The goal is to ensure that everyone has exactly the same copy and the ledger is append-only, *i.e.*, more transactions can be added to the ledger, and once a transaction is recorded on the ledger, it becomes immutable.

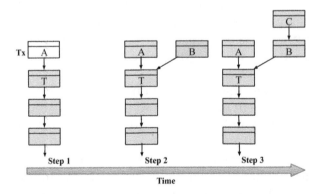

Figure 8.20   The double-spending attack steps.

For Bitcoin, the only way to successfully launch a double-spending attack is to own more than half of the hashing power of the entire Bitcoin network. The attacking steps are illustrated in Figure 8.20. First, let's assume that the attacker spend some cryptocurrency in a transaction Tx. Presumably that is a large-value transaction. Otherwise, it will not be economical for the attacker to commission such huge computing resources (*i.e.,* more than half of the hashing power of entire network) for the attack. For the transaction to be successful, the transaction must have been confirmed, *i.e.,* it has been included in a block that is newly mined and is (temporarily) added to the blockchain. Let this block be A. and its parent block be T. It is conceivable that the vender who accepted the large quantity of cryptocurrency would wait at least for one confirmation to deliver the goods or services in exchange. If the vendor insisted for more confirmations, such as six as normally recommended for large-value transactions in Bitcoin, the cost for the double-spending attack would no longer make any economical sense. This is the first step.

As soon as the attacker has received the goods or the services corresponding to the transaction Tx, the person would instruct its partners that collectively control more than half of the hashing power to mine a new block, and the miners will be informed to *not* include the transaction from which the attacker received goods/services. The attacker could opt to create a transaction that uses exactly the same set of transaction inputs as the ones used in the original transaction Tx to hide its trace, and asks the miners that it has control over to include this new transaction instead of Tx. This new transaction would have one or more transaction outputs that bear addresses belonging to the attacker (*i.e.,* this new transaction would pay to the attacker itself). This new block B would choose A's parent block T as the parent too. The presence of B forced a fork in the system because both block A and block B point to the same parent T. The miners would have to choose either A or B as the parent block. This is step 2. At this point, the decision can be arbitrary because both branches would have equal cumulative difficulty.

Because the attacker has control over more than half of the hashing power, it will ask its miners to continue mining for one more block that uses B as the parent. Chances are that a new block C that uses B has the parent will be created before those miners that are not controlled by the attacker could mine a new block. If this is the case, then the attacker will have succeeded in launching a double spending attack because the $C - B - T$ branch will be favored over the $A - T$ brach due to containing more cumulative difficulty. This is the last step of the double-spending attack.

The double-spending attack is also referred to as 51% attack to emphasize that it requires the attacker to have control over more than half of total hashing power. Once an attacker has this much hashing power, it can launch other forms of attacks. One of them is sustained denial of service attack against some users. The attacker could intentionally exclude all transactions that come from one or more users. If by any chance some of the transactions are included in a block created by a miner that is not controlled by the attacker, the attacker could create a fork and abandon that block, just like the way it does the double-spending attack.

Of course, an attacker could attempt to double spend by literally creating two or more transactions using the same transaction input within a short period of time. Each cryptocurrency system has its own way of detecting such fraudulent behaviors. In Bitcoin, each mining node maintains a UTXO pool containing all transactions outputs that have not been spent yet. Once an output is spent, it is removed from the UTXO pool. Therefore, except the very first transaction, all later arrived transactions from the double-spending attack would be deemed invalid. It is possible that different miners would select different transactions in the new block, but no miner would include two or more conflicting transactions in the same block.

Selfish mining [18] is a more subtle (and less damaging) attack. The goal of selfish mining is to increase an unfair share of block reward by colluding with a group of miners. Such miners would first mine a new block but reveal it only among themselves instead of publicly announcing the new block to the entire network. When they have successfully mined more blocks (the blocks that they have mined would form a chain), they could decide to reveal them all at once to the public network. To be more profitable than honest miners, the selfish miners must possess a significant fraction of the total mining power. Obviously, if they possess over half of the hashing power, they could effectively take all the block rewards of the system. The open question is whether or not if exists a threshold that is lower than 50% for the selfish miner to be profitable.

In [12], the authors analyzed how the traditional eclipse attack can be used to attack the Bitcoin networks. In an eclipse attack, the attacker aims to control the connections of the victim node with the rest of the world to effectively isolate the node. After all, the blockchain systems run on top of the Internet. In addition to denying the services to the victim node, the eclipse attack could impose a number of damages to the blockchain network, including causing forks, splitting hashing power, facilitating selfish mining, or even helping on double-spending attacks.

References

1. A. M. Antonopoulos. *Mastering bitcoin: Programming the open blockchain.* " O'Reilly Media, Inc.", 2017.

2. A. M. Antonopoulos and G. Wood. *Mastering ethereum: building smart contracts and dapps.* O'reilly Media, 2018.

3. A. Back. Hash cash postage implementation. http://www.hashcash.org/papers/announce.txt, March 1997.

4. A. Back. Hashcash - a denial of service counter-measure. http://www.hashcash.org/papers/hashcash.pdf, Aug. 2002.

5. V. Buterin et al. Ethereum white paper. https://ethereum.org/en/whitepaper/, 2013.

6. M. Castro and B. Liskov. Practical byzantine fault tolerance and proactive recovery. *ACM Transactions on Computer Systems (TOCS)*, 20(4):398–461, 2002.

7. D. Chaum. Blind signatures for untraceable payments. In *Advances in cryptology*, pages 199–203. Springer, 1983.

8. D. Chaum and S. Brands. 'minting'electronic cash. *IEEE spectrum*, 34(2):30–34, 1997.

9. W. Dai. B-money-an anonymous, distributed electronic cash system. http://www.weidai.com/bmoney.txt, 1998.

10. M. Dameron. Beiepaper: An ethereum technical specification. https://github.com/chronaeon/beigepaper/blob/master/beigepaper.pdf, Aug. 2019.

11. C. Dwork and M. Naor. Pricing via processing or combatting junk mail. In *Annual International Cryptology Conference*, pages 139–147. Springer, 1992.

12. E. Heilman, A. Kendler, A. Zohar, and S. Goldberg. Eclipse attacks on bitcoins peer-to-peer network. In *24th {USENIX} Security Symposium ({USENIX} Security 15)*, pages 129–144, 2015.

13. N. Koblitz. Elliptic curve cryptosystems. *Mathematics of computation*, 48(177):203–209, 1987.

14. L. Lamport et al. Paxos made simple. *ACM Sigact News*, 32(4):18–25, 2001.

15. S. Nakamoto. Bitcoin: A peer-to-peer electronic cash system. https://bitcoin.org/bitcoin.pdf, 2008.

16. M. E. Peck. The cryptoanarchists' answer to cash. *IEEE Spectrum*, 49(6):50–56, 2012.

17. R. J. Rybarczyk. Bitcoin p2pkh transaction breakdown. https://medium.com/coinmonks/bitcoin-p2pkh-transaction-breakdown-bb663034d6df, Sept. 2018.

18. A. Sapirshtein, Y. Sompolinsky, and A. Zohar. Optimal selfish mining strategies in bitcoin. In *International Conference on Financial Cryptography and Data Security*, pages 515–532. Springer, 2016.

19. Y. Sompolinsky and A. Zohar. Secure high-rate transaction processing in bitcoin. In *International Conference on Financial Cryptography and Data Security*, pages 507–527. Springer, 2015.

20. N. Szabo. Smart contracts: building blocks for digital markets. *Extropy*, 1996.

21. N. Szabo. Bit gold. https://unenumerated.blogspot.com/2008, 2008.

22. W. Wang, D. T. Hoang, P. Hu, Z. Xiong, D. Niyato, P. Wang, Y. Wen, and D. I. Kim. A survey on consensus mechanisms and mining strategy management in blockchain networks. *IEEE Access*, 7:22328–22370, 2019.

23. G. Wood. Ethereum: A secure decentralised generalised transaction ledger. https://ethereum.github.io/yellowpaper/paper.pdf, Sept. 2020.

24. Z. Xu and C. Zou. What can blockchain do and cannot do? *China Economic Journal*, pages 1–22, 2020.

25. W. Zhao. *Building dependable distributed systems*. John Wiley & Sons, 2014.

26. W. Zhao. Fast paxos made easy: Theory and implementation. *International Journal of Distributed Systems and Technologies (IJDST)*, 6(1):15–33, 2015.

27. W. Zhao. Performance optimization for state machine replication based on application semantics: a review. *Journal of Systems and Software*, 112:96–109, 2016.

28. W. Zhao, L. E. Moser, and P. M. Melliar-Smith. Unification of transactions and replication in three-tier architectures based on corba. *IEEE transactions on Dependable and Secure Computing*, 2(1):20–33, 2005.

29. W. Zhao, S. Yang, and X. Luo. On consensus in public blockchains. In *Proceedings of the 2019 International Conference on Blockchain Technology*, pages 1–5, 2019.

9

Consensus Algorithms for Blockchain

Distributed consensus is the most fundamental issue in distributed computing. There has been a strong interest on distributed consensus since early 1980s [31]. Milestones in this line of research are many. We can easily name of few: the logical timestamp concept proposed by Lamport [18], the Byzantine generals problem and the earliest algorithms also proposed by Lamport [21], the impossibility result for asynchronous distributed systems by Fischer, Lynch, and Paterson [11], the group communication systems by Birman [6], Moser, and Melliar-Smith et al. [23], the practical Byzantine fault tolerance algorithm (PBFT) by Castro and Liskov [7], and the Paxos-family of algorithms by Lamport [19, 20].

To remove trivial solutions to the distributed consensus problem, such as everyone always decided on a particular value, it requires that the value chosen by a member must have been proposed by someone in the system. If there is only a single member that always proposes some value, then the solution to the distributed consensus problem is also trivial. However, such assumption is obviously not fault tolerant, *i.e.*, if that member fails, the system stops operating. Hence, at least a subset of the members must share the responsibility to propose values dynamically. Once we allow more than one member to propose, we are risking of different members in the system choose values proposed by different ones. Hence, the distributed consensus is a complex problem. In an asynchronous system where there is no bound on networking delay, no bound on processing time, and no restriction on the clocks used by different members (*e.g.*, the clocks can be different and there is no bound on the clock drift rate), the famous FLP impossibility result stated that a distributed consensus is impossible because one cannot differentiate a slow member from a crashed one. To bypass this impossibility result, there are two approaches. One is to use an unreliable failure detector to remove a member from the current membership when necessary [8]. The other is to use a randomized algorithm that does not use time in anyway in the operation of the algorithm [3]. The failure detector could mistakenly remove a running member that is temporarily slow from the system, and that member might not even know that it has been removed from the system, which significantly complicates the task of reaching consensus. The latter algorithm is probabilistic, in that it may run many rounds and there is no consensus reached if the system is very asynchronous, which is expected due to the FLP impossibility result.

Classical solutions to the problem of distributed consensus all require a concept of membership where a member would know: (1) who else is in the membership; (2) its own role; (3) the roles of other members; and (4) how to connect to other members. Usually, one of the members would carry additional role, which is typically referred to as the primary, coordinator, or leader. As such, there must be a leader election algorithm defined. If a system allows dynamic membership, a membership protocol must also be defined. All these membership related algorithms/protocols are by themselves consensus problems.

The PoW-based consensus algorithms (used in Bitcoin and Ethereum, for example), are completely different from the classical solution. The reason can be easily understood. The membership required by classical algorithms inevitably make the system tightly-coupled and can be easily attacked if deployed on the Internet, and the algorithms are not scalable due to the use of multiple-rounds of message exchanges. The PoW-based consensus algorithms do not use any notion of membership. Instead, they run on a peer-to-peer network where every mining node is equal in responsibility, and there is no additional message exchange just for the sake of reaching consensus (other than relaying valid transactions and blocks received, and propagating the blocks it has mined). This sounds rather unbelievable. How can a system magically achieve consensus without a membership and without making multiple rounds of message exchanges to ensure that all members agree on the same value?

In blockchain, the consensus is established probabilistically by converting the consensus problem into a stochastic process similar to winning a lottery. Everyone is allowed to participate the competition by investing on hardware, installing the blockchain software, and running the protocol. The PoW algorithm would use a carefully designed hard puzzle where it is impossible to cheat other than using a computer that has more computing power to gain some advantage over other nodes (the higher hashing rate and higher memory bandwidth, the better chance of winning the puzzle competition). Furthermore, the puzzle is designed so that the puzzle solving process is a stochastic process in that no one can predict what kind of input would lead to an output that meets the difficulty target. The only way for a node to solve the puzzle is to try out different nonce (and some other parameters allowed). The security, fairness, and the randomness of the puzzle solving process are protected by the use of cryptographic hash functions such as SHA2 or SHA3.

Of course, there is always a tradeoff. The PoW-based consensus algorithm is probabilistic in that it does not always produce a single winner in each round. It could happen that two or more blocks are mined almost at the same time. In this case, the system would have inconsistency in that some nodes in the system might choose one of the competing blocks, and other nodes would choose some other blocks at the same block height. This situation is actually not new to the research community on distributed systems. Optimistic replication has been extensively studied [26]. The key idea is to resolve the inconsistency when it occurs, which is often called a fork illustrating the fact that the single chain started to have two or more branches, using some conflict resolution mechanisms. In Bitcoin, this is achieved by using a simple rule: whichever branch that has the most cumulative difficulty should be chosen as the main blockchain. In Ethereum, a variation of a more sophisticated protocol (called GHOST) [29] is used where the total computation of each subtree is compared to select a winning block.

Another tradeoff is that no one would know for certain that when a consensus is definitively achieved in PoW-based algorithms, which is also because the consensus achieved is probabilistic. Theoretically, if someone has possession of an overwhelming computing power, the person could create a branch right after the genesis block and essentially render all existing transaction records obsolete. Fortunately, in reality, this is virtually impossible because the cost of doing so could very well be a lot greater than the financial gain anyone could obtain. It is also foreseeable that someone, some organization, or certain state would want to demolish a blockchain platform. In this case, there are much cheaper means to achieve the goal, such as shutting down the Internet connection to all mining nodes or disable the DNS system for these nodes.

Yet, another tradeoff is the energy consumption. If there are 1,000 mining nodes competing to create the next block, then 999 of them will waste their computation in Bitcoin. This effectively creates 99.9% waste (or only 0.1% energy efficiency) for reaching consensus. To address this energy consumption issue, many alternative consensus algorithms have been proposed [30]. Including PoW, these algorithms can be divided into two approaches: one is based on proof of resources, the other is referred to as virtual mining [30]. There are also hybrid algorithms that span the two approaches. Unfortunately, many of these are not well documented, and some are pure theoretical work without an implementation. We are also aware of a lot of proposals on using traditional consensus protocol such as Paxos or PBFT. They might be fine working in a private blockchain that has very small number of nodes. However, one would question the value of using such a private blockchain. The well-touted benefit of the immutability of blockchain is made possible with a large scale public blockchain where it is virtually impossible to subvert the consensus established by the many mining nodes (with huge amount of energy devoted to computation). The small-scale private blockchain would only resemble a public blockchain in data structure itself, without the true benefits of the public blockchain.

In this chapter, we first introduce a set of requirements for blockchain consensus algorithms. Then we comment on PoW and a few better documented alternative blockchain consensus algorithms. We also provide a detailed description of the PoS algorithm implemented in PeerCoin. The PeerCoin is in fact the very first PoS-based consensus algorithm proposed although it is far less well-known than the PoS algorithm proposed by Ethereum, which has been touted as their future consensus algorithm. Our description of the PeerCoin PoS algorithm is based on the latest source code of PeerCoin. In our opinion, the PeerCoin PoS algorithm ought to be better recognized being a self-contained PoS algorithm not only having been implemented, but having gone through revisions and the tests of being part of a practical system.

9.1   Model on Blockchain Consensus

To support a public blockchain, the consensus algorithm must work with an open dynamic and large system where any node could join or leave at any time. Currently, the Bitcoin network has over 10,000 mining nodes as reported by `https://bitnodes.io/ dashboard/`, and the Ethereum network has over 5,000 mining nodes as reported by `https://etherscan.io/nodetracker`. No classical consensus algorithm can operate in a network of this scale.

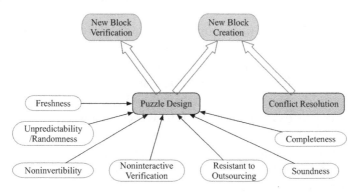

Figure 9.1   A model for public blockchain consensus.

Figure 9.1 presents the model for public blockchain consensus. We recognize that there are two corner stones for the consensus algorithm: (1) a puzzle design; and (2) a conflict resolution mechanism. The puzzle design is what makes it possible to use a puzzle-solving competition to replace traditional voting-based solutions. Because the puzzle-solving competition is inevitably probabilistic, consensus is not guaranteed. When inconsistency occurs, an additional mechanism must exist to select only one of the proposed values. In PoW, the puzzle is based on computation. Bitcoin uses pure hashing, and Ethereum uses a combination of hashing and a memory-bandwidth-limited operation. As we will see later, researchers have investigated other forms of puzzles. The essence is the proof of possession on some valuable resources. In [30], these algorithms are referred to as Proof-of-Resources or Proof-of-Concepts. Regardless how it is designed, the puzzle must exhibit a set of characteristics, which we enumerate and explain below.

9.1.1   Requirements on Puzzle Design

Unpredictability. The most fundamental requirement on the puzzle design is that the puzzle solving process must be stochastic. More specifically, the puzzle must define a rule on how it is considered solved. In PoW, a difficulty target is defined and a miner would have to find a right nonce so that the hash of the new block header is smaller than the target difficulty. Unpredictability means that given the puzzle-solving objective, one cannot predict what input would meet the objective. The only way to solve the puzzle is to try out many different inputs.

Freshness. While this requirement might have been implicitly covered by the unpredictability requirement, it is worthwhile to single this requirement out to emphasize that no one should be able to start solving a puzzle much sooner than others. If some miners could start working a puzzle ahead of others, then the consensus process is no longer fair, which eventually will lead to the destruction of the system. For blockchain, freshness means that the input must include information about the new block. After all, the consensus is about which block should be the next block. In essence, the freshness requirement means that one cannot reuse any resource that it has already used to mine a previous block.

Noninvertibility. This refers to the requirement that the puzzle must be very difficult to solve while very easy to verify. On the one hand, the difficulty level should be so difficult that statistically it takes a block-interval amount of time to solve among the miners (thousands or more of them). Otherwise, the network would fork easily and as a result, many stale blocks would be produced [1]. Ultimately, this is detrimental to the security of the network [12]. On the other hand, a new block would be verified by thousands of nodes. It is important that the verification must be efficient. Otherwise, the miners would be disincentivized to verify new blocks.

Noninteractive verification. Considering the scale of the network, and the nature of the problem where there is one puzzle solver and thousands of verifiers for each new block, the verification of the solution presented by the solver must be noninteractive. Otherwise, the solver would be bombarded with messages, essentially killing the scalability of the system.

Soundness. This requires that if a mining node claimed falsely that it has solved the puzzle with a wrong solution, the proposed solution can be detected as wrong and therefore will be rejected during the verification process.

Completeness. This requires that if a node has presented a valid solution to the puzzle, then the solution will be accepted by all verifying nodes.

Resistant to outsourcing. This is a rather subtle one. Unlike previous requirements, the violation of any of which would immediately render the puzzle design unacceptable for practical use, the violation of this requirement will not. This requirement should be considered desirable and but not absolutely a must. In fact, the PoW algorithm used by Bitcoin does violate this requirement. By outsourcing, we mean that to solve the puzzle, one can divide the solution space into multiple partitions, and assign the tasks on checking for solution in each partition to other nodes. This is the basis for forming mining pools in Bitcoin. This is indeed a concern because pooling of resources could lead to centralization, which is exactly what Bitcoin and the like wanted to avoid.

9.1.2   Zero-Knowledge Proof

The puzzle design in blockchain can be regarded as a form of noninteractive Zero-Knowledge Proof (ZKP) [25]. ZKP was originally designed as an interactive system that consists of a prover and a verifier [13]. The prover would somehow present some evidence for the possession of certain secrete without revealing it, and the verifier can be certain based on the presented evidence whether or not the prover indeed has possession of the secrete. Note that the prover must not simply reveal the secrete (*i.e.,* the knowledge of the secrete), which is why this scheme is called zero-knowledge proof. According to the original scheme, ZKP would inevitably require an interactive session, where the verifier would provide a challenge to the prover so that the prover could respond accordingly.

In context of blockchain, the prover in ZKP must prove the possession or consumption of some minimum amount of digital resources. If it is to prove possession, there must exist a mechanism such that the resources used to prove for possession cannot be reused. Classical ZKP systems typically require the existence of a trusted third party to generate random seeds or keys that will then used to derive a common reference string at both the prover and the verifier. In blockchain, the need for a trusted third party is replaced by a random oracle model where the random oracle would respond to a unique query with a random response uniformly selected from the output space. An ideal cryptographic hash function would serve as the purpose of the random oracle. Strong cryptographic hash functions such as SHA2 and SHA3 (including Keccak) would be used to approximate the ideal hash function.

9.2   Proof of Work

The puzzle design for PoW in Bitcoin is entirely based on the cryptographic hash function. The theoretical foundation is that for an ideal cryptographic hash function that produces an L-bit string, the search for a preimage of a given hash value cannot be more efficient than exhaustively trying out all combinations of the bit patterns in the L-bit space [30]. In contrast, the verification of a solution to the puzzle takes only a single hash operation. The Ethereum PoW added an additional step in random memory access, but the puzzle design still follows the same principle (with much reduced difficulty target in Ethereum than that in Bitcoin). Hence, the PoW algorithm satisfy the requirements on unpredictability, noninvertibility, noninteractive verification, soundness, and completeness. Because what is being hashed is the new block header, the freshness requirement is satisfied as well (i.e., previous work cannot be reused to mine the new block). The only issue for PoW is that it lacks resistance to outsourcing. By introducing a memory-limited additional step, Ethereum PoW significantly reduced this issue.

9.3   Proof of Resources

There has been many attempts of using other means of digital resources to replace the computing resource used in the PoW algorithm. The general objectives are not just make the puzzle consumes less energy, but also to make the puzzle-solving competition to do useful work such as for distributed file storage or computing some hard problems which can be useful for research. We categorize the approaches on proof of resources into two camps, one relying on data storage, and the other relying on computing. As we will see in this section, the proposed algorithms relying on data storage consist of various deficiencies. The other direction is to still rely on the computing resource, but computing something useful in some ways instead of using hashing, which would waste the computing resource. The latter is actually quite promising and deserves a lot more further research.

9.3.1   Using Storage as Resource

The proof of space [10] asks the prover (*i.e.*, the miner) to present evidence that it has indeed dedicated the required amount of disk space to store the information as requested by the verifier. Unfortunately, this uses an interactive ZKP design involving an initialization phase to ensure that both the prover and the verifier could deploy the data structure (typically a hard-to-pebble graph), and a challenge-response phase where the verifier would challenge the prover on the accessibility of certain information in the graph. Hence, this scheme is simply impractical for use in the public blockchain, where noninteractive verification is a prerequisite. It is also unclear how easy it is to ensure the freshness needed to mine each new block.

Miller et al. proposed a scheme called Permacoin, based on the proof-of-retrievability (PoR) concept that involves distributed storage [22]. PoR grew out of the idea of proof of storage designed for secure file systems where a client could verify indeed its files are reliably stored remotely at the server prior to the creation of Bitcoin [9, 27]. In [22], the authors attempted to adapt the PoR concept for consensus in blockchain in the form of a noninteractive ZKP scheme. In this scheme, there exists a trusted file dealer that would divide the files into a sequence of segments and somehow publishes these segments for provers to store at their sites. For easy retrieval and verification, the segments would be constructed into a Merkle tree and the root hash would also be made public and immutable. A verifier could then verify whether or not the prover has stored the required segments by checking the Merkle proof presented by the prover. The scheme also assumes the existence of a publicly known, non-precomputable puzzle ID that is somehow a function of the block height. Furthermore, a client would have a fixed number of random challenges for the oracle.

It is apparent that Permacoin is incompatible to the requirements for public blockchain consensus. Even though the design is a noninteractive ZKP, it is not a full stochastic process [30]. Besides the intrinsic limitation on the puzzle design, the assumptions made in the scheme is not practical for a system that aims to achieve decentralization. The assumption of a trusted file dealer for file distribution is a contraction to the design principle of public blockchains. Furthermore, how to produce a non-precomputable puzzle ID is by itself a problem on par with the consensus problem. We should note that there is no publicly-known implementation of Permacoin for blockchain.

KopperCoin [17] is a follow-up work by addressing several deficiencies of Permacoin. The main extension in KopperCoin is to make the ZKP scheme a full stochastic process. First, it introduced a distance metric between the index of a locally stored segment and a publicly-known random challenge. Second, it introduced a mechanism to generate public and unpredictable random challenge by hashing the header of the most recent block.

FileCoin [4] is a practically deployed system designed for secure storage of files. It has built-in mechanisms for a client to challenge a storage server to make sure that the client's files are indeed stored at the site and the files are indeed replicated for fault tolerance and reliability. It introduced the concepts of proof of replication and proof of space time. However, we note that these concepts are designed for a client to challenge the storage server. They are *not used to achieve consensus*, which is a sharp contract to Permacoin and KopperCoin. Instead, what the FileCoin white paper [4] is advocating is a consensus scheme rather similar to the proof-of-stake. Different from PoS, which uses the amount of coin as the stake for a cryptocurrency system, FileCoin uses the file storage power as the stake.

In FileCoin, the power of a mining node is defined as the sum of the miner's storage assignments. The election for the miner that is to create the next block is determined by the following precedure. Given a miner i at round t (which is referred to as epoch in FileCoin and each epoch has a maximum fixed duration) with power $P_i(t)$, the miner i would be given permission to create the block for the round if $Hash(< t||rand(t) >_{Sig})/2^L \leq (P_i(t)/\sum_j P_j(t))$, where it is assumed that the cryptographic hash function produces an L-bit string. As can be seen, a mining node has no opportunity to try out different schemes hoping to win the lottery. Each mining node could only try once and if the condition is met, then it would proceed creating the block for round t. Otherwise, it waits for the next round. Apparently, this scheme could lead to multiple miners to be given the permission to create a block, or no miner is given the permission. The while paper stated that in case no miner is selected, an empty block will be created. However, the white paper did not specific who is in charge of creating the empty block. Furthermore, the white paper failed to elaborate how to break the tie if two or more blocks are created in the same round. We note that these problems are equivalent to the forking scenarios in PoW and a conflict resolution mechanism must be defined. Otherwise, the network cannot recover from the inconsistent state.

9.3.2   Using Computing as Resource

Primecoin [15] proposed a puzzle design on the search for three types of prime number chains (*i.e.*, the Cunningham chain of the first and the second kind, and the bi-twin chain). Unfortunately, the puzzle design suffered from two major issues [30]: (1) the puzzle does not follow a random distribution on leader election; (2) the verification violates the soundness requirement.

Proof of exercise proposed a puzzle design on finding solutions for some matrix product problems offered by clients [28]. Unfortunately, the computing tasks are not guaranteed to have the same complexity level and hence the puzzle-solving process is not a stochastic process. Furthermore, the puzzle design failed to provide an efficient verification scheme.

The useful proof of work (uPoW) [2] is a very promising puzzle design that rivals the PoW algorithms used in Bitcoin and Ethereum. It aims to find specific mathematical problems that are both useful and fulfill the puzzle design requirements for a noninteractive ZKP scheme as we have laid out previously. The k-Orthogonal Vectors (k-OV) problem happen to fit the requirements.

To find a solution to k-OV, a miner would have to perform exhaustive search over k-sets of vectors for a vector that would make the vectors in the set k-orthogonal. To make the puzzle-solving as a stochastic process, a cryptographic hash function is used, where the elements in a vector are regarded as coefficients of polynomials, and the first element in each vector is generated based on publicly-known input string. Other coefficients would be generated using the hash function. Besides k-OV, the paper also elaborated several other mathematical problems that are eligible for uPoW, including 3SUM and all-pairs shortest path.

9.4   Virtual Mining

In [30], Wang et al. referred to a category of alternative consensus for public blockchains as virtual mining. This is to emphasize the fact that the puzzle does not force a miner to dedicate computing or storage resources for solving the puzzle. Instead, how likely a miner solves a puzzle is based on what the miner possess (*i.e.*, something valuable and aligns with the best interest of the system), which is referred to as stake. That is why this scheme is called proof of stake (PoS). Another way of doing virtual mining is to resort to hardware-based attestation, which is referred to as proof of elapsed time. This issue with the latter is that it depends on a particular hardware vendor, which is more or less equivalent to trusting a third party.

In this section, we first discuss PoS algorithms, and then briefly on the proof of elapsed time scheme. We will take the opportunity to provide a detailed description on the PoS algorithm introduced as part of PeerCoin. This is the first PoS algorithm that was implemented in a public blockchain and has gone through many years' of tests and revisions. We then go over the alternative PoS approach and comment on the issues with this scheme.

9.4.1   PeerCoin PoS

PeerCoin was the first blockchain system that incorporated PoS in block creation. Unfortunately, there is no detailed description on how PoS works in PeerCoin. The PeerCoin white paper [16] only presented the high-level idea. In this section, we fill this gap by providing a detailed description on how the PeerCoin PoS works based on our study of the PeerCoin source code, which is available at GitHub (`https://github.com/peercoin/peercoin`). We also dispel the misconception that the PeerCoin PoS is still based on Proof of Work (PoW) and hence would consume a lot of energy. In fact, it adopted a genius design by following the concept of PoW where mining nodes would compete to solve a puzzle of certain difficulty to achieve consensus. Instead of hashing the block header with different nonce until the hash value meets the difficulty target, PeerCoin PoS relies on CoinAge to drastically reduce the difficulty target. Here CoinAge is the product of the coin amount that the miner holds and the duration that the miner has already held on to the coin.

Although the PeerCoin PoS-based algorithm resembles PoW in terms of finding a solution based on hashing where the hash value must meet the difficult target, the two differ significantly on what is being hashed and how it is done. In PoW, the new block header is hashed repeatedly with different nonce in the hope of meeting the difficulty target and the mining node would do so continuously as quickly as it can. The PeerCoin PoS on the other hand, does not use nonce and only hashes a finite set of items related to each stake transactions in each round. Hence, the energy consumption of the PeerCoin PoS is significantly less compared with PoW. As will see later, a larger CoinAge would significantly improve the likelihood of meeting the target.

The most fundamental concept used in the PeerCoin PoS algorithm is CoinAge. Like Bitcoin, PeerCoin also uses the Unspent Transaction Output (UTXO) model for balance tracking. If someone received some cryptocurrency in a transaction and has not yet spent it, then there is an associated CoinAge with the transaction output in the transaction. The CoinAge would drop to 0 as soon as the cryptocurrency amount is spent (i.e., the transaction is used as an input in another transaction). To be able to track the CoinAge accurately for each transaction output, PeerCoin added a transaction timestamp field.

Figure 9.2 illustrates part of the main loop used by a mining node to compete in the creation of a new block using PoS in PeerCoin. The mining node starts with calling a function `CreateNewBlock` on creating a new block. If the function returns true, it means that it wins the competition in creating the next block and subsequently creates one. Then it will sleep for 1-3 minutes randomly before it attempts to create the next block. Unlike Bitcoin, which offers

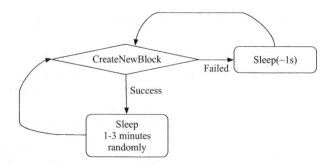

Figure 9.2   Main loop used by a mining node to compete in the creation of a new block using PoS in PeerCoin.

a fixed reward per block, PeerCoin offers a block reward that is proportional to the CoinAge. Previously it was set to be slightly over 1% of the CoinAge and recently it is increased to 3% of the CoinAge plus 0.25% of the money supply per block [24]. To prevent a mining node from increasing the CoinAge by holding on to a small amount of coins for a long period time, the age of the coin is capped at 90 days.

If the function returns false, the mining node would have to wait for roughly 1 second before it attempts again. More specifically, the wait time is determined to be $500+30 \times sqrt(\#coins)$ milliseconds. If the number of coins is 9, then the wait time would be $500 + 30 \times 3 = 590$ milliseconds.

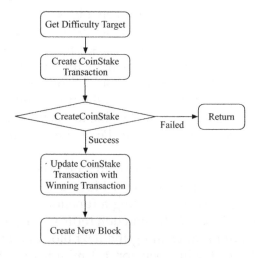

Figure 9.3   Major steps in the CreateNewBlock function in PeerCoin PoS.

Figure 9.3 shows the detailed steps in the `CreateNewBlock` function. First, the current difficulty target is retrieved. Then, a CoinStake transaction is created. Similar to the CoinBase transaction used in Bitcoin for the block reward, PeerCoin uses a CoinStake transaction as the very first transaction in a block. At this point, the CoinBase transaction is only a placeholder. Next, the `CreateCoinStake` function is invoked, which is defined as part of the wallet module. The purpose of this function is to find if one of the transactions that is held in the wallet satisfies the requirement that can be used as the coin stake (the details will be explained next). If an appropriate transaction is found, the `CreateCoinStake` function would return the transaction, and the CoinStake transaction will be updated accordingly. The final step is to create a new block. If no coin stake transaction can be found, the `CreateNewBlock` returns immediately.

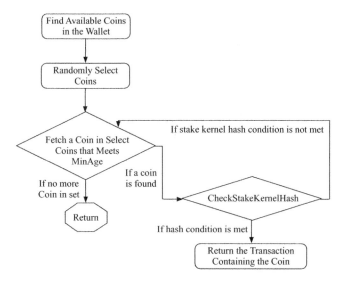

Figure 9.4   Major steps in the CreateCoinStake function in PeerCoin PoS.

The details of the CreateCoinStake function are shown in Figure 9.4. First, all available coins in the wallet are retrieved and a subset of the coins are randomly selected. PeerCoin stated that this random selection is not fundamental to the security of the system, but nevertheless helps in policing the behavior of the mining nodes. Then, the selected coins are looped through and each of the coin that meets a minimum age is passed to a function called

`CheckStakeKernelHash` to see if it meets the hash condition as defined in the PeerCoin Kernel protocol (which will be explained in detail next). This hash condition check is equivalent to the requirement of the PoW where the hash of the new block header must meet the target difficulty. Just like the mining node that first finds the solution to the PoW puzzle gets to win an award and create the new block, the coin that meets the hash condition first will lead to its owner to gain the right to create the new block and win a stake award. The loop terminates immediately when a coin is found to meet the condition, or it ends when there is no more coin in the selected coin set.

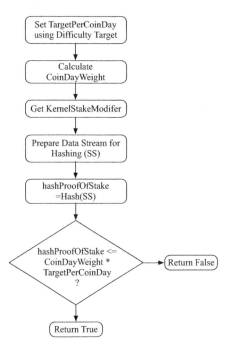

Figure 9.5   Major steps in the CheckStakeKernelHash function in PeerCoin PoS.

Figure 9.5 shows the main steps in the `CheckStakeKernelHash` function. First, the `TargetPerCoinDay` is computed based on the current blockchain difficulty target. The difficult target is changed dynamically based on the actual amount of time used to create new blocks and the target block period. For PeerCoin, the block period is set to be 8.5 minutes (the block period in Bitcoin is 10 minutes). Then, the

`CoinDayWeigth` is computed as the product of the coin value and the age of the coin divided by a constant. The constant is currently set as $1,000,000 \times 24 \times 60 \times 60$.

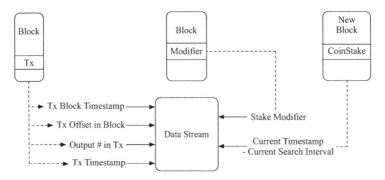

Figure 9.6   Information included in the data stream for computing PoS hash.

The next step is to create a data stream for hashing. What to put in the data stream requires carefully planing and PeerCoin has gone through three revisions on this mechanism. As shown in Figure 9.6, the current version (v0.5) includes the following items: the stake modifier, the timestamp of the block where the stake transaction resides in, the position (i.e., offset) of the stake transaction in the block, the timestamp of the stake transaction, the output number of the stake transaction, and the timestamp of the current transaction minus the current search interval. There are primarily two purposes for including these items: (1) minimize the chance of two mining nodes finding the stake transaction in the same round; (2) provide a fair competition ground for all mining nodes based on the stake they hold and how long they have held (however, the mining node that possesses the largest coinage is not guaranteed to win). It is important to understand that the information included in the data stream comes from three blocks:

- The block that contains the transaction used as the stake by the mining note. This is the oldest block among the three blocks. It must be older than the minimum age imposed by PeerCoin, which is currently set to be 30 days.
- The block that contains the modifier. This block is much newer than the first block. It is the block that is slightly older than the current timestamp minus the stake modifier selection interval, which is set to be 21 days in v0.5. Please

> note that every block in PeerCoin contains a field of stake modifier and the modifier is recalculated very 6 hours or so.
>
> - The current block to be created. The timestamp is used as the timestamp for the block and for the CoinStake transaction.

The data stream is then hashed to produce `hashProofOfStake`, which is subsequently compared with the product of the `CoinDayWeight` and `TargetPerCoinDay`. If `hashProofOfStake` is equal to or smaller than the product, then it is said that the PoS target is met and hence, the stake transaction is found. The mining node that owns this stake transaction gets to create the new block.

Stake modifier. To help ensure that the PoS winner selection process is a stochastic process, PeerCoin introduced a stake modifier. The stake modifier is designed to make it difficult for a mining node to precompute future PoS at the time of the coin's confirmation. Every block has a stake modifier of 64-bit-long that is computed based on a set of 64 blocks. A block is randomly selected from a given block group in the blockchain based on the time they were created., and each block contributes exactly one bit to the modifier. The stake modifier is recomputed roughly every 6 hours. An important design consideration for the stake modifier is to prevent an adversary from being able to control some of the bits if it could generate a chain of blocks. By dividing the blocks into 64 groups based on the time they were created and selecting only one from each group could effectively achieve the objective.

9.4.1.1   Conflict resolution

Because the winner selection is stochastic, there is no guarantee that there is only a single winner per round. When two or more mining notes have built a new block concurrently, PeerCoin specifies that the chain with the highest total consumed CoinAge should be chosen as the main chain.

9.4.1.2   Security of PeerCoin PoS

Obviously, PoS must be safe-guarded to prevent malicious mining nodes from dominating new block creation, which could lead to double-spending attacks. The first question that might come to mind is why in PeerCoin PoS the new block header is not part of the hash like Bitcoin PoW considering that PeerCoin inherited most of Bitcoin codebase.

To understand why, we need to understand and compare the design philosophy of the two approaches. We start by pointing out the similarity between the two. Both aim to use a stochastic process to select the winner for each block height among possibly a huge number of competitors (*i.e.,* minding nodes) and this winner gets to create the block and win an award for the round, which is an ingenious way of solving the distributed consensus problem in a trustless, large scale network. In PoW, both the work and the verification are on the new block only. The work involves finding the right number that makes the current block header meet the target difficulty. The verification is also self-contained in each block, i.e., one could simply verify if the hash of the block header is smaller than the target difficulty. This design is extremely simple and elegant. However, the tradeoff is the huge energy consumption in PoW competition and the problem would become more serious in the presence of more mining nodes because the block interval remains the same and yet only a single winner is expected for each round.

In PeerCoin PoS, however, the winner is randomly selected from those that possess cryptocurrency and have held on the coins long enough. Inevitably, those candidate stake transactions must be verified and some of their characteristics (such as timestamp and the offset in the respective blocks) will need to be retrieved in earlier blocks to determine if the transaction meets the hash difficulty target. The verification process is rather similar to finding the right stake transaction. However, by only using historical information, which is known to all mining nodes, is not secure based on our previous analysis [32] and the work by Want et al. [30]. We pointed out that the stochastic process must include information regarding the current state of the block, which we call freshness. In PoW, this requirement is easily met because the current block header is being hashed. In PeerCoin PoS, this requirement is at least partially satisfied by including the current timestamp as part of the data stream to be hashed. This might be sufficient to prevent a mining node from performing PoS ahead of the time compared with other mining nodes because it will be used in the new block as the timestamp of the block.

It is interesting to note that in the PeerCoin source code, the PeerCoin developers pointed out the reason why the block hash is not included in the data stream. It warns that using block hash would degrade the system back into a PoW situation because the hash "can be generated in vast quantities so as to generate blocks faster." (PeerCoin supports both PoW and PoS mining, albeit PoW is discouraged).

In addition to using the current timestamp, PeerCoin introduced the stake modifier as a random source into the data stream for hashing. Intuitively, this enhances the stochastic process for finding the winner of each round.

Nothing-at-stake issue. A general vulnerability of PoS algorithms is a potential nothing-at-stake issue exactly because it is much cheaper to meet the target requirement than that for PoW. To address this concern, PeerCoin PoS introduced two mechanisms: (1) only the coin that is old-enough can be used as a stake, which is currently set at 30 days; (2) once the coin is used as a stake, the CoinAge for the coin is said to have been consumed and the mining node can no longer use the same coin as a stake for another block anymore.

Grinding attack/stake burn-through vulnerability. PeerCoin releases earlier than v0.3 has a vulnerability that enables an adversary to search the limited search space without waiting the required time between different attempts, which is why it is referred to as stake burn-through or grinding attack. This was possible because the input to the data stream for hashing to see if the result meets the target is deterministic. Jutarul demonstrated a successful attack in December 2012 [14]. Starting v0.3, PeerCoin introduced a stake modifier as one of the inputs to the data stream, which essentially eliminated this vulnerability. As we have discussed earlier, the stake modifier is computed from multiple blocks and is used as an unpredictable entropy source to the data stream. Hence, the search space is so greatly increased that it is virtually impossible to launch the grinding attack.

9.4.2   Fixed-Epoch Time Based PoS Schemes

We are aware of some PoS schemes that assume a fixed block time in that the system somehow would produce one new block (but could be 0 or more than 1) for a pre-defined fixed amount of time, typically referred to as an epoch. We argue that this assumption is very dangerous for any system that run on the Internet, and particularly dangerous for a large-scale open system like a public blockchain. The reason is simple. The clocks are loosely synchronized at best even for a small network in the laboratory setting, let alone on the Internet. The clock drift rates differ as well. For a distributed algorithms to work robustly and securely, ideally the asynchronous system model should be used where there is no assumption on the bound of message propagation, on the bound of local processing, and on the bound of clock drift rate. Any assumption on any of these bounds would be asking for attacks.

That said, a practical system must ensure progress in terms of time (this is often referred to as liveness of the system). How to resolve this conflicting requirements then? The Bitcoin PoW algorithm gives a practical solution. The design does not dictate a fixed block interval (or a bound on the block interval), but aims to achieve a target block interval of 10 minutes. It achieves this objective by adjusting the difficulty level for every 2,016 blocks. Why every 2,016 blocks? This is because if the system indeed produces exactly one new block every 10 minutes, then it will take exactly two weeks (*i.e.*, 14 days) to create 2,016 blocks. Please note that the difficulty adjustment period is set in terms of the number of blocks that have most recently created, not some pre-defined time in terms of some time unit. Hence, if the system is very asynchronous or due to the nature of the stochastic process, it could take significantly more time than 14-days to produce 2,016 blocks, in which case, the difficulty target will be reduced to make the system more likely to take less time to produce a new block on average. As can be seen, in no place does Bitcoin dictated a hard time limit on its operation, particularly on the consensus operation. This is how a practical, robust, and secure system should be designed.

The follow-the-satoshi PoS scheme was introduced as part of the proof of activity [5]. In this scheme, a fixed-epoch time is assumed, and the goal is to ensure the creation of exactly one block per epoch time. The scheme's operation uses several parameter: (1) a group size of l blocks, the creators for a future group of l blocks are determined based on previous group of l consecutive blocks; (2) a minimal block interval time G_0; (3) a minimal stake amount C_0; (4) a double-spending safety bound T_0. To determine the next group of block creators, first a $k - bit$ string B_i is produced somehow by combining the bits contributed by each block of a previous group of l blocks. One way for producing such bits is to simply hash the block. The next group of block creators are determined by hashing three parameters: i, z, and B_i, where i is the block height of the last block in the group of block used to determine the next group of block creators, z is a sequence number starting from 1 and ending at l (*i.e.*, the group size). The parameter G_0 is used to make sure that no block is created within G_0 amount of time after a new block. The size l is actually defined as the product of k and another parameter w, where $w \geq 1$. The recommended parameter values are: $k = 51$, $w = 9$, $l = k \times w = 459$, $G_0 = 5$, and $T_0 = 5,000$. There is an additional parameter on block reward C_1, which does not impact the correctness of the algorithm.

A big difference between this scheme and the PoW or the PeerCoin PoS algorithms is that the block creators are determined by algorithms instead of a miner actively competing to be the creator of a new block. As such, there is a chance that the block creator determined this way is either offline or is unwilling to do the job. To deal with this potential problem, the follow-the-satoshi algorithm specifies a "three-strike" blacklisting rule. If a miner has been selected for creating a new block and failed to do so, then the node is blacklisted after three strikes. However, it is not clear what would happen if the expected block creator failed to create a new block at all or failed to create a new block on-time. How long would the next expected block creator have to wait in this case to add its own block? The system is bound to have forks in this situation and it is not caused by the stochastic process of the puzzle-solving process, but due to the use of time in the algorithm design.

The follow-the-satoshi PoS scheme does offer a conflict resolution rule where the network should choose the branch that has the longest chain (*i.e.*, whichever branch that has the most number of blocks). However, the work did not describe how a conflict could happen because the scheme is designed to have only a single miner that is eligible to create a block per epoch to overcome the rational forks problem: "only a single stakeholder identity may create the next block, and solidifying the random choices for these identities in the earlier ledger history via an interleaving mechanism." [5]. The requirement on a minimum time gap in block creation is also problematic. The rule stated that there is a minimum time gap G_0 between two consecutive blocks. The only way to verify if the rule has been abided by the miners is to compare the timestamps of the two consecutive blocks. However, because the clocks are not strictly synchronized, two blocks could be created with a time gap of G_0 or larger in reality, but the timestamps might appear to be smaller than

G_0. In this case, one of the blocks would have to be abandoned. There is no rule on which block should be abandoned, which by itself could lead to inconsistency in the network. This issue is also caused by using time explicitly for the correctness (or safety) of the consensus process.

The consensus scheme outlined in FileCoin [4] is also a form of PoS. The difference is instead of using cryptocurrency stake, FileCoin uses the storage power as the stake. The FileCoin PoS also assumes a predefined epoch time and aims to determine the miner for each epoch. However, the method to determine the next miner is probabilistic in that there could be 0, 1, or more miners that satisfy the condition. The FileCoin PoS is not as fully described and rigorously analyzed as the follow-the-satoshi PoS. Nevertheless, it does offer an alternative of stake to be considered.

9.4.3   Proof of Elapsed Time

Proof of elapsed time (PoET) simulates the stochastic process on the leader election (*i.e.*, which miner gets to create the new block) as required by ZKP-based probabilistic consensus for blockchain using essentially a trusted hardware blackbox instead of using a mathematical puzzle. More specifically, PoET relies on the Intel Software Guard Extension (SGX), which has a software developing kit (SDK). Intel SGX allows a piece of code running in a trusted environment, and it can create an attestation for the trusted code execution. The full specification of PoET can be viewed at `https://sawtooth.hyperledger.org/docs/core/releases/1.0/architecture/poet.html`. We should note that PoET can only be used for permissioned blockchain where the membership is known and controlled. One reason is that its key operation of PoET requires the knowledge of the membership size (not necessarily very accurate size, to decide on the mean wait time).

In PoET, a miner would setup the required computing environment with SGX SDK with the code for the blockchain with PoET consensus. All PoET related computing will be done in an enclave, which is a protected area in the application's address space that ensures security even in the presence of malware with administrative privilege. Each enclave has a `SealKey` used to encrypt confidential information.

Then, the miner must call the function `generateSignUpData()` to obtain a set of signup data. When this function is invoked, the enclave generate a pair of ECC public and private keys (called PPK and PSK, respectively), and create a monotonically increasing counter called MCID. Then, the enclave encrypts PPK, PSK, and MCID using the SealKey. The encrypted PPK, PSK, and MCID are called sealedSignUpData. Besides the sealedSignUpData, the enclave also generates a report and a PSEmanifest. From the PoET specification, it is not clear exactly what information is included in the report and the PSEmanifest. Presumably they are used for the purpose of attestation. Finally, the miner broadcast a join request to the network (signed with the miner's PPK), including the necessary authentication information.

Other nodes in the network would verify the join request. If successful, the new miner is accepted and an internal signup certificate is generated for the new miner. The newly joined miner would then have to wait for c number of blocks to be published on the blockchain before it is allowed to participate the competition for new block generation. When it is ready to do so, the miner would first call createWaitTimer() function with a local mean value of the wait time. The call returns immediately with a waitTimer object. Even though the PoET specification did not say explicitly, presumably the miner would proceed to creating the new block while waiting for the timer to expire. When the timer expires, it would call createWaitCertificate() with the digest of the new block just created as input. The enclave then returns a signed waitCertificate to the miner. The miner would subsequently broadcast the waitCertificate and the new block to the network. The miner whose waitCertificate with the lowest value of wait duration will be taken as the winner for this round of competition.

This design has one potential issue because the wait call takes a localMean parameters, which a malicious miner could manipulate with a much smaller value than it should be. To mitigate such threats, the system uses a statistical test, called z-test, to determine if a miner has been winning the competition disproportionally, and if so, blacklist the miner.

As can be seen, the PoET design does satisfy the noninteractive ZKP design requirement. The distribution of the wait time is a perfectly stochastic process as controlled by the SGX environment assuming all miners would use the localMean honestly. It also satisfies some of the requirements we have enumerated, including freshness, unpredictability, noninteractive verification, resistant to sourcing. Since, PoET does not really use any puzzle, the noninvertibility, completeness, and soundness requirements on the puzzle design are irrelevant.

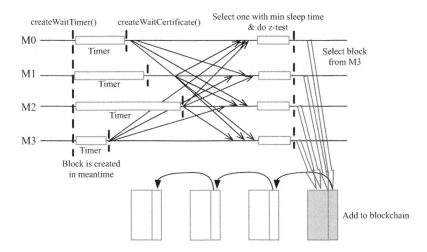

Figure 9.7   Major steps in PoET consensus.

Figure 9.7 illustrates the main steps in PoET consensus with four miners and when there is no fault during the consensus process. On surface, PoET appears to be a well-designed scheme for reaching consensus for a permissioned blockchain. However, it suffers from several issues. First, the PoET design has an apparent scalability issue. This is because by design of PoET, every miner would broadcast a new block with the waitCertificate for each round. The winner of this round of election can then be determined after the broadcast messages have been collected. That would be a lot of broadcast messages if the number of miners is large. Perhaps PoET is not designed for a large network in the first place as revealed by the terminology used in the PoET specification, where the miner is referred to as a validator. There is an even more serious problem than the scalability issue in fact. When deciding on the winner for each election, the PoET specification did not describe the condition for the time to perform such a check. Should a node wait until it has received input from every single miner in the network? If so, the design is not fault tolerant because a single crashed node would prevent the system from making progress. Let's say the system is designed to tolerate up to f faulty nodes and would calculate the winner when each node has collected $n - f$ inputs, where n is the total number of miners. Due to the asynchrony of the system, different nodes could collect different sets of $n - f$ inputs, then their decision could be completely different! The PoET specification failed to describe this issue at all and there is no recover mechanism given. The PoET specification used the term "server" when describing the winner determination step. Perhaps it is assumed that a single server is in charge of doing the task, which would avoid the correctness issue at the expense of being a single point of failure. Either way, the PoET design has intrinsic technical issues.

References

1. E. Akbari, W. Zhao, S. Yang, and X. Lou. The impact of block parameters on the throughput and security of blockchains. In *Proceedings of the 2020 International Conference on Blockchain Technology*, pages 13–18. ACM, 2020.

2. M. Ball, A. Rosen, M. Sabin, and P. N. Vasudevan. Proofs of useful work. *IACR Cryptol. ePrint Arch.*, 2017:203, 2017.

3. M. Ben-Or. Another advantage of free choice (extended abstract) completely asynchronous agreement protocols. In *Proceedings of the second annual ACM symposium on Principles of distributed computing*, pages 27–30, 1983.

4. J. Benet and N. Greco. Filecoin: A decentralized storage network. *Protoc. Labs*, pages 1–36, 2018.

5. I. Bentov, A. Gabizon, and A. Mizrahi. Cryptocurrencies without proof of work. In *International conference on financial cryptography and data security*, pages 142–157. Springer, 2016.

6. K. P. Birman, R. van Renesse, et al. *Reliable distributed computing with the Isis toolkit*, volume 85. IEEE Computer Society Press Los Alamitos, 1994.

7. M. Castro and B. Liskov. Practical byzantine fault tolerance and proactive recovery. *ACM Transactions on Computer Systems (TOCS)*, 20(4):398–461, 2002.

8. T. D. Chandra and S. Toueg. Unreliable failure detectors for reliable distributed systems. *Journal of the ACM (JACM)*, 43(2):225–267, 1996.

9. Y. Deswarte, J.-J. Quisquater, and A. Saïdane. Remote integrity checking. In *Working conference on integrity and internal control in information systems*, pages 1–11. Springer, 2003.

10. S. Dziembowski, S. Faust, V. Kolmogorov, and K. Pietrzak. Proofs of space. In *Annual Cryptology Conference*, pages 585–605. Springer, 2015.

11. M. J. Fischer, N. A. Lynch, and M. S. Paterson. Impossibility of distributed consensus with one faulty process. *Journal of the ACM (JACM)*, 32(2):374–382, 1985.

12. A. Gervais, G. O. Karame, K. Wüst, V. Glykantzis, H. Ritzdorf, and S. Capkun. On the security and performance of proof of work blockchains. In *Proceedings of the 2016 ACM SIGSAC conference on computer and communications security*, pages 3–16, 2016.

13. S. Goldwasser, S. Micali, and C. Rackoff. The knowledge complexity of interactive proof systems. *SIAM Journal on computing*, 18(1):186–208, 1989.

14. Jutarul. Ppcoin - stake burn-through vulnerability. https://bitcointalk.org/index.php?topic=131901.0., Dec. 2012.

15. S. King. Primecoin: Cryptocurrency with prime number proof-of-work. http://primecoin.io/bin/primecoinpaper.pdf, July 2013.

16. S. King and S. Nadal. Ppcoin: Peer-to-peer cryptocurrency with proof-of-stake. https://www.peercoin.net/whitepapers/peercoin-paper.pdf., Aug. 2012.

17. H. Kopp, C. Bösch, and F. Kargl. Koppercoin–a distributed file storage with financial incentives. In *Proceedings of the International Conference on Information Security Practice and Experience*, pages 79–93. Springer, 2016.

18. L. Lamport. Time, clocks, and the ordering of events in a distributed system. *Commun. ACM*, 21(7):558–565, July 1978.

19. L. Lamport. Fast paxos. *Distributed Computing*, 19(2):79–193, 2006.

20. L. Lamport et al. Paxos made simple. *ACM Sigact News*, 32(4):18–25, 2001.

21. L. Lamport, R. Shostak, and M. Pease. The byzantine generals problem. *ACM Transactions on Programming Languages and Systems*, 4:382–401, 1982.

22. A. Miller, A. Juels, E. Shi, B. Parno, and J. Katz. Permacoin: Repurposing bitcoin work for data preservation. In *Proceedings of the IEEE Symposium on Security and Privacy*, pages 475–490. IEEE, 2014.

23. L. E. Moser, P. M. Melliar-Smith, D. A. Agarwal, R. K. Budhia, and C. A. Lingley-Papadopoulos. Totem: A fault-tolerant multicast group communication system. *Communications of the ACM*, 39(4):54–63, 1996.

24. Ngalim. Proof-of-stake reward adjustment (peercoin rfc-18). https://github.com/peercoin/rfcs/blob/master/text/0018-pos-reward/0018-pos-reward.md., Apr. 2020.

25. C. Rackoff and D. R. Simon. Non-interactive zero-knowledge proof of knowledge and chosen ciphertext attack. In *Annual International Cryptology Conference*, pages 433–444. Springer, 1991.

26. Y. Saito and M. Shapiro. Optimistic replication. *ACM Comput. Surv.*, 37(1):42–81, Mar. 2005.

27. H. Shacham and B. Waters. Compact proofs of retrievability. In *Proceedings of the International conference on the theory and application of cryptology and information security*, pages 90–107. Springer, 2008.

28. A. Shoker. Sustainable blockchain through proof of exercise. In *Proceedings of the IEEE 16th International Symposium on Network Computing and Applications (NCA)*, pages 1–9. IEEE, 2017.

29. Y. Sompolinsky and A. Zohar. Secure high-rate transaction processing in bitcoin. In *International Conference on Financial Cryptography and Data Security*, pages 507–527. Springer, 2015.

30. W. Wang, D. T. Hoang, P. Hu, Z. Xiong, D. Niyato, P. Wang, Y. Wen, and D. I. Kim. A survey on consensus mechanisms and mining strategy management in blockchain networks. *IEEE Access*, 7:22328–22370, 2019.

31. W. Zhao. *Building dependable distributed systems*. John Wiley & Sons, 2014.

32. W. Zhao, S. Yang, and X. Luo. On consensus in public blockchains. In *Proceedings of the 2019 International Conference on Blockchain Technology*, pages 1–5, 2019.

10

Blockchain Applications

The blockchain technology has attained huge interest in the last several years. In an early book on blockchain applications published in 2015 [60], which has been cited nearly 3,000 according to Google Scholar, Swan painted a rosy future for blockchain. She regarded blockchain systems that offer cryptocurrency as the main functionality (such as Bitcoin) as blockchain 1.0, blockchain systems that offer smart contract (such as Ethereum) as blockchain 2.0. She envisaged a new type of systems that take advantages of the many intrinsic properties of the blockchain technology, which she terms as blockchain 3.0. She further divided blockchain 3.0 into two types of applications, one she terms as justice applications, and the other as efficiency & coordination applications. The former primarily includes organizational or governmental services, such as a decentralized domain name system, digital identity verification and document attestation, and blockchain-based governments. The latter spans any applications that could exploit the blockchain technology for higher efficiency and more reliable coordination (with smart contract). Indeed, from the economic point of view, any technology that can be used to reduce transaction cost could potentially play a big role in the society. A great example for such technology is the Internet and World Wide Web. In the book, Swan placed great emphasis on the value of decentralization. While decentralization is attractive, not everyone agrees with such a view considering how our societies are organized. By all means, we do need many services and protections from the governments. Digitally technology, not matter how trustworthy it can bestow on a system, cannot be extended to physical activities in our everyday life that require trust on governments or trusted third parties. In a recent paper authored by Xu and Zou [68], they provided an excellent discussion on the value and potential of the blockchain technology from the economic point of view, particularly regarding decentralization and the trust outside the blockchain platform.

In this chapter, we first introduce our insight on the value of the blockchain technology in terms of different levels of benefits it can bring to applications. Second, we review the existing proposals on various blockchain applications for cyber-physical systems (CPS). With the permeation of the digital and Internet technologies in our society, more and more physical operations are cyber-enabled. We are using Internet of Things (IoT) to collect data and to control various home and industrial devices [50]. Hence, most of the applications can be regarded as some form of CPS [83]. Third, we summarize the work on addressing the limited blockchain throughput issue using various means. Finally, introduce the work by Xu and Zou [68] on their view of what blockchain can and cannot do and their opinion on the balance between decentralization and the trust on third parties.

10.1   The Value of Blockchain

The value of blockchain is reflected from the benefits that it could bring to applications. Instead of itemizing all of the benefits in a monolithic manner like most of the published literature did, we create a structure on the numerous benefits, as shown in Fig. 10.1. First, we differentiate between non-functional and functional benefits. By non-functional benefits, we mean the properties that describe the quality of services of a system, and such properties are independent from the functionality of the system. The most well-known non-functional properties are security and dependability. By functional benefits, we mean the benefits that can be

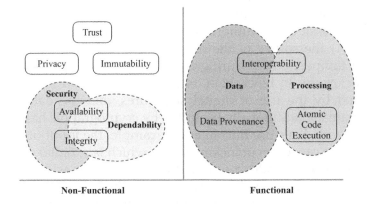

Figure 10.1   Main benefits of blockchain for applications.

employed to implement the functionality of the system. In other words, the functional perspective refers to what the system does (*i.e.,* services), and the non-functional perspective refers to how well the system does its job (*i.e.,* the quality of services).

10.1.1   Non-functional benefits

The non-functional benefits can be roughly divided into three levels. At the bottom level are the most obvious benefits of blockchain: security and dependability. At the middle level are privacy and immutability. At the highest level is trust.

A closer look at what blockchain can provide regarding security and dependability reveals that the benefits at the bottom level are availability and integrity. As we have elaborated in Chapter 1 of this book, availability and integrity are properties of both a secure system and a dependable system. However, the interpretations for these two terms are actually slightly different. In the context of dependability, availability refers to the probability of the system is ready to serve its clients at any given time, and the integrity largely refers to the correctness of the services a system provides. Due to the massive degree of replication (there are around 10,000 miners in the Bitcoin network, for example) and the various verifications (the most relevant being the cryptographic hash of the block header) ensure that each copy of the blockchain has not been tampered with. The availability and the integrity of the system, if it is enabled by blockchain, are guaranteed this way.

In the context of security, the availability means that information is accessible by authorized users, and integrity means two things: (1) the source of the data is legitimate, and (2) the data are not tampered with during transmission and while stored on the blockchain. In blockchain, both availability and integrity are protected by the use of digital signatures, and the data on the blockchain are additionally protected by cryptographic hash of the block header. Let's use Bitcoin as an example, the input of a transaction must carries an unlocking script, which is a digital signature corresponds to the address of the fund to be spent as specified by the input. This ensures that only the user who has the corresponding private key can spend the fund and therefore, can create the transaction. In blockchain, the transaction is always the primary form of data. Even on blockchain platforms that support smart contract, such as Ethereum, the contract is created and invoked by transactions. By ensuring only legitimate user can generate transactions, the system would ensure that the source of data are genuine. When a node receives a transaction, the node will verify the transaction before it accepts and propagates the transaction. Similarly, a new block just created will be verified before it is accepted and propagated as well. These verifications would make sure the data are correct and are not tampered with during propogation. Once a block and all the transactions included in the block are placed on the blockchain, it can no longer be altered without being detected. A block might be rendered stale due to a fork, but it cannot be altered. Hence, the integrity is guaranteed by blockchain.

As can be seen from Figure 10.1, blockchain does not offer any mechanism for confidentiality. Indeed, public blockchains such as Bitcoin and Ethereum do not encrypt the transaction and blocks. Hence, one can argue that blockchain does not protect the confidentiality of transaction data. Indeed, the transaction ledger (i.e., the blockchain) is designed to be a public ledger on purpose. However, with smart contract, confidential data may be encrypted. The lack of confidentiality on the transaction data does create concerns for the adoption of the blockchain technology in the financial sector.

Sometimes privacy is considered a property of secure system, but we prefer to use the authoritative definition of security [12], which does not include privacy. The mechanism used to protect the privacy of a user is quite different from those that ensures the three fundamental properties of a secure system, i.e., confidentiality, integrity, and availability. Privacy does not equate to confidentiality, although it does relies on confidentiality. For example, Bitcoin uses the UTXO model for account balance tracking where a user is advised to create a new address every time it wanted to receive some fund. The identity of the user is protected not only by using a seemingly random identifier (*i.e.*, the address), but by using many different identifiers for receiving funds as well. The user does need confidentiality to protect its private keys.

Immutability is a much stronger form of protection to data. It goes beyond traditional security that ensures the the integrity and availability of the data because it establishes the context in which the data resides. In many cases, if the context where the data reside is altered, such as the relative ordering with respect to other data items, the system integrity would be lost. Blockchain makes sure neither a transaction nor its context can be modified.

For non-functional properties, trust stands at the highest level. Although trust has been used to describe a system or service very pervasively, there is no authoritative definition for trust [14]. Quite often, it means different things in different literature. In this chapter, we use trust to refer to the level of assurance of a system on what it has promised to its users [72] in terms of security and dependability. Trust may be evaluated based on historical performance of a system, based on reputation of the system, but it could also be analyzed and established from the design and implementation of the system. The former two are looking at a system from outside and treat the system as a blackbox, while the last one looks at trust from the internal construction of a system. In the context of blockchain, we prefer the latter. From the algorithm perspective, blockchain offers unprecedented level of security and dependability transparently. Furthermore, considering that the purpose of public blockchains is to enable cryptocurrency, the implementation must be nearly impeccable. Indeed, in over ten year's operation, the Bitcoin network experienced no major incidents thanks to its ultra-conservative design. Ethereum had to do a major hard fork to overcome a significant issue due to a vulnerability in its early smart contract design [10], it has been getting much more reliable since. Hence, a blockchain-enabled application that relies on an established public blockchain would have a great foundation to offer good trust level to its users.

10.1.2   Functional Benefits

In addition to non-functional benefits, blockchain could also facilitate the design and implementation of core functions in a blockchain-enabled application. We first group functional benefits into two: (1) data-related, and (2) processing-related. Then, there is another benefit that span both data and processing. The data-related benefit primarily refers to data provenance. Data provenance [57], or end-to-end traceability [8], refers to the property that the chronology of the ownership, custody and/or location of a data item can be fully established and attested. Data provenance can be implemented based on immutability. Blockchain records the original owner of a data item and the timestamp when the item is placed in the blockchain. What is more, blockchain essentially totally orders all data items (*i.e.*, the transactions). Hence, the chronology can be easily established. The transfer of cryptocurrency ownership can be tracked and the records cannot be changed. Hence, the custody of data items (*i.e.*, if the data can be encoded via cryptocurrency) can be unambiguously tracked. Hence, data provenance is an essential functionality for regulatory applications (*e.g.*, to meet governmental regulations) and accounting applications.

In addition to the protection of data, an application can use smart contract to ensure atomic execution of code as defined in the contract. Previously, fault tolerant processing has attracted tremendous amount of research and development, as can be seen in chapters 3-7 in this book. Unfortunately, few practical systems that ensures fault tolerant processing are available to the public. One reason is that general purpose computing (via programming languages and operating systems) supports multithreading (*i.e.*, concurrent processing) and many forms of asynchronous interactions that render the processing of a program nondeterministic, and as such, it is incredibly difficult to replicate such processes and still ensure consistency among the replicas [17, 18, 19, 20, 73, 75, 77, 81, 82, 84, 85, 86, 90]. Ethereum can be viewed as the first platform that supports secure and fault tolerant large-scale processing. Indeed, the design goal for Ethereum is to run as a world-wide computer under decentralized consensus and storage that supports arbitrary state and is capable of executing code of arbitrary and unbounded complexity. A key design choice is to ensure deterministic processing where transactions and smart contracts are executed via an Ethereum Virtual Machine (EVM) *sequentially.* In effect, Ethereum runs as a single-threaded deterministic global computer, which is much needed to ensure fault tolerance computing. As hoped by the Ethereum community and outlined by Swan [60], many Dapps and DAOs could be developed based on smart contract and blockchain.

Another benefit that has been documented in the literature is interoperability [24]. This is because the public blockchain used by the application would force a standard way of storing data and inter-process communication. Obviously, one can argue whether or not this is desirable in the long-run.

10.2   Blockchain-Enabled Cyber-Physical Systems

In this section, we first provide our interpretation on what constitutes a CPS, then we review recent development on the integration of blockchain and CPS. Finally, we identity key operations in blockchain-enabled CPS and explain how such operations can benefit from the blockchain technology.

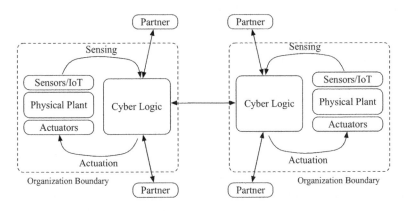

Figure 10.2   A model for cyber-physical systems.

10.2.1   Cyber-Physical Systems

Similar to the term "trust", "CPS" is another term that has been very loosely defined and few publications actually define what it is before engaging in lengthy discussions about CPS. We propose a CPS model based on what is defined by Skowronski [58], as shown in Fig. 10.2. While a CPS that is controlled by a single organization is common, we believe the potential of CPS can be significantly expanded if different organizations start to collaborate, hopefully with the help of blockchain. Hence, our CPS model emphasize on the interactions across organization boundaries where multiple CPS can work together. A CPS could also interact with non-CPU systems. Each CPS would consists at least one close-loop component and one cyber logic unit that is in charge of making decisions on the closed loop as well as interacting with other partners, which could be a CPS in a different organization. The closed-loop unit consists of a physical plant, sensors and IoT devices for measuring the state of the physical plant [40, 48], and various actuators for enacting changes to the physical plant. The data collected regarding the status of the physical plant by the sensors and IoT devices are transmitted to the cyber logic unit. The cyber logic would then compute the necessary actuation decisions to be applied back to the physical plant. The closed-loop operation typically requires a timely response to ensure correctness and often even the safety of the system. The interactions with external partners may or may not have stringent timing requirement depending on the nature of the interaction. For example, timing would be critical if the partner system is also a CPS system, but non-CPS partners could tolerate potentially longer delays in communication. Going beyond the organization boundary has always been a challenge due to the concern on trust. The blockchain technology could potentially alleviate the trust concern because it is designed to bring trust to computing and data. The closed-loop operations in a CPS, and interactions between two CPS must be made fault tolerant and secure while requiring timely delivery of messages and processing.

In the following, we characterize the challenges facing CPS, and argue how the blockchain technology could offer unprecedented help in addressing these issues. First, traditional fault tolerance algorithms are expensive and not scalable, as we have elaborated in Chapter 8 [15, 38, 79, 87, 78]. Second, ensuring atomic execution of a set of time-sensitive operations among multiple processes is very difficult, which poses a particularly challenging issue for CPS closed-loop operations [11, 61, 62, 80]. Third, it is difficult to attain the high degree of trust required to facilitates collaboration across the organizational boundary. Previous works on this area are typically designed for a single administrative domain and are not scalable [16, 72]. Fourth, conventional identity-based system design would require a public-key infrastructure (PKI) to issue and manage public-key certification. Due to the possibility of certificate revocation and expiration, certificate management is a complex issue, and the reliance on PKI creates external dependency and potential single point of failures.

Blockchain can potentially enhance the level of security, dependability, and trust of CPS without resorting to the use of any trusted third party or centralized control. First, fault tolerance for both data and processing can be achieved via the blockchain's massive redundancy and deterministic execution of smart contracts. The second challenge can be addressed by using smart contract at least partially. Atomicity of computing can be ensured via a smart contract, however, the timeliness of computing cannot be strictly guaranteed. For the third challenge, a CPS application can use blockchain as a trust platform where all transaction records will be made immutable in a decentralized manner, and all smart contracts will be executed atomically with their state reliably logged. Regarding the fourth challenge, a CPS application could adopt the blockchain-way of separating the identity management from secure communication by using a wallet-like component. In Blockchain, all communication is message-based instead of session-based. Therefore, every message is self-contained in that it must carry sufficient information for user authentication (typically via a public key) and it is processed without having to consult with other entities. For systems using the UTXO model, each transaction is associated with a unique pair of keys. Hence, this eliminates the need for checking on the validity of some public-key certificate, which would in turn eliminates the need for a PKI.

10.2.2   Application Categories

To find out how the blockchain technology has been accepted and impacted the broader industry, we did a literature search specifically in the context of cyber-physical systems. As mentioned earlier, we believe that in this area blockchain could play a more critical role in making the applications more secure and dependable, and ultimately, more trustworthy.

The literature search was done in early 2020 using the Web of Service core collection. We first used the search term *"blockchain cyber physical systems"*. The search result contains 76 publications. We again searched using the term *"blockchain IoT"*, which returned a total of 764 papers. Then, we narrowed the search with a term *"cyber physical systems"*, which led to 33 papers. After removing irrelevant papers and low quality papers, we selected 40 papers as the basis for the review on blockchain applications in CPS.

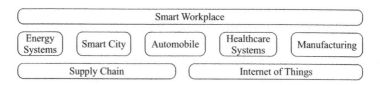

Figure 10.3   Blockchain-enabled CPS applications.

The application areas are summarized in Fig. 10.3. Not all works can be easily categorized into a particular industry sector, for example, the work on supply chain [47, 63] and IoT [37, 42, 44, 65] can be used in many industry sectors. Likewise, the work on generic workplace [4] is applicable to most industry sectors. There are also papers having a high level discussion on considering blockchain as one of the enabling technologies for general purpose CPS systems [2, 3, 27, 29, 53, 54, 67, 76]. Comparatively, there are fewer publications that have focused on a specific industry sector. What we have seen include energy systems [39, 46, 70, 92, 93], smart city [25, 52], automobile [24], healthcare systems [21, 51], manufacturing [3, 21, 43].

The following tables show the key operations that are enabled by blockchain as well as relevant references for each category of applications. Table 10.1 shows the key operations for blockchain-enabled IoT. As we can see, blockchain has been used or proposed to use in a wide variety of aspects of IoT operations, from secure communication, to access control, to the overall architectural design of IoT systems.

Table 10.2 shows the key operations of blockchain-enabled supply chain operations. Only two papers have been founded in this category [47, 63]. One focused on general discussion on how to use blockchain to make supply chain operations more efficient with machine-to-machine interaction [63]. The other focused on primarily software management by exploiting the immutability feature of blockchain [47].

Table 10.3 shows the key operations of blockchain-enabled manufacturing [3, 21, 43]. The operations that can benefit from

Applications	Blockchain-Enabled Operation/Key Points	References
IoT	Identity and attribute management	[37, 32, 7]
	Data-facilitated assessment	[42]
	Secure communication for IoT	[55, 56]
	Secure edge-to-cloud communication	[35]
	Secure publish-subscribe communication	[41]
	Proposed a service-oriented architecture	[65]
	Enhance business processes	[64]
	Access control with smart contract	[63]
	Overview of blockchain-enabled IoT applications	[63]

Table 10.1   Blockchain-enabled IoT-based applications.

Applications	Blockchain-Enabled Operation/Key Points	References
Supply Chain	Supply chain software management	[47]
	Software patch management	[47]
	Software configuration management	[47]
	Digital supply chain	[63]

Table 10.2   Blockchain-enabled supply chain applications.

Applications	Blockchain-Enabled Operation/Key Points	References
Manufacturing	Vertical and horizontal system integration	[22]
	Design and engineering stages integration	[22]
	Secure communication in machine-to-machine interaction	[43]
	Securing sensing in production environment	[43]
	Data sharing among partners	[43]
	End-to-end tracking in manufacturing supply chain	[43]

Table 10.3   Blockchain-enabled manufacturing applications.

Applications	Blockchain-Enabled Operation/Key Points	References
Automobile	Data management	[24]
	Automobile supply chain end-to-end transparency	[24]
	Smart contract between partners	[24]
	Access control with smart contract	[24]
	Automobile parts production traceability & data provenance	[24]
	Financial management between buyer and seller	[24]

Table 10.4   Blockchain-enabled automobile production.

integrating with blockchain range from securing communication, enabling data sharing, end-to-end tracking in manufacturing supply chain, to system design and integrity.

We found only a single paper in the automobile sector [24], which is shown in Table 10.4. The paper discussed a full-range of application of the blockchain technology in this sector from data management, to data provenance for parts production tracking, to automobile supply chain end-to-end transparency, to the use of smart contract for access control and partner interaction, and to financial management between buyers and sellers.

There are more interests in integrating blockchain with energy systems [39, 46, 70, 92, 93], including smart grid, traditional power plant operation, and energy trading. The operations identified by these papers are shown in Table 10.5, and they range from sensor

Applications	Blockchain-Enabled Operation/Key Points	References
Energy	Sensor data acquisition and logging	[46, 70, 92]
	Energy resource management (direct load control)	[92]
	Microgrid operation and control	[46]
	Eletric trading among electric vehicles & charging stations	[46, 93]
	Electric energy trading	[46, 39]
	Reliable data provenance for power delivery	[39]
	Privacy in home area network	[39]
	Power generation and distribution monitoring	[58]
	Power system control	[58]

Table 10.5   Blockchain-enabled energy systems.

Applications	Blockchain-Enabled Operation/Key Points	References
Smart Health	Smart clothing	[21]
	Secure sensing data acquisition and logging	[21]
	Data sharing (for occupational therapy)	[51]
	Patient status monitoring (with smart contract)	[51]

Table 10.6   Blockchain-enabled healthcare systems.

data collection, to power generation and distribution monitoring, to data provenance on power delivery, to microgrid operations, to operations in home area networks, to energy trading.

We found two papers on blockchain-enabled healthcare systems [21, 51], and the key operations they identified are shown in Table 10.6. One focused on collection of sensing data regarding a patient's biological status using smart clothing [21]. The other concerns increasing health IT operation efficiency with blockchain for data sharing and for patient status monitoring [51].

Table 10.7 summarizes the key operations in smart city related applications [25, 52]. Smart city is becoming a more popular topic and it appears that it has encompassed intelligent transportation systems [25] and practically includes everything that could happen

Applications	Blockchain-Enabled Operation/Key Points	References
Smart City	Data analytics based on IoT data for sharing economy	[52]
	Collaborative traffic information gathering & sharing	[25]
	General discussion	[66]

Table 10.7   Blockchain-enabled smart city.

Applications	Blockchain-Enabled Operation/Key Points	References
Workplace	IoT sensor data secure acquisition and logging	[4]
	Behavioral tracking and liability attribution	[4]

Table 10.8   Blockchain-enabled workplace.

in a modern city, even on IT operations for the sharing economy [52]. There is also a paper engaged in general discussion regarding how blockchain could impact smart city operations [66].

There is one paper that discusses an application for employee accountability tracking in workplaces [4], as shown in Table 10.8, including sensor data collection and employee behavior tracking, facilitated by the blockchain technology. In case there is a serious incident, liability attribution can be conducted based on the collected and stored on the blockchain.

Finally, there are a relatively large number of papers that discussed how blockchain could transform or enhance CPS in a general way [2, 3, 27, 29, 53, 54, 67, 76]. The major focuses are outlined in Table 10.9, which include the the control-loop operation in CPS, securing communication in CPS, using smart contract to ensure sophisticated access control.

10.2.3   Blockchain-Enabled Operations in CPS

The operations that we have extracted from the literature are highly application dependent, as shown in the tables in the previous section. It is beneficial to condense them into a set of common and fundamental key operations in CPS applications. We then establish their relationship with the set of benefits brought by blockchain

Applications	Blockchain-Enabled Operation/Key Points	References
General CPS	On-demand control loops operation	[44]
	CPS closed-loop operation	[3]
	Secure & automated machine-to-machine interaction	[71]
	Smart contract design for CPS (access control)	[27]
	General discussion	[2, 29, 53, 67, 54, 76]

Table 10.9   General discussions on blockchain-enabled CPS applications.

as we have outlined previously. Furthermore, we align these key operations along with two dimensions, one on timing sensitivity, and the other on throughput requirement. This alignment would give decision makers a better idea on whether or not to integrity with the blockchain technology, and be aware what potential issues one might encounter when developing blockchain-enabled applications.

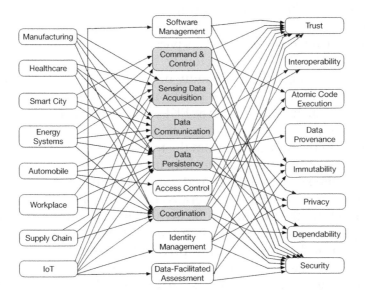

Figure 10.4   Key operations and their relationship with the CPS applications and the blockchain benefits.

We come up with 9 basic operations: sensing data acquisition, data communication, data storage, command and control, coordination, access control, identity management, data-facilitated assessment, and software management. The relevant CPS applications for these basic operations and their relationship with the blockchain benefits are summarized in Fig. 10.4. We believe that these basic operations could be used in virtually CPS applications, even though some of them are not explicitly mentioned in the papers that we have reviewed.   Five of the basic operations are the most fundamental and are colored with light green in Fig. 10.4.

Sensing data acquisition is an important part of the closed-loop CPS operation so that the status of the physical plant can be determined. Not all CPS applications would have a traditional closed-loop with very tight timing requirement, for example, supply chain could use day as the unit for the timing requirement. There are two major security challenges in this operations: (1) the data are typically transmitted wirelessly, which may be tampered with by adversaries during transmission; and (2) the identity of the sensors could be spoofed and therefore fake data might be injected into the system. Blockchain has built-in mechanisms that address both concerns. For the first concern, all messages contain the sender's digital signature, which would enable the receiver to detect any tampering of the message during transmission. For the second concern, blockchain has a unique way of doing sender authentication, which we will elaborate as part of the identity management.

Data communication is obviously a must for any networked system, including CPS. The beauty of using blockchain to facilitate data communication is that it can be made secure without relying on any centralized entity, such as PKI. Anyone that wanted to verify a transaction can retrieve the public key for verifying the digital signature in the transaction from the transaction itself. This is made possible because by design, blockchain removed the identity of the owner of the keys from the consideration, which makes it unnecessary to rely on a certificate generated by a trusted third party such as PKI to bind the identity of the owner and a public key used for verifying a digital signature. A tradeoff of this design is that the protection of the corresponding private key becomes paramount. Anyone who has possession of the private key can claim to be the owner of the public key because anyone who has the private key can generate a valid digital signature. Another tradeoff is that the private key cannot be lost because if that happens, the owner would be unable to spend the cryptocurrency that he or she might have, and in the context of secure communication in a CPS, the sensor would be unable to generate any more valid messages.

Data persistency is important for any system that wanted to preserve its state, including CPS. When data are recorded on the blockchain, they become immutable, which is much more secure and reliable than storing it in some local database. In addition, the relationship between different data items can be determined because all data recorded in the blockchain are totally ordered and timestamped. Furthermore, data provenance can be achieved by establishing the sequence of events as reflected by the immutable data.

Command-and-control and coordination are needed to facilitate the interaction with multiple entities in the CPS according to prede-fined application logic. We group them together for discussion because of their similarity. Command-and-control is used in closed-loop control, while the coordination is used in other context. We differ the two primarily because their requirement on timeliness could be drastically different. Smart contract could play a big role for these operations, which enables their security, dependability, and atomicity of the execution.

The remaining four are higher level operations. *Identity manage-ment* is a challenge in any networked system. Identity manage-ment is particularly challenging for CPS applications that use IoT and wireless sensors to collect system state. It is well-known that wireless sensor networks are vulnerable to various identity-related cyber attacks such as Sybil [71] and spoofing attacks [89]. In blockchain, the identity management is done via public-key cryptography and stateless document-based communication where each message is self-contained. The public and private key pair generation and management in blockchain are done via a digital wallet. The integrity of the message (*i.e.*, the transaction) is partially protected by the use of digital signature. The message can be veri-fied and processed without relying on any other third party. The separation of sensor identity and the security keys also protect the privacy of the sensor owners (for example, if used in a smart home for health related data collection).

Furthermore, while some blockchain platforms such as Bitcoin does not mandate a transaction fee, many others such as Ethereum do require a transaction fee. If we model the message transmitted by a sensor as a transaction where the sensor must pay a transaction fee, then it would significantly increase the cost for an external adversary to launch Sybil attacks and spoofing attacks.

Several other identity management methods have been proposed [7, 32, 37, 94]. One way to do so is to derive a unique identifier from the sensor hardware, which is commonly referred to as physical unclonable functions (PUF) [32]. Each sensor is then authenticated by comparing the device id submitted with that stored on the blockchain. However, one should not simply to include device id in the message for authentication because an adversary could easily intercept the message and extract the device id, which would open the door for spoofing attacks. The current approach often relies on a trusted node that stored the device id (derived from PUF) during the device enrollment step [45, 69]. We are not in favor of this approach because once the "trusted node" is compromised, the entire system will become compromised. We think that the sensor authentication problem can be formulated as a non-interactive zero-knowledge proof problem where a sensor would include some form of information related to the device id, but not the device id itself, in the sensing message for verification.

Another way is to include identity assertion information in all transactions issued by the sender [37]. The sender reputation and the relationship between senders are established by examining previous transactions recorded in the blockchain. There is also work on a decentralized framework for identity verification [7, 94].

Access control is another import task in securing a system that allows remote access. The rules for access control can be highly complex because there are many different users in an organization and a user might have several different roles. Again, smart contract can be a big help in doing complex access control because the access control can be enforced automatically among multiple entities [24, 33, 63, 27].

Software management is applicable to all computer systems. It consists of software module processing, software integration, software transfer, software patch management, and software configuration management. Blockchain can help software management by recording all important software management decisions, such as software module processing changes, patch releases, and configuration changes [47]. In addition to recording key information, smart contracts can be used to automate the patching and configuration processes. Hence, blockchain can significantly increase accountability, standard conformance, auditability of CPS software.

Data-facilitated assessment. Objective assessment on the quality of a service, for example, by collecting system performance data and analyzing the data, is much more reliable because reputation based measures can be manipulated. In [42], the authors proposed to assess the quality services provided by a CPS by mining transactions recorded on the blockchain. Because the data on the blockchain are immutable, the assessment is more trustworthy.

Next, we go over the relationship between the basic operations and the blockchain benefits. Some of the apparent benefits from blockchain have already been mentioned while we describe each basic operation.

- *Security.* All basic operations could benefit from the enhanced security brought by blockchain.
- *Dependability.* While all basic operations could also benefit from the enhanced dependability brought by blockchain, we highlight three operations, coordination, command and control, and data persistency as the ones that most directly benefit from the enhanced dependability.
- *Privacy.* Blockchain is designed with protecting the privacy of the user in mind. Hence, sensing data acquisition and data persistency will directly benefit from blockchain's privacy protection. In addition, blockchain also facilitates identity management that could potentially enhance privacy further.
- *Immutability.* All operations that would record data on the blockchain will enjoy the immutability benefit, including data-facilitated assessment, identity management, data persistency, and software management.
- *Data provenance.* Data persistency could be made much stronger with data provenance where the relationship of different data items can be determined, in addition to immutability.
- *Atomic code execution.* Operations that focus on run-time processing (in comparison to data) would benefit from this blockchain property tremendously, including command and control, coordination, and access control.
- *Interoperability.* The use of blockchain provides an opportunity for interoperability among sensing devices due to the

use of the same format as required by the blockchain [24]. Hence, data communication would directly benefit from this property. Furthermore, the use of blockchain has been recognized to facilitate higher level cooperation (such as data sharing) beyond the organizational boundaries, which is related to coordination.We anticipate that data sharing, enabled by interoperability (and the increased trust level), could enable new types of CPS that span across multiple organizations.

- *Trust.* Trust is a high level benefit of using blockchain. The trust level will be increased across all basic operations.

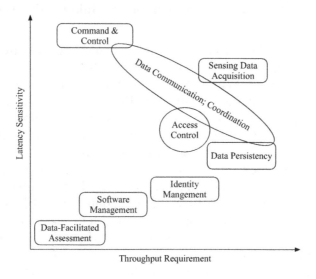

Figure 10.5   Basic CPS operations with respect to the latency and throughput requirements.

Next, we discuss the basic operations with respect to the latency and throughput requirements, as shown in Fig. 10.5. We single out these two requirements because they are highly relevant to both CPS and blockchain operations.

Data-facilitated assessment [42], software management [8, 47, 63], and identity management [7, 32, 37, 94] are at the bottom level because they are not on the critical path of a CPS. Because data-facilitated assessment can be done offline by examining the transactions on the blockchain, it does not impose a strong latency restriction and has no throughput requirement on blockchain. Software management does not impose significant throughput requirement because the number of transactions to be placed on the blockchain is fairly limited. Software management related operations do not impose a tight latency requirement (on when the corresponding transactions should be placed on the blockchain). Similarly, the identity management scheme relies on the use of blockchain to record relevant information. Because software changes happen much less frequently than identity-related changes and verifications, software management is less sensitive to the latency and has less throughput requirement on blockchain compared with those for identity management.

Compared with the above three operations, data persistency [24, 46, 70, 92] happens much more frequently. Therefore, data persistency could require much higher throughput. Considering the large amount of sensing data that could be collected, they could exceed the throughput capacity of most current blockchain platforms. Fortunately, some sensing messages could be queued for logging at the blockchain when the arrival rate is temporarily higher than the blockchain throughput. Therefore, the operation is not sensitive to latency as much as the remaining operations, including access control, data communication, coordination, sensing data acquisition, and command and control. Nevertheless, the data persistency operations are more sensitive to latency than that of software management and identity management because prolonged delay in placing the transactions on blockchain would ultimately impact the operations on the critical path of the CPS.

Smart contracts have been used to automate the logic of access control of IoT devices [24, 33, 27, 63]. Because access control usually happens only when an entity requests to access certain resources during a communication session, its throughput requirement would be significantly below that of average data communication or coordination operations, but the latency requirement should be similar.

If blockchain is used to secure sensing messages (*e.g.*, for system state monitoring), the operation is becoming part of the critical path of CPS, which is very time sensitive [58]. The throughput requirement is also higher than data storage because queueing might not be acceptable in this case. That said, due to the redundancy of sensors, as long as sufficient portions of the data can be collected in time, the state of the system may still be estimated fairly accurately. Hence, the time sensibility for state monitoring is not as high as that for command and control, and for some forms of data communication. Furthermore, sensing data acquisition may have additional considerations such as data aggregation.

Data communication could happen both on and off the critical path. For those on the critical path of the CPS, the latency requirement would be much tighter than that for off-critical-path operations. Data communication has overlap with sensing data acquisition, data storage, and command and control operations. Coordination has rather similar requirements on the latency and throughput because it is about communicating with multiple partners.

Command and control operations are on the critical path of a CPS by design [58], therefore, it has the the most strict requirement on latency. However, because the actuation commands are periodic and are sent to a limited set of actuators, the throughput requirement is moderate. Command and control are more complex than data communication because it may need to coordinate with multiple actuators, which requires the atomicity of their operations on multiple actuators (which can be facilitated by smart contract).

10.3   On Blockchain Throughput

The throughput limitation on public blockchain is intrinsic because of the PoW design. How many transactions the blockchain can handle is limited by the capability of creating new blocks per unit of time. In Bitcoin, interval between two blocks is targeted at 10 minutes. In Ethereum, the block interval is much shorter at 12 seconds. If we take the medium transaction size of 275 bytes as we have mentioned in Chapter 8, one Bitcoin block could include 3,737 transactions. This would lead to a throughput of 6.2 transactions per second, which is fairly close to the widely publicized 7-transaction-per-second Bitcoin throughput limitation. Ethereum does not impose a hard limit on the block size. Instead, it allows the miner to set the maximum gas that can be included in a block provided that the the gas limit is within $1/1024$ of the gas limit of the previous block. Currently, the average gas limit for each block is about 10,000,000 and the minimum transaction gas charge is 21,000. That would limit the maximum transactions per block to around 476. Considering that the block interval is about 12 seconds, the maximum throughput for Ethereum is about 39.7 transactions per second. As can be seen, the transaction rates for Bitcoin and Ethereum are far below the credit card processing rate, which could reach 47,000 transactions per second [34].

There has been a lot of efforts on increasing the throughput of blockchain. We can roughly divide the work into two camps: (1) On-chain approach: those that would literally increase the throughput by altering the block size, block interval, or even the consensus algorithm, and (2) off-chain approach: those that reduce the number of transactions that have to be placed on the blockchain and handle most transactions by other means.

10.3.1   On-Chain Approach

This is the most intuitive approach. There are two obvious parameters, block size and block interval, can be altered for better throughput. Some also proposed to use traditional consensus algorithms such as Paxos or PBFT in small-scale permissioned blockchain. Some projects, such as Hyperledger, even offer a pluggable interface for users to plug in their own consensus algorithm. Apparently, replacing the PoW consensus algorithm with a traditional consensus algorithm is a not viable solution for the limited throughput problem in public blockchain. Other than the scalability issue with traditional algorithms, they do not guarantee a latency bound as many would have expected. While during periods of strong synchrony, which is termed as "normal operation," these algorithm might exhibit excellent latency and throughput [15, 82], the algorithm might not be able to terminate during periods of strong asynchrony or worse yet, in the presence of cyberattacks. One symptom would be continuous view changes. The view change algorithm is typically highly complex and expensive [15, 74, 91]. This fact is rarely acknowledged in the proposals for adopting traditional consensus algorithm for blockchain operation.

Increasing the block size is the most intuitive and straightforward way of increasing the throughput because the larger the block size the more transactions could be confirmed in one block interval. Initially, Bitcoin did not impose a hard limit on the block size, and the maximum block size could reach 36MB. Due to a number of concerns, in 2010 Nakamoto imposed a 1MB hard limit on Bitcoin block size. In 2015, Gavin Andresen proposed the Bitcoin Improvement Proposal (BIP) 101 [9] with a plan to increase the block size as the network grows over time. The proposal was not adopted by Bitcoin and the status of the BIP shows that it has been withdrawn. There are several Bitcoin forks due to this type of disagreements, for example, Bitcoin Cash is a fork that imposes an 8MB limit. More stories on the Bitcoin block size dispute is available at https://blocksdecoded.com/what-bitcoin-block-size/.

Another closely related parameter is the block interval, which is the target latency for solving the PoW puzzle. Obviously, the shorter the block interval, the higher the throughput. Ethereum uses a 12-second target block interval, Litecoin (a Bitcoin fork) uses a block interval of 2.5 minutes, and Dogecoin uses a block interval of 1 minute.

The block size and the block interval cannot be arbitrary set because they together would determine how likely a fork would happen, *i.e.*, two or more miners concurrently discover new blocks at the same block height. While the block interval will directly impact the probability of forking because a shorter target block interval would mean a lowered difficulty target, a larger block size could also increase the likelihood of forking because the transmission latency is proportional to the block size, and when it takes longer for a miner to receive a new block from another miner, it increases the chance for the miner to keep mining until it finds a solution to the puzzle at the same block height.

Frequent forking could be exploited by adversaries to damage the security of the blockchain. Several papers presented the investigation results on the relationship between the system security and block generation rate [6, 28, 34]. The intuition is that when the block interval is approaching the time it takes for mining nodes to share with each other transactions and blocks, the system becomes more vulnerable to malicious attacks. A symptom when the block interval is too short is the presence of frequent forks, which means there are more blocks that would have to be abandoned (*i.e.*, they are not on the main chain), and such blocks are referred to as stale blocks. Due to the conflict-resolution rule used by blockchain, there is a non-negligible probability that a block might be deemed as a stale block for a little while and later becomes a block on the main chain if some miners have used this stale block as the parent and have grown a longer branch than the original branch. In fact, an adversary could attack the system exactly this way. Therefore, the presence of stale blocks would reduce the security of the system.

To study the impact of different block sizes and block intervals, we need a carefully designed simulator because such experiments simply cannot be done in an actual blockchain platform. The work by Gervais et al. filled this gap [30]. They presented a quantitative framework with a publicly available simulator for researchers to study the impacts of various parameters in PoW-based blockchains. The framework has two components, the blockchain and the security model. The input to the blockchain includes various network and consensus parameters. The output from the blockchain component includes the stale block rate, the block propagation times, and the throughput. The input to the security model includes security parameters. The output from the security model consists of security provisions and optimal adversarial strategy. The authors recognized that the network and consensus parameters will directly impact the stale block rate, which in turn has strong security implications.

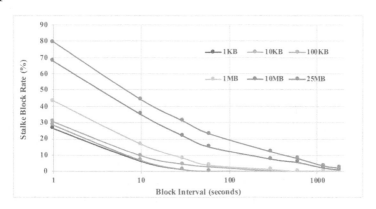

Figure 10.6   Stale block rate for different block sizes and block intervals.

We used the simulator to study what combinations of block size and block interval could potentially be acceptable using the stale block rate as a criteria. The larger the block size, the longer block propagation time, which would lead to higher stale block rate. The smaller the block interval would lead to higher stale block rate. In the simulation, we assumed that the transaction size is 500 bytes. Figure 10.6 shows the simulation result. We varied the block size from 1KB to 25MB, and the block interval from 1 second to 1800 seconds. The throughput for the combinations of these parameters in the table format is shown in Figure 10.7. Based on the stale block rates, we use the green color to highlight the combinations that would lead to stale rate of 10% or below, and use red for the others. The green region are safe parameters from the security perspective where the stale block rate is small. As can been, the highest throughput of 83 transactions per second can be achieved with the 25MB block size and the 10-minute block interval combination. Hence, the maximum achievable throughput is 25 times of the current Bitcoin maximum throughput with the 1MB block size limitation and 10-minute block interval.

Block Interval (Sec)	Block Size				
	10 KB	100 KB	1 MB	10 MB	25 MB
1	20	200	2,000	20,000	50,000
10	2	20	200	2,000	5,000
30	0.67	6.7	67	667	1,667
60	0.33	3.3	33	333	833
300	0.07	0.67	6.7	67	167
600	0.03	0.33	3.3	33	83

Figure 10.7   Throughput for different combinations of block sizes and block intervals.

10.3.2   Off-Chain Approach

The essence of all off-chain approaches is to use a small set of transactions recorded on the main blockchain to ensure the security of transactions stored off-chain. The most well-known and mature approach is state channel [49]. It is also referred to as payment channel because the channel's primary functionality is to facilitate payment between two-parties. The state of the channel is the balance of the cryptocurrency specific to the blockchain and it changes during the operation of the channel. The security of the state channel is protected by two transactions recorded on the main blockchain. One transaction is used to create the channel, which is referred to as the anchor or funding transaction. The other is a transaction created at the termination of the channel to settle the payments between the two parties involved in the channel, which is referred to as the settlement transaction.

Figure 10.8 shows the steps and usage of the state (payment) channel. The state channel is actually a one-way channel in that one party (with symbol A) would pay the other party (with symbol B) for certain service provided by B with the cryptocurrency. For trustless operation, A and B would have to agree on a special address that requires two keys to unlock the fund transferred to that address. This address is referred to as the 2-of-2 multisignature address. A would have one key and B would have the other key. A is responsible to create the anchor transaction where A would deposit some amount of cryptocurrency that is enough to cover the fees incurs during the operation of the channel to this 2-of-2 multisignature address. Once this anchor transaction is confirmed, *i.e.,* it has been included in a newly mined block that is added to the blockchain, the channel starts. A would then create a commitment transaction, and send it to B. The commitment transaction contains payment to the multisignature address (intended for B) for the amount of service that B could immediately deliver. Upon receiving this transaction, B would add its own signature, return the signed transaction back to A, and deliver the agreed-upon service. A would then sends one or more commitment transactions for more services until A decides to end, at which point, A would create a settlement transaction and send it to the network to be included on the blockchain. On sending the settlement transaction to the blockchain network, the channel terminates. The transactions between A and B sent during the channel operation will not be sent to the blockchain, therefore, they can happen very quickly and in the mean time, alleviate the need for the blockchain to support high throughput.

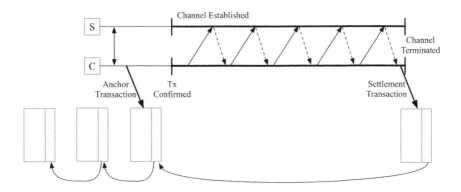

Figure 10.8   Payment channel operation.

The scenario we illustrated in Figure 10.8 are actually a little bit of naive and it works only if both A and B are cooperative and honest, and there is no failure during the channel operation. For example, A will not be able to get the deposit in the anchor transaction back unless B signs the transaction. To put it another way, for A to spend the deposit in another transaction in the future, A would need B to co-sign to unlock the fund. If B disappears or refuses to cooperate, A effectively has lost the deposit. Once the channel is operating, A could have send any of the commitment transaction that B has signed to the blockchain network. In this case, A could cheat by paying for only a single segment of service unless B is vigilantly monitoring such a commitment transaction that is transmitted to the blockchain network. One way to solve the problems mentioned is to use a timelock, which Bitcoin already supports. To create a new payment channel, A would actually create a pair of transactions: an anchor transaction as well as a refund transaction. A would send the refund transaction to B and B should sign it. Obviously, B wanted to prevent A from getting paid by sending the refund transaction to the blockchain network. To address this concern, the refund transaction is post-dated with a timelock. If A used a timelock of 4320 blocks, it means A will not be able to get the refund until 30 days later if Bitcoin is used. When B co-signs the refund transaction, A then sends the anchor transaction to the blockchain network. Furthermore, the refund transaction would be the first commitment transaction, and all subsequent commitment transaction would bear a decreasing timelock value.

The use of timelock can be considered as a smart contract between A and B. The purpose of this method is to ensure that the fund in a more recent commitment transaction can be spent prior to that of the older one. This method to ensure a trustless payment channel works, but it would limit the lifetime of the channel and how many commitment transactions can be used in the channel. Furthermore, forcing the commitment transactions in a sequence makes the payment channel difficult to use. A more flexible method is to have the newer commitment transaction revoke the earlier transaction. This is achieved using a revocation key, which can be used to punish the cheating party. The technical description of the mechanism is beyond the scope of this book.

Another approach is to use multiple blockchains to parallelize the processing of transactions. The most well-known work in this approach is sidechain [13]. In addition to support independent blockchains that each runs a PoW consensus, sidechain has a more ambitious goal of facilitating the transfer of cryptocurrency between different sidechains. The authors proposed a two-way pegging mechanism, which provides proof of value locking and redeeming. The mechanism proposed in [13] relies on the Merkle path originally designed in Bitcoin to enable simplified payment verification of a transaction at a lightweight client that does not have possession of the entire blockchain.

The work of Back et al. [13] was later extended with a hierarchical two-level blockchains [31]. The low level blockchains do not disseminate all transactions to the entire network. The main blockchain is used only to resolve conflicts. The paper is more of a review paper on off-chain solutions for increasing the blockchain throughput than providing a new way of solving the throughput issue.

The idea on using multiple relatively independent blockchains to increase the effective throughput is rather intuitive. Previously, we proposed a hierarchical blockchain architecture to accommodate the scalability needed for electronic voting [5]. The hierarchy would align with the voting scale such as precinct, county, state, and the national level. The lowest level of blockchain would operate at the precinct level.

In [88], we proposed a two-level logging system that is designed specifically for IoT and wireless sensor networks where sensing data are massively produced. The raw data are logged locally and they are aggregated periodically. Only the aggregated data are recorded on the blockchain. Hence, effective throughput could be orders of magnitude higher than the blockchain would normally provide. A key innovation is a strong linkage mechanism between the aggregated data on the blockchain and the corresponding raw data logged locally. This linkage would afford the locally stored raw data the same level of security as those on the blockchain.

The basic idea is illustrated in Figure 10.9 assuming that 8 samples, $d1$, $d2$, $d3$, $d4$, $d5$, $d6$, $d7$, $d8$, are aggregated. The goal is to produce a digest of these samples with a Merkle tree. Each sample is first hashed. The hash of these samples, $H(d1)$, $H(d2)$, $H(d3)$, $H(d4)$, $H(d5)$, $H(d6)$, $H(d7)$, $H(d8)$, would form the leave nodes of a Merkle tree. Subsequently, they are hashed pairwise to create 4 intermediate nodes, i.e., $H12 = H(H(d1), H(d2))$, $H34 = H(H(d3), H(d4))$, $H56 = H(H(d5), H(d6))$, $H78 = H(H(d7), H(d8))$. These four nodes are further hashed pairwise to create two additional intermediate nodes at a higher level, i.e., $H1234 = H(H12, H34)$, $H5678 = H(H56, H78)$. Finally, the Merkle root is created by hashing $H1234$ and $H5678$. How the

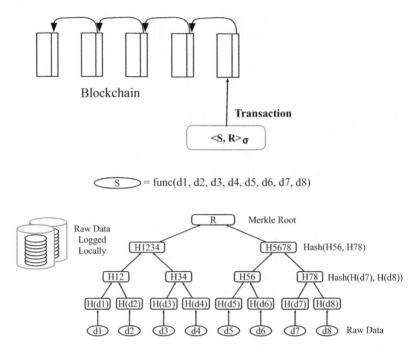

Figure 10.9   Two level logging for sensing data with blockchain.

samples are aggregated is application-dependent. For example, one can choose to include some basic statistical information regarding the set of samples, including the mean and standard deviation. The aggregator would create a transaction including a signed tuple with the aggregated value and the Merkle root corresponding to the set of samples $< S, R >_\sigma$ (where σ is the digital signature), and sends the transaction to the blockchain network. After a little while, the transaction will be included in a new block and placed on the blockchain. Furthermore, to facilitate searching for raw data based on the aggregated data, and vice versa, the set of raw data and the corresponding aggregated data tuple are logged sequentially together, *i.e.*, the aggregated data would be logged right after the set of raw data, as shown in Figure 10.10. For instance, the data in the example would be logged on the disk as $d1$, $d2$, $d3$, $d4$, $d5$, $d6$, $d7$, $d8$, $< S, R >_\sigma$.

The blockchain technology ensures that once a record is placed on the blockchain (after a few confirmations usually), it becomes immutable (*i.e.*, no one can alter it or remove it from the

Raw Data Set   Raw Data Set

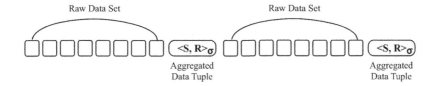

Aggregated   Aggregated
Data Tuple   Data Tuple

Figure 10.10 The format for the raw data (together with the aggregated data tuple) for local logging.

blockchain), and furthermore, no one could alter its relative ordering with respect to other transactions on the blockchain. This same set of guarantees applies to the raw data items. Next, we present an informal proof that this linkage protects the raw data with the same security strength as the aggregated data on the blockchain using the example shown in Figure 10.9.

Proof: If a raw data item is altered, deleted, or inserted into the raw data store, one can verify the record by recomputing the Merkle tree for the corresponding aggregated data item. To be more precise, let the set of raw data items that have been aggregated with a transaction placed on the blockchain be: $< d1, d2, d3, d4, d5, d6, d7, d8 >$, and the aggregated data tuple included in the transaction be $< S, R >_\sigma$, where $S = func(d1, d2, d3, d4, d5, d6, d7, d8)$. Without loss of generality, we first consider $d4$ being altered. When checking the integrity of the local data, each set of raw samples are hashed to produce a Merkle tree root. Because $d4$ has been modified, the computed root hash must be different from the originally computed root R. Hence, this attack will be detected.

Next, we consider the cases where a sample, say, $d4$, is removed from the log or a faulty sample is injected into the log. This is even easier to detect because each set of raw samples that are aggregated are demarcated by the aggregated data tuples. If it is found that the number of samples is not the designated number, apparently the log has been tampered with. One can further verify the integrity by recomputing the Merkle root and compare with the tuple logged. The adversary could delete a sample and replace it with an injected faulty sample. This case is treated as if a sample is altered.

Note that because the aggregated data tuple is protected by the digital signature, any alternation of the tuple can be easily detected. However, an adversary could remove the entire set of raw data together with the corresponding aggregated data tule, or reorder different sets. To detect such attacks, the records on the blockchain are retrieved and compared with the locally logged aggregated data tuples periodically. Ultimately, the integrity of the locally logged data is tied to the $< S, R >$ tuple stored on the blockchain. If the tuple is immutable, then the locally stored data are also immutable to the same degree because they are linked to the tuple. ∎

This mechanism can be extended to facilitate multiple-level sensor data processing and logging, when the aggregated data at a lower level is further condensed at a higher level using the same mechanism until the final highest-level aggregated data are placed on the blockchain.

10.4   A Critical Look on Blockchain from Economy Perspective

In their paper [68], Xu and Zou first presented a rather sobering view of the blockchain application development. The blockchain technology is still largely limited to the cryptocurrency market. According to https://coinmarketcap.com, there are currently 7,371 cryptocurrencies and the total market cap is $358B (as of early October 2020). Bitcoin is still dominating with a 58.5% share of the market. In contrast, according to https://dappradar.com/, there are a total of 3819 Dapps with only 31 of them having more than 1,000 users (as of early October 2020). Furthermore, the Dapps are largely in the crypto exchange, gambling, and games categories. According to [68], these apps have little to do with the real economy, and they attributed the reason for the slow development of blockchain applications to the limited throughput of public blockchain systems, which they term as "low efficiency." Nevertheless, they do recognize the value of the blockchain technology, particularly its tokenization functionality. They highly regard the work led by the Libra association, which will launch a global cyptocurrency and financial infrastructure, as well as the creation of central bank digital currencies. They pointed out that for practical applications (that actually have a real impact on the economy) that use smart contract and the tokenization idea cannot be completely decentralized. It is inevitable for such applications to rely on trusted third parties to enforce the execution of the physical world actions as defined in the smart contract, and to provide legal guarantees needed in cases of contract disputes.

Xu and Zou reviewed the blockchain technology from three perspectives: (1) understanding the blockchain technology from the economy point of view; (2) the economic functions of blockchain; and (3) the use of blockchain as a financial infrastructure.

10.4.1 Blockchain Technology from the Economic View

From the economic point of view, blockchain created a new token paradigm, where the token could be cryptocurrency or the digital presentation of some assets. Public blockchains all share three key features:

- Blockchain consensus is about agreeing on the state change due to token transfer between different addresses. The consensus ensures that token transactions inside blockchain are not subject to the traditional settlement risk. The settlement risk occurs because a traditional transfer of fund between two accounts happens in two distinct steps, one withdrawal and another deposit, and if the deposit step does not occur as expected, the settlement of the transfer fails. Transactions in blockchain are executed atomically in a single step. Hence, the settlement risk is avoided.
- Smart contracts and tokens are inseparable. First, some form of token (*i.e.*, gas in Ethereum) is used to ensure that no smart contract would run indefinitely (*i.e.*, a potential risk of enabling Turing-complete computation). Second, higher level tokens in tokenization-based applications rely on a smart contract to create and manage tokens.
- Information that is not related to tokens in a transaction is not protected by the consensus algorithm in blockchain. Actually, what concerns Xu and Zou is not consistency of such information across different miner (because all miner would see exactly the same transaction content even for information unrelated to token transfer). They are concerned about the integrity and validity of the token-unrelated information placed in a transaction. Such information could be fake and it requires an oracle mechanism to ensure fake information is never accepted into a transaction. That is, they hope that such information is validated to

be correct before a transaction is included in a mined block.

Xu and Zou also pointed out that blockchain-based systems not only need the consensus algorithm, which they termed as machine consensus, but also two additional forms of consensus, *i.e.*, governance consensus and market consensus, for their operation. The blockchain code and algorithms are developed and managed by the respective developers community. The community must agree on key parameters, such as the maximum block size and block interval, the consensus algorithm itself, and rules for operation. This is referred to as governance consensus. When the community cannot reach a consensus, the community would split and each would manage its own version of the blockchain system. This has happened to Bitcoin, with Bitcoin XT, Bitcoin Classic, and Bitcoin Unlimited have been forked out of the original Bitcoin. Market consensus is about cryptocurrency pricing. Issues with machine consensus and governance consensus would directly impact the market consensus.

Another very interesting topic discussed in [68] as part of the token paradigm is what it means by trustlessness. Four characteristics of trustlessness in public blockchains are identified:

- The rules of blockchain are not subject to human intervention because they are enforced by computer code (until a software fork happens).
- All valid transactions will be processed and included in the blockchain. Hence, the blockchain system is resilient to censorship.
- Transactions do not incur settlement risk because they are processed atomically.
- The blockchain (*i.e.*, the distributed ledger) is public. Hence, it is accessible to all and the blockchain is immutable.

Xu and Zou warned that the trustlessness for within-blockchain operations cannot be extrapolated to scenarios involving assets in the physical world. The latter operations would inevitably bear counterparty credit risk. This risk can be mitigated by setting up escrow accounts to hold up fund to sellers until the goods have been shipped/delivered.

They also examined the functions of smart contracts and their shortcomings. Smart contracts have primarily three functions:

(1) property rights management; (2) procedural control; and (3) economic and social functions.

- *Property rights management.* A smart contract could issue a new token, destroy a token, and exchange property rights between users.
- *Procedural control.* To make a payment, the smart contract must include provision to make sure the source address or account for the payment has sufficient fund. The smart contract could also implement sophisticated contingent plan to ensure the payment will happen.
- *Economic and social functions.* These include voting, token collateralization, and token lockup and release. Voting can be simulated by designating addresses for the candidates, and then one would vote by sending a token to one of these addresses. Token collateralization refers to the procedure that a user first deposit some predefined number of tokens with a refund condition. The user will get the tokens deposited back when the condition is met. Tokens can also be locked up for some predefined time. The owners of the tokens would temporarily lose liquidity and will get the tokens back after the time expires.

They pointed out three major shortcomings on smart contracts.

- *Lack of decentralized oracle mechanisms to ensure outside information is correct.* External information can be recorded into the blockchain through smart contract. To make sure such information is correct, an oracle mechanism is needed. To be consistent with the decentralization design goal, the current approach to accomplish the goal is to use economic incentives and some voting schemes. However, Xu and Zou pointed that this solution could not stem the systematic biases in votes.
- *Unable to eliminate credit risk.* For example, a smart contract states that one address or account should pay someone certain amount of tokens. However, that address might not have enough tokens to make the required payment. To mitigate such risk, over-collateralization could be used. But the amount needed to set aside is difficult to determine in advance.
- *The issue on incomplete contracts.* Due to human nature, complex contracts will be intrinsically incomplete. That is

why traditional contracts have provisions for unforeseen situations and the judicial system could be the last resort to resolve contract disputes. Unfortunately, smart contracts in blockchain do not have such provisions.

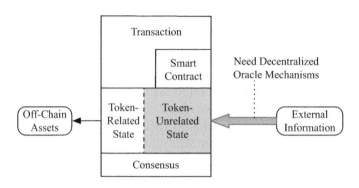

Figure 10.11   Summary of the token paradigm.

The token paradigm can be roughly summarized in Figure 10.11. Token is the most essential concept in blockchain. The power and value of the blockchain technology lies in tokenization, *i.e.*, using token to represent off-chain assets. The foundation of the token paradigm is the consensus on the state of blockchain (*i.e.*, machine consensus) as well as the consensus on the blockchain project governance and the market consensus. The state of the blockchain consists of token-related and token-unrelated state. Although the consensus algorithm ensures the consistency of the state among all copies of the blockchain (*i.e.*, the distributed or shared ledger), the validation mechanisms used in blockchain can only guarantee the integrity of token-related state. There is a need for decentralized oracle mechanisms that validate the information that comes from outside the blockchain so that faulty, incorrect, or inaccurate information is never written to the blockchain.

10.4.2   Economic Functions of Blockchain

Xu and Zou discussed five issues on the economic functions of blockchain. First, they provided a classification of blockchain applications based on whether or not, and how tokens are used in the application, which is quite enlightening. Second, they reviewed the token's monetary features. Third, the discussed the token's impacts on blockchain systems. Fourth, they looked into the governance functions of blockchain. Finally, they summarized the efficiency and security issues of blockchain systems.

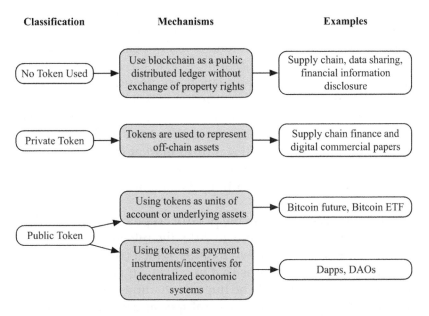

| Classification | Mechanisms | Examples |

Figure 10.12   A classification of blockchain applications based on token usage.

The classification of blockchain application by Xu and Zou is quite interesting [68], as shown in Figure 10.12. Most classification is done via the application sectors like what we have done [83], their classification is based on token usage. They recognized that not all blockchain applications would use token as the building block. Such applications would use the blockchain as a distributed ledger to share or disclose data to partners. The economy value for these applications is to help alleviate information asymmetry among the constituents in the society, which could encourage cooperation and reduce transaction cost.

For applications that do use tokens, they separated them with respect to whether or not the token is publicly issued/traded. In all applications that use tokens, the token would represent some off-chain asset. Private tokens could be used in applications that the owners do not wish to make the information on the blockchain public. The opposite is those that use publicly issued and traded tokens. One way is to use tokens as cryptocurrency, for example, Bitcoin could be traded on the market. A more promising approach is to use tokens as forms of payment or incentives in decentralized systems that have economic impacts, such as Dapps and DAOs.

The most prominent monetary feature of tokens is that it functions as a digital gold. However, tokens as cryptocurrencies lack flexibility in supply, and they do not have sovereign support by design. Because the cryptocurrencies are not backed by any asset, they do not have any intrinsic value. Due to the anonymity feature and the lack of government regulation, cryptocurrencies have been used for illegal activities. As reported in [23], 44% of Bitcoin transactions were found to be related to illegal economic activities. The volume of illegal Bitcoin transactions in 2017 is around $72 billion, close to the size of illegal drug market in Europe and the US combined in that year. Since 2017, newer cryptocurrencies that promise stronger anonymity attracted some of the illegal activities away from Bitcoin.

There is also a concern that the price of cryptocurrencies could be manipulated [26]. For example, in 2013, the Bitcoin price increased from $150 to $1,000 within two months, which could be attributed to the suspicious transactions that involved 0.6 million Bitcoins at the Mt. Gox exchange [26]. The huge fluctuation of cryptocurrency price has led to the creation of several special cryptocurrencies that are backed by traditional money (referred to fiat money) reserve, such as USTD issued by Tether. These cryptocurrencies are called stable coins. Finally, allowing the exchanges between cryptocurrencies and fiat money without sufficient regulation could open the door for money laundering.

The tokens' impacts on blockchain platforms stem in their dual roles. First, organizations could use tokens as a financing tool by doing initial coin offerings (ICO). Second, tokens are used as a payment tool within the blockchain system. Unfortunately, these dual roles of tokens would bring instability to their price because there exist multiple equilibriums [59]. ICO has become a common strategy to launch new blockchain platforms. Unfortunately, due to lack of regulation, many projects funded by ICO have been abandoned [36]. A big reason for this to happen is that the founders could cash out their tokens rather quickly.

Blockchain's governance functions are fairly limited compared with traditional monetary tools such as common stocks. Theoretically, smart contracts could be used to issue tokens with dividend rights and governance rights. Not surprisingly, blockchain suffers from several problems. First, the large volatility of token price could impact the effectiveness of using tokens as an incentive mechanism. Second, smart contracts have intrinsic limitations on implementing governance mechanisms that have been used in real world economy. Third, as we mentioned earlier, the lack of regulation on cashing out tokens after an ICO impairs the interest on the ICO investors. Fourth, how to combine on-chain and off-chain governance is largely unknown.

Regarding the efficiency and security of blockchain, an important observation is the impossibility trinity hypothesis proposed by Abadi and Brunnermeier [1]. An ideal record-keeping system would have three properties: (1) correctness, (2) cost efficiency, and (3) decentralization. Correctness means that the system must record data correctly and the recorded data must be valid. Cost efficiency means that the cost of operating the system is low. Decentralization is the strategy used to develop the system. A fully decentralized system is more robust to hardware failures, cyberattacks, and human corruptions (such as the too-big-to-fail problem and the corresponding bailout).

As shown in Figure 10.13, Abadi and Brunnermeier observed that to ensure correctness, one either would trust a centralized entity to do so by submitting a rent to the entity, or to achieve the goal via pure waste of physical resources [1]. Therefore, they claimed that it is impossible for any record-keeping system to achieve all three properties, which is referred to as the impossibility trinity.

Their hypothesis is that for a centralized ledger, the record keeper would be incentivized to maintain the ledger correctly to ensure future profit. Unfortunately, a centralized solution would limit competition because it essentially has monopoly power over the records it is keeping (*e.g.*, by using proprietary format) and the barrier to create a similar system is high, which is not in the best interest of users of the system.

While using a decentralized public ledger would significantly lower the barrier to entry, the solution requires a sound and robust consensus algorithm so that all copies of the ledger are the same. The dominating way of achieving the consensus is via proof of work, which inevitably wastes on energy. From the economic point of view, A decentralized ledger replaces the risk of having users to pay rents disproportionally with wasteful cost on energy.

However, as we have shown in Chapter 9, there are two promising works that address the cost efficiency issue, one is to make the proof of work to actually do useful work, and the other is to do virtual mining, especially PoS based consensus algorithm. Although it takes more work to analyze the cost efficiency of PoS-based blockchains (such as PeerCoin and perhaps a future version of Ethereum), we believe that PoS-based blockchain could become a ledger that satisfy all three properties, thereby, solving the impossibility trinity problem.

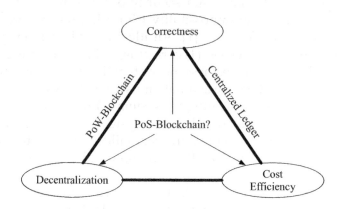

Figure 10.13   The impossibility trinity hypothesis.

Because PoW-based consensus is virtually the de-facto standard in blockchain systems, its impacts have been well studied, including on the energy cost (the energy cost is proportional to the number of miners instead of the PoW difficulty) and on the transaction fees (the larger the blockchain network becomes, the higher the average transaction fees). The low throughput is necessary for Bitcoin (and similar PoW-based blockchains) to guarantee operational sustainability.

10.4.3   Blockchain as a Financial Infrastructure

For blockchain to be used as a financial infrastructure, tokens are representing off-chain assets such as fiat money and financial securities. This way, the tokens will have intrinsic values because the value would be derived from off-chain assets they are linked to. This linkage must be protected legally and economically. Hence, a centralized trusted institution (such as a central bank) is essential for this type of blockchains. The blockchain as a financial infrastructure (BaaFI) has the following features:

- Account-based balance tracking (on the number of tokens owned) is used, similar to that in Ethereum (and different from the UTXO model used in Bitcoin).
- Tokens can be transferred between different accounts.
- Unlike fiat money, tokens can be used across the borders of different sovereign countries.
- The security of the blockchain is ensured by consensus algorithms like PoW.

The most well-known example for BaaFI perhaps is Libra proposed by Facebook. Libra is managed by Libra Association, and will consists of 100 verification nodes (one node from each member of the Libra Association) and aims to support 1,000 transactions per second. Hence, Libra is intended to run as a consortium blockchain and adopts some PoS consensus algorithm. As such, we are concerned on the immutability of the blockchain used in Libra. It certainly will not be the same as that for Bitcoin.

References

1. J. Abadi and M. Brunnermeier. Blockchain economics. Technical report, National Bureau of Economic Research, 2018.

2. G. Aceto, V. Persico, and A. Pescapé. A survey on information and communication technologies for industry 4.0: State-of-the-art, taxonomies, perspectives, and challenges. *IEEE Communications Surveys & Tutorials*, 21(4):3467–3501, 2019.

3. M. Y. Afanasev, A. A. Krylova, S. A. Shorokhov, Y. V. Fedosov, and A. S. Sidorenko. A design of cyber-physical production system prototype based on an ethereum private network. In *2018 22nd Conference of Open Innovations Association (FRUCT)*, pages 3–11. IEEE, 2018.

4. G. Ahmadi-Assalemi, H. M. Al-Khateeb, G. Epiphaniou, J. Cosson, H. Jahankhani, and P. Pillai. Federated blockchain-based tracking and liability attribution framework for employees and cyber-physical objects in a smart workplace. In *2019 IEEE 12th International Conference on Global Security, Safety and Sustainability (ICGS3)*, pages 1–9. IEEE, 2019.

5. E. Akbari, Q. Wu, W. Zhao, H. R. Arabnia, and M. Q. Yang. From blockchain to internet-based voting. In *2017 International Conference on Computational Science and Computational Intelligence (CSCI)*, pages 218–221. IEEE, 2017.

6. E. Akbari, W. Zhao, S. Yang, and X. Lou. The impact of block parameters on the throughput and security of blockchains. In *Proceedings of the 2020 International Conference on Blockchain Technology*, pages 13–18. ACM, 2020.

7. N. Alexopoulos, S. M. Habib, and M. Mühlhäuser. Towards secure distributed trust management on a global scale: An analytical approach for applying distributed ledgers for authorization in the iot. In *Proceedings of the 2018 Workshop on IoT Security and Privacy*, pages 49–54, 2018.

8. B. Alotaibi. Utilizing blockchain to overcome cyber security concerns in the internet of things: A review. *IEEE Sensors Journal*, 19(23):10953–10971, 2019.

9. G. Andresen. Increase maximum block size. https://github.com/bitcoin/bips/blob/master/bip-0101.mediawiki, June 2015.

10. A. M. Antonopoulos and G. Wood. *Mastering ethereum: building smart contracts and dapps*. O'reilly Media, 2018.

11. D. Arney, M. Pajic, J. M. Goldman, I. Lee, R. Mangharam, and O. Sokolsky. Toward patient safety in closed-loop medical device systems. In *Proceedings of the 1st ACM/IEEE International Conference on Cyber-Physical Systems*, pages 139–148, 2010.

12. A. Avizienis, J. C. Laprie, B. Randell, and C. Landwehr. Basic concepts and taxonomy of dependable and secure computing. *IEEE Transactions on Dependable and Secure Computing*, 1(1):11–33, 2004.

13. A. Back, M. Corallo, L. Dashjr, M. Friedenbach, G. Maxwell, A. Miller, A. Poelstra, J. Timón, and P. Wuille. Enabling blockchain innovations with pegged sidechains. *URL: http://www. opensciencereview. com/papers/123/enablingblockchain-innovations-with-pegged-sidechains*, 72, 2014.

14. M. Blaze, J. Feigenbaum, and J. Lacy. Decentralized trust management. In *Proceedings 1996 IEEE Symposium on Security and Privacy*, pages 164–173. IEEE, 1996.

15. M. Castro and B. Liskov. Practical byzantine fault tolerance and proactive recovery. *ACM Transactions on Computer Systems (TOCS)*, 20(4):398–461, 2002.

16. H. Chai, H. Zhang, W. Zhao, P. M. Melliar-Smith, and L. E. Moser. Toward trustworthy coordination for web service business activities. *IEEE Transactions on Services Computing*, 6(2):276–288, 2013.

17. H. Chai and W. Zhao. Interaction patterns for byzantine fault tolerance computing. In *Computer Applications for Web, Human Computer Interaction, Signal and Image Processing, and Pattern Recognition*, pages 180–188. Springer, 2012.

18. H. Chai and W. Zhao. Byzantine fault tolerance for session-oriented multitiered applications. *International Journal of Web Science*, 2(1-2):113–125, 2013.

19. H. Chai and W. Zhao. Byzantine fault tolerance for services with commutative operations. In *2014 IEEE International Conference on Services Computing*, pages 219–226. IEEE, 2014.

20. H. Chai and W. Zhao. Towards trustworthy complex event processing. In *2014 IEEE 5th International Conference on Software Engineering and Service Science*, pages 758–761. IEEE, 2014.

21. T. M. Fernández-Caramés and P. Fraga-Lamas. Towards the internet of smart clothing: A review on iot wearables and garments for creating intelligent connected e-textiles. *Electronics*, 7(12):405, 2018.

22. T. M. Fernández-Caramés and P. Fraga-Lamas. A review on the application of blockchain to the next generation of cybersecure industry 4.0 smart factories. *IEEE Access*, 7:45201–45218, 2019.

23. S. Foley, J. R. Karlsen, and T. J. Putniņš. Sex, drugs, and bitcoin: How much illegal activity is financed through cryptocurrencies? *The Review of Financial Studies*, 32(5):1798–1853, 2019.

24. P. Fraga-Lamas and T. M. Fernández-Caramés. A review on blockchain technologies for an advanced and cyber-resilient automotive industry. *IEEE Access*, 7:17578–17598, 2019.

25. A. Fujihara. Proposing a system for collaborative traffic information gathering and sharing incentivized by blockchain technology. In *International Conference on Intelligent Networking and Collaborative Systems*, pages 170–182. Springer, 2018.

26. N. Gandal, J. Hamrick, T. Moore, and T. Oberman. Price manipulation in the bitcoin ecosystem. *Journal of Monetary Economics*, 95:86–96, 2018.

27. P. Garamvölgyi, I. Kocsis, B. Gehl, and A. Klenik. Towards model-driven engineering of smart contracts for cyber-physical systems. In *2018 48th Annual IEEE/IFIP International Conference on Dependable Systems and Networks Workshops (DSN-W)*, pages 134–139. IEEE, 2018.

28. J. Garay, A. Kiayias, and N. Leonardos. The bitcoin backbone protocol: Analysis and applications. In *Annual International Conference on the Theory and Applications of Cryptographic Techniques*, pages 281–310. Springer, 2015.

29. M. García-Valls, A. Dubey, and V. Botti. Introducing the new paradigm of social dispersed computing: Applications, technologies and challenges. *Journal of Systems Architecture*, 91:83–102, 2018.

30. A. Gervais, G. O. Karame, K. Wüst, V. Glykantzis, H. Ritzdorf, and S. Capkun. On the security and performance of proof of work blockchains. In *Proceedings of the 2016 ACM SIGSAC conference on computer and communications security*, pages 3–16, 2016.

31. L. Gudgeon, P. Moreno-Sanchez, S. Roos, P. McCorry, and A. Gervais. Sok: Layer-two blockchain protocols. In *International Conference on Financial Cryptography and Data Security*, pages 201–226. Springer, 2020.

32. U. Guin, P. Cui, and A. Skjellum. Ensuring proof-of-authenticity of iot edge devices using blockchain technology. In *2018 IEEE International Conference on Internet of Things (iThings) and IEEE Green Computing and Communications (GreenCom) and IEEE Cyber, Physical and Social Computing (CPSCom) and IEEE Smart Data (SmartData)*, pages 1042–1049. IEEE, 2018.

33. R. Gupta, S. Tanwar, F. Al-Turjman, P. Italiya, A. Nauman, and S. W. Kim. Smart Contract Privacy Protection Using AI in Cyber-Physical Systems: Tools, Techniques and Challenges. *IEEE ACCESS*, 8:24746–24772, 2020.

34. A. Kiayias and G. Panagiotakos. Speed-security tradeoffs in blockchain protocols. *IACR Cryptol. ePrint Arch.*, 2015:1019, 2015.

35. P. Kochovski, S. Gec, V. Stankovski, M. Bajec, and P. D. Drobintsev. Trust management in a blockchain based fog computing platform with trustless smart oracles. *Future Generation Computer Systems*, 101:747–759, 2019.

36. L. Kostovetsky and H. Benedetti. Digital tulips? returns to investors in initial coin offerings. https://ssrn.com/abstract=3182169, 2018.

37. D. W. Kravitz and J. Cooper. Securing user identity and transactions symbiotically: Iot meets blockchain. In *2017 Global Internet of Things Summit (GIoTS)*, pages 1–6. IEEE, 2017.

38. L. Lamport et al. Paxos made simple. *ACM Sigact News*, 32(4):18–25, 2001.

39. A. Laszka, S. Eisele, A. Dubey, G. Karsai, and K. Kvaternik. Transax: A blockchain-based decentralized forward-trading energy exchanged for transactive microgrids. In *2018 IEEE 24th International Conference on Parallel and Distributed Systems (ICPADS)*, pages 918–927. IEEE, 2018.

40. S. K. Lo, Y. Liu, S. Y. Chia, X. Xu, Q. Lu, L. Zhu, and H. Ning. Analysis of blockchain solutions for iot: A systematic literature review. *IEEE Access*, 7:58822–58835, 2019.

41. P. Lv, L. Wang, H. Zhu, W. Deng, and L. Gu. An iot-oriented privacy-preserving publish/subscribe model over blockchains. *IEEE Access*, 7:41309–41314, 2019.

42. A. Maiti, A. Raza, B. H. Kang, and L. Hardy. Estimating service quality in industrial internet-of-things monitoring applications with blockchain. *IEEE Access*, 7:155489–155503, 2019.

43. G. D. Martins, R. F. Gonçalves, and B. C. Petroni. Blockchain in manufacturing revolution based on machine to machine transaction: a systematic review. *Brazilian Journal of Operations & Production Management*, 16(2):294–302, 2019.

44. J. J. Mendoza and F. Núñez. Blockchain-driven on-demand control loops over iot environments. *IEEE Access*, 7:157524–157534, 2019.

45. S. P. Mohanty, V. P. Yanambaka, E. Kougianos, and D. Puthal. Pufchain: A hardware-assisted blockchain for sustainable simultaneous device and data security in the internet of everything (ioe). *IEEE Consumer Electronics Magazine*, 9(2):8–16, 2020.

46. A. S. Musleh, G. Yao, and S. Muyeen. Blockchain applications in smart grid–review and frameworks. *IEEE Access*, 7:86746–86757, 2019.

47. M. Mylrea and S. N. G. Gourisetti. Blockchain for supply chain cybersecurity, optimization and compliance. In *2018 Resilience Week (RWS)*, pages 70–76. IEEE, 2018.

48. H. Ning, Z. Zhen, F. Shi, and M. Daneshmand. A survey of identity modeling and identity addressing in internet of things. *IEEE Internet of Things Journal*, 2020.

49. J. Poon and T. Dryja. The bitcoin lightning network: Scalable off-chain instant payments, 2016.

50. T. Qiu, N. Chen, K. Li, M. Atiquzzaman, and W. Zhao. How can heterogeneous internet of things build our future: A survey. *IEEE Communications Surveys & Tutorials*, 20(3):2011–2027, 2018.

51. A. Rahman, M. Rashid, J. Le Kernec, B. Philippe, S. J. Barnes, F. Fioranelli, S. Yang, O. Romain, Q. H. Abbasi, G. Loukas, et al. A secure occupational therapy framework for monitoring cancer patients quality of life. *Sensors*, 19(23):5258, 2019.

52. M. A. Rahman, M. M. Rashid, M. S. Hossain, E. Hassanain, M. F. Alhamid, and M. Guizani. Blockchain and iot-based cognitive edge framework for sharing economy services in a smart city. *IEEE Access*, 7:18611–18621, 2019.

53. D. Ratasich, F. Khalid, F. Geissler, R. Grosu, M. Shafique, and E. Bartocci. A roadmap toward the resilient internet of things for cyber-physical systems. *IEEE Access*, 7:13260–13283, 2019.

54. H. Rathore, A. Mohamed, and M. Guizani. A survey of blockchain enabled cyber-physical systems. *Sensors*, 20(1):282, 2020.

55. D. B. Rawat, M. S. Parwez, and A. Alshammari. Edge computing enabled resilient wireless network virtualization for internet of things. In *2017 IEEE 3rd International Conference on Collaboration and Internet Computing (CIC)*, pages 155–162. IEEE, 2017.

56. E. Reilly, M. Maloney, M. Siegel, and G. Falco. An iot integrity-first communication protocol via an ethereum blockchain light client. In *2019 IEEE/ACM 1st International Workshop on Software Engineering Research & Practices for the Internet of Things (SERP4IoT)*, pages 53–56. IEEE, 2019.

57. Y. L. Simmhan, B. Plale, and D. Gannon. A survey of data provenance in e-science. *ACM Sigmod Record*, 34(3):31–36, 2005.

58. R. Skowroński. The open blockchain-aided multi-agent symbiotic cyber–physical systems. *Future Generation Computer Systems*, 94:430–443, 2019.

59. M. Sockin and W. Xiong. A model of cryptocurrencies. Technical report, National Bureau of Economic Research, 2020.

60. M. Swan. *Blockchain: Blueprint for a new economy.* " O'Reilly Media, Inc.", 2015.

61. E. Y. Vasserman, K. K. Venkatasubramanian, O. Sokolsky, and I. Lee. Security and interoperable-medical-device systems, part 2: Failures, consequences, and classification. *IEEE security & privacy*, 10(6):70–73, 2012.

62. K. K. Venkatasubramanian, E. Y. Vasserman, O. Sokolsky, and I. Lee. Security and interoperable-medical-device systems, part 1. *IEEE security & privacy*, 10(5):61–63, 2012.

63. W. Viriyasitavat, L. Da Xu, Z. Bi, and D. Hoonsopon. Blockchain technology for applications in internet of thingsmapping from system design perspective. *IEEE Internet of Things Journal*, 6(5):8155–8168, 2019.

64. W. Viriyasitavat, L. Da Xu, Z. Bi, and V. Pungpapong. Blockchain and internet of things for modern business process in digital economythe state of the art. *IEEE Transactions on Computational Social Systems*, 6(6):1420–1432, 2019.

65. W. Viriyasitavat, L. Da Xu, Z. Bi, and A. Sapsomboon. New blockchain-based architecture for service interoperations in internet of things. *IEEE Transactions on Computational Social Systems*, 6(4):739–748, 2019.

66. J. Xie, H. Tang, T. Huang, F. R. Yu, R. Xie, J. Liu, and Y. Liu. A survey of blockchain technology applied to smart cities: Research issues and challenges. *IEEE Communications Surveys & Tutorials*, 21(3):2794–2830, 2019.

67. L. D. Xu, E. L. Xu, and L. Li. Industry 4.0: state of the art and future trends. *International Journal of Production Research*, 56(8):2941–2962, 2018.

68. Z. Xu and C. Zou. What can blockchain do and cannot do? *China Economic Journal*, pages 1–22, 2020.

69. W. Yan, N. Zhang, L. L. Njilla, and X. Zhang. Pcbchain: Lightweight reconfigurable blockchain primitives for secure iot applications. *IEEE Transactions on Very Large Scale Integration (VLSI) Systems*, 2020.

70. T. Yang, F. Zhai, J. Liu, M. Wang, and H. Pen. Self-organized cyber physical power system blockchain architecture and protocol. *International Journal of Distributed Sensor Networks*, 14(10):1550147718803311, 2018.

71. S. Yin, J. Bao, Y. Zhang, and X. Huang. M2m security technology of cps based on blockchains. *Symmetry*, 9(9):193, 2017.

72. H. Zhang, H. Chai, W. Zhao, P. M. Melliar-Smith, and L. E. Moser. Trustworthy coordination for web service atomic transactions. *IEEE Transactions on Parallel and Distributed Systems*, 23(8):1551–1565, 2012.

73. H. Zhang and W. Zhao. Concurrent byzantine fault tolerance for software-transactional-memory based applications. *International Journal of Future Computer and Communication*, 1(1):47, 2012.

74. H. Zhang, W. Zhao, P. M. Melliar-Smith, and L. E. Moser. Design and implementation of a byzantine fault tolerance framework for non-deterministic applications. *IET Software*, 5:342–356, 2011.

75. H. Zhang, W. Zhao, L. E. Moser, and P. M. Melliar-Smith. Design and implementation of a byzantine fault tolerance framework for non-deterministic applications. *IET software*, 5(3):342–356, 2011.

76. J. J. Zhang, F.-Y. Wang, X. Wang, G. Xiong, F. Zhu, Y. Lv, J. Hou, S. Han, Y. Yuan, Q. Lu, et al. Cyber-physical-social systems: The state of the art and perspectives. *IEEE Transactions on Computational Social Systems*, 5(3):829–840, 2018.

77. W. Zhao. Application-aware byzantine fault tolerance. In *2014 IEEE 12th International Conference on Dependable, Autonomic and Secure Computing*, pages 45–50. IEEE, 2014.

78. W. Zhao. *Building dependable distributed systems*. John Wiley & Sons, 2014.

79. W. Zhao. Fast paxos made easy: Theory and implementation. *International Journal of Distributed Systems and Technologies (IJDST)*, 6(1):15–33, 2015.

80. W. Zhao. Towards trustworthy integrated clinical environments. In *2015 IEEE 12th Intl Conf on Ubiquitous Intelligence and Computing and 2015 IEEE 12th Intl Conf on Autonomic and Trusted Computing and 2015 IEEE 15th Intl Conf on Scalable Computing and Communications and Its Associated Workshops (UIC-ATC-ScalCom)*, pages 452–459. IEEE, 2015.

81. W. Zhao. Optimistic byzantine fault tolerance. *International Journal of Parallel, Emergent and Distributed Systems*, 31(3):254–267, 2016.

82. W. Zhao. Performance optimization for state machine replication based on application semantics: a review. *Journal of Systems and Software*, 112:96–109, 2016.

83. W. Zhao, C. Jiang, H. Gao, S. Yang, and X. Luo. Blockchain-enabled cyber-physical systems: A review. *IEEE Internet of Things Journal*, 2020.

84. W. Zhao, P. M. Melliar-Smith, and L. Moser. Fault tolerance middleware for cloud computing. In *Proceedings of the IEEE International Conference on Cloud Computing*, pages 67–74, 2010.

85. W. Zhao, P. M. Melliar-Smith, and L. E. Moser. Low latency fault tolerance system. *The Computer Journal*, 56(6):716–740, 2013. in press.

86. W. Zhao, L. Moser, and P. M. Melliar-Smith. Deterministic scheduling for multithreaded replicas. In *Proceedings of the IEEE International Workshop on Object-oriented Real-time Dependable Systems*, pages 74–81, Sedona, AZ, 2005.

87. W. Zhao, L. E. Moser, and P. M. Melliar-Smith. Unification of transactions and replication in three-tier architectures based on corba. *IEEE transactions on Dependable and Secure Computing*, 2(1):20–33, 2005.

88. W. Zhao, S. Yang, and X. Lou. Secure hierarchical processing and logging of sensing data and iot events with blockchain. In *Proceedings of the 2020 International Conference on Blockchain Technology*, pages 52–56. ACM, 2020.

89. W. Zhao, S. Yang, and X. Luo. On threat analysis of iot-based systems: A survey. In *Proceedings of the IEEE International Conference on Smart Internet of Things*, 2020.

90. W. Zhao, W. Yang, H. Zhang, J. Yang, X. Luo, Y. Zhu, M. Yang, and C. Luo. High-throughput state-machine replication using software transactional memory. *The Journal of supercomputing*, 72(11):4379–4398, 2016.

91. W. Zhao and H. Zhang.   Proactive service migration for long-running Byzantine fault tolerant systems. *IET Software*, 3(2):154–164, 2009.

92. D. Zhaoyang, L. Fengji, and G. Liang. Blockchain: a secure, decentralized, trusted cyber infrastructure solution for future energy systems. *Journal of Modern Power Systems and Clean Energy*, 6(5):958–967, 2018.

93. Z. Zhou, B. Wang, M. Dong, and K. Ota. Secure and efficient vehicle-to-grid energy trading in cyber physical systems: Integration of blockchain and edge computing. *IEEE Transactions on Systems, Man, and Cybernetics: Systems*, 50(1):43–57, 2019.

94. X. Zhu and Y. Badr. Identity management systems for the internet of things: a survey towards blockchain solutions. *Sensors*, 18(12):4215, 2018.

Index

Printed and bound by CPI Group (UK) Ltd, Croydon, CR0 4YY

19/04/2023

03211841-0001